# TRANSFORMING KNOWLEDGE

*Second Edition*

ELIZABETH KAMARCK MINNICH

# Transforming Knowledge

SECOND EDITION

TEMPLE UNIVERSITY PRESS  PHILADELPHIA

ELIZABETH KAMARCK MINNICH is Senior Fellow, the Association of American Colleges and Universities. She has spoken and consulted on developing more inclusive curricula at colleges and universities in the U.S. and abroad. She has served as Chair of the North Carolina Humanities Council, and on both the Executive Committee of the Society for the Study of Women Philosophers and the Committee on the Status of Women, which are associated with the American Philosophical Association. In addition, she is the co-editor of *Reconstructing the Academy: Women's Education and Women's Studies.*

Temple University Press
1601 North Broad Street
Philadelphia PA 19122
*www.temple.edu/tempress*

Text design by Kate Nichols

⊖ The paper used in this publication meets the requirements
of the American National Standard for Information Sciences—Permanence of Paper
for Printed Library Materials, ANSI Z39.48-1992

Library of Congress Cataloging-in-Publication Data

Minnich, Elizabeth Kamarck.
Transforming knowledge / Elizabeth Kamarck Minnich. — 2nd ed.
p. cm.
Includes bibliographical references.
ISBN 1-59213-131-X (cloth : alk. paper) — ISBN 1-59213-132-8 (pbk. : alk. paper)
1. Critical thinking.   2. Methodology.   3. Feminist theory.   I. Title.
BC177.M55 2005
305'.01–dc22            2004049836

2   4   6   8   9   7   5   3   1

F OR FORTY YEARS and more of unwavering friendship
that is the foundation of our home, and for the work
he does to make the world a safer, fairer place for us all,
I dedicate this book to Si Kahn.

Without those who were already there when I was
just beginning, without those who never even considered
giving up, what would I have done? To Hannah Arendt,
Jane Gould, Gerda Lerner, Eve Merriam, admiration, love,
and gratitude.

*In philosophizing we may not* terminate *a disease of thought
. . .* slow *cure is all important.*

—LUDWIG WITTGENSTEIN

*The old woman's silence is so long, the young people have
trouble holding their laughter.*

*Finally she speaks, and her voice is soft but stern. "I don't
know," she says. "I don't know whether the bird you are
holding is dead or alive, but what I do know is that it is
in your hands. It is in your hands."*

—TONI MORRISON

# CONTENTS

# PREFACE AND
# ACKNOWLEDGMENTS

## A Note on Sources

B OOKS AND ARTICLES are by no means the only or even the primary
sources of ideas that change us. At least as often—and probably more
so—such ideas come to us in conversation. But when it comes time to
list sources, to give credit, to adduce examples, we turn to published works. I
am sorry about that, although I understand it; we can hardly offer introduc-
tions to all those with whom we have talked as we can list the works we have
read and wish to recommend to others. Unfortunately, though, such listings
can falsify the history of ideas—and miss almost entirely histories of thinking—by making it appear as if all Important Ideas are in texts and *only* in texts.
They also inaccurately and unfairly privilege those who write over those who
think, talk, act, and teach with such involvement that they do not pause to
produce the texts that in some cultures confer that peculiar thing, ownership
of ideas.

I have settled on using endnotes to give basic bibliographic information
as well as to surround what I say with generally accessible examples and sources
of the thinking of others. I intend these notes to be evocative—no more, no

less. They are in reality surrounded at every moment by memories I have that are recognized—if incompletely—in the listing of friends, colleagues, organizations, and institutions in the Acknowledgments that follow.

# A Note on Usage

I am no more satisfied with some decisions I have made about usage, but I did the best I could when it came time to stop enjoying the complexities of language and *do* something.

## "We"

Several readers of an early version of my manuscript commented on a confusing use of "we" throughout the text. They were right, and I made a lot of changes in accordance with their suggestions, but I could not find a way to clear up entirely the confusion caused by my membership in and/or choices to ally with differing communities. I say "we" when I wish to stand with a group, such as women, that has been constituted as a *kind* of human despite serious and significant differences among its members. To me that seems the only response that recognizes some significant realities, whether they are chosen or desired realities or not (certainly they are neither constant nor immutable). I have little respect for those who disclaim or deny their membership in groups they fear it may be disadvantageous or politically or theoretically uneasy to identify with. Politically potent identifications are perpetuated by denial as well as by uncritical adoption, as history has too often taught us when categorically oppressed people try to assimilate on the terms set by the dominant. Standing together is as crucial to rejecting categorical prejudices as recognizing differences is to confounding them. It is because both are important that my own use of the only apparently simple "we" changes, but of course I do not pretend to have gotten it right.

I also use "we" when it would be wrong, as well as ridiculous, to pretend that I do not belong to a group—such as white, middle-class U.S. women who have participated in some power and privilege—whether or not I am always proud of that identification. Yet confusion unavoidably lurks here: I stand within the "we" of all women at the same time I know perfectly well that I am also a part of particular, noninclusive groups within it. I am, in the United States, apparently white, female, and able-bodied, and usually I am taken to be middle class or "higher." This is how I grew up and live; it informs my daily reality and more of my sense of self than I can know. But I do know that I will not always be able-bodied; that could change tomorrow, and will change as I age in any case. Being white in the United States confers some privileges; I have traveled and lived where that was less the case, where people stared at me, isolated me, evidently did not want even to be in physical proximity to me. Sex/gender has wobbled, too. When I lived in India, I was once assigned, at a wedding, to sit where the men did and was given the gifts deemed appropriate to them (including tobacco paan, which I dutifully chewed but was not able to spit out the copious—and to my taste, foul—juice, which I therefore had to swallow). A friend told me later that I had caused confusion because I am too tall for a woman and had been observed not acting like one. In some parts of the United States, the codes that mark me as middle or upper-middle class instead mark me otherwise. In Appalachia, I have been taken to be a poor mountain woman. Where wearing makeup—which I do not use—is essential to being a "lady," I am lowered on the class scale. Religion also complicates things. In the United States, the default assumption is that one is Christian. I am not. I come from Russian Jewish and Polish Catholic immigrants who chose in this country to "be American," as well as longer-term "Americans" who were originally English and German Protestants of some sort. We lived within none of these identifications, which have been all too potent and at violent, deadly odds with each other. I have also lived as a heterosexual, protected and limited by that set of requirements and privileges, although on rare occasions I have had threatening experiences with people who see feminists and other notably independent women as lesbians who trigger their fear, hatred, and potential violence. But with all that, I have lived most of my life as a professional-class, "normally" abled white woman assumed to be—as "proper" members of that "kind" are mostly assumed to be—acceptably Christian and heterosexual. My own sense of *this* "we" can wobble, can trouble me, can lead to assumptions I must openly refute—but it is still a "we" that I cannot with any honest realism disavow.

I also use "we" to identify with feminism and other chosen affiliations that allow me to stand in opposition along with others, again recognizing as I do so internal differences—even conflicts—within and among those groups. I also recognize that sometimes I have no obvious claim to belong to such groups. But I do not intend to slide into complicity with the efforts to divide and conquer that surround feminists and others who refuse domination. At the same time, I refuse to renounce my participation in the "we" of academics, of teachers, of those who work within as well as on and against dominant traditions. I have participated in the privileges of my profession (although fewer than usual, given that I chose to spend most of my career at a university that took as its mission "serving the underserved," socially and politically relevant scholarship, interdisciplinarity, and "learner-centered" doctoral programs—hence, an institution that was radically underfunded and all too vulnerable). I choose to be a part of academe, with which I have an insider/outsider relationship; to struggle for as well as with it; to believe that the values that animate me are at least as basic to education as are those of others with whom I differ.

And sometimes I use "we" because I wish to speak with people, with you, on a level at which, despite all our differences, we are all natal and mortal, relational, communicating beings who live, love, work, and have our being on this earth. That I hold particular views and have had particular experiences does not mean that I *am* those views, that we have no shareable ground even when we must try very hard to create rather than assume it. This "we" may be no more or less than a horizonal, aspirational ideal, but as such, it both holds and challenges us in ways that I do not wish to forgo.

Underlying the use of "we," then, is the age-old tension of particularity with generality, even universality, as well as with related political realities that both express and distort individualities and group memberships. I have not found, and I neither expect nor desire to find, a simple way to resolve such conceptual/political tensions. They call for a life lived attentively and not for any kind of theoretical, ideological 'solution.' It is scary to appear in public in print or in any other way when we know we will be interpreted through so many differing lenses—that we *will* be mis-taken—but of course recognition is also possible when we act, and "going public" is essential to the openness of learning, the undoing of privatizations. The bumps go with the territory: I may never be comfortable spitting tobacco paan juice and surely hope I won't have to swallow it again, but that's a small price for the experience my superbly generous hosts at the Indian wedding gave me when, faced with such an odd duck, they figured out a way to be hospitable nevertheless.

## "Black"/"White" and Entwined Racializations

The terms by which groups of people are created and named *as* groups matter a great deal. Very few words (if any) are personally, intellectually, historically, culturally, politically neutral, and certainly racial labels are not. They reflect the meanings of the times and situations in which they come into use, and they accrete multiple, even contradictory, meanings over time, across cultures and subcultures, in movements. They can wound and heal, liberate and entrap, threaten and promise, clarify and mystify and do so differently for differing people at different times and in different situations.

Even though I prefer to remain open to changing and multiple usages and try to follow the lead of those who have the right to name themselves and to expect that name to be honored, writing a book that will be with people when I am not requires me to make choices. I have most often chosen to use "Black" rather than "black," "Afro-American," or "African American" because "Black" was used by many of the people I admire during the time I began the thinking that led to this book. I have also chosen it because it recalls the powerful anger and pride that burst forth in the U.S. Civil Rights Movement; "Black" in this country is a term chosen within a liberation movement. I use it to honor that choice, even though I realize that it can also seem to oversimplify the enormous complexities of ongoing, shifting racial formulations. Howard Winant writes: "The dissolution of the transparent racial identity of the formerly dominant group, that is to say, the advancing racialization of whites in Europe and the United States, must also be recognized as proceeding from the increasingly globalized dimensions of race. As previous assumptions erode, white identity loses its transparency, the easy elision with 'racelessness' that accompanies racial domination. 'Whiteness' becomes a matter of anxiety and concern."[1] Revolutions, rebellions, social movements, new scholarships, economic changes, migrations of the formerly colonized to the lands of the colonizers—all of these revalue and complicate "Black," "white," and "race" as it has been understood and used.

"People of color" is increasingly being used as a more inclusive term; clearly, it is useful in recognizing a "we" that many more have chosen to stand within in solidarity. I sometimes use "people of color" as well as other terms for that reason. However, I am also aware that "people of color" can (as all more capacious terms do) blur and even seem to deny the significance of some real political, economic, cultural distinctions. For example, for high-caste/upper-class urban Indians and highly educated Japanese from Tokyo, it may not be convincing to make common cause *on the basis of identities* with poor rural Black people from the Mississippi Delta, even though they can indeed stand together wholeheartedly as equal allies who share critiques and visions. Class and caste and education can also, of course, make identifications among Black people tricky: contrary to popular white "wisdom," not all Black people are poor and "ignorant." Nevertheless, in the United States' racist systems,

Black people have had a common identity forced on them for so long that solidarity may still be claimed on the basis of that stubborn reality.

"African American," while neatly reminding whites that (as John Dewey put it at the turn of the last century) there are many "hyphenated Americans" from all over the globe, can leave out people who in the United States are Black but do not trace their roots to Africa or identify with common ancestors. So perhaps the time has not yet come when we can safely give up "Black," with all its pride, complexities, and historical rawness.

I have not capitalized "white" because I do not believe or wish to pretend that it is a parallel term to "Black." White people have not been oppressed in the United States *because* we are members of a racially defined group. Nevertheless, some white people have suffered for other reasons, including one that has for too long been suppressed through a process that Loree Miltich has called "social silencing." Being stripped of sustaining cultural, family, and community identities other than *white* leaves those who underwent this sea change with an ascription that is simultaneously fiercely held and mystified as 'natural.' The children of parents who had to give up identities such as Irish, German, Finnish, Swedish, Hungarian, Polish to "fit in," but who did not then "succeed," have sometimes turned a painful sense of shame into anger against those to whom they were taught that they should (even must) be superior. In the Southeast, "poor whites" and "rednecks" are terms of opprobrium that reveal the scorn of white people who have "made it" for those who have not, even when they are used by progressives who think their scorn is aimed only at "redneck racism." But such regional and class-based prejudice of whitened people against other whitened people is not the same as that against Black people: it reflects the sense that "poor whites" have failed properly to improve themselves, not the belief that "their kind" could not do so, no matter what.

Analyses by Roediger, Ignatiev, Frankenberg, Lopez, Jacobson, Allen, Winant make it evident that *whiteness* is finally being studied as the twisty, dangerous construct it is. But when it is capitalized, it is often (not always) being claimed, not analyzed, and in its most dangerous form, as in its use by "White supremacists," neo-Nazis, the Ku Klux Klan—most, if not all, of whom conflate their defiant White identity with Christianity. These hate groups' anti-Semitism is too often "overlooked"—it is certainly there to be seen—by some white and Black Christians who do not want to deal with their own anti-Semitism. They thereby remain implicated with the very White guys they are otherwise determined to oppose. Neither white–Black racism nor anti-racism is simple.

By emphasizing "white/Black" complexities, I do not mean to ignore the many other related racial formations in the United States and elsewhere. I do, however, recognize that there are racial divides and hierarchies that apparent skin tone persistently signifies—through however many gradations and however many related signifiers of 'proper,' racially stratified 'place'—a 'high' to 'low' scale, with "white" or "light" or some related term marking 'high,' and "black" or "dark" marking 'low.' This is patent nonsense and leads to truly absurd systems demarcating all sorts of gradations and counts of "drops of blood" and so on. Yet it is real nonetheless, both socially and politically. And that reality plays out in the relations other "non-white" people(s) have had with both white and Black people. Indigenous peoples have had complex inter-relations with Black people in the United States since Anglo-Europeans imposed their color-coded, divisive categories—"Negro" and "red" and "brown" and "yellow"—in ways that took "white" as the norm and ideal for "mankind" to which other constructed 'kinds' of people collectively, but also differentially, did not and could not measure up. Anthony F. C. Wallace writes about "the moral dilemma that bedeviled white Americans in Jefferson's time: . . . what ultimately to do about the presence of black slaves and free Indians." He sets this "dilemma" in context: "The process of encroachment, followed by war, followed by land cession, never ceased. . . . And as justification of the United States' commitment to expansionism, Jefferson and Madison helped to establish the belief in the redeemer nation's manifest destiny to move westward." He concludes: "Jefferson resolved this problem, in his own mind, by favoring the separation, or elimination, of disparate ethnic groups—Indians and blacks—who refused to disappear through civilization and assimilation, or were, in his view, incapable of participating as citizens in the republic. Too many national leaders of the twentieth century have also sought such final solutions."[2]

Like ever more fevered characterizations of "The Enemy" in wartime, conceptualizations of people(s) subjected to dominance of varying kinds tend to lose subtlety and complexity, becoming grossly singular evocations of inferiority, if not of full-blown Evil. And still the differentiations persist, sometimes undercutting, sometimes understood as requiring, solidarity. There were Indian tribes that sheltered and fought for "runaway" slaves; there were Indian tribes that became "slave catchers"; there were enslaved Indians and Indians who owned slaves; there are Indian tribes that have refused to deny tribal membership to "Black Indians"; there are Indian tribes that have denied full tribal status to "Black Indians" to gain recognition premised by government agencies on that old racist standard, the 'purity' of "bloodlines." Racializations entangle us all. If we do not recognize that as we try now to tell all our stories, we will remain implicated with the "social silencing" that has for so long denied and distorted histories and other scholarship.

Identities entangled with such histories can hardly be expected to change with changes in nomenclature. Even so, the terms we use for ourselves and for others matter a great deal. Like the use of "she or he" rather than "he" (which reminds us that in English, as in some other languages, we cannot speak without divisively gendering: note that "or"), speaking against the grain of thinking that carries histories within it is crucial to the daily, fine-grained work that is necessary to transform knowledges and all the systems that produce and use it. Objections to choices of identifying terms (and pronouns) constitute occasions to continue thinking together about the old errors that still divide us.

## Scare Quotes

I have used scare quotes (single quotation marks) in this book to flavor words or phrases with irony, to recognize sensitivities, to dissociate myself from a familiar usage—to call attention to usage and to invite the reader to think about how it may be too blithe, or wrong. For example, 'proper' woman: the scare quotes mean I wish to open the term to critical attention, to bring forward the prescriptions of propriety, so we can see them at work. I use double quotation marks when I am referring to a word or phrase *as* a word or phrase: for instance, "Black power" as a phrase chosen to reclaim and revalue meanings of "Black" as well as to name a general goal for a movement.

In a book in which I am thinking about the ways we think—including the words we use (in this context, it is difficult *not* to use scare quotes around *we*)— it seemed important to ask the reader to join me in hearing language as it vibrates among levels and across situations and realms of meaning.

# Acknowledgments

It is impossible to do this adequately and accurately, but still I must try. I owe a great deal to family, friends, teachers, students, and colleagues with whom I have worked and talked through the years. My family taught me to care about justice on a local as well as a global scale, to love reading, to need art, to talk over dinner endlessly, to laugh a lot. Sarah Lawrence College; the University of California, Berkeley; and the Graduate Faculty of the New School University allowed me to follow my passions, informed them, challenged them. A Fulbright Fellowship to India cracked open assumptions I never knew I had, opening spaces I have since tried not to fill once again but, rather, to keep expanding so I can take in still more. Work at the New School College (now Lang College) and at Sarah Lawrence, Hollins, and Barnard colleges as an administrator and teacher helped me realize the congruence of my love of philosophy with my fascination with institutional systems, the lively relation of thinking and acting. The Graduate College for Interdisciplinary Arts and Sciences of the Union Institute and University, for which I worked for a startlingly long time, gave me a home among colleagues and learners whose intellectual, moral, and political passions refused compartmentalization, disengagement, standardization.

I have had the privilege of studying in Florence, Italy, on a Doris Riker Scholarship from Sarah Lawrence; teaching and studying in India on the Fulbright (already mentioned); teaching for a semester at Scripps College as the Hartley Burr Alexander Professor of the Humanities; participating in a seminar and doing research as a visiting scholar at the Getty's Institute for the History of the Arts and Humanities; teaching as the Whichard Visiting Distinguished Professor of Humanities and (for my year) Women's Studies at East Carolina University; and holding shorter-term "Distinguished Professor" appointments at Rollins College and the University of Hartford.

I cannot list all the schools, groups, colleges, universities, and higher-education and other professional associations at which I have spoken and, gratefully, participated through all these years of my fieldwork philosophizing. But I should certainly mention the Association of American Colleges and Universities, which through the years has provided leadership for most of the significant changes in which I believe and which honored this book when it first came out with its Frederic W. Ness award for best book on liberal learning for that year. I also learned enormously from being on the AAC&U's National Panel for its multiyear project on "American Commitments: Diversity, Democracy and Liberal Learning," under the brilliant, skillful, committed, and staggeringly energetic leadership of Carol Geary Schneider (who subsequently became president of AAC&U).

For support of projects that provided me and others with occasions for thinking and talking with invaluable people, I am grateful to the Ford Foundation, the Soros Open Society Institute, the National Endowment for the Humanities, the American Council on Education, the American Association for Higher Education, the Great Lakes Colleges' Association, and the Women's Colleges Coalition, as well as to the journals for which I have been privileged to read: *Signs, National Women's Studies Association Journal, Feminist Studies, Hypatia, Soundings, Transformations,* and the American Philosophical Association's *Newsletter on Women and Philosophy.* I am grateful to have served on the North Carolina Humanities Council as both member and chair. All of these have kept me thinking and have offered challenges—far too tempting to resist—to rethink just about everything.

Even harder than naming all of these institutions, projects, and organizations (incompletely, but there we are) is naming individuals. I cannot bear to leave people out, but the longer the list, the more obvious the omissions. There is no way around it: decisions must be made. In addition to those I thanked in the first edition, I now have the pleasure of publicly thanking, for their good work and wonderful thinking: Rita Arditti, Margaret Blanchard, Evelyn Torton Beck, Suzanne Benally, Mayra Bloom, Jan Brooks, Mary Ellen Capek, Carlos Cortes, Bonnie Thornton Dill, Troy Duster, Liza Fiol-Matta, Luis Galanes, Ramon Gutierrez, Lyndall Hare, Patrick Hill, Joseph Jordan, Esther Kingston-Mann, Lee Knefelkamp, Loree Miltich, Chandra Talpade Mohanty, Satya Mohanty, Caryn McTighe Musil, Margo Okazawa-Rey, Michael Q. Patton, Minnie Bruce Pratt, Stephen Rowe, Carol Geary Schneider, Debra Schultz, Beverly Guy-Sheftall, Rosemarie Garland Thomson, Lynne Westfield, Judy Whipps.

My good friends Nancy Barnes, Gayle Greene, Martha Crunkleton, Debra Schultz, and Esther Kingston-Mann were especially helpful, as always even beyond the advice they gave so generously at a critical juncture. Ongoing conversations also with Sara Ruddick, Simi Linton, Helena Meyer-Knapp, and Janet Francendese have held me and consistently startled me back into thinking, and rethinking—a gift without measure.

Valerie Jones nobly worked and thought with me (and put up with my railings) throughout the technological as well as some conceptual challenges involved in the process of revision. She and the other magnificent women in my classes at East Carolina University gave me the great gift of thinking with me about some very hard subjects. I miss them—their courageous honesty, humor, and integrity.

Thank you, Elizabeth Rhymer, for allowing me to use our grandfather's study: what peace, inspiration, and blessed quiet!

With lasting sadness that we have lost her—leavened only by the ongoing excitement of thinking with her—I cannot but repeat that I am indebted beyond measure to my teacher, Hannah Arendt. As she once said, if I had to be grateful, I would be utterly helpless.

# INTRODUCTION

# Still Transforming Knowledge

THERE IS NOTHING "merely academic" about how we think and what we think we know. We are creatures and creators of meaning. Among the many meanings that interweave our varied worlds, the meanings of *human being* are central. They can sustain us in peaceful, caring, just relation with others and with the earth we share. They can divide and rank us within systems of dominance. They can open us to love, friendship, respect, justice, nurture. They can enable us to enslave, exploit, rape, kill those who have been defined as less than fully human. We are called by inspiring and by disturbing meanings of *human being* to keep thinking, to hold horizons open. We, who are conscious creatures and creators of meaning, remain responsible.

# THINKING:
## AN INTRODUCTORY ESSAY

### Thinking about *Women,* or,
### "Women's Work Is Never Done"

THIRTY YEARS AGO, when I began thinking with some colleagues and friends about *women* as an under-studied subject, I discovered that a remarkable number of other colleagues responded to this topic—so evidently, it seemed to me an exciting call to rethink what we thought we knew about meanings of *human being,* to look hard at tired old clichés—with thoughtless jokes, awkward silences, and other defensive reactions. Some colleagues with whom I tried to share my excitement thereafter avoided me as if I had revealed myself to be not just unsound but contagiously so. Some allies in various causes, from academic politics to the Civil Rights Movement—people who had hitherto accepted me—became suspicious of my loyalties. I was subjected to patronizing lectures to the effect that I was at risk of taking a politically dubious as well as career-threatening turn. And I noticed, too, that where—like it or not—I had drawn attention as a female, once I became marked as a woman interested in women (a characterization in which "interested in" was charged quite differently from, say, "interested in philosophy," my academic field), I repelled not a few. I could hardly fail to notice such reactions: the question that fascinated and hooked me was what they meant. After all, if we do not study women, with all our differences, how can we believe that our studies adequately concern humankind? However we have made meaning of the diversities of humankind, however those meanings have themselves differed through time and across cultures, where they exist they are real in their effects.

In the first edition of this book (1990), I wrote about what I had learned during the personal, moral, political, philosophical quest I had taken up well before I sat down to write: the quest to figure out how meanings of humankind could exclude the majority of us and still stand as sound, adequate, and truthful. How, I kept asking, could so many of us not see what was so obvious? What ways of thinking kept us from making changes even when we did see that they needed to be made, and even when we genuinely wanted to make them? Now, after fifteen more years' work in this time of extraordinarily fruitful scholarship and ongoing progressive activism (in stark counterpoint to horrifying repression, exploitation, wars, sexualized violence, and genocidal regimes around the globe), I am grateful for the chance to rethink and rewrite.

Having started this work because I encountered weird difficulties in thinking about women and, in trying to think those through, recognized the obvious need to rethink meanings of humankind, I still believe we need to keep focusing on women. It worries me that women's studies is yet again under attack as intellectually unsophisticated and "politically correct." I cannot but notice that today's attacks on women's studies—however different the terms in which they are cast—are still aimed at its intellectual adequacy and political purposes. If nothing else, this seems to suggest that thinking about women remains a disturbing exercise. I stubbornly take that to indicate that we should keep it up.

Thinking about differing women disturbs most systems of dominance (including, it must be said, all too many regimes that emerge from revolutions against dominant orders). We cannot reframe meanings of *human being* without remembering the many meanings of *women* that continue—as Alice Kessler-Harris wrote in 2001—to inform "gendered ways of thinking that stretched into every nook and cranny of the public imagination."[1]

## Thinking as Philosophical Fieldwork

During the years of work on transforming courses and curricula to make them adequately inclusive—work that I took up after my initial discovery of the revelatory power of thinking about women—I was not aware that I was using any kind of method. Now, however when people ask, I respond that what I do is fieldwork philosophizing. This works rather nicely to make it clear that I do not pretend to be doing social science research while suggesting a different kind of legitimacy (there are traditions here, of course) for free-range thinking as philosophical. I do believe thinking that is stung awake by encounters with people whose certainties appear untroubled by questions about the meanings that inform their knowledge and their actions is philosophical. I remember and still love Socrates, who reminds us of the gadfly effect of thinkers, of the need for intellectual midwifery to discover whether our ideas are babies or only "wind eggs." He also said that thinking is like a wind that blows everything down. We honor Socrates now; Athens put him to death for corrupting its youth. It is helpful to remember that, as long as one also recognizes that being charged with corrupting anyone is always a call to the most serious self-examination and by no means proof that one is a Socrates.

So, philosophical fieldwork—thinking with others out and about in the *agora* and then reflecting in solitude with them in mind—is not about learning philosophical systems and then applying them, nor is it about trying to derive a theory from experience. It is neither deductive nor inductive, nor is it held within any other single logic. Rather, it is about listening and hearing, looking and seeing, taking in and trying to comprehend without rushing to interpret, to translate into familiar terms, to explain. In Simone Weil's sense, it is about being *attentive.* Such attentiveness is philosophical also because it entails listening for *meanings* and, as philosophers do, for *moves*—for what is being done conceptually, as well as for what someone is wanting to mean.

As in reading philosophy, one is then trying to comprehend a (re)framing of available meanings, a task that requires attention to each word, each line, each section within the context of the entire work, itself read within its own multiple contexts. In this process of reading, listening, opening to take in *what is going on here,* philosophical readers, like effective political actors, attentive parents, good teachers, artful psychological and pastoral counselors, listen for how what is said coheres, and does not; how it is familiar, and strange; how it invokes and suggests, and suppresses things not directly said. They listen for recurring images and for what sorts of relations those images privilege (mechanical? organic? rigid? fluid? oppositional? transactional?). They pick up on language use and what it suggests: why the colloquialism here, the technical term there? Why that rhythm in those sentences, another in these?

We do all of that—and more, of which we are rarely aware—to be fully present within a conversation as it is happening here and now, with these particular people. We can do that because and insofar as we also always hold in mind other, differing conversations. Making sense with one another—which is both enabled and limited by culturally framed interactions—is an ongoing project that can never be completed. It is a transactional process that has no products but does have crucial effects. And those effects are of great importance: through them, we can be deformed as well as informed, and sometimes even transformed.

There is nothing trivial or 'only' theoretical about how people in their daily lives make sense together, and this ongoing process is particularly significant when we are trying to make sense of who and what "we" are, of who and what "they" are. In doing so, we are making and remaking our lives and possible relations with others and with the earth we share. So, calling on every art of listening I have learned or found myself to possess, and trying always to practice it better, I do philosophical fieldwork to locate where and how efforts to connect with others are distorted into prejudicial—preformed, unreflective, and so potentially dangerous—forms.

I certainly do not claim that this project is original; on the contrary. Sophisticated as well as unreflective daily methods and methodologies for making particular kinds of sense abound. These methods characterize and delimit all professions and established practices related to all sorts of conventions. But no one formalized method can or should lead us to renounce, disable, or scorn the arts we possess and practice whenever we engage fully in the effort to comprehend each other and to make sense together. Formalized methods are necessary to protect us from imposing what we think we already know (even without realizing it) on that which we seek freshly and more fully to understand. But the informal arts of being together that we also have are necessary to protect us against the thoughtlessness that trained technical and theoretical proficiency, as well as other internalized conventions, can lead to. The danger lies in mis-taking what is before us by forcing it into frames of meaning within which it cannot reveal its unruly uniqueness.

Recently, I found this in Foucault's *Fearless Speech*:

> The history of thought [in contrast to the history of ideas] is the analysis of the way an unproblematic field of experience, or a set of practices, which were accepted without question, which were familiar and "silent," out of discussion, becomes a problem, raises discussion and debate, incites new reactions, and induces a crisis in the previously silent behavior, habits, practices, and institutions. The history of thought, understood in this way, is the history of the way people begin to take care of something, of the way they become anxious about this or that.[2]

This is helpful: Foucault's "archaeological" and "genealogical" methods can be powerfully illuminating, particularly—as I am confident he would have agreed—when they are taken to call us into recurrently fresh thinking, instead of being adopted as yet another method to be learned and applied.

Some aspects of ethnomethodology are useful as well. They can remind us to watch, in particular, for how meaning systems deal with being disrupted—how they readjust themselves to neutralize, absorb, and/or recast challenges as mere additions, thereby maintaining themselves at base just as they were. At such moments, systems are showing us not so much what they are as how they do what they do. Psychoanalysis, as a highly honed way of listening for the most elusive meanings that are nevertheless sustaining dysfunctional meaning systems, also comes to mind as useful. So do some other methods developed in social psychology, anthropology, history, philosophy, cultural studies. Each of these, among other fields, offers a plethora of helpful methods for trying to figure out, as I am trying to do, how dominant systems do their work and are legitimated by knowledge. I find all these fields and their methods fascinating and suggestive; I consider them also, along with social conventions and personal beliefs, subject to critique. Methods, too, can be rooted in old errors, which they will perpetuate if we do not dig them out.

In practicing such critiques, I recognize, of course, that I am personally implicated within some of the systems about which I think most. I remember very well one of the moments that crystallized my interest in this work. It came when I realized that in all my years of study, clear through the doctorate in philosophy and despite growing up in a family long committed to working for equality, *I had not noticed* the eloquent absence of women and some 'kinds' of men from what I was studying. This first amazed, then appalled, and then *interested* me. It struck me as a philosophical issue of the first order, like bumping into the walls of the fly bottle (as Ludwig Wittgenstein put it), or, by Toni Morrison's analogy, like noticing the fishbowl in which I had been swimming. It was, it seemed evident to me, a call to philosophize, which is to say, to think.

Many have been doing so in recent years, stung awake by their own disturbing moments and thinking them through in many differing ways. We are not out of the fishbowl yet, but yes, it has indeed been changing.

## Thinking in the New Academy

Higher education is both shaped by and influential in defining and responding to ongoing struggles over knowledgeable responses to crucial questions. What has it meant to be human? How have these meanings changed through time and across cultures? How can and should we live together not despite but with all our differences? Who are "we"? How should we think if we wish to think together? How, by whom, and to what effects is knowledge legitimated? How do thinking and knowledge relate to "the real world"? Why do such questions matter; why should we care?

Over the past thirty years, I have seen transformations in education designed to increase its inclusiveness and its depth begin, and begin to take. Around many campuses today there are old houses with neatly printed signs set out front or propped in windows: Women's Center; Center for Intercultural, Interracial Communication; Conflict Resolution and Mediation Institute; Center for the Study of Social Change; Black Culture Center; Institute on Technology and Human Values; Diaspora and Nationalism Research Center; Disability Studies Center; Gay, Lesbian, Bisexual, and Transgender Student Center; Distance Learning Center; Center for Multicultural Research; Ethnic Studies Institute; Native American/Indian/Indigenous Peoples' Culture and Research Center; Service Learning Office; Community/Campus Coordinating Office. . . . No campus has a complete set; most campuses have at least a few. The names for these centers and institutes, gathering places for people and resources, vary, and there are ongoing discussions, often impassioned, about the names neatly printed on the signs that identify them.

Some of today's students already take these hard-won provisions for granted. Some understand their fragility as well as their importance. Some resent them and the passionate discussions they invite as distractions from or even perversions of the 'real' business of education.

Still, there they are, these outposts of the academy spreading into the community. People go through campus gates, cross busy streets around campuses, to get to them. On campus, faculty teach in classrooms and lecture halls (many still with seats bolted to the floor, precisely lined to face the lectern, the screen, the stage) in larger, more solid classroom buildings. But some of the same faculty also teach in the liminal houses, around round tables, in somewhat shabby living rooms with a few overstuffed armchairs among awkward folding chairs and footstools.

Growing numbers of faculty in all fields also now teach "distance learning" courses, reaching students sitting in their own chairs, sometimes with friends and family members, who can (invisibly, for free) join them. A woman taking a women's studies course that way told me that her male partner started checking out what she was doing, and now they are having some of the best discussions they have ever had. Simultaneously, a movement for "engaged learning" is spreading, taking students and faculty into communities to discern what all can learn by studying and acting together.

Clearly, cross-fertilization is going on, and hybrids are developing, some of which will prove hardy, others unable to thrive. On campus, a remarkable number of courses and some faculty appointments (often joint appointments) now correspond to those neatly lettered signs set out not so long ago on those houses' lawns. Literature and history and philosophy and biology and psychology and mathematics and economics and history of art are of course still there, naming and claiming groups of carefully planned, sequenced courses, minors and majors, and so also job slots, tenure lines, budget and administrative units. But what all those established provisions support increasingly includes courses, materials, and analyses developed in women's studies, peace studies, disability studies, Native American/Indian studies, inter- and multicultural studies, queer studies, many ethnic studies, gender studies, environmental studies and ecology, science studies, postcolonial studies, critical legal studies, cultural studies, white studies, Holocaust studies, acoustic ecology . . . and more. The list is long and getting longer. It is also changing: the names of these areas, too, are being hotly contested. For good and for ill, few of us are quite as sure as we once were of who and what "we" are.

Things have changed.[3] Chaos and conflict and faddishness and divisiveness, declare some. Behind closed doors at a meeting of influential educators, an eminent scholar whose works are often cited in these new fields called them "the academic equivalent of talk radio"—a clear slam, in his view. But scornful critics are fewer than they were. "Interdisciplinarity" and "engaged scholarship" are, if not established, no longer out of bounds. Their achievements make it hard not to see them as legitimate.

Students look different, too. More of them are over twenty-one; more of them are people of color; more of them are visibly women of all groups (on faculties, too, and in administration); more of them are differently abled people using government-mandated ramps and other badly belated provisions for accessibility. Administrators and faculty go to meeting after meeting to discuss "diversity issues," "multiculturalism," "globalizing the curriculum," "differing learning styles." Local, regional, national, and now international projects for and studies of service learning and civic engagement are taking on the task of "preparing citizens for a more interrelated and diverse world." On many campuses there are now "learning communities," and differing modes of assessment are being designed to recognize and support collaborative as well as individual and/or competitive learning.

Our campuses—the virtual as well as the physical—are lively, less tightly disciplined places. All sorts of ideas and bodies and identities and issues and works once excluded and devalued are making their presence felt in transformative ways.

But forms—both new and old—of "top-down" power persist and in some cases are increasing. Corporatized boards of trustees and some legislatures are applying pressure to undo faculty powers. More and more administrators are happy to encourage this trend; they tend to think of themselves as CEOs and CFOs (and as deserving equivalent pay). These "executives" and "officers" see themselves as pressed to be responsible not for educational leadership but for raising money, lobbying legislators, marketing the 'product' of their 'industry,' and generally holding education "more accountable to the bottom line." Pressures to standardize in order to measure "output" and "outcomes" and "deliverables" so as to be able to 'prove' accountability in terms appropriate to businesses are growing concomitantly. Aggressively for-profit schools are springing up, further blurring what is left of the business–academy boundary, even as the broader business–public realm distinction also blurs in favor of the former. Public universities are taking funds from corporations to support research, which those corporations then control lest potentially profitable findings leak to competitors. As a result, some scholarly gatherings and peer-reviewed journals are seen not as guardians of sound scholarship for the public good, but as threats to future corporate profits (in which universities increasingly yearn to share).

In the United States today, it can seem that capitalist fundamentalism—whose devotees practically worship the "free market" and take the "bottom line" to be an unquestionable moral imperative—has been conflated with democracy and with freedom. Schools are now being pressed to serve not the conservation and creation of knowledge, the reflective life, the public good, but economic growth and competitiveness. Professional faculties—whose members have been supported and protected in giving their lives to thinking, learning, questioning, and creating—are under assault, and little is being done to preserve them and the invaluable contributions such lives make possible. Tenured positions are being cut or allowed to disappear with retirements while more and more part-time and adjunct faculty are being hired. Faculty are becoming part of a "flexible, market-responsive delivery system," and as such are being reduced to fungible, easily replaceable functionaries. There are superstar faculty at one extreme of the academic world; at the other extreme (with little in between) are grossly underpaid, uninsured "instructional personnel" with no job security and little professional standing, however good they are. As Lyotard put it: "One thing seems certain. . . . [T]he process of delegitimation and the predominance of the performance criterion are sounding the knell of the age of the Professor: a professor is no more competent than memory banks in transmitting established knowledge."[4]

In academe, too, the rich have gotten richer, and the poor have gotten poorer—and increasingly vulnerable. Meanwhile, those in the middle, as a reaction to their more and more precarious position, are becoming either more docile or more defiant (or, spasmodically, both). Women and men of some groups among the more recently hired suffer these changes along with and often more than others; they are also, weirdly, charged with responsibility for causing them. Mutters a white man: "I'd have gotten that job they gave to a woman if it weren't for affirmative action," or "That Black man took my job." It may feel safer to be angry at the more vulnerable rather than the more powerful, but it leaves untouched the dynamics—and the interests—that are actually pitting us against each other for ever less secure jobs. ("Crabs in a barrel don't even need a lid," says a friend of mine. "If one scrabbles toward the top, the others pull it back down.")

## Some Reframings of Thinking from the New Academy

From the new fields that are nevertheless taking root in higher education today, new ways of thinking are indeed emerging. In the hope that it will help you read what follows in today's context, here is a kind of bird's-eye view of shifts that have become possible.

### From the One to the Many—Abstract Singulars to Plurals

We have been learning to pluralize terms so that we are less likely to forget— or to collude in devaluing—the complex differences among us that remain hidden by singular terms. In particular, plurals such as "citizens" rather than "the citizen," "students" rather than "the student," help us avoid reducing differences to lowest common denominators or denying their relevance while we dream of transcendent unity. We speak more commonly and carefully now, for example, of sexualities, genders, races, ethnicities; of histories, cultures, societies; of truths, meanings, faiths, logics. We remember more readily that "woman" is a changing and enormously complex construct that includes people from vastly different traditions as well as multiple, even contradictory, overlapping meanings.

To 'pluralize' in this sense is not just a call to iteration—to list, say, under the singular "woman" Kenyan women and lesbians and blind women and queens and some transgendered people and Victorian women and poor women and indigenous women and working women and mothers and abused women and cross-dressers and prostitutes and migrant women and revolutionary women and Roma women and bearded women and Brahmin women. Such a list can neither be completed nor a source of any one adequate abstraction: there are too many crucial differentiations really at play. Issues of categorization, of multiple and/or co-constructing identities, of differing levels and kinds of cultural (and national, and individual) meanings, and, with them, differentials of power, make such lists almost as problematic as singular terms. It is not enough for us to become collectors of examples (of what?). We cannot think better about all of us if we simply tack "and women," "and disabled women," "and minorities," "and other people of color" onto the same old exclusive meanings.

"and Staff"

To pluralize is to hold open the question of whom we really mean to include, and why. It is a beginning, no more, no less, like holding that women everywhere must have the vote without knowing how they will exercise that power or what may emerge to reconfigure political life as a result.

## From Nouns to Verbs—Static to Active

We have also begun to see what turning nouns into verb forms—"race" into "racializing," "gender" into "gendering"—may be able to do for us. Perhaps it may help us remember human agency (and so responsibility) by focusing our attention not on static things, products, abstractions but, rather, on the processes, histories, and complexly interrelating systems that create and sustain so much of our world. Some scholars are now studying why and how some people(s) *became* white after they arrived in the United States, while others, enslaved or not, became no longer Ashanti or Ibo (for example) but "Negro" or "Black." We can also now try to deal with problems of "sexualized violence," and not 'only' "trauma" but also "traumatizing experiences" and "retraumatizing situations." And we can work to promote "democratic practices" rather than the static, singular "democracy."

We may then realize that changing our language practices entails changing epistemologies and ontologies. When we try using active rather than static terms, we are shifting toward asking not what "knowledge is," but how it "*becomes* knowledge," and what difference that makes. Foucault, who thought not about "problems" but about "problematizing," said: "The question I raise is this one: How and why were different things in the world gathered together,

characterized, analyzed, and treated as, for example, 'mental illness'?"[5] Throughout this book I will be asking, "Why and how were, and recurrently are, the
*kinds* of humans that have been thought of as singular, static, and unchangeable
created?" "Kind," I cannot resist saying now, is a word that English etymology
relates at root to *gender,* which is related to "engender"—that is, "to birth" and
"to produce." On this, more later.

## From External (Additive) to Internal (Transactional) Relationalities

Singular, static entities (people, categories, problems, things, modes, constructions, fields/disciplines, systems) can only be externally related, iterated,
added, juxtaposed. Being singular, they are defined by what they are not; being
static, they are defined as if they could not be otherwise. Locked into their separateness by such definitions, things, people, events, systems seem able to be
related and held together only by rules, laws, or some other kind of imposition from without. Thus that curious phrase, "the laws of nature," which seems
to imply that patternings of relations that scholars and observers have discerned
(or postulated) within nature are, like human positive law, imposed by fiat and
take on a moralistic tone.

But sex/gender, race, able/disabled, ethnicity, nation, and class/caste can
be, and often now are, recast as complex, ongoing, historically created processes
that we can study not as separate things or identities or qualities but, rather,
as mutually and intimately co-constructing. For example, a female who is
marked as "disabled" by the culture into which she is born will be gendered
differently from another girl from the same culture whose body is judged to
be "normal" and so also "normally" female. What it *means* to be "Black" differs for males and females; so does what it means to be Chinese or Chinese
American. These identities are imposed, internalized, and more or less freely
chosen; they are woven of many strands, sustained, and challenged through
many sorts of daily interactions. They are not 'kinds' that we simply *are,* one
by one, additively, nor do they intersect only at some points.

Using analyses that reveal such mutually co-constructing phenomena, the
historian Linda K. Kerber writes about "rethought histories" that reveal relations among "asymmetrical education of men and illiteracy of women, the ways
in which understanding of male honor and respectability are shaped by placing boundaries on women's choices, how the globalization of sweatshops rests
on the employment of women in harsh industrial conditions, and the vast

transnational flow of traffic in women," as well as "sexual assault on women as central to the way conquering armies have established control."[6]

## From Divided to Mutually Formative Theory and Practice

When we focus on transactional relations—on processes rather than solely on static 'things'—we are also enabled to see the practical, applied, and political dimensions of abstractions and theories. Generalizations, which theories relate on a still more abstract level, are intellectual abstractions from and of concrete, historical particulars. Which particulars are selected to be generalized about and abstracted from, by the few who are legitimated as scholars at a particular time and place, has effects on the subsequent theory. Any theory is thus already related to, and carries within it, past practices; if a theory is then applied, it may implicitly confirm and continue what it was supposed to explain or help improve. For example, a theory about the behavior of "the labor force" in a particular country at a particular time in history deals with preestablished generalizations about *labor*. Since those generalizations were made from a variety of gendered and racialized class/caste prescriptions that shaped who does and does not "labor," the subsequent theory may fail to illuminate the socioeconomic injustices that preceded and continue to support exclusions from "the labor market."

Theories have their own histories of implication in the particular social realities from which they arose. Remembering that, we are better prepared to use them effectively; to choose not to use them when they are inappropriate; and to keep expanding and refining the practices of theorizing and the theorizing of practices.

I CANNOT RESIST noting here, as an example of how against the grain much of the new scholarship still is, that my computer's word-processing program has highlighted a fair number of the words I have just used: racialized, racializing, gendered, gendering, narrativizing, ethnicities, significations, pluralize, logics. Wrong, says the programmed red pen. I resent being intruded on that way, but I must also say that I, too, resist some wrenchings of language that I nevertheless value precisely *because* they go against the grain. Dominant languages can require the linguistic equivalent of physical therapy (which I have undergone, so I know how painful it can be). Living languages must remain

limber, must at times be realigned to correct twists and bends that have locked in. But the purpose of such changes is not to substitute a new rigid posture for the old. On the contrary: it is to get our minds moving, to get us thinking more flexibly and more responsively.

## Questioning "Theory"

Today, the value (and even the possibility) of thinking about women is again in question, and so, too, is women's studies. Among those raising the questions are postmodernists, to use a shorthand. This complex school of thought has convinced many scholars (if far fewer people outside the academy) of its usefulness. That it has done so means that its challenges cannot be ignored without losing professional credibility as well as the real benefits of the (initially wrenching) rethinking such challenges entail. At the same time, women's studies and feminist scholarship in general have come under attack by anti-feminists and by some anti-"gender ideology" scholars who still claim to be feminists.

I should say right out, then, that I have some disagreements with post-modernist feminists as well as—although less than—with anti-feminists and anti-"gender ideology" feminists.[7] I do not "do Theory," and I remain uncomfortable with the appropriation of theorizing by any one example thereof. I do read and admire some of postmodernism's key theorists and works. (I have quoted a few already.) I respect its analytical power, and I recognize that it has brought with it what some feminists and other cultural critics have craved as I do not: a thoroughgoing, philosophically grounded, coherent theoretical/ideological approach capable of yielding often startlingly telling insights. I drew my sketch of shifts in thinking characteristic of the new academy from experiences I have had primarily with people who have not engaged with postmodern "Theory," but of course I recognize how consonant they are with it.

I can hardly argue that "postmodern" is not a broadly descriptive term that may loosely cover a great deal. But "postmodern Theory" arose in these times along with, and not as the source or warrantee for, many other schools of thought, analysis, and action. I value many of these (from "old left" analyses to highly local movements that focus on reclaiming, not dissolving, identities, such as those in Ecuador and Colombia). I do not want to see any thoughtful, courageous struggles against real oppressions discredited and silenced yet again, whether by entrenched interests or by allies who believe their theory is or should be universally applicable (even if denying universals is part of their creed).

So, I have refrained from conversion to postmodernism, just as I have to any other single school of thought. To give all my reasons would require more discussion than I can offer here. But I will say that, at this point (I continue to read, to listen), there are some things that trouble me, not so much about "the postmodern" as it reaches to provide a name for this age or as it relates to movements in art and architecture, but in its guise as a curiously singular, capitalized "Theory." That this "Theory" appears to be leading some of its adherents to denigrate women's studies certainly concerns me, but that derives from and suggests other problems as well.

I am uncomfortable with some of the philosophical roots of postmodernism, and especially with its evident adoption of key Heidegerrian moves, terms, and, in my view, dangerous contradictions.[8] I see the effects or echoes of these moves and related contradictions in a worrisome aspect of postmodernist "Theory" that Chandra Talpade Mohanty and M. Jacqui Alexander describe this way:

> Postmodernist theory, in its haste to dissociate itself from all forms of essentialism, has generated a series of epistemological confusions regarding the interconnections between location, identity, and the construction of knowledge. Thus, for instance, localized questions of experience, identity, culture, and history, which enable us to understand specific processes of domination and subordination, are often dismissed by postmodern theories as reiterations of cultural 'essence' or unified, stable identity.[9]
>
> If we dissolve the category of race, for instance, it becomes difficult to claim the experience of racism.[10]

Such undercutting of grounded political realities and experiences, and so of some actions—which I do trust that many postmodernists do not intend—may correspond to a contradiction in Heidegger, whose focus on developing a method that would "let Being, be" blinded him to the realities of the disastrous political events of his murderous era instead of illuminating their meaning. Heidegger read the rise of the Nazis as a "withdrawing" of Being that would sweep away deadening old forms of life, just as he intended his philosophizing to do. And so, briefly but influentially, he moved out into public life to serve the Nazis as rector of the University of Freiburg. Faced with the same historical realities, Hannah Arendt saw them more clearly. Early on, she recognized the deadly threat of what she called the opening of the gutters of Europe (which, we must also recognize, were fed by and spread back to the United States—as, for example, in the eugenics movement—as well as other countries). I believe that Arendt's actions then and throughout her life, as well as her many works of political philosophy, need to be taken fully into account when assessing both Heidegger and the postmodernism he so profoundly influenced. Arendt provides us with antidotes we need to avoid their tendency to obfuscate (or, worse, substitute themselves for) rather than illuminate the very realities they are meant to help us see.[11]

Foucault, in whose thinking Heideggerian influence can readily be seen, was sometimes criticized for "a form of 'historical idealism'" of the sort that can blind adherents to concrete realities. Late in his life, he responded: "When I say that I am studying the 'problematization' of madness, crime, or sexuality, it is not a way of denying the reality of such phenomena. On the contrary, I have tried to show that it was precisely some real existent in the world which was the target of social regulation."[12] Thus, he recognized the validity of this criticism even while responding to it: "real existents" such as racist practices should not disappear into, or be cast only in terms of, discourses, philosophical ideas, historical logics, or anything else.

Unfortunately, in some postmodern writings it is hard not to fear that that is exactly what is happening to "real existents" and our actual experiences of them—as when someone speaking about and for women's experiences in our still highly gendered world is charged with "essentialism," with "reinscribing" that which she claims to be critiquing. In such cases, "Theory" seems to be taking on the role of arbiter of what is real, and of imposing only one way of speaking to that reality, for allies as well as opponents. In denying that they play that role, postmodernists too often disappear into a cloud of inky dicta. Chris Hables Gray, whose work I respect, uses a postmodernistic juxtaposition of quotes to 'define' his simultaneously powerful and elusive subject (non-subject?): "Postmodernism is whatever you want it to be, if you want it bad enough," and "Postmodernism is the intellectual equivalent of nervous laughter."[13]

I am all for increasing the latitude of thinkers. But "Theory" does not reliably work to do that, I fear. Too often, I have found myself troubled by the wholesale adoption and subsequent autopilot use of postmodernist language by some of its adherents, and too many graduate students seem to have been taught few alternatives to that language. I worry about the intolerance I have encountered among some postmodernists for those who do not "speak postmodern." One example: I encountered such intolerance at a conference in Budapest at which I spoke. Having heard nothing but postmodern-informed papers before mine, I started by saying that I was not going to speak postmodern. I was later told by several participants that I was "very brave": this from women living through the turmoil of Eastern Europe. Of course, postmodernists are not the only ones who are guilty of secular dogmatism; it is the temptation, the risk, the threat of any powerful theoretical engine. This is one reason I continue to value philosophizing in the field rather than "doing Theory" of any kind: what interests me is what theories as well as other kinds of systems take for granted, take off from, create, foreclose, make possible. I have not found that I need to adopt any one technical language to do that work. On the contrary: I have found that I need to be able to hear and draw on as many as possible. In this, I should find allies among postmodernists, and I sometimes do. As Jane Flax writes: "Contemporary feminists join other postmodern philosophers in raising important metatheoretical questions about the possible nature and status of theorizing itself."[14]

But some postmodernist feminists question whether women's studies is sustainable at all. This doubt apparently derives from the radical avoidance of "essentialism" that Mohanty and Alexander discuss. For example, Wendy Brown writes:

> Women's studies as a contemporary institution . . . may be politically and theoretically incoherent, as well as tacitly conservative—incoherent because by definition it circumscribes uncircumscribable 'women' as an object of study, and conservative because it must resist all objections to such circumscription if it is to sustain that object of study as its raison d'etre. . . . [Women's studies] consolidates itself in the remains [left it by "Critical Race Theory, postcolonial theory, queer theory, and cultural studies"], impoverished by the lack of challenges from within, bewildered by its new ghettoization in the academy—this time by feminists themselves.[15]

This troubling depiction has some truth to it. But there is not to my mind anything *necessary* about it. The women's studies programs I know do teach "Theory" along with other theories. They do take care to complicate understandings of "women." They do draw on the scholarship of, and form various kinds of relations with, the other new fields (which for some reason Brown apparently does not see as similarly self-contradicting). And they also insist, rightly in my view, on speaking with students in multiple ways, starting with them where they are—which usually includes a sense of themselves as women, living in a highly gendered world as they do. Instead of teaching one theory, capitalized or not, most women's studies faculty are working hard to encourage students to find their own differing voices in conversation with many. To do so beyond the circle of a few scholars, they need, as we all do, to be able to speak far more than (if also) "postmodern."

Furthermore, that the subject, women, is "incoherent" makes it no different from any other field: all fields work with subject matter that has been, and not infrequently still is, seen quite differently, and incompatibly, from differing angles and stances. There are multiple schools of history, of philosophy, of psychology, of economics even in one culture and certainly among many, and not a few of these constitute refutations, rather than additions to or variations, of each other. No field or theory possesses the essence of its subject, but few therefore reject useful, historically derived names that gesture toward subject matter. Why, then, should the subject *women* be seen as less legitimate than any other? And why should being "incoherent" constitute a problem for a postmodernist, anyway? Perhaps what we see here is a suppressed premise: that the only acceptable ground of "coherence" derives from one kind of theory. That would be a suspiciously hegemonic move on the part of those who do so much good work questioning hegemonies.

So although I agree that there are risks and anomalies in establishing women's studies, I see similar risks and anomalies in establishing any discipline, any interdisciplinary or antihegemonic method. And if women's studies is aware of and troubled by such issues (as indeed it is), that marks it as more trustworthy, not less. May it remain so, and may more others become so. Whatever is done with the category *women* in theories, in academe, people marked as, and/or choosing to identify as, women continue in the real world both to be oppressed and to resist as women. Our cause is not a distraction but a necessary corrective, constituent of and correlative to all others. We cannot renounce thinking and speaking as, about, and for women just because "essentialism" is now taboo among some theorists any more than we can believe that we are beyond race and racism because geneticists have finally rejected as incoherent the category of race.

Politically, there can be a pincer effect to questioning feminism and women's studies today. Conservatives want us to stop focusing on injustices that they claim are now past; they want to dismantle all aspects of affirmative action so we can get "beyond such divisiveness." They do not want us to speak about women; they want us to show loyalty to 'higher' causes by speaking about humans (as if speaking about women were not doing so). Simultaneously, others want us to stop studying women because doing so is conceptually "incoherent" in terms of what they take to be a more radical epistemological and political perspective. Both groups seem to want to define women yet again out of order. I do not entirely reject either of these views, but I do believe that we should continue to observe how all such critics, including the most progressive, themselves define *women,* to what purpose, and to what effect, because none of us, and no theory, suffices to get it right.

As Lyotard has said, we should avoid "zero-sum games." He believes that this is possible, even in a world of many closed "games" that would seem to be able only to contend, because "the reserve of knowledge—language's reserve of possible utterances—is inexhaustible."[16] Yes, and not only "language's reserve," but the reserves of actual examples across times and cultures; of human imaginations; of the possibilities that cooperation across all the old divisions enables; and the reserves of emotionally courageous thinking that clears a space of freedom at the heart of the most sedimented experiences, the most dominating knowledges, the most unjust political systems. No "game" is entirely closed as long as someone is still thinking, because—as Heidegger and Arendt agreed—"thinking is out of order." There is always also a great deal to be learned with those with whom we sometimes disagree.

## Returning to the Field

To take us back out into the field with the new scholarships in mind, I close this section of the introduction with 1) two contrasting statements by powerful U.S. public figures; followed by 2) reflections I recently heard (and am reporting from notes and my memory) by activists about their participation in the Civil Rights Movement. I will also mention, as one exemplary resource among many that help us make theoretical sense of these examples, 3) an anthology of papers by women activists/theorists from around the globe who draw more explicitly from, even as they challenge, feminisms and women's studies. Together, these differing voices suggest why we do need to keep thinking for ourselves with many others if we really wish to comprehend and to change our worlds, and how relevant for that calling is remembering to hold women, with all our differences, in mind.

1. IN SEPTEMBER 2002, the White House issued the Bush administration's National Security Strategy statement, an annual event mandated by Congress. Authored by Condoleezza Rice, National Security Adviser, it began by "asserting that there is 'a single sustainable model for national success'—America's—that is 'right and true for every person, in every society.'"[17] In proclaiming the rightness of one nation, one view of history, one kind of success, the statement assumed that the Bush administration's understandings of *nation* and of *success* are not particular to itself, or one among others, but that those understandings are inclusive and define the only legitimate meanings, norms, and ideals for all. All other nations, all other understandings of success, if judged against this proclaimed standard, can be seen only as lesser, their differences marking their failure to be what they ought to be.

In stark contrast but at about the same time, on September 13, 2002, an article titled "A Network of Global Solutions" appeared. In it, Jean-François Rischard gave his views on the world situation. Rischard, vice-president for Europe of the World Bank, spoke of a "crisis of complexity" and suggested as a response *not* the dominance of a single superpower justifying its unilateral stance by proclaiming itself to be the only true and right model for all but, rather, a system of global "networked governance." He took this transnational, active, plural, relational approach to be appropriate for the following reasons:

    I. Hierarchical organizations will be unable to respond quickly or nimbly enough to the changes taking place. . . .

    II. Nation-states, committed to the idea of territorial sovereignty, will struggle because most of the pressing problems—among them, global climate change, the spread of diseases, the control of electronic commerce—have no geographical boundaries.[18]

Here we have, in the most public, worldwide arenas, an example of thinking premised on a domination-serving mono-vision countered by an alternative that proposes changes deriving from thinking that is remarkably similar to that which has been developing in the new academy. I find the White House statement terrifying, threatening, and outrageous; this whole book constitutes an effort to dig out the roots of that kind of thinking about others, about differences, about "us" not only *versus* but *above* "them." The Rischard statement offers hope that thinking attuned to complex interrelations rather than dominance can be found in influential places. Both statements show how epistemological and policy positions inform each other: there is nothing merely academic about how we think. Both also fail to make it evident that they have remembered to hold women, half of humankind, in mind.

Rice left an administrative position at Stanford University—a site of significant struggles over "the new academy," which she strongly opposed—to take up her post in the White House. I do not think this history is irrelevant to her selection for that job. There is nothing, I repeat, merely academic about how we think and what we teach. Those who seek to legitimate domination know that.

2. AN AFTERNOON PANEL, "Women in the Sit-Ins," was held at the Levine Museum of the New South in Charlotte, North Carolina, on February 1, 2003. It was part of a public gathering designed to contribute to oral histories of, as well as to celebrate, the Charlotte and Rock Hill, South Carolina, sit-ins of 1960–61 that launched "Jail, No Bail" actions across the country. That afternoon, Elsie White Springs, Thelma Johnson, and Betty Houchins Lundy, holding their own experiences and those of other women in mind, tactfully and tellingly complicated and recast the more familiar stories told in other sessions. Remembering the women, and not just the highly visible, charismatic males who were cast as leaders, they also saw more of the real stories of the movement.

They remembered that it was the students who, while continuing to attend classes and go to jobs essential to paying for their education, made the sit-in movement. They were supported by administrators and faculty at Johnson C. Smith University (a historically Black university in Charlotte), but, fearful of losing the funding on which the university was dependent, university officials stayed behind the scenes. The faculty did not mark their students absent when they had to miss classes. One woman remembered taking a test while in jail: "He brought it to me. He said, 'You can take it there. I know you can't cheat in jail'!"

The Black women also remembered receiving support from "white women who came out from Charlotte and did all they thought they could," and from the Jewish community. An audience member stood up and told us that she had gone to her job one day despite her involvement with the sit-ins, but while she was putting on her uniform, she was fired. She was promptly hired by the

Blumenthals, a prominent Charlotte family who had hired several other students whose activism had cost them their jobs. Someone remembered the role in the Civil Rights struggle played by Harry Golden, crusading editor of the *Carolina Israelite*: "One time a big old white boy took Harry by the shoulder and said, 'What's a Jew doing around here?' Harry, never at a loss, said, 'Starting a crusade to preserve Christian ethics.'"

A light-skinned, red-haired African American woman remembered being asked whether she would go with a light-skinned man to try to get served in a lunchroom in one of the most vehemently anti-desegregation department stores. She described walking past the ropes that had been set up to protect the entrance to the store from civil rights picketers and on into the lunchroom. There they sat down, ordered, and were served. "We sat there for about an hour," she said. "I was shaking, but no one told us to leave." When they had finished, they walked outside and joined the picketers. "*Then* they noticed us!" she said. When asked later about what she had learned from her experiences, she said, "I'm not a leader. I'm a follower. But I'm proud to have been part of something so important." Her male companion is now a well-known minister, still very much a leader and far more often interviewed by those studying the movement.

We also heard about a Black man in a wheelchair who rolled himself up to a lunch counter and asked to be served. Refused, he said, "I'm not sitting on your stools at your counter." This "confused them; they could throw out the others and be following the law, but he made it hard on them!"

An audience member stood up to remind us that Black maids in white homes were a crucial source of information. "They didn't think they even had to be careful what they said around us," she said. "They thought we were so dumb."

Another woman said that, at the university, "we were really respected. The faculty called us 'Miss and Mrs.,' and they really treated us well." That women were "respected" and "protected" was a major theme at this conference. The women's participation in planning meetings was limited because they, unlike the men, were required by the university to be in their rooms early every night. Nevertheless, they attended meetings when they could: "And when we were there, there wasn't any cussing, and we would not let them fall into violence. We told them, 'You're not coming if you can't get yourself under control.' And they didn't go if we said they couldn't."

Another woman said: "They wouldn't let us do some things. They didn't want us to get hurt. There weren't any of us there when they did the Rock Hill sit-in to get arrested and refuse bail." These women, 'protected' as they were, do not often appear in the histories; they still are not recognized as some of the men are.

A preacher in the audience asked whether the men had done wrong even though they meant to do right by treating women the way they had been brought up to do. One woman replied: "Black men mean well; they don't always do well. . . . Men have egos, you know, and we are cool." "Black women," she said, "are gifted." And then they all assured the preacher that they loved him.

More than once a man said: "If you have nothing to die for, you have nothing to live for." One of the women, focusing on how she lives rather than on death, said: "You know, I have faith, and that keeps me going. I respect every plant, every animal, every person—and my husband would say, 'and every machine,' so OK. We all need to do that."

Clear the space for such voices, and the ways we can think and so also act, as well as the values that inform both, begin to shift. In academe, too, such voices are finally being heard.

3. *FEMINIST GENEALOGIES, COLONIAL LEGACIES, DEMOCRATIC FUTURES,* an anthology edited by M. Jacqui Alexander and Chandra Talpade Mohanty, offers highly diverse but at the same time deeply consonant examples of more such "reserves of knowledge" from women who are still resisting whenever, whomever, and however they must and can.[19] The discussions in the anthology focus on the situation of women in postcolonial nations; they offer highly specific analyses of precolonial cultures, colonial conquest and rule, liberation struggles, and postcolonial regimes under which women still suffer sexualized violence, economic hardship, educational deprivation, constricted political power. For example, Amina Mama writes about an often hidden and denied continuum of sexualized violence that encompasses rapes during military conquest; rapes to threaten, punish, and humiliate colonized men by 'taking' 'their' women; rapes that act out the deadly mix of attraction to the exoticized Other with disgust for the 'inferior'; and rapes that continue to violate and subjugate women under postcolonial regimes. Amina Mama rejects simplistic labeling that 'explains' any of these as "just another instance of 'male violence.'"[20] Her multifaceted analysis challenges theories to take fully into account both the commonalities and the differences we need to comprehend the real experiences of specifically located women.

If we are to have a world in which no 'kind' of human is taken to be the defining, ideal type and standard for all, and no others are defined as 'kinds' whom it is legitimate for the few to use and abuse, we have a stake in such inclusive, complex thinking. It is not only a requisite for fine-tuned, effective action; such thinking is in itself a reason, a justification, for acting against mind-stopping domination. Hannah Arendt wrote: "Contrary to what is currently assumed about the proverbial ivory-tower independence of thinkers, no other human capacity is so vulnerable, and it is in fact far easier to act under conditions of tyranny than it is to think."[21]

## *STILL TRANSFORMING KNOWLEDGE: CIRCLING OUT, PRESSING DEEPER*

THE WOMEN WHO SPOKE on the "Women in the Sit-Ins" panel made it evident that turning off the spotlight on the singular figures of male leaders, and turning up the house lights in a gathering place with mobile microphones, allows us all to see and hear and try to comprehend more meaningful stories. Like others, I have continued to have such experiences through these years, and they have led me to extend and sometimes rethink what I had found before. I have tried to interweave these gleanings and reconfigurations throughout the rewritten book that follows, but it seems important also to discuss some of them separately here to give them more space to appear in their own light. I do not want to slip my changes by you; I want to be sure they are open to your thoughtful, critical attention so we can keep the work that invites us all going.

Here, then, is an introduction to some of the basic shifts that continue to transform *Transforming Knowledge.*

## Classifying Humans by Kind

Most important, I have changed what I take to be the root conceptual error that feeds knowledges that—as I now say more insistently—derive from and legitimate systems of domination. Earlier, I located that basic error in taking a few privileged males to be *Man* and then using "Man" as if it were nevertheless the inclusive term, the norm, and the ideal for all of us, as if a noninclusive, singularized abstraction from the great diversities of humanity could possibly be other than wrong in all senses of the term. I now realize—and wonder how I did not before—that this very serious error is preceded by another that entailed it: dividing humans into 'kinds,' not in the form of flexible, mutable distinctions, but as real divisions that are taken to be given (by gods, by a supreme deity, by nature—that is, not by the human agency and choice that make us responsible). This fraught move now seems to me evident: how else would we have wound up with the idea that some groupings of humans (recurrently sex/genders, races, class/castes, the 'disabled') are 'naturally' both different from and inferior or superior to others despite evidence that such categories of 'kinds' never hold for all individuals, not even those most viciously forced into lives in which it is extremely difficult, and deadly dangerous, to appear and to act differently from the prescriptions for their 'kind'?

Having been persuaded that such an error was still at work, but now curious about how it evolved, I worked on a brief sketch of how the division into 'kinds' developed in the dominant Western tradition. This, I think, is a history we need not to dismiss as if it did not, and does, not matter.

In *The Philosophical Roots of Anthropology* (1998), William Y. Adams argues that in Western cultures this error can be traced at least as far back as fifth-century, pre-Christian–era Greece. It took firm hold with the Neo-Platonic hierarchy that moves up from inanimate nature to plants, then animals, then humans, then angels, all under the gods/God.[1] Jumping forward to thirteenth-century Europe, we encounter Albertus Magnus, who in *De animalibus* discusses the idea of a "missing link" between animals and humans. This quest for not-quite-humans was itself further inscribed into dominant European culture with Sir William Petty's *The Scale of Creatures* (1676) and Sir William Tyson's *Orang-outang, sire homo silvestris, or, the Anatomy of a Pygmie* (1708). Carl Linnaeus, in *System of Nature* (1735), consolidated these moves toward a classificatory science that both divided 'kinds' from each other and related them externally on terms set by the neat boxes of a static order.

In 1802 in London, a doctor named William Turton issued an "amended and enlarged" version of Sir Charles's work that purported to show the "System of Nature through the three grand kingdoms of animals, vegetables, and minerals systematically divided into their several classes, orders, genera, species, and varieties with their habitations, manners, economy, structure, and peculiarities." It is striking that this systematic division of "Nature" included "manners" among the markers for the various 'kinds.' No doubt, since "manners" were also being used to categorize "minerals," he meant something like 'way of being' rather than social behavior. But when applied to human animals, it opened (or failed to close) the door to scientific validation of the cross-cultural ignorance and prejudices of the times in which these men (you will have noticed) wrote.

Thus, under "Mammalia, Order I. Primates, 1. Homo. Sapiens," we find in Linnaeus's system the "European" characterized as "fair, sanguine, brawny; hair yellow, brown, flowing; eyes blue; gentle, acute, inventive. Covered with close vestments. Governed by laws." We also find, among others, the "African":

"Black, phlegmatic, relaxed. Hair black, frizzled; skin silky; nose flat; lips tumid; crafty, indolent, negligent. Anoints himself with grease. Governed by caprice." And the "Asiatic": "Sooty, melancholy, rigid. Hair, black; eyes dark; severe, haughty, covetous. With loose garments. Governed by opinions."

Obviously, the categorizer here was not considering how "the European" appeared to those he observed. Nor was he thinking about females, who were not then likely to have been characterized as "brawny," as the "European" was.[2] These elaborations of ranked levels of 'kinds' of men were themselves evidently preceded by sex/gender hierarchies, as well as by other systems of oppression, including (always also gendered) slavery and caste.

The old roots are also evident in the Darwinism we are all taught (although for religious reasons, some still resist accepting it to hold on to their own hierarchies). As the sociologist Troy Duster writes, Darwin's *On the Origin of Species* presented "at once a meticulous classification system of organisms and a theory of the evolving relationships between them." That this "Theory of Evolution" put forward such relationships made it highly controversial: "man" was insulted by the idea that "he" was continuous in any sense with the "lower" animals. But Darwin still gives us a hierarchy, which Duster characterizes as follows: "At the bottom of the rung are the single-celled amoebae; at the top of the heap is the magnificently complex human. In between are all the combinations and permutations and mutations that form an intricate hierarchy of organisms. It is intricate. It is most decidedly hierarchical." Social Darwinism picked up the less static but still hierarchical order from biological Darwinism. In the hands of Herbert Spencer, the Englishman who "dominated the social thought of his age [the late 1800s] as few have ever done," social Darwinism also differentially placed humans, "the races and the cultures, societies, tribes, and nations in which they live" on an ascending scale. The "primitive savage" was at its base; the "civilized person" at its apex. And this was 'explained' and justified by what Spencer (not Darwin) called "the survival of the fittest." Thus, capacity for "civilization" defined in terms that glorified the categorizers' culture was defined in 'natural' terms as a capacity of the "fittest." And thus, in 1869, Spencer could note that "black children in the United States could not keep up with whites because of the former's biological and genetically endowed limits." This judgment, which is predicated on circular reasoning (one of the basic errors discussed in this book), has surfaced yet again in Arthur Jensen's work on racial "intelligence quotients," or IQs.[3]

Scientists have continued to root out such deforming errors, and we do not lack for histories and studies of stratification systems (as sociologists refer to them).[4] But they have a nasty way of reappearing: their roots go deep, and pruning does not suffice.

Western colonialism sought legitimacy from such classificatory hierarchies (among other rationalizations) and went on to concoct a still more complex brew. In "Murder in India," Pankaj Mishra writes: "The nineteenth century changed everything in South Asia, as it did in Europe. Western-style education under the auspices of British colonialism created a middle-class intelligentsia in India for the first time in its history. . . . This intelligentsia was also the first to embrace the modern [i.e. European] idea of nationalism: the idea, essentially, of a community that defines itself as a nation and aspires to form a state." This abstract, secular, imported/imposed idea of *nation* premised on the political relevance of a people was received as both promise and threat. It seemed to offer an identity for many on impartial terms—one with the potential to replace the old hierarchies from which the new middle classes were already escaping. But to others, that promise was belied by what they saw as a contradiction embedded in its claims to "impartiality." Mohammed Ali Jinnah, leader of the Muslim League and an advocate for a separate Muslim nation, suspected the Congress Party's nationalism of being no more than "slogans that concealed the ambition of an upper-caste Hindu elite to wholly supplant the British."[5] When the era of colonial domination ended, it left behind new as well as old roots of communal strife. Apparently inclusive meanings that are actually partial are dangerous in all forms. Mishra's article focuses on Hindu–Muslim conflict today in the Indian state of Gujarat. Kashmir, too, remains a battleground of nationalisms.

I am not seeking to discredit all ideals, all capacious notions, all claims to inclusiveness. On the contrary. My concern here is with the mystifications that arise when *partial* definitions and interests inform/deform supposedly impartial categories and institutions, and particularly when groups and 'kinds' of people are thereby rendered "unsuitable" for inclusion in "the people."

Here is another example of tangled legacies In "Pedagogy of Domination," Mokubung Nkomo lists the objectives of apartheid education in pre-liberation South Africa. His list makes it clear how hierarchical classification systems become deeply inscribed both in and through education. Apartheid education, Nkomo says, was designed:

1. To produce a semi-skilled black labor force to minister to the needs of the capitalist economy at the lowest possible cost. . . .
2. To socialize black students so that they can accept the social relations of apartheid as natural. . . .

3. To forge a consciousness and identity accompanied by a sense of "supe-riority" among whites. . . .
4. To promote the acceptance of racial or ethnic separation as the "nat-ural order of things." . . .
5. To promote black intellectual underdevelopment by minimizing the allocation of educational resources for blacks while maximizing them for whites.[6]

*Mutatis mutandis,* such purposes can be found across eras and national boundaries wherever classificatory systems of 'kinds' of humans exist as mir-rors of and supports for gendered, racialized, hierarchical social, political, cul-tural, educational, religious, and economic orders—in other words, sad to say, almost everywhere. In many countries—those that have allowed females any education at all—schools for girls and women have followed the same basic prescriptions as any apartheid system to train females for, and to accept, their 'natural' roles.

But efforts today to reject this naturalizing of imposed, unequal identities and roles can generate their own problems. For example, they can lead to the mistake of assuming that conceptual refutation of a root error need—and, indeed, *must*—not take differing forms in response to differing manifesta-tions of that error. For example, when a U.S. feminist speaks about "women" (let alone "woman"), she is liable to be charged with "reinscribing" static, essentialized, ranked, gendered, Eurocentric 'kinds'—that is, with preserving instead of recognizing them in order to challenge them. Right enough: we need to be careful here. But in some contexts, "disaggregation" of identities can work all too well with good old "divide and conquer" strategies. Nkomo there-fore chose to use "black" to refer to "all of the oppressed groups, namely: Africans, coloreds and Asian/Indians" because of "a desire to unify in the com-mon project of dismantling apartheid."[7] Domination is protean; sometimes resisting it requires an insistence on solidarity in identity.

## Conceptual Errors as
## Psychotic Conceptualizations

I am more tentative about the following shift in terms for the skews in think-ing that concern me, but so far I have found that it provokes intense and fruit-ful thinking, so I continue to try it out. The term *psychotic conceptualizations* seems to me to recognize the strange fusion of (on the one hand) dominance-serving prejudicial systems that fiercely insist on false and simplistic "principles" and definitions, with (on the other hand) remarkably fertile, often fast-changing interpretations, explanations, and actions. This conjunction of core rigidity and switchbacks to defend it can leave those who are trying to comprehend, to resist, or even to obey such systems feeling as if they are wrestling with Proteus. Grab on *here,* and the system sometimes kicks back with deadly force, sometimes simply melts away only to show up over *there.* An example: the hypersexualizing of women in the United States that holds us in our 'proper' role as sex objects has shifted under pressure from the women's movement, but it has diminished not at all.

To be 'acceptable' and 'attractive' (both coded also to signal racialized class), Euro-American females need no longer exaggerate our curves by wearing unhealthy, miserably uncomfortable corsets under wasp-waisted dresses. Similarly, we need no longer avoid developing 'masculine' muscles or wearing 'men's' trousers. Instead, we are supposed to sculpt ourselves into fat-free bodies that are to be as uncovered as is thus far allowable (more and more all the time). It is only apparently inconsistent that padded push-up bras and corsets (now displayed, not hidden) and dangerously destabilizing stiletto heels are making a comeback. The signals we are supposed to send that we are "real [need I say heterosexual?] women" have changed somewhat; the requirement that we send such signals as visibly as possible has not. And despite changes in styles, in our muscle development, in our own belief that we, too, have a right to be sexual when and as we choose, our vulnerability to sexualized violence has not lessened. It is endemic and stunningly, horrifyingly common.

Such cultural shiftings serve to avoid, not to make, changes in dominant systems. When we find them doing so most stubbornly and over time, they call to my mind the reality-resistant elaborations of psychoses. I precisely do not mean that they reveal individual pathologies. On the contrary. When what is taken to be 'rational,' 'correct,' 'sane,' and 'normal' has been distorted in a thoroughgoing, systemically enforced way, it is a whole dominant culture that has gone 'mad.' Things have turned topsy-turvy: it is those who resist an 'insane' reality—those who think and question and act on their consciences, by moral principles—who are labeled 'crazy' while those who go along with the madness are considered 'sane' and 'sensible' and 'sound.'

More than one political dissident has been locked up without trial or appeal in an "insane asylum." More than one worker has lost a job because, in choosing not to accept prescriptions for her 'kind,' she appears to her boss "unstable." And I have known more than one professor who has been written off as "having a chip on her/his shoulder" because she or he persisted in speaking up for the concerns of the long excluded. This is nutty, never mind how often it has been put forward as a defense of the sound, the sane, the sensible. I find it a relief to say that right out: these errors, reproduced in established systems, do not open us up to realities—they *resist* realities.

I repeat: we are not dealing with individual pathology here; we are dealing with pathologically closed, rationalizing systems, and it helps to recognize that so we can see how they do their work. McCarthyism, and the twenty-some–year reign of the U.S. House Un-American Activities Committee (from the late 1940s to the 1960s), is an example of a protean, rationalizing, crazy system now finally recognized as such. For such systems to work, they must turn knowledge to the purposes of dominance by rewarding intellectuals, artists, and "opinion leaders" who conform while discrediting and isolating others and sometimes even hounding them to death. The intellectual groundwork for these systems can be, and almost always has been, laid beforehand, and as hard as it is, we must recognize that, too. In *The Origins of Nazi Genocide,* Henry Friedlander cites, to chilling effect, how the U.S. eugenics movement directly contributed to "science"-based justifications for the Holocaust as well as to forced sterilizations and other egregious practices in the United States.

Here is one instance Friedlander discusses: Harry Hamilton Laughlin, the director of the Eugenics Record Office in New York ("financed with Carnegie, Harriman, and Rockefeller money"), authoritatively "'compared human racial crossing with mongrelization in the animal world' and argued that 'immigrants from southern and eastern Europe, especially Jews, were racially so different from, and genetically inferior to, the current American population that any racial mixture would be deleterious.'" Determined to accept this spurious knowledge, scholars such as the Princeton psychologist Carl C. Brigham found themselves with the kind of problem that erroneous scholarship produces when it has been created to control rather than illuminate reality: what, then, is to be done with the counterevidence? In this situation, Brigham had to deal with the documented achievements of Jewish intellectuals. He chose to reinterpret that evidence to fit with the tests his prejudices (and perhaps his career ambitions) led him to credit. He "theorized that 'the able Jew is popularly recognized not only because of his ability, but because he is able and a Jew,' and concluded that 'our figures, then, would rather tend to disprove the popular belief that the Jew is highly intelligent.'"[8] That "would rather tend" indicates that he knew he was stretching things, but his redefinition of documentary evidence as a discreditable "popular belief" propped him back up. By this forced interpretation, he tried to legitimate mutually intensifying fears of Jews, of immigrants generally, and of miscegnation so that government action against these "threats" could claim scientific justification.

While researching this book, I found it impossible to avoid this next point, which you will encounter again. Driving the eugenics movement, as exemplified by Brigham's studies, was an obvious fear of uncontrolled and uncontrollable *breeding.* It was believed at the time (and to some extent still is) that "miscegenation," "cross-breeding," "intermarriage" between 'kinds' of humans would lead to the "mongrelization" of 'real' Americans. This possibility, so dreaded by not a few men in charge, did more than threaten to mix 'good' stock with 'bad'; it also seems to have threatened 'proper' sex by calling to racist minds visions of rutting animals. Control of "well-bred" women was thereby reconfigured as 'protection' from dangerously 'animalistic' men—revealing yet again the implication of racializations with sex/gender.

Another prime example of psychotic conceptualizations implicating racializations with sex/gender control systems is starkly laid out in an exhibition of historical postcards of lynchings in the United States. In "No Sanctuary" (2001), curated by Joseph Jordan, the postcards on display had been made by someone ordinary from photographs that someone ordinary took, that ordinary people bought, that were routinely handled and delivered by the U.S. Postal Service, that were received by ordinary people, and that bore mundane, and often cheerful, messages. Lynching was ordinary; it was supported by knowledge, by faith, by convention, and, more or less explicitly, by government and legal officers. It was also mad, insane, glaringly immoral and unjust but accepted by those who did not suffer it as the opposite.

When I talk about "psychotic conceptualizations," I do not mean to suggest that these ways of imposing 'sense' on the world are 'irrational' in a way that would sideline appropriate moral judgments. The Nazis who were tried at Nuremberg were held responsible for promulgating and for following orders—orders that were legitimated by utterly fallacious "science" as well as by the state. The moral madness of a collective order does not exculpate the individuals who go along with it.

I am also not using social psychology, although doing so can be very interesting and suggestive as long as it does not reduce explanations to psychological causes that fail to implicate ways of thinking that are broadly accepted as 'rational.' As the social psychologist James Waller writes in *Becoming Evil: How Ordinary People Commit Genocide and Mass Killing,* we do not need a "single broad-brush psychological state to explain extraordinary human evil." Waller proposes that understanding the "ordinariness" of some evil entails becoming "aware of our own capacity" for it. He suggests that such awareness requires us to understand "the dispositional and situational factors that foster it."[9] Yes, and my own focus—which I offer not to compete with but to complement such explanations—is on the conceptual, rationalized factors that prepare minds for, legitimate, and perpetuate domination that can turn genocidal. This is why I have chosen a term, "psychotic," that names not an individual or a social-psychological causal factor but a kind of thinking.

I could have written about "ideologies," which can also be defined as closed meaning systems that brook no contradictory interpretations, no interruptions by mere realities. But still, I think "psychotic" is useful. It helps to capture that sense we have, when confronted with some ways of thinking, that nothing we say or do can get through and the paralysis that can set in when those we feel the most urgent need to reach, to stop from doing great harm, keep changing without ceasing to harm, becoming more dangerous as they reinterpret reality ever more sweepingly.

I do not want my use of "psychotic" for erroneous conceptualizations that resist change to reinforce fears of individuals suffering the terrible world-loss of psychiatric illness. We are at far, far greater risk from closed meaning systems accepted by many, legitimated by some knowledges, and used by those in power for their own ends.

I realize that there is a significant difference in dramatic force between "conceptual errors" and "psychotic concepts." The new term came to me after years spent studying the connections among acts of violence sustained by unjust systems and their strikingly similar roots in some congruent established, supposedly disinterested knowledges. It speaks to the need I felt to find a term for rationality in the service of thought systems that have lost touch with realities, those about which outsiders are reduced to saying: But that's mad! Nevertheless, I do not want to lose the call to simple, good, clear thinking suggested by my earlier term, "conceptual errors." Nor do I wish to undercut the crucial point that deadly errors can and do appear in obvious, even obviously foolish, form—as "errors," "mistakes." If we remain alert to such errors and are willing to remember how very serious they can become if not set right, we may be able to focus more effectively on undoing them wherever we encounter them.

The cure for closed systems of thought that keep shifting on the surface to defend some very basic underlying errors is not individualized psychological analysis; nor is it the substitution of some other system of thought or belief.

It is a reawakened capacity to think and act responsively, responsibly, appropriately, and respectfully in relation to anything and anyone we encounter. It requires us to remain critical of the conventions, concepts, and theories—right along with the laws and policies—that preshape realities for us. We cannot avoid abstractions and generalizations: we make them as spiders spin webs, because that is how minds, languages, and cultures do their work. Even to scorn abstractions requires abstraction—as does thinking, "It's time for lunch." But we should question, challenge, and keep reconfiguring abstractions in an ongoing, open fashion as we encounter the 'more' that we are capable of perceiving and thinking and dreaming, and that resists capture in any conceptual/emotive web.

As Hannah Arendt said, not only can we "unfreeze concepts," but we can also "think without a banister." We are socialized creatures—sometimes insanely so—but there is always someone who is thinking, and we can always do so ourselves if we will. Surely the most crucial purpose of education is to increase the number of thinkers among us and to strengthen us all in the courage as well as the arts that thinking requires. In that sense, education is called to be therapeutic and to remember that we cannot unfreeze old, or newer, erroneous conceptualizations of what it means to be human without thinking through even—particularly—the roughest patches.

A professor who heard a paper I gave at a philosophy conference in which I introduced the notion of psychotic conceptualizations, using the exhibit of lynching postcards to illustrate it (as I have done here), came up to me afterward to say that she agreed with those who, during the discussion, had said they did not like "psychotic conceptualizations" as a term. "Good," I said. "Thank you. Why not?" "Oh," she said, "well, you know—lynching was so very, very horrible. I cannot bear to think about it." And then she talked about lynching with the kind of rawness we feel when our usual categories have been disabled. Finally, someone else virtually shoved her aside to tell me with equal intensity what she was thinking. OK, I thought: if a phrase with which I found myself after being rubbed raw by what I was studying throws others into struggling again with questions that are painful and essential to face, I had better stick with it awhile.

## Including Nature

It is common in the new scholarships to speak of "naturalizing" identities such as racialized sex/genders, and to analyze the effects of thus explaining them as *necessarily* the way they are. It was evident from the outset to me and to other feminists that "nature" explanations were significantly in play whenever people thought about women. That is why the distinction between *sex* and *gender* was so important: we needed to detach physiological differentiations from the extraordinarily elaborate prescriptions for how we were to enact what we supposedly just were "by nature" in order to show how those prescriptions served not sexual reproduction of a species, but gendered production of inegalitarian social orders—which, we can now say, then turn around to affect and to control reproduction and sexualities in all their expressions.

It was also clear early on that being defined as "closer to nature" meant being shifted down on a scale of human worth. This was one of the ways women and some 'kinds' of men were mutually feminized—that is, over-determined as sexual, as emotional, as primal, and as less rational in contrast to 'civilized,' 'rational' Man. I now believe that we cannot undo the old, mutually implicating hierarchies unless we rethink the radical division of Man from Nature that persists not only despite Darwin but in Darwinism's very own hierarchies, especially as they keep reappearing in versions of social Darwinism.

In the dominant culture of the United States, "humans and nature" is still a common locution, as if our relation to all that makes up and lives on the earth were external to our own definitively (not "naturally") different human being. This ampersand division persists despite transforming scholarships and movements such as ecology, ecofeminism, science studies (with feminist critiques closely engaged), and studies of as well as by peoples with very different understandings of the human–nature nexus (for example, Native American and Indigenous studies [First Nations studies in Canada]; African studies; and more specific studies of traditions such as Wicca, Vodun, alchemy, animism, and shamanism).

In what is clearly circular reasoning, sex, race, and disabilities (for prime examples) are defined within cultures and languages and read into nature; then categorically unequal treatment is explained as appropriate to and legitimated by the very nature into which it has been inscribed. Thus, in her introduction to *Race: The Origins of an Idea, 1760–1850,* H. F. Augstein writes about nineteenth-century racial theory, which set out to "answer . . . questions about the biological nature of man" posed in the preceding century—that is, "the [pre-existent] notion that mankind is divisible into a certain number of 'races' whose characteristics are fixed and defy the modifying influences of external circumstance." Circular reasoning again: what is 'proved' is what was already believed, but now it is cast in scientist terms that license those beliefs.

I said that the old classifications have not gone away. In a footnote on the same page, Augstein observes what we have already noted: that "the biologically founded racial theory developed in the nineteenth century lasted well into the twentieth century culminating in the racial ideology of the German National Socialists." She adds: "In recent years, there have been attempts to revivify pseudo-scientific notions of racial theory."[10] And where races are defined as natural, breeding is at issue: racialization is precisely not about individuals; it is about "stock," "bloodlines," "genetics," and "genealogies" that are used to explain how 'kinds' of people are, and why they should remain, separate and unequal. And where breeding is of concern, gendering systems for directing and controlling it are already there: racialized, class/caste, nationalistic, and other hierarchies of abilities and functions are informed by and serve gendered systems of control.

Yes, contemporary Western science has declared *race* to be a concept that is scientifically unsustainable. Augstein reports that, although "specific genetic configurations can be discerned in various populations, . . . they are far more diverse" than racial theory would have them be, running into "many thousands."[11] They are also, of course, mutable through time as a result of reproductive activity (breeding)—unless, as in the United States until 1967 (when the Supreme Court finally ruled them unconstitutional), antimiscegenation laws keep supposedly natural but socially and legally (and extralegally, often violently) enforced divisions among 'kinds' from becoming naturally blurred. Caste systems and some religions that proscribe "intermarriage" have the same effect, of course; there are, around the world, many systems that forbid (albeit never successfully) "what comes naturally." The circularity then mutates socially. Races, castes, classes, ethnicities, and 'normalcy' (of body, of brain/mind, of social behavior) are constructed as necessary to 'purity' and propriety. These are read into nature *not* (if we look more closely) as created by it but as always potentially subverted by it. They are then explained and justified as efforts to maintain the best of nature, especially by insuring "good breeding" and the "purity of the line."

Bimorphic classifications of sex that are taken to be the basis of and warrant for natural heterosexuality are not always mentioned as foundational to such circularity; nor are they always seen as themselves circular, but I now find it hard to avoid thus characterizing them. Insofar as breeding is of concern, complex and profligate sexualities are vulnerable to being forcibly reduced to the single goal of reproduction. In humans, this obviously privileges heterosexuality, which is socially prescribed in defiance of natural variations even as it is defended as the only 'natural' kind of sex.

This sort of circularity can intensify to the level of psychotic systems that predefine realities and that admit fewer and fewer contradictions from any kind of evidence. In the United States, "inter-sexed" infants have been operated on to 'fix' their naturally 'unnatural' bodies—a striking example of the social construction and medical (re)construction of sexual realities. And once such systems have been established as natural (in the sense of necessary as well as "healthy," "right," and "good"), not even retraction by scientists (or religious figures, or any other authority) suffices to root them out.

Nature, that figuration of the undomesticated and uncontrolled, is commonly referred to as "she," as "Mother Nature," a designation that—like gendering anything or anyone female in more than one dominant meaning system—simultaneously reflects scorn, fear, and romanticized reverence. Karen J. Warren sums up a discussion of "sexist-naturist language": "Language which feminizes nature in a (patriarchal) culture where women are viewed as subordinate and inferior reinforces and authorizes the domination of nature: 'Mother Nature' is raped, mastered, conquered, mined; her secrets are 'penetrated' and her 'womb' is to be put into service of the 'man of science.' . . . The exploitation of nature and animals is justified by feminizing them; the exploitation of women is justified by naturalizing them."[12]

More circular reasoning here, supported by yet another of the basic errors to be discussed later: faulty generalization. Man having been taken to be not just one among other 'kinds' of humans but humankind itself—and humankind at its best—Woman could only be defined as outside that representative, normative, ideal category. "Woman" was thereby moved down the scale of human worth to come closer to the nature that Man has not quite dominated and that has threatened him not only by its awe-full powers but also by surrounding him and reminding him of his dependence. In Western literatures and in some other strongly patriarchal, masculinist cultures, "man who is of woman born" is a reminder not of life-giving and sustaining connection, but of shame. Eve, it has been written, caused shame to enter the world.

"Natural man" was equated with childhood, with "the primitive," the "animalistic," the "lower drives of human nature"; as a result, "civilized," "mature," "cultivated," "high-caste," "mandarin" man felt a need to control himself by mastering both his 'lower' "animalistic" natural desires and those he blamed for arousing them. Hence all the man-made laws that deny women the right even to be seen in public—a domain in which people emerge from privacy to appear among others, and long (and still in significant parts of the world) held to be properly for males only. In the United States, "the man in the street" still means an "ordinary" citizen; "a woman of the streets" refers to a prostitute. And people who might suggest and arouse desires not legitimated by association with 'natural' reproduction have been closeted.

We should note that the Man/Nature constructions with which we still contend are not true dualisms. They are hierarchies, at the bottom of which is, literally, "rock bottom," "mindless," "inanimate," "lifeless" nature. But even the great divide between "man" and *inanimate* nature does not assure would-be superior "Man" that there is no threat or possibility of slipping down toward it. Such crossings are taboo, not impossible: taboos exist only where one might transgress.

Such taboos need reinforcing by knowledge as well as social and religious proscriptions. Animals *must not* be interpreted through human categories, Western science has told us: that is the heresy of anthropomorphism. "Must not" is, of course, a proscription that precludes studies that could possibly question it. Why lock that door? What is being protected? Animals were long ago defined as nonconscious, nonintelligent, noncommunicative creatures, so radically different from and inferior to Man that he could make use of them without any moral qualms. And as exemplars of what it meant to be radically lacking in the qualities required for moral personhood, to be a subject rather than an object, animals could be and were used to signify low status for some 'kinds' of humans: "he is an animal" means that he is out of control and that we are licensed to do anything to protect ourselves from him. Animality was thus both thrown out of Man's nature, and known to implicate him: Man *could* fall to that level. That weird external/internal division is also evident at a very basic level in man's relations with women: she "tempts" him; he "falls"; he blames and punishes and restricts her.

New research on animals, much like feminist research, is breaking through these morally fraught definitions. Scientists now tell us that animals do not use what humans (some of us) have defined as language, but they do communicate; that they do not have written ethics, but they do cooperate, make up after conflicts, and work at maintaining relationships. Consider research by Jane Goodall (chimpanzees), Birute Galdikas (orangutans), Dian Fossey (gorillas), Irene Pepperberg (the grey parrot), and Denise Hertzing (dolphins), among many others (notably, Frans de Waal, Marc Hauser, Sarah Blaffer Hrdy, David Mech). These scientists are demonstrating to us what some nonhuman animals can indeed do; in doing so, they are also complicating and enriching our understanding of what potent notions such as *consciousness, intelligence,* and *reasoning* (and the moral systems premised on their possession or lack thereof) can mean and do for us. Man's—actually, only a few men's—great escape clause from moral responsibility for all defined as other and less than him is finally beginning to fail. But it is by no means completely gone, and even where it totters, systems of all sorts are propping it up despite the efforts of feminist, indigenous, environmental, and animal rights scholars and activists.

The work needed to free ourselves from the partial knowledge skewed by conceptual errors of the sort traced in this book will not be completed, I therefore believe, until nature, too, has been rethought quite literally from the ground up. I have mentioned a few nondominant traditions and movements. These and others are themselves now the subject matter of many scholars, writers, and activists grounded in them (for example, Linda Hogan, Paula Gunn Allen, Winona LaDuke, Leslie Marmon Silko, among Native Americans). Among efforts to take up the call to rethink nature by thinkers situated *within* dominant traditions, let me mention just one, which I select because it demonstrates an effort to hold together "nature, polis, ethics" in a determined way. Strachan Donnelley, founder of the Center for Humans and Nature, writes that "we are groping for a new substantive 'world view' ethics and a new art of 'moral ecology.'" To that end, he insists that "we must forever critically ask of present regional perspectives, 'What has been left out of account?'"; that we must recognize "not only the plural values and moral obligations relating to nature and different spheres of human activity, but also the different historical and cultural perspectives and values of [a] region's various human communities . . . and ethnic groups"; and that we "need to think regionally, systemically, pluralistically, and historically."[13] You will have observed how attuned this very complex approach is to the kinds of thinking I sketched earlier as emerging in the new academy: here you can see them put to work as a philosophically informed methodology. But what is lacking, yet again, is a feminist critique that is itself informed by critiques of constructions of nature that cross all these lines, and that will be required if we are to keep our critiques inclusive and drive them deep enough.

Gloria Anzaldua describes poetically what such efforts may be like: "The thrust toward spiritual realization, health, freedom, and justice propels you to help rebuild [a] bridge. . . . You realize that 'home' is that bridge, the in-between place of constant transition, the most unsafe of places."[14]

## Reordering Historical Time

Having realized that rethinking nature is essential to feminisms, I began to recognize that placing some expressions of nature 'lower' than others also affects dominant chronologies (logics of time). Threading some dominant notions of nature and history together is a strangely disordered sense of time of which I think we need to be aware, and critical.

The conflation of "closeness to nature" with the inferiority of women and "primitives" produced the notion that some people(s) are, as Andy Smith puts it, "'early' people." Smith, in discussing the persistence of this view even in some ecofeminisms, observes that "one would not describe white people as 'early' people." Why are Natives labeled 'early' people when they are "contemporary people who face contemporary problems"?[15] Here we have a picture of a few normative, self-defined–as–ideal humans surrounded in their present by leftovers from the past, by childlike "throwbacks" and "missing links" who have not developed 'properly.' Common terms such as "less-developed nations" and the way some people still say "girls" when they are talking about adult women reflect not just a notation of some people's lack of modern technologies or America's youth fetishism, but also the paternalism that goes with patriarchy. Both continue the old notion that the few—now cast as the only ones who have properly "grown up," developed in the 'right' ways—should therefore 'protect,' condescend to, and play the role of forceful tutor and guardian for all others.

One can of course hold various views about "development." My point here is that when "development" is at issue, a kind of conceptual pincer effect can be activated that makes it hard for even the best-intentioned people to avoid colluding with the dominance systems with which this book is concerned. Reviewing *Globalization and Its Discontents* by Joseph E. Stiglitz, Benjamin M. Friedman wrote: "The IMF [International Monetary Fund], [Stiglitz] argues ... adopt[s] a 'cookie cutter' approach in which one set of policies is right for all countries regardless of their individual circumstances." The thinking behind such "cookie cutter" policymaking is ideological: a belief in the superiority of free markets, which Stiglitz views as a quasi-religion "impervious to either counterarguments or counterevidence."[16] The conceptual 'pincer' effect results, on the one hand, from an uncritiqued (dis)ordered historical logic of "development," and on the other hand, from an analysis that takes one system—that of the "First World" (often narrowly construed as the United States)—to exemplify economic development. There's the old root error again, acting psychotically (as it too often does) to blind adherents to counterarguments or counterevidence.

Equality doesn't stand a chance of being taken seriously as long as people(s) are categorically seen as throwbacks, as leftovers, as childlike and immature. By this logic, "they" must be helped or forced to become the *same* as the proper, self-defining few before equality can even be considered, a misunderstanding of equality we will encounter time and again.

## Rights, Public/Private—and Privatization

That women and devalued men have been defined as "closer to nature" and as "backward" both historically and developmentally has contributed to rationalizations for denying us public life. This matters a great deal: *privatizing* serves domination by disabling people from making their cause apparent to others, denying them basic rights, and thereby keeping them vulnerable to the power of those who do have public lives and rights. It should not surprise anyone that movements for full public rights and recognition are experiencing backlashes. Too many people, too many long-standing injustices, too many connections between these and the beliefs and systems predicated on justification for denying their claims are out "in the streets" with such movements.

These backlashes are also linked to increasing efforts by the powers that be to "shrink" government, although these efforts are usually discussed in terms of saving tax dollars, making governments more efficient, and 'liberating' citizens from the state. Perhaps—but they are, and more importantly, also a way to deal with all those troublesome, newly public people without openly trying to take away our hard-won rights. Shrinking the sphere of public governance also shrinks the spheres in which people can exercise rights that are granted and protected by governments.

The critical legal scholar Patricia Williams writes: "In the law, rights are islands of empowerment. To be un-righted is to be disempowered, and the line between rights and no-rights is most often the line between dominators and oppressors. Rights contain images of power, and manipulating those images, either visually or linguistically, is central in the making and maintenance of rights."[17] It matters—and it is progress—that rights have been extended to those long defined as the wrong 'kinds' of creatures to hold them. It matters that there is growing international recognition of human rights that transcend national borders and legal systems. But this is not simply an additive process: it takes something away from those who have benefited from having populations of "un-righted" people, and they know that.

Changes in who and what is public are also changes in who and what is genuinely private. If you do not have a legally recognized, protected public and work life, you do not have a safe private life, either. Everywhere and always, people who have no public rights to invoke are subject to those who do. Women of most groups know this, and so do men of categorically excluded groups. "Public" and "private" are nondualistic terms. Like humans/nature, man/woman, Black/white, European/"Oriental," 'normal'/'handicapped,' heterosexual/homosexual, "public" and "private" mark points on a scale that slides down from possession to dispossession, from power to powerlessness, from recognized boundaries to constant vulnerability to the violation of intrusion.

To be *privatized* is to be shoved down the scale toward the extreme of being rendered "civically dead" (the term applied to penitentiary inmates who are stripped of their rights as citizens). It has also meant to be owned, closeted, domesticated, removed to reservations, shut in, and it is what being married or widowed has meant for women in many cultures. Patricia Williams also observes that to be privatized is to become vulnerable at any moment to intrusion, violation, and exploitation without recourse other than appeals to the conscience of the publicly empowered. Those who lack rights can only beg for favors—which places a premium on being ingratiating, pleasing, apparently loyal and grateful. It seems apparent that the qualities of femininity—those qualities that in a man signal "emasculation"—derive not from being female but from the need faced by those without rights to propitiate and, if possible, to manipulate those who have them. Femininity is then a strategy, not a 'natural' quality.

This age of movements for equality and recognition has profoundly disturbed systems of dominance. As old maps used to say, here there be dragons—and they are not sleeping. In the United States a very curious alliance has been developing between exceedingly wealthy corporate interests and religious fundamentalists, whose base is generally among the lower middle class and the poor. Corporate interests want rights-providing, publicly accountable governments to get out of their way so they can pursue the "efficiency" and "flexibility" that allow them to put profits above all. Fundamentalists seek 'freedom' from government so they can enforce their own creeds and hierarchies without hindrance. Both tend to see their own interests as justifiably overriding state and national boundaries; both tend to be headed by powerful leaders; both can and do adduce doctrines that forecast a better life for those who join them. Few spheres of public life, few "islands of empowerment" that protect differing values, lives, views are safe when these interests make common cause against them.

Schools, prisons, welfare systems, public lands, social security, the military (right after I wrote that, I saw in the October 13, 2002, issue of the *New York Times* a report on "America's For-Profit Secret Army," subheaded "Military Contractors Are Hired to Do the Pentagon's Bidding Far from Washington's View")—these and more are now the focus of privatization in the United States (and, for that matter, elsewhere, often as a result of American pressure, sometimes exerted through international organizations such as the IMF). When these resources and services are privatized, so are people. Privatizing prisons, for example, means that some people can be legally used against their will to generate profits for owners. Privatizing public lands means less freedom of public movement, of use and enjoyment; it also shuts out those whose traditional faiths were once celebrated on those lands. Privatizing exploitation of natural resources directs profits away from public projects and services and into private pockets, and makes it difficult to protect the possibility of future generations of citizens enjoying differing relations to the earth.

The struggle to keep a publicly empowered, rights-wielding few from controlling crucial public goods by restricting the rights of others is ongoing and hardly new. Nevertheless, it is grounds for hope that new fields of knowledge are developing along with movements for rights and justice that speak for the protection of the differences that should and do appear in public when equality, not sameness, is protected. We see these developments coming together in the efforts being made by and on behalf of displaced peoples, whose unrighted status illustrates all too clearly that being privatized means not having a protected place where one's civic rights are protected, where one's civic powers are recognized. People who lack national status in this age of nation-states become, as Hannah Arendt put it, "worldless"—they become "pariah" peoples who are vulnerable at every moment to intrusion; to repeated displacement; to vicious stereotyping; to social, cultural, and educational exclusion; to economic exploitation; and to suffering violence without recourse. We do not, as the popular saying has it, have "a right to be here" independent of systems that grant, protect, and conceptually underwrite such a right.[18]

Clearly, the notion that freedom means shrinking the sphere of government rather than the liberty to exercise public rights guaranteed by government can be a dangerous one. Of course, governments can intrude unjustly: totalitarian regimes have shown us just how thoroughly and devastatingly they can do to all people what those who have historically been un-righted have suffered. But the cure for unjust intrusions by governments is the establishment of public rights, laws, and protections; it is not privatized domination by people and powers that cannot be held publicly accountable. This can be hard to keep believing, even for those who remember having few or no rights. Where we have governmental, legal protections that are still new, what we too often see when we call on those protections is, yet again, just how deep and resilient the old systems still are. As Alice Kessler-Harris writes in a review of a book on *Jenson v. Eveleth Mines* (the case that established the right of women "to sue as a class for sexual harassment and . . . placed the burden of proof on the company, not the victims"), by the end of the thirteen-year struggle, "the women were ill, exhausted, bitter and resentful." Their work situation had not improved but deteriorated over the course of the trial, as threatening sexualized hostilities by male miners were compounded by the failure of management and the union to protect them. The tactics used in court against the women included "vicious cross-examination in which every aspect of their emotional life was explored [in an effort to 'prove' that] they had histories of emotional disturbance"[19]—proof that the legal systems whose task it is to enforce rights are still permeated with the same problems we need those rights to combat.

At such times, it can be helpful to remember—as civil rights workers in the United States did—that Gandhi called the tactics of India's anticolonial struggle "experiments in truth." Actions were planned to be educational rather than immediately corrective. Through acting, people publicized the values they chose to serve and practiced resistance, believing this to be important whether or not those actions succeeded in the short run. Truth and justice are, I believe, propaedeutic for each other. It is not that we must know, or have, one before we can establish the other. Rather, as the progressive pragmatists in the United States also taught, we make our meanings through our actions, and we act in light of what we hold to be meaningful. John Dewey taught that "ends" are no more than a special kind of "means"—they are "ends-in-view" and subject to ongoing emendation. One lesson we can take from histories of successful resistance to domination is not that "one person can change history," but that it takes an ongoing movement—the support of many people who are in for the long haul—to keep us from being crushed one by one by the systems we are challenging.

Rita Arditti writes about the Grandmothers of the Plaza de Mayo in Argentina and their "Struggle against Impunity," against the power that allows dominant orders to replace one another without genuinely changing the old, deforming systems. The *abuelas* went public with their search for the grand-children who were born in prison before their mothers were "disappeared." They demanded that those children be found and rescued from the families that had adopted them. Some of those adoptive families contained the very people who had murdered or supported the murderers of the parents. The *abuelas'* courageous actions made the "right to identity" a public matter: emerging from privatized lives as traditional women, they wrested genealogy—the basic logic of gender control—from the hands of those in power. And they did not stop when they won some victories or retreat in the face of some terrible losses. Arditti quotes the *abuelas*: "We must not forget or be silent. Our duty is to keep the memory, to keep talking tirelessly about the horrors of the Argentine genocide. We will not let any episode, insignificant as it may seem, go by without expressing our views. We will clarify and spread the truth, the whole truth, to enlighten the minds of those who still refuse to understand."[20]

# Religion

I mentioned religion in relation to privatization, and I would have had to discuss it at length had I told the full story of the *abuelas*. In thinking about logics of domination that make use of categorizations of humans by hierarchically ranked 'kinds,' I have not been able to avoid the realization that religions have at times been deeply implicated in authorizing those hierarchies. *In God's Name: Genocide and Religion in the Twentieth Century*, edited by Omer Bartov and Phyllis Mack, is only one recent study of this troubling, hotly contested issue that brings to the surface the sorts of connections I am tracing. It is a present as well as a historical fact that some religions teach and enforce the inferiority (not the equal difference) of women; that they teach that it is proper to subjugate some 'kinds' of men to others; that they preach that some "unbelievers" (who may well be believers in a different faith) can and should be shunned, cast out, even slaughtered. In more than one country and era, various religions have condoned slavery and underwritten the privileges of the few as reflecting a deity's will or reward. I do not need to rehash all of this; these things are known, and they are of deep concern to many believers in the same way that scientific authorizations of divisions by 'kind' are of deep concern to many scientists. But we cannot leave corrective work only in their hands. These are increasingly transnational problems; furthermore, believers, like all experts—like all of us—can too easily fail to see their own most form-ative assumptions. We need one another's help for such work.

Religions can carry within them in an extreme form the error of conflat-ing partial truths with Truth-itself. That error is as hard to avoid as it is dan-gerous. Whenever we express high-level abstractions in images, in words, in stories, in rituals—whenever we give them socially and culturally compre-hensible content—we particularize them. In doing so, we exclude: particulars are by definition not general, let alone universal. But problems arise when some particulars then come to partake of the Truth, and others do not. Depic-tions of a white male Jesus Christ in a world stratified by race and gender ineluctably comes to signify that there is something divine about whiteness and maleness. Religions that forbid depictions of G_d or the use of His name (that's a particularization right there) are recognizing that reduction and reject-ing it. But it happens anyway: there are particular believers in nondepictable deities, and there are non-believers; there are religious laws prescribed in par-ticular forms that make it possible to follow them (eat this, but not that; say this, but not that). And all this, which makes a religion something other and more than a system of conceptual abstraction (mathematics, for example, can express relations, functions, and laws without concretizing them), also dis-tinguishes one religion's universal truths from those of others. Thus have emerged plural claims to possession of differently expressed universal truths. This is dangerous and is not rendered any less so by claims that "we all wor-ship the same God." Whether we do so or not, we do so differently, each group believing that its way is warranted by true universality. Thus, religion poses in acute form the question of whether it is possible (conceptually, emotion-ally, socially, politically) to have an equal pluralism of universalized claims to truth and goodness. I do not deny that it is possible, nor do I deny that some religious people are deeply engaged in just such efforts to avoid pitting one particular set of universal claims against the others. Many have struggled to right the wrongs that result from religious intolerance justified by claims to possession of "the one true faith." Some have died for their efforts; some have been excommunicated and otherwise silenced. It is in their spirit that I remem-ber that, and look for how, history as well as contemporary struggles over inclusiveness cannot avoid critiquing religious establishments, beliefs, and theologies as well as all other systems.

When religions fail to root out prejudicial exclusions that were taken to be right and proper by the humans who turned them into human institutions, the result is a blending of prejudices with the unavoidable particularity already in risky tension with claims to universality. This brew can then confound the efforts of adherents to be true to the best of their faith. It can also, as we know too well, license deadly acts by those with no qualms about claiming universality not only for their particular practices, but for their prejudices. The same is true for philosophical and scientific universals: when they are actually derived through abstraction from an already exclusive, partial sample, the result is partial universals. That this is self-contradictory is more than a logical, linguistic observation: the conjoining of contradictory terms can indicate that there is another, more potent logic actually at work. Religions that preach love and respect for all individuals even while prescribing unequal roles and possibilities for women, and/or categorically refusing full inclusion of homosexuals, are contradictory on their face; they are, however, also consistent with old, naturalized hierarchical sex/gender logics. It is these logics, the ways of thinking that support exclusion, exploitation, domination that should concern us most of all. Without their continuing, if sometimes hidden, deformations of our minds, we would do better at seeing—a crucial step in renouncing—such obvious contradictions as hating in the name of a just and loving deity.


SO, IT IS TIME to move on to the book that keeps transforming itself in my mind, and has done so all too often in my computer, as I have continued to listen, to read, to think.

# I

# No One Beginning

THERE ARE BEGINNINGS we must struggle to unearth and to uproot because they were, and could again be, deadly. Paula Gunn Allen, in her introduction to an anthology of American Indian literature, writes:

> The very influential work of the American historian Frederick B. Turner played a large role in the redefinition of Native people as forever beyond the pale of 'civilized' culture, as did a dramatic rise in xenophobia, cultural chauvinism, and white supremacist thought that culminated in the establishment of the Third Reich in Germany but was by no means confined to that unhappy nation.[1]

There are also beginnings on which we still draw. For instance, Ann J. Lane writes of the American historian Mary Beard (1876–1958):

> Without much support from the woman's movement, without a large body of ideas upon which to build, without models of any kind to follow, virtually alone, she audaciously placed women at the centre of history and society, and then she insisted that the world look again from her

perspective. . . . Beard's life and work embody her thesis: women are neg-
lected in the writing of history, but the effect of their existence is a reality of history.[2]

Both troubling and inspiring works such as these remind us that there are
fault lines in what established scholars and their students have known, taught,
and believed. These fault lines are deep; they run through and across disciplines, cultures, and countries. Too many communities, too many textured,
layered tales have begun, developed among courageous groups that have refused
to be silent, only to be erased from the "story of mankind," from the records
of those who control access to public memory, oral and written. Discontinu-
ity, disruption, loss have marked our stories and so our self-perceptions just
as surely as have discovery, achievement, and courage.

The curious thing is not that the dominant have silenced those they use
for their own purposes. It is hardly surprising that men have not wanted
women to be heard; that imperial powers have suppressed the languages and
cultures of those from whom they steal; that racially privileged groups do not
want those from whom they demarcate themselves so fiercely to appear and
speak as equals. The curious thing is how hard it is to integrate all those who
have for so long been silenced, privatized, and oppressed into legitimated public knowledges, into public lives in all their dimensions, even when some realize that this should—indeed, must—be done for the sake of justice, and because
otherwise what is known is radically—from the root—falsified.

This is a book about transforming knowledges, not just trying to extend
them or correct them here and there. It is about changing *what* and, just as
important, *how* we think so that we no longer perpetuate the old exclusions
and devaluations of the majority of humankind that have pervaded informal
as well as formal schooling in the United States and around the world. But to
change education involves more than changing a text or two, a course or program or two. Behind and within curricula are complex cultural, intellectual,
and political traditions. We must consider multiple contexts if we are to understand what we wish to change more than superficially.

Changes are necessary, I believe, not only to transform what is accepted
as knowledge by any dominant culture and what is passed on to new generations, but for the sake of thinking itself. We cannot think well about anything
or anyone as long as we are locked into old errors that are so familiar as to be
virtually invisible. It is my particular purpose to bring those errors to the

surface, to characterize them as *conceptual* errors—and, in their most virulent, totalized forms, as culturally *psychotic conceptualizations,* or radical ideologies—and to show how they have to varying degrees worked and still work
to distort, limit, and in extreme instances to paralyze our thinking, distorting
our knowledge, our selves, and the worlds we would share.

Change does not happen at once just because some of us change our minds.
But as long as minds are informed, and deformed, in ways that persistently serve
systems of dominance, transforming remains literally inconceivable.

## Centering Critique

Let me say here, in highly condensed and abstract form, what I wish to suggest about *why* and *how* we need to change our minds—what the fundamental conceptual errors are. This sketch may seem both too simple, even simplistic, and too difficult because too abstract. Nevertheless, it states the
conclusions I had come to when I began to write and that guided my thinking throughout. I hope that by the end of the book, the basic insights I sum-
marize here will be as clear and suggestive (not definitive—that is no more
desirable than possible) as I can make them.

A single-sentence version of the theme of this book might go as follows:

*Thesis of book*

The problem we still have today in thinking ourselves free of hierarchical systems of dominance so that we can comprehensively recognize and equalize the rich diversities of humankind within our
interrelations with nature derives from radically dividing (not just
distinguishing) humans from nature; dividing and ranking humans
into 'kinds' that 'ascend' from nature; and taking a particular group
to be not only the "pinnacle of creation" but the *inclusive* term or
kind, the *norm* and the *ideal* for all, a tangle of injustice-serving
errors that perpetuates itself, even when its original premises are
denied, through *faulty generalizations, circular reasoning, mystified
concepts,* and the *partial knowledges* that result.

Thinking through what all that means, approaching it in different ways, setting it in different contexts (specifically, not only, as it is evident in curricula) will
take the rest of this book. Such thinking entails quite literally changing our minds.
Minds are, of course, extraordinarily complex things, as are cultural and polit-

ical systems. I do not pretend for a moment to have covered all the errors that are built into dominant traditions, let alone to be in possession of truth against which error can be seen as such. What I do believe is that, in the thousands of conversations about feminist and other critical scholarships I have had on campuses, with scholarly and professional associations, in communities in the United States and elsewhere, I have found some of the central errors that make it difficult *despite good intentions* to open many systems to all those who have been privatized—who have been denied public recognition, rights, freedoms and been made subject to others—for so long, in so many cultures and countries. And I believe that the basic errors that have worked to perpetuate the silencing and the privatization of women do the same for the men of some groups, albeit without erasing gender hierarchies *within* those groups. This, then, is an invitation to engage in thinking ourselves free of errors that construct and perpetuate dangerously disordered, dominance-serving systems that affect us all.

## More Personal Beginnings

In the early 1970s, when I first discovered that a few women were beginning to uncover and to create knowledge that speaks of and for us, I had a calm and uncomplicated reaction. Why not? I thought: That is very interesting. But I soon discovered that my initial reaction was by no means the norm, and that there was a great deal of work to be done before it might become so. I began to speak publicly about the new scholarship on women—an effort that required me to think through why I found such scholarship interesting and so obviously important, and thus to think about thinking as well as about scholarship and activism. I began to realize that what truly engaged me was the apparently simple observation that before I could think well about what needed to be studied about women, I had to understand how on earth I (as well as others) had managed, through many years of education, not to *notice* that I had not studied them/us. I mean, there I was, in a gender- and race-obsessed culture in which those two markers of 'kind' were *never* ignored, studying only men who were white and not noticing it. Truly weird, that; I've been trying to discover what made it possible ever since.

Initially, I thought in conversation with those who were raising new questions and doing new research on women (in particular, Gerda Lerner, Joan Kelly, Sherry Ortner, and Amy Swerdlow, who were working at Sarah Lawrence College then, as was I), and also with those who were skeptical about and even hostile to such work. I began to give workshops for faculty members else-where. Through encountering their questions and exploring the ways they thought, I became deeply engaged in trying to understand the puzzle. Why was it not obvious that, if we do not know much about more than half of humankind, we do not know much about humankind? Why was it not obvi-ous that this new (*renewed*, actually) effort was intellectually as well as per-sonally, morally, and politically exciting and necessary?

During those years, I wrote almost as many talks and papers as I gave workshops, because every time the conversations ended, I rethought what had seemed clear to me in order to take into account why and how some people had had trouble understanding and accepting it. I became more conscious of the ways we tend to think, of the assumptions we make without knowing it, of the judgments that underlie what seems merely obvious. I began to realize that what I was finding was and is by no means restricted to scholarship or to the thinking of faculty members. Through the problems faculty members were having in rethinking their courses, I was seeing the workings of what I have come to call *dominant meaning systems*—systems of meaning that are in the ascendant and that serve domination. At first, I simply referred to "tradition," but that, of course, indicates precisely where the root problem lies. There are *many* traditions: it is erroneous to refer to only one without qualifiers, as if it were the inclusive term, the norm, the ideal, just as it is erroneous to refer to *women* when we mean *white* women, to *philosophy* when we mean Western philosophy, to *men* when we mean heterosexual men.

I began to realize that curricula can be approached as 'texts' through which one can read some of the critical conceptual constructions—the chosen-to-be-dominant systems of meaning—of cultures, of nation-states, of established religions.

My work became an intellectual, political, and very personal cause. I set out to discern, analyze, and clear away what I increasingly saw as simple errors deeply rooted within every discipline, in the very construction of the disci-plines, throughout the most influential thinking outside the academy—errors that were startlingly isomorphic with (that is, similar in form to) most sys-tems of dominance.

This kind of analysis, this search for why and how people think and con-strue knowledge, carried out by extensive and very careful listening to what they/we say, differs in some ways from that for which I was trained as a philoso-pher, but in other ways it is profoundly related. I draw constantly on my years of work with Hannah Arendt, and on Dewey, Wittgenstein, Kant, and

Plato/Socrates in particular. These are philosophers who thought about think-ing, who wanted to know not only what we know but how and why we can know it, and *why it matters* that we know it this way and not that way. That is, they are all profoundly political and ethical philosophers whose lives as well as work reflect the intensity of their care not only for freedom *of* thought, but for freedom *for* thought.

If, as these philosophers held, we are thinking creatures in a way that is pro-foundly and intricately related to the fact that we are also creatures of com-munication—creatures and creators of the shareable meanings within which we live—and so of society and politics, then education is of critical importance. It is in and through education that a culture, and polity, not only perpetuates but enacts the kinds of thinking it welcomes and discards and/or discredits the kinds it fears. Arendt, Dewey, Wittgenstein, Kant, and Plato/Socrates played often on the lines between what was acceptable and what was not. In many senses of the term, they were critical thinkers who placed the quest for freedom of and for thought before loyalty to any system of any kind. That, I believe, is not only one of the expressions of their greatness, but one of the reasons they under-stood how thinking is political in particularly acute and important ways.

As I began this work, I was, then, in direct and (it sometimes seemed) unending conversation with faculty members and community groups, and, at the same time, with philosophers who were helping me think about why and how thinking is political, why and how it matters in the world. And through-out, I was also talking with feminist thinkers and activists, with those who were critiquing constructions of race and other creations of 'kinds' of humans. We shared emerging insights that it would be impossible to disentangle now. What I learned from those who were just curious about or even hostile to this work—a particular weave of philosophical, feminist, and other insurgent thought—also wove in and out of the writing, speaking, conversing, and rewriting I had undertaken. The sharpest moments of focus, of illumination, almost always came to me at faculty workshops or after a public speech, when I was suddenly asked a question or faced with a serious rejoinder for which I did not have a response. These challenges helped me see the limitations of my analysis and brought for-ward different ways of thinking about meanings of human being.

I did not consider myself ready to write anything other than talks turned into papers until I found that it had been a good while since I had been asked anything new or encountered objections to which I had no response at all. Only then, when it seemed that I had become reasonably able to think with many, seriously differing other people, did I feel ready to trust my own understandings.

It was not that I had found ways to coerce agreement; I can assure you that this kind of work will always make that impossible even if it were desirable (which it is not). It was not agreement I was seeking but a genuine possibility of mutual recognition informed by comprehension. That, rather than a sense that I had read everything pertinent, indicated to me that I had done my research.

It was an exhausting and largely very lonely time, for all that good talk. Such thinking takes one to one's own roots, surfaces assumptions, turns established beliefs inside out and upside down, and it must, finally, be done alone if it is to make sense, to become coherent and consistent. I realized that the praise I sought—because one does listen carefully to praise when doing controversial work that often provokes highly personal as well as intellectual hostility—was, "That makes sense. Of course. It really is obvious, isn't it?" *That* was what I wanted—not to be 'right' but simply to be part of a common effort to make sense. Making sense meant that I had found and spoken *with* what people were thinking in a way that allowed them to change their minds on their own if also with me.

That is the kind of thinking, the kind of relationship—political and moral as well as intellectual—in which I believe. It is also, I now want to say, a kind of work that I want to be doing, to name and to make accessible. I now call such work *fieldwork philosophizing* and see it as a confluence of philosophy, in its concern for thinking through and about meaning systems; political and moral critique, in its questioning of how meaning systems inform and can deform our living together; and psychoanalysis, in its efforts to bring into consciousness complexes from the past that are distorting our present relationships.

*Transforming Knowledge* continues my reporting of and reflections on some results of that method, all that talk, all that thinking, all that effort to help us make sense together. I accept responsibility for my own thinking without pretending for a moment that thinking ever proceeds without contexts much broader than even (or perhaps especially) the thinker can know.

## Speaking as and for Ourselves

Paula Giddings says of her book *When and Where I Enter*:

> For a Black woman to write about Black women is at once a personal and an objective undertaking. It is personal because the women whose blood runs through my veins breathe amidst the statistics. They struggled north

during the Great Black Migration, endured separations, were domestics and schoolteachers, became pillars of their community, and remained ordinary folks. Writing such a book is also an objective enterprise, because one must put such experiences into historical context, find in them a rational meaning so that the forces that shape our own lives may be understood. *When and Where I Enter* attempts to strike a balance between the subjective and the objective. Although it is the product of extensive research, it is not without a point of view or a sense of mission. A mission to tell a story largely untold. For despite the range and significance of our history, we have been perceived as token women in Black texts and as token Blacks in feminist ones.[3]

Paula Giddings writes to claim her voice specifically as a Black woman among others. In 1892, Anna Julia Cooper, recognizing the differences among us, chose nevertheless to speak of a singular "woman's voice": "It is not the intelligent woman vs. the ignorant woman, nor the white woman vs. the black, the brown, and the red—it is not even the cause of woman vs. man. Nay, 'tis woman's strongest vindication for speaking that *the world needs to hear her voice*."[4] We come together intellectually, personally, politically—and we separate to think for ourselves, alone and with others whose voices we fear have also not been heard. Generative as well as divisive tensions continue along the fault lines—between the past and the present, the particular and the general, the individual and the group, the concrete and the universal, the historicized and the decontextualized, between sameness and difference, between research on specific groups and conclusions that might offer us common ground. It has been a great struggle for women to speak with individual voices; it has also been a struggle to stand together, sometimes with, sometimes against our brothers, who have too often demanded that we serve them in political struggles as they would have us submit to them at home.

To re-member ourselves, separately and together, is more than to await a corrected scholarship, however crucial such an effort indeed is. In a strikingly personal yet simultaneously political and philosophical voice that feminisms have helped establish as legitimate, Jeffner Allen explores *remembering*:

Touching, feeling, imagining, fighting, thinking, caressing, I remember myself. I remember the possibilities in my future, the actuality of my past, the openness of my present. I remember the members of my body, the actions that form my body as lived. In remembering, I am.

Remembering shapes my existence within a temporal horizon. The horizon of temporality is not neutral. Whenever the profiles of my memory, like the horizons of time, are erected by men, I cannot remember myself. At such moments, male domination not infrequently forces me to remember myself as essentially and "by nature" the Other who "is" only in relation to men. I, dismembered, disappear into nonexistence.

Yet, quite clearly, I am here. In everyday life I undergo and envision an experience of stopping the time and memories of patriarchy and of unfolding a temporality in which I am myself.[5]

Such quests, we have learned, must be more than corrective, more than additive; they are and press toward transformations because it has turned out that moral and political generosity do not suffice in systems premised on the 'normalcy' of one falsely universalized 'kind.' As Rosemarie Garland Thomson writes, in *Extraordinary Bodies: Figuring Physical Disability in American Culture and Literature*, "The moral generosity that seeks to compensate for physical differences makes cultural outcasts of its recipients by assuming that individual bodies must conform to institutional standards, rather than restructuring the social environment to accommodate physical variety."[6]

Listening to the voices of differing people(s), we also notice the easily forgotten obvious: even when we are all speaking the same languages, there are many other 'languages' at play behind and within what the speakers mean and what we in turn understand. Becoming aware of the levels upon levels of different meanings in even the most apparently simple and accessible utterance, we try to renounce the hegemony of "the time and memories of patriarchy" so as to hear better, comprehend better. But then we run the risk of finding ourselves in "no-time," with no place that is our own to stand, with no tongue to speak that does not entrap us the minute we open our mouths. It helps then to remember that, inspired by voices that have spoken for themselves despite dominant systems, we can also proceed, if carefully, to make use of the languages we wish to change.

In doing so—perhaps particularly if we are professional scholars and teachers—we tend to adopt the conceptual language that seems most promising. There are feminists who have worked within, and always also on, most if not all of the established schools of thought—including Marxism, Freudianism, object relations theory, liberal democratic theory, literary criticism, and, increasingly, the newer schools that are themselves attempting to undo much that characterizes the dominant culture and curriculum, such as poststructuralism and deconstructionism. Emerging from the fear that we can only misspeak ourselves if we speak at all because of the power of the dominant 'language,' we face the next problem: the coexistence of a veritable babble of conceptual tongues.

For my own work, I have chosen no one of the available systems, or 'languages,' of conceptual analysis/synthesis, although of course I do to some extent speak culturally from my own (hardly monovocal or unmixed) background. I do not believe that one can make sense, or find it, in only one theoretical, conceptual frame at a time, however valuable such particular meaning constructions are. I do believe that we can speak sensibly to each other across some cultures and most disciplines, through theories, beyond technical languages, including those now developing within feminist scholarship itself (to the despair of those who fear the establishment of just one more exclusive language where many had hoped to find their voices). If we could not speak to each other across these conceptual languages, intellectual work and achievement would be a great deal more alienated and alienating than they already are. If we give up on the effort to speak across fields, theories, systems, 'isms,' and to people in many different communities, we also give up our responsibility as thinkers who care about as we depend on democracy, especially in today's highly specialized, technologized, fragmented, yet simultaneously ever more interdependent world.

Choosing to try to speak with many people, I risk speaking adequately to none. I know that, of course, but for me, the effort to keep up the conversation, to widen and deepen it, is too important—I must try. I refuse to think that I have only one voice because I am a particular 'kind' of woman or because of my academic training and predilections, and I refuse, too, to believe that you can only hear one kind of voice, one mode of speech.

Thinking is political because it is a capacity we all share, a need we all have, and a responsibility we can all accept or flee. To express thinking primarily and persistently in any one 'language' is, in my view, often politically irresponsible, if sometimes forgivable. It is, however, also sometimes important and sometimes even liberating, as when those who are regularly silenced in the dominant culture get together to speak their own language free of the incomprehension and uninformed judgment of those who stand guard over 'standard' speech and 'proper' academic writing—as if there were not always enriching alternatives.

I hope, then, that you will find ways to think with me throughout this prolonged essay in thought. To increase the openings to the center of what I want to say, I included the voices in the quotations above (a mere gesture: so many are available now) as well as a bit of my own story. Now I would like to offer several different ways to move into the conceptual center by exploring some of the contexts from which women's studies, like Black/African American and other multicultural and insurgent studies, arose. I do so because conceptual analysis always takes some, if not all, of its meanings from its real contexts, even when those contexts are not apparent because the language of the analysis is abstract. When we do not at least point toward those contexts, it is far too easy to misunderstand not so much what a conceptual conclusion states as what it *means* and *does*; as a result, we are less able to make use of it in the immediate world in which action takes place.

Just as there are many beginnings for any realization that is of broad significance and use, there are many contexts. But there is no need for everyone to explore all of them; we think, as we act, differently. If none of what follows engages you, or if it is frustratingly familiar and introductory (although I hope it will at least be evocative), please feel free to jump to Part III, "Conceptual Approaches: Thinking Through," where I begin exploring the basic conceptual errors I sketched earlier, or to Part IV, "Errors Basic to Dominant Traditions," which focuses on them, although there, too, there will be circlings in and out: we are exploring a tangled whole here, not tracing a line or making an argument or proving a point.

## Why Do Curricula Matter?

All too often, a quick way to lose the interest even of people who care about education is to announce that one is about to discuss the curriculum. The curriculum has become the purview of experts; specialists in curriculum or members of particular fields have been held to be the only ones qualified to prescribe it. Even scholars who make their salaries teaching usually think about curricular matters beyond their own courses only when they must, as a result of departmental planning and hiring needs, or when their institution draws them into discussion of, say, the desirability of a "core curriculum." But whenever we fail to continue critiquing and correcting the curriculum, the framework of meaning behind particular questions of what to teach to whom will continue to prove inhospitable to all those who have been excluded from legitimated knowledge and knowledge making, and so also from effective participation in understanding and exercising power at a basic cultural level.

I believe that unless feminist and other critical scholarship is informed by ongoing work on why and how dominant curricula are not and, without fundamental reconception, *cannot* be receptive to study of the majority of humankind, today's new fields remain at risk of disappearing or simply masking inequities behind new specialized languages. As we produce new knowledge, we must continue to work to understand why it is recurrently "new" rather than a further unfolding of all that has gone before. Throughout this book, I ask: what is it that functions so effectively in dominant meaning systems, including newer ones, to hold knowledge of, by, and about women—with all our differences, which always also implicate us with some 'kinds' of men—outside that which has been and is being passed on, developed, and taught? How have meanings of *human being* that cast the majority of us out of the definitional category and down a scale of human worth persisted? How have such meanings continued to shape intellectual, moral, religious, legal, political, economic systems?

These are questions for curricula. They are also obviously more than that. The conceptual blocks to comprehension and full inclusion of women and many 'kinds' of men that we find in some scholarly theories and arguments, as well as in organizations and systems (political, economic, legal), are at root the same blocks that can be found within the curriculum. The same can be said of the culturally psychotic complexes that radically shut out women and some 'kinds' of men. If we do not remove such distortions from the curriculum, much if not all that we achieve elsewhere may prove to be, once again, a passing moment. It is, after all, to a significant extent through what we teach new generations that we bridge past and future. That which is actively excluded from the curriculum is very likely to be forgotten, seen as deviant and marginal.

Our educational institutions—those inspiring, impossible, frustrating, appealing, appalling systems within which we usually try simply to find the space and time to do our work of teaching and learning—are not the only shapers and guardians of cultural memory and hence of cultural meanings, but they are the preeminent ones. Here too, then, we must do our work of critique, re-membering, creation. As we do so, we will encounter both temptations and risks. Linda Gordon observes that "existing in between a social movement and the academy, women's scholarship has a mistress and a master, and guess which one pays wages."[7] That these risks and temptations are complex and challenging of our values does indeed need to be recognized. It is difficult to sustain work against the grain of what, after all, stands preeminently for "the life of the mind," especially when one has had to struggle to achieve access to those institutions that have claimed to define that life and that indeed have succeeded all too well in marking it as their own and rewarding well those who succeed. I do not mean to trivialize even for a moment the struggle for access, the continuing difficulty of 'getting in,' or the recurrent "backlashes" that even mild changes always evoke. But I also do not want to overlook or underrate the risks that feminist and other critical, creative scholars have warned one another about since the beginning of curriculum change movements. These difficulties ought not to surprise us, and we must not let them unnerve us: comprehension of some of their intellectual, political, moral, and psychological/individual roots helps prepare us for them.

The dangers of such projects are indicated by the difference between the term "mainstreaming" and the one that superseded it, "curriculum transformation." "Mainstreaming" implies that there is one real stream, and that our goal is to achieve the 'normalcy' of becoming invisible in the big river. This framing is painfully familiar to people with disabilities, just as it has been, *mutatis mutandis*, to successive groups of immigrants and refugees; to sex/gender 'transgressive' identities; to 'fat' people; and to others marked in various ways as nonnormative. "Transformation," in contrast, places the emphasis not on joining what is, or on adding something onto it, but on changing it.[8]

Teresa de Lauretis characterizes the problem, the risk (and again I add, the temptation), of "mainstreaming" as "the appropriation of feminist strategies and conceptual frameworks within 'legitimate' discourses or by other critical theories" in a way that "deflect[s] radical resistance and . . . recuperate[s] it as liberal opposition," which is "not just accommodated but in fact anticipated and so effectively neutralized."[9] That, indeed, would be the result of "mainstreaming." But it is something else again to work on transforming the curriculum fully realizing that the 'kinds' of humans defined as 'lower,' as 'lesser,' cannot be added to present constructions of knowledge because knowledge of, by, and for the motley lot of us is not simply more of the same; is not only knowledge of a subset of "mankind" that is conceptually compatible with that of which it is misdefined as a subset; is not a category of exotica that can be tacked onto courses without implications for that which remains safely 'normal.'

The belief that the knowledge that defines women's studies—and the knowledges characteristic of all the other new fields with which it shares (or should share) a basic critique of dominance—is simply additive to, or a new subset of, or a complement to knowledge about dominant men has been and is held both by nonfeminist scholars and educators and by some feminists involved with women's studies and curriculum-change projects. I understand those beliefs and know that some good work can indeed be done by those who hold them. For instance, it remains important to find the women who did what women were not allowed to do so as to "prove that we can do it." But I do not believe such work is, by itself, adequate: exclusive systems cannot tolerate those whom they were designed *not* to include.

It is precisely to continue work on transforming the curriculum—not simply to achieve access to it or to join its 'mainstream' or provide it with an oppositional perspective that it can accommodate in the sense de Lauretis rightly fears—that I have written and keep revising this book. Let me repeat here what I first wrote in 1979: what we are doing is as radical as undoing geocentrism, the notion that the earth is the center of the cosmos. If the earth— if Man—is neither a genuinely inclusive category nor the center, then everything predicated on taking it or him to be so no longer stands as originally formulated or as it persists at the root of knowledge founded on it. This is not to say that there are no schools of thought with which we can join, or that there is nothing in existing traditions for us to draw on, use, and choose ourselves to perpetuate. It is not even to say that all feminist scholarship is or ought to be that radical, that it ought to work at that fundamental level. It *is* to say that as we do our work, we need to hold on to the radical critique, the effort to go to the root (*radix*) of traditions that are premised on our exclusion, or the tree of knowledge will continue to grow exactly as before,[10] even if it has a few elaborate new branches and flowers.

Making the case for that position is what this book is about, so I will leave the point now with the statement that refusal to engage in, or at least support, work on transforming the curriculum leaves us not pure but vulnerable to being, once again, excluded, rendered marginal, or brought into and utterly lost within the mainstreams that have through the ages flooded and washed away the recurrent spring growths of scholarship and thought critical of dominance-preserving systems, and with them the possibility of rethinking basic meanings of human being that still carry deadly errors within them.

# II

# Contextual Approaches

## Thinking About

## Access to the Curriculum: Some Background

In a history of the curriculum in the United States, Frederick Rudolph reminds us that neither Black people nor white women were included in the curricula even of institutions designed for us:

> By 1900, the curriculum of the black colleges was shaped by a policy of apartheid in a society sufficiently democratic in the abstract to encourage the development of a class of responsible professional leaders. But the models for these institutions were those of the dominant caste: Fisk University's music department concentrated on classical European music to the exclusion of the music that expressed the black experience in America, and black history and sociology courses were rare and exceptional until after World War I.

Similarly:

> As was true of the colleges for blacks, colleges for women were often colleges in name only; those that deserved the name, having survived the

opposition of critics who sought to discredit them with accusations of having failed to live up to the curricular standards of men's colleges, soon found themselves criticized for imitating the men's colleges too well and for not providing a course of study appropriate to women's work.[1]

*Women's work,* in Rudolph's words, was "whatever men would not do."[2]

Thus, the majority of humankind was forced absurdly into proving that we were indeed fully human, that we could indeed think and learn, in curricula that either took no account whatsoever of us or were designed to keep us in our 'proper' places. The virtues (understood in a way that fluctuated between the classical sense of *excellence of kind* and the Christian sense of *moral goodness*) of white middle- and upper-class women and those of Black men and women, however different they were from each other, had in common that they were defined as different from the virtues of man-qua-citizen, or the scholar. They were defined as virtues of service, not in the generalized Christian sense that calls on all of us to act with *caritas,* but in a narrower, more specific sense: those who were to serve the lives and interests of the small group of scholar–citizens were to develop the specific virtues of the 'naturally' servile.

This was the case even when some real pride and privilege went with fulfillment of the service role. For example, Patricia Palmieri notes: "The American revolution made the entire society aware of the need to educate a populace capable of exercising democratic principles." Yet such civic arts and the virtue of their exercise were not to belong directly to all: "Women were to exert social influence through raising and educating sons. . . . Thus by 1800, while the vote was reserved for white men, white women could add to their domestic roles the role of 'Republican Mother.'"[3] Such provisions for influence—as distinct from power—were by no means extended to all those who served the dominant few. Even those who could proudly claim the mantle of "Republican Mother" did so through their relations to white male citizens, their rearing of male children, and the services they rendered the dominant male order through those relations. Linda Kerber has located for us the telling twist in such thinking:

> Discussions of female education were apt to be highly ambivalent. On one hand, republican political theory called for a sensibly educated female citizenry [from the privileged groups] to educate future generations of sensible republicans; on the other, domestic tradition condemned highly

educated women as perverse threats to family stability. Consequently, when American educators discussed the uses of the female intellect, much of their discussion was explicitly anti-intellectual.[4]

Black women in the United States, as always even more than privileged white women, have always struggled not only with the difficulty of achieving access to any education at all, but also with the task of defining what Black people should be educated for. This was so even after slavery was abolished and they could openly seek and provide some education. They did so with great fortitude and ingenuity. Paula Giddings writes about the well-known debates over Black education around the turn of the last century:

> Though in many instances there was accommodation to [Booker T.] Washington's ideas—and power—Black women also operated independently of his influence. The educators, for example, believed in industrial education, but they also believed that Blacks should attain the highest academic level possible. One foot was in Booker T. Washington's camp on this issue, the other with W.E.B. DuBois, who supported the concept of the "talented tenth," a well-educated cadre of Black leaders. Anna Julia Cooper, for example, may have believed in industrial education with all her heart, but as an educator, and principal of Washington, D.C.'s The M Street School, she was best known for her success in channeling Black students into the most prestigious universities in the country. Mary McLeod Bethune advocated "domestic science," but she also confronted (successfully) her White board members who wanted to maintain her school's curriculum below university status.[5]

Clearly, mere access to schooling has never been enough. And it will not become so as long as any vestiges remain of the old assumptions that some 'kinds' of people are by nature inferior and ought to be *trained* rather than *educated,* and that in the process they must be stripped of independent identifications supported by "different" cultures, religions, and languages. The boarding schools to which American Indian children were taken—often forcibly—remind us that "access" has in the past been the opposite of liberating and strengthening in any terms other than those of the dominant culture. The present status hierarchy within and among institutions of higher education reflects a continuation of this history of exclusion, which is perpetuated by those who bemoan the difficulty of finding 'qualified' women of all groups,

and 'qualified' African American, Latino, Native American, and other male candidates to be hired or admitted. Old assumptions, built into institutions, systems, and standards of judgment, keep discrimination functioning long after
many have honestly renounced, even denounced, it.[6]

But resistance has also continued to provide resources for critique and
change. Roger Gottleib writes: "Shaped by history and embodying the spirit
of the radical movements that created them, [critical theories] each have in
them some of the truth we need in order to face the darkness of the current
social world and the ominous threats to the earth."[7]

## Contemporary Movements:
## Equality, Recognition

In the 1950s and early 1960s in the United States, the distortions afflicting
human lives, minds, and spirits—distortions arising from blithely as well as
viciously inegalitarian social, political, educational, and economic systems—
began once again to inspire social movements. Out of these movements swelled
a great deal of the passion and vision of feminist and other insurgent new scholarships; from them, too, arose some of the tensions that remain with us.

The Montgomery bus boycott took place in 1956; the struggle to desegregate Little Rock High School in 1957; the sit-in movement that triggered
mass civil rights protests took off in early 1960. These were pivotal events for
which civil rights organizers had been preparing for years.[8] Betty Friedan published *The Feminine Mystique* in 1963, providing a rallying point for middle-
class white women suffering from "the problem without a name." Educators
such as Melissa Richter, Esther Rauschenbush, and Jean Walton tried to do
something about the inadequacies of women's education that were evident
even at elite U.S. colleges such as Sarah Lawrence, Barnard, and Pomona. The
(largely white male) beatniks and their male and female successors, the hip-
pies of the late 1960s and early 1970s (who had their own peculiar notions
about what was 'proper' to men and to women), defied conventionality in
cultures that seemed obsessed with material success and war.[9] Black nationalism gained new political and cultural impetus, often apart from, even in
opposition to, efforts to desegregate white America.[10] The year 1968 saw the
founding of the Third World Women's Alliance. In 1971, the Vancouver
Indochinese Women's Conference was held, drawing "a contingent of 150
Third World and white women from North America." Also in 1971, Asian

Sisters emerged from the Asian American Political Alliance. In 1974, WARN (Women of All Red Nations) was formed.[11]

These (and more) were complex, multivoiced movements that were at times at odds with one another even while sharing a passion for justice and equality. The changes they were all demanding would require systemic transformations as well as full recognition of those excluded from dominant cultures. These movements were felt within the academy. The long quest for educational equality in the United States had by no means ended with the entrance of a few members of the excluded groups into the halls of 'higher' learning, any more than the quest for political equality had ended with the winning of the franchise, first by Black men and then by all women.

In the middle and late 1960s, some women involved in the Civil Rights Movement and other movements became aware that prevailing generalizations about equality, about justice, somehow did not hold for women. That seed of critique released an intense and unstoppable energy:

> We've talked a lot, to each other and to some of you, about our own and other women's problems in trying to live in our personal lives and in our work as independent and creative people. In these conversations we've found what seem to be recurrent ideas or themes. Maybe we can look at these things many of us perceive, often as a result of insights learned from the movement.[12]

The "recurrent ideas or themes" that white women began to see seemed at first not to speak to some of the Black women in the movement. For Black women, the Civil Rights Movement was their movement, and they well knew they had some real power in it. However, despite particular and by no means trivial differences in how it was experienced, discrimination based on sex/gender affected all women. "Opposite ends of the spectrum" was Cynthia Washington's description of Black and white women's complex and differing realities. Nevertheless, many women were beginning to realize that there was a problem:

> During the fall of 1964, I had a conversation with Casey Hayden about the role of women in SNCC [Student Nonviolent Coordinating Committee]. She complained that all the women got to do was type, that their role was limited to office work no matter where they were. What she said didn't make any particular sense to me because, at the time, I had my

own project in Bolivar County, Miss[issippi]. A number of other black women also directed their own projects. Certain differences result from the way in which black women grow up. We have been raised to function independently. The notion of "retiring" to housewifery someday is not even a reasonable fantasy. Therefore whether you want to or not, it is necessary to learn to do all of the things required to do to survive. It seemed to many of us, on the other hand, that white women were demanding a chance to be independent while we needed help and assistance that was not always forthcoming. We definitely started from opposite ends of the spectrum.... [Yet even though] we did the same work as men, usually *with* men, when we finally got back to some town where we could relax and go out, the men went out with other women. Our skills and abilities were recognized and respected, but that seemed to place us in some category other than female.[13]

When some of the women in the movements of these times began to talk to each other, to explore their experiences *as women,* and to take those experiences and one another seriously, tensions rose, splits developed even between long-time coworkers—and change was on the way. Expressions of personal and then of social discontent became increasingly politicized as movements carried by strong convictions and courage ran into the need to deal not only with those who crudely and sometimes violently opposed civil rights for all in the United States, but also with the contradictions and tensions that many movement activists had internalized in a segregated, class-divided, rigidly gendered land in which colonizers and colonized, recent and longer-term immigrants, and differing traditions and religions were simultaneously jumbled together and pitted against each other.

Long and often agonizing debates developed out of the earlier quiet, more personal conversations, and were sometimes broken up by confrontations that led to stunned silence, to deep hurt and anger, between and among individuals and groups. Women of color and white women; men of color and white men; southerners, northerners, easterners, and westerners; Christians, Jews, Muslims, atheists; civil rights workers, ethnic group activists, disability activists; students and nonstudents; political sectarians and those who avoided all doctrinal rigidity; gay and "straight"—struggled to work together, broke apart to work separately. The deep divisions hidden behind "the American dream," exacerbated as well as repressed by the economically and socially enforced norms of the "melting pot," cracked open in the crucible of the age of movements. These divisions were not created only then; the fault lines were older, and they ran deep. But still it felt to some as if both a false dream of unity premised on imposed sameness and a dream of unity premised on difference-respecting equality were shattering. Victories now recognized as such and celebrated by most Americans then seemed, sometimes, too little and too late. Demands as well as opposition to those demands escalated; hope mixed with fear and despair.

Those of us who lived through those times remember them vividly, and some of the dreams and nightmares, divisions and alliances, that developed then remain with us today. Much as some might like to think so, the 1960s and early 1970s were not an aberration that is now, thank goodness, entirely over and done with; nor were those decades unambiguously successful or good. Like all serious political issues, those we tried to deal with then were not settled at the time, nor can they ever be for as long as we retain any meaningful freedom. While traveling around the country working with faculty members and community groups, I have often encountered people who are still struggling to understand and learn from what happened then, when movements succeeded in undoing most legally enforceable segregationist practices; converted many people to a lasting commitment to equality (but not to the same understandings of what that might and should mean); ended a war that the majority of Americans had come to believe was morally wrong; and spawned thousands of grassroots organizations that today range across the political spectrum.[14] Some who became faculty members then did so because they believed that education is indeed where and how cultures create themselves, and they wanted to be part of and have an effect on that critical process.

I have also met many faculty members who are still hurt, still angry, still frightened, by what happened in the late 1960s and early 1970s. Among these have been some of the major opponents of curriculum transformation, and they continue to find allies across the nation and around the globe. Thus, some of us were enlivened by dreams as well as by struggles for equality and justice; others were traumatized and remain terrified of anything that seems even vaguely "like the '60s," or, in 1990s parlance, "political correctness." In 2000, I was invited to a gathering in Poland of educators from Eastern Europe and several former Soviet countries to debate "postmodernism" versus "the Classics." "Postmodernism," I found, was being used as a near-synonym for "political correctness." One of two keynote speakers, a college president from the United States, warned participants in no uncertain terms about its grave dangers. This, needless to say, was heard with great concern by people who had emerged so recently from repressive, ideologically driven regimes. Fortunately, the Eastern European Classics scholar with whom I had been paired for this debate—which drew an overflow crowd—was as respectful and at the same time as critical of "the Classics" as I am of "postmodernism," so instead of debating, we had a lively discussion. The organizer of the conference told me later that some attendees were disappointed at the lack of a fight.

But a fight is surely not what most of us want, or any of us need. When women's studies and Black studies, ecology, peace studies, postcolonial studies, queer studies, ethnic studies of many kinds—and the other insurgent, critical fields that have now reshaped scholarship and so curricula—began to appear on U.S. campuses, their creators were often motivated primarily by the renewed dream of an equitable world that had emerged, with pain as well as hope, from the Civil Rights Movement as well as the growing movement of women—most visibly, privileged women in the United States but also, and very importantly, Black, Latina, disabled, Asian, indigenous, and other women whose activism tended to be 'overlooked' by the U.S. press. There was a shared realization that equity requires more than access to unchanged structures. But this does not mean that equity itself was understood in one way. Becky Thompson wrote in 2002, citing Chela Sandoval's 2000 criticism of "hegemonic feminism": "This feminism is white led, marginalizes the activism and world views of women of color, focuses mainly on the United States, and treats sexism as the ultimate oppression. . . . [It also] sees equality with men as the goal of feminism, and has an individual rights-based, rather than justice-based vision for social change."[15] For others, among them women and men who consider themselves the real and proper feminists, "equality with men" does and should provide access to "individual rights-based" systems on the same terms that have held for included men.

As both a concept and a political issue, "equity" is stubbornly contentious. For example, it can be argued that white women's liberationists' early emphasis on finding fulfilling work outside homes defined by heterosexual marriage undercut a more general meaning of political and economic equity that could include women of color and all poor women—most if not all of whom had never enjoyed either the luxury or the prescriptive necessity of working only in their own homes for no pay.[16] Still, those who became involved in women's studies saw that in the academy, as elsewhere, all women were denied full and equal entrance, and that even once 'inside' they were not well treated as students, workers, teachers, and administrators—experiences still with us and today discussed by those new to them as "backlash." Sometimes naively assuming that the emerging new knowledges will be as inclusive as the old were exclusive, we continue to struggle as we did earlier not only to be present but to be *recognized* in the fullest sense.[17]

While we, all of us, remained strangers to the academy, even if some of us were present in it, we could expect no more than token efforts toward such recognition. And tokenism reveals not so much bad faith as a profound lack of understanding. Tokenism, after all, assumes that exclusion—which is an effect of complex hegemonic systems—is itself the problem. The assumption then is that adding a few of those who have been excluded solves the problem, even though it actually leaves untouched the systems that, left unfixed, will go right on producing it. That is why tokens, even those included in (uncomprehending) good faith, even those who themselves fully intend otherwise, become available to play the role of "exceptions that prove the rule."

So to our work for political and professional equity we added efforts to bring full recognition of our highly diverse half of humankind into the body of what is taught. Some privileged women worked for women's studies without making adequate efforts to learn from and with other women, but not entirely without awareness of the importance of doing so (a statement intended as neither excuse nor judgment). Undoing exclusions in the women's movement is a task as complex and ongoing as undoing them anywhere else. This is a call for change that must be made, no matter how painful it is.[18] Equity demands that we keep learning, keep trying.

It is in the feminist and other movements' challenges to the academy in all its aspects—and especially in the knowledge the academy preserves, enriches, and passes on—that I locate one important context for the extraordinary explosion of thinking and new knowledges that no one should ignore any longer. Much has changed, but commitment to transforming education so that it supports rather than undermines egalitarian democratic aspirations remains alive, and needed.

## Early—and Continuing—Questions

There is yet another way to move into the subject of transforming knowledge and the ways we think. We can change our perspective from the times in which this commitment reemerged, and focus on the unfolding thinking itself. To do so, it may be helpful to return to some of the early questions we encountered. There are always lots of ways to begin, different contexts within which to locate that which we wish to understand, many perspectives on what we are trying to see. And although more and more histories are being written about our age of movements, most of them—curiously—omit the critical thinking within and about the academy that is home to many of the authors of those histories. This, I think, is risky: generations turn over quickly in schools, and the very same issues and questions with which many struggled earlier tend to recur. If we do not pay attention to this history too, we may have to deal with it again (although it may wear different clothes).

## Scholarship versus Politics?

From the beginning, the commitments of feminist scholars have been complex and often in creative, demanding tension with each other. For example, an early conference in a continuing series run by the Barnard College Women's Center took on the question of the relation of scholarship to politics. The conferences, led by Jane Gould as director of the center, were, in the late 1980s, still called "The Scholar and the Feminist," as if *scholar* and *feminist* were perforce separate identities. Were we, as many of those opposed to women's studies held, threatening to 'politicize' scholarship and the academy in some new and dangerous way? Is it true that formal scholarship as traditionally conceived and practiced is disinterested and objective—that it is and should be removed from the political realm? Are scholarship and action two separate human activities, and should they be? Can one serve both equity and excellence, or does commitment to one threaten to undermine the other? To respond to such questions, we were faced with the need to rethink what scholarship has meant and should mean. That effort led us to undertake analyses and critiques of constructions of knowledge.[19]

## The Disciplines

Among the most evident characteristics of the prevailing construction of knowledge is its disciplinary nature—a characteristic that is given power by the discipline-based departments that are at the heart of academic institutions. Hence, we were faced with an obvious intellectual and institutional problem. Women's studies placed the study of women at the center as no then-existing discipline did. In what disciplinary department were we to work? Women as authors, as scholars, and as subject matter were largely or wholly invisible in all of them. Furthermore, the search for any one disciplinary/departmental home quickly came to seem peculiar, since it is quite obvious that women cannot be studied adequately in only one discipline any more than men can. That is in part why Florence Howe issued her call to "break the disciplines," and why we claimed early on that women's studies must be interdisciplinary.

But then we had also to ask whether even interdisciplinary work would suffice. How could an amalgam of fields—none of which had proved open or adequate to the subject, women—transcend its component parts? It seemed clear that we would have to create a new field, not a pastiche of old ones, to free ourselves to locate and, when necessary, create the theoretical frameworks, the methods and techniques of research and of teaching that we might need to illuminate our complex subject.

A new debate arose. Should the goal of women's studies be to create a new discipline, and a new department, rather than to transform all the other standing disciplines? But the scholars who worked on women's studies had themselves been trained in those disciplines, and the students who might take women's studies would also be taking other courses—courses that would continue to exclude and/or devalue women. The task at hand seemed to require us not only to create a whole new field, but also to rethink each and all other disciplines—separately, in relation to each other, and as they reflected and perpetuated cultural understandings of knowledge. We realized that scholarship that refuses old exclusions and invidious hierarchies not only does not fit into any of the old fields, but also, for that very reason, has the potential to transform them all.

So we worked both to establish a new discipline, women's studies, and simultaneously to spread the new scholarship on women to all fields by transforming curricula. Despite the concern of some feminist activists and scholars that woman-focused work would get lost in the work of transforming curricula, both undertakings have flourished, one reinforcing the other. The academy has been changed by the burgeoning of feminist scholarship in general, by women's studies programs in particular, and by the effects of both on all disciplines, including other new ones. The decision as to which kind of work to undertake has in fact usually been the result of realistic assessments of what is most possible and most likely to succeed at a particular institution at a particular time.[20]

## "Lost Women"

Both projects—the creation of women's studies programs and the transformation of courses in and across all disciplines—depend, of course, on the availability of works by and about women. At first it seemed that whatever anyone's intentions, it might be impossible to include knowledge of women in any courses at all until generations of dedicated scholars had produced enough sound new knowledge. Across the country, some women and a very few men (notably, William Chafe and Joseph Pleck), while teaching what they had been hired to teach and struggling to continue the research on which jobs, promotions, and tenure depended, turned to finding the "lost women" whose lives, works, and perspectives could be brought into the curriculum. There was a sense that we had to prove that women and women's works really did exist; even more important, there was an urgent desire to find our history, both in general and within each field. Stunning works of retrieval emerged with equally stunning speed; for example, Ann Sutherland Harris and Linda Nochlin's work locating, documenting, and studying women artists resulted in a groundbreaking show of women artists at the Brooklyn Museum of Art. The catalogue for this show, *Women Artists: 1550–1950,* was immediately picked up and used as a text. Crucial works of research, testimonies, stories powered by activism that centered on interlocking constructions of identities also started emerging. All of these enriched the categorical identity of "woman," thereby challenging simplified uses of that identity. More direct challenges pressed thinking, and action, toward more complexity, more accuracy. These included works by Cherrie Moraga, Audre Lorde, Sherry Ortner, Gloria Anzaldua, Gerda Lerner, Paula Gunn Allen, Joan Kelly, Winona LaDuke, Robin Morgan, Florynce Kennedy, Evelyn Torton Beck, Alice Walker, Barbara Smith, Maxine Hong Kingston, Angela Davis, Minnie Bruce Pratt, Wilma Mankiller, Mab Segrest, Chandra Talpade Mohanty, Miya Iwataki, Linda Hogan, Rayna Rapp. Documentation and resource projects were also undertaken, such as Dorothy B. Porter's monumental long-term work that made available the stories of Black women and men through the Moorland Spingarn Research Center at Howard University, and Gerda Lerner's research locating the primary sources published in *Black Women in White America.*

As such work began appearing, it deepened critiques of constructions of bounded fields of knowledge, thus putting in question the notion that what had been taught was the product of apolitical, objective scholarly judgments of significance, of quality. Nochlin's early essay, "Why Are There No Great

Women Artists?" questioned definitions as well as evaluations of art, encouraging others to think and speak about why there seemed to be no "great women" philosophers, musicians, political leaders, scientists in ways that put the question itself in question.[21]

We began to realize the full, complex implications of the obvious statement "Women have always been here," and so to refine our understanding of the intellectual problems that arose once we had seen the obvious—that as women, with all our differences, we have largely been invisible in the bodies of knowledge passed on by the educational and research institutions whose purview is supposed to be the preservation, transmission, and enrichment of *humankind's* knowledge.

## "Add Women and Stir"

In a now famous line, Charlotte Bunch characterized the problem. "You can't," she said, "just add women and stir."[22] It was an apt observation, crystallizing what many had learned in their own efforts to find 'lost' women and add them to their courses. The women could in fact be found, but, once 'found,' they often didn't *fit*—they couldn't simply be dropped into standing courses. Why not? In looking for individual women who had done what men had done, we had not after all shifted anything very radically (as we would later and by now have). The problem was that although the "found" women seemed to prove something that needed proving yet again—that women are by no means and in no ways inferior to men—we had not actually learned much about *women*. In fact, we had not even proved anything about female abilities; exceptions, as we know, can easily be used simply to prove the rule. If some women were mathematicians, why were not more mathematicians women? There must be something about most if not absolutely all females that disqualifies us. That was not, of course, a sustainable conclusion. In finding the 'lost' women, we had also found more about why and how they were 'lost': we began to know and to think more about systemic practices of exclusion.

But was the point of all our efforts to document that women had not performed as men had in all the 'important' areas of life because we were discriminated against and actively excluded? Yes, of course that needed—and still needs—to be acknowledged, studied, comprehended. But it leaves untouched some other critically important questions. What were women who led the lives prescribed for women—differently across cultural, group, and class lines, but always differentially from males—doing in the past? What were *those* lives like? What do we all need to learn *from* as well as *about* them/us? Those were the questions we could not ask within the constraints of the familiar courses and fields. We realized that we needed not only to find the few women who did what men did, but also to ask, "Where *were* the women?" "What can we know about *women*?" We needed to undo the blinding definitional conflation of some few men with humankind, the ongoing delegitimizing of the significance of the category *woman* in real lives.

What was required was a complete rethinking, first of the basic models of reality, truth, significance, and meaning in dominant traditions, and then of all the knowledges predicated on them. *If it is an intellectual, moral, and political error to think that a highly partial construction of Man has been, is, and should be the representative 'kind' of human, then we must rethink not only the bases of all systems predicated on those errors, but also all knowledges that derive from, legitimate, and perpetuate them.*

To be additive, knowledge must rest on the same basic premises, be of the same basic sort, as that to which it is to be added. But in the language most often used in the earlier days of women's studies, knowledge about women cannot be added to knowledge about men, because the center of the system shifts radically when women are moved from "margin to center" (to use the phrase adopted by bell hooks for her second book). This holds for critical theories as well.

The basic errors that established some men as the falsely universalized, singular Man needed to be explored directly and in depth along with their conceptual consequences. Those errors began to appear as we realized that problems in each field were not unique to them, that at a deep level there were striking commonalities across all fields and outside the academy as well.

Many more issues were debated, and many more questions were raised, as we continued the effort to rethink traditions that had excluded and invidiously ranked so many for so long, but perhaps the ones I have discussed will suffice for our purposes. What is important, we had realized, is the task of thinking through how scholarship and politics have always been related; why the new scholarship on women could not (and should not) become only a subspecialty within the standing disciplines; why finding things that women had done that were as similar as possible to men's achievements did not tell us enough about the lives of women; and why, then, it would not suffice—was not even possible—simply to add women or "a feminist perspective" to scholarship that was premised on our devaluation and exclusion.

# Critique and Reflexive Thinking

In addition to the personal, historical, political, and intellectual contexts in which efforts to change the curriculum developed, there has also been a philosophical context. No one sets out to understand anything without bringing to that effort some more or less formulated, more or less conscious, philosophical assumptions, tools, frameworks, and values. Certainly I do not; in fact, as I have said, some of the primary conversations that have informed my work have been with the philosophers I have always in mind. Furthermore, *even more now than when I began, I believe that the effort to find out why and how our thinking carries the past within it is part of an ongoing philosophical critique essential to freedom and to democracy.* As we work on the curriculum—and thus on understanding dominant traditions—maintaining critical philosophical perspectives allows us to avoid tripping ourselves up precisely when we most need to think creatively and (often) in radically new ways.

## Thinking with and without the Tradition

We need not give up all that has come to be known, or all the ways and forms and techniques of thinking that have been developed. Quite the contrary: we need to make use of whatever can help us think not only within but also about dominant traditions. There is no articulable, communicable stance for us to take that is *utterly* outside of traditions. Were we to try to find such a position, we would risk falling back into silence; were we to think we had found one, we would risk silencing others. This is true just as surely as it is true that if we were to speak only within the established terms of dominant cultures, we could not transform them, or ourselves. Furthermore, if we lock ourselves into established traditions—into any one system—we also betray their own creative, questioning spirit.

Fortunately, we humans are creatures of translation—that is, we are transitive creatures capable of understanding more than one language, of moving between languages without losing either what is unique to each or what is common enough to make translation possible. We are able to apprehend more than can be spoken in any one language, and we can stretch that language in ways that change and enrich it. There are many ways to be both within and outside our own cultures.

I found my thinking in this book on a commitment to critique in a generally Kantian sense, asking, "What is *behind* this knowledge, this mode of thought?" "What were and are the conditions of its possibility?" "What makes, and keeps, it what, and as, it is?" And *I take the ground for the possibility of philosophical critique to be the gift of reflexive thought, which is, I believe, not only a given possibility for us all but one of the primary sources of both the idea and the personal experience of freedom.* Neither critique nor reflexive thinking suffices to make us free, but they enable us to comprehend and experience the freedoms we require to realize our full human being. Indeed, it may be the experience of reflexive thinking that is available to us all from which, time and again, people have abstracted ideas and principles of political and moral freedom in the first place—ideas and principles that can be found even among people who have lived only under tyrannical systems.

Reflexive thinking about thinking allows us to escape even from our own assumptions, habits, and conventions, which uninterrupted can keep us running around in circles like a squirrel in a cage. It enables us to see particular ways of thinking as well as knowledge from a standpoint that is relatively, not absolutely, outside them. Contrary to many philosophical and theological teachings, as well as conventional moralities, we do not require 'higher' or absolute knowledge in order to "rise above" ourselves, our times, our cultures. We begin, at least, to do so when we observe ourselves becoming angry, or notice how we see something, or pay attention to how we learn and make discoveries—or finally hear everyday prejudicial statements as such.

More simply, I do not believe that we are trapped by the fact that we learned to think in particular ways in a particular culture and/or in schools, nor do I believe that we can simply decide to be free of our formal and informal educations. There is no either/or here, no "We are free or we are determined." Such dilemmas, created by abstracting two possible positions from all that grounds them in real experiences and then placing them artificially in opposition to each other, are part of a pattern of thought whose coercion we can reject. We all know perfectly well that although we can and too often do think in conventional, clichéd, prejudiced, and/or highly technical ways, we can also think *about* these blinkers. And when we do, we rediscover that some apparently hard, apparently profound problems simply dissolve. For a prime example, some troubling generalizations about women's (or "less-developed" peoples') inability to be properly 'rational' dissolve when we recognize that those generalizations were based not only on evaluations of people who were not allowed education or were differently educated, but also on definitions of "rational" that were too narrow. We are not then left with no criteria for good thinking: we are enabled to derive such criteria from a more adequate array of examples. This is the same kind of realization we came to when we saw that feminist work by and about women is not just missing from an academic canon to which it could simply be added: it is incompatible with some of the canon's basic, founding, and too narrow, assumptions.[23]

I had the notion behind the latter idea for quite some time, but, as with many such flashes of understanding, it illuminated my thought only fitfully. I had not thought it through. But one day, after I had given my talk at a conference opening a curriculum transformation project and was listening to other speakers on changes taking place in specific disciplines, I found myself whispering to the sociologist Margaret Anderson, who was sitting next to me, "We weren't *omitted*. We were *excluded*."

What had blocked me from seeing the epistemological implications of the fact that women were not overlooked through a prolonged fit of the famous academic absentmindedness (much like that attributed to the British to 'explain' how they ended up with an empire) was the use of the word "omitted." I became better able to see that, and how, women were excluded from lives of scholarship—as from significant subject matter, as from positions of authority and power—when the basic ideas, definitions, principles, and facts of dominant traditions were being formulated. But does that mean that all the creators and transmitters—and even some critics—of dominant traditions were and are personally animated by the consistent, purposeful intention to exclude women, and many men, every moment (a nasty thought that we probably both doubted and avoided so as not to antagonize people who already used the epithet "angry women" to discredit us)? No, it does not, although it does not preclude the observation that some individuals indeed were so animated and, I fear, still are. It reminds us that *the principles that require and justify the exclusion of some 'kinds' of people, and the results of those principles' shaping of the complex artifices of knowledge and culture, are so locked into dominant meaning systems that it has for a very long time been irrelevant whether or not any particular person intended to exclude anyone.* The exclusion was and is effected by the forms and structures within which we all try to live, work, and find meaning—which is, of course, why reflexive thinking is so essential.

Thus, although it at first sounds as if using the strong term "excluded" might divide us radically from one another, such that all who are not part of the solution are seen as actively, consciously, and willfully part of the problem, in fact it reminds us of something quite different. We are all to some (albeit importantly varying) degree a part of the problem. Insofar as we speak and think and act in ways that make sense to other people within dominant meaning systems, we cannot avoid participating—again to varying degrees—in precisely that which we wish to change. We have all at times thought, said, and done things that, as our consciousness grew through the use of our ability to think reflexively, we wish we hadn't thought, said, done. And that "we" includes (again in critically different ways, and with critically different results) not only those who benefit but also those who suffer from the dominant system. One of the struggles of the oppressed, excluded, and colonized is always to break free of internalized oppression—which does not mean that "women are their own worst enemies," a ridiculous exaggeration of the reasonable insight that we tend to learn what the dominant culture teaches us (and reteaches us, sometimes harshly, when we begin to struggle free).

This is, of course, only another way of saying that prejudicial systems such as sexism and deeply related homophobias, racisms, ableisms, class and ethnic hierarchies—along with the radical division of 'higher' humans from nature that so often underwrites them—are not just personal problems, not just sets of peculiar and troubling beliefs. Exclusions and devaluations of whole groups of people by 'kind' as 'lower,' 'degenerate,' and/or 'abnormal' are systemic: they shape the worlds within which we all live and find meaning. Albert Memmi wrote: "Racism, on whatever level it occurs, always includes [a] collective element . . . ; there must be no loophole by which any Jew, any Colonized, or any Black man [or woman] could escape this social determinism."[24]

I and other women who (or whose forebears) in the United States became 'white' benefit to varying degrees from the system of racism, however strongly we oppose it, just as all men benefit to varying degrees from the sex/gender system. And those of us who work in various ways within the academy benefit from it, too, however much our work is designed to change it. That all these systems also, and profoundly, damage those who benefit from them is something we can recognize without thereby excusing those systems or ourselves from responsibility—just as lack of individual responsibility for past enslavement of Africans does not erase responsibility for present-day privileges conferred by thoroughly racialized economic, social, political systems.

Men and women sometimes say to me, "But men suffer, too. They aren't allowed to cry or be nurturant; they die younger than women; they (especially men of color) are incarcerated at much higher rates." I recognize those problems. But let us note that although privileged white men can understand and feel the harm done to them, most seem to want to get rid of the harm without giving up the privilege. By itself, such awareness tends to make those in power guilty and grumpy—harder, not easier, to live with, and more likely to become defensively righteous. Although it should be everyone's goal to change systems that so egregiously racialize poverty, violence, and law enforcement, we are less likely to achieve that goal if we deny the potent role of racialized sexism, of dominant-mode heterosexual gendering, in all too much violence, including that of some oppressed men against women, against gays and lesbians, against children. Awareness of how interrelated injustices too often divide those who most need to stand together helps strengthen movements, which can then work to deal with them all, internally as well as externally. For example, labor unions that have histories of racism, sexism, and homophobia narrow their possible bases, fail to serve all their members equally, and seriously undercut their moral and political claims to be serving justice. Similarly, the anti-Semitism used by some Black leaders strengthens rather than attacks deadly histories of racialization that have long served up Jews as scapegoats for those who prefer vague, false, hate-driven conspiracy theories that demonize "Others" to analyses of the real dynamics of oppression that must be addressed. Sadly, no oppressed group is safely free of such self-defeating, politically and morally self-contradictory divisiveness: here as everywhere, the old roots go deep and feed many branches.

The questions of 'harm' and 'benefit,' of 'consciousness' and 'false consciousness,' of 'oppression' and 'internalized oppression' are extraordinarily complex. These complexities are painful, but they are also important. They hold us to the level of systemic analysis without allowing us to forget that it is individuals who participate in and rebel against systems: we are responsible on both levels. They also remind us that we can critique these systems even as they shape us. There may be "false consciousness," for example, and "internalized oppression," and conspiracy theories instead of analyses, but in diagnosing such phenomena, we are also recognizing that consciousness can be not only in but also of itself (I *can* catch myself in moments of "false consciousness"). In this way, we learn to see, and so can question and consider changing, the terms by which we live.

In the case of the academy, we can know that knowledge that is claimed to be objective and inclusive yet reflects and perpetuates societal discrimination and prejudices fails even on its own terms. In what it covers, how it treats its subjects, and how it explains and judges, it replicates the most basic assumptions of the dominant culture—but neither entirely nor absolutely. Such knowledge is almost certainly blind to some of its own basic assumptions and methods, but those assumptions and methods are there to be found when, thinking reflexively and then critically, we become able to *see* what and how we know.

Consider the example of geocentrism. Copernicus's arguing that the sun, not the earth, is at the center was taken as a challenge to many of the most deeply held beliefs of his culture, to a remarkable range of systems of explanation, knowledge, faith, mores and morals, and so to the authority of established powers. His transforming perspective was thus both a refutation of particular standing beliefs and a kind of dye that made them, and much more that was implicated with them, visible as it had not been before. Darwin's theory of evolution had—and for some, still has—the same devastating but also illuminating effects. It dethrones Man by suggesting that he is not the center, not a unique creation that is discontinuous with and superior in kind to all else. Shifting from an invidiously hierarchical view of humankind, and of humankind 'above' nature, required then, and enables now, a concomitant shift in all areas of knowledge, of ethics, of religion, of politics. Consider, too, the deep differences between the knowledge of the British and Europeans who colonized the United States and the knowledges of Native Americans. One set of cultures saw the land as given to Man to tame, to use, to make his own so that thinking about the earth and other animals—and people defined as closer to those animals—tended to be instrumental. Indigenous cultures saw the land as sacred; thinking about it tended to be descriptive, celebratory, mythic, with the instrumental entering, when it did, in the mode of propitiation, not mastery. Many indigenous and nonindigenous activist conservationists, seeing both systems, and thereby also becoming able to imagine others, can now counter hierarchical divisions in a similar spirit and so call for relational cooperation of humans with the nature of which we are all equally a part. Today, ecofeminists are also trying to learn with such differing traditions, in the hope of weaving a more sustaining web of meaningful life.

## Public/Private

The critical, reflexive turn of mind that is awakened by just as it calls for action to change systems that divide and rank humans—systems that set us against each other as well as against a weirdly estranged nature—can be seen as well in the early women's movement insight that "the personal is political." Much opens to view when we reflect on our own life stories with others and find in them—different as they always are—striking commonalities. In this way, many women in the early days of second-wave feminism came into political consciousness. "It's not just me" is a deprivatizing recognition, especially for those whose 'kind' has been in several senses domesticated—that is, defined as essentially as well as 'properly' nonpublic.

Not to have an empowered public life does not mean that one nevertheless has a private life, as domesticated women were taught to believe by the privileged men who, oh, so nobly, took on the "dirty" work of politics with which 'proper' women ought not to besmirch themselves—and with which 'lower' "kinds" of women and men ought not to be entrusted. In many cases, the obvious contradiction in taking public life, politics, to be too important to be opened to 'lesser' people and, at the same time, as too 'rough' and 'dirty' for 'pure' women, did not derail those who thereby protected their paternalistic, dominating power over others. In reality, whenever the powerful have withheld from the many full rights of citizenship—including freedom of speech among equalized friends and strangers; freedom of movement and of access; freedom of opportunity; freedom from violating force at home as well as elsewhere—people grouped as women, "inferior races," "illegal aliens," "freaks," sexual "deviants" have had no safe place of retreat, no protected privacy. To be privatized means to be made vulnerable to use, to exploitation, to abuse without recourse to generalized legal, governmentally enforced protections. An only apparently trivial, or benign, example: I confess to feeling a chill when workplace "personnel offices" are renamed "offices of human resources." "Resources" are not the kinds of things that have rights—although my computer sometimes acts as if it does. "Human resources," like "natural resources," are considered to be—have been defined as being—available for use, which slides quickly into abuse where there are no rights to set firm limits.

"The personal is political" and "It's not just me" can become, then, realizations that open a great deal to clearer view. They can become invitations to think, to join and act with others in breaking out of the radical vulnerability of un-righted privatization, in coming out into public life. Only then can we also return safely to private lives with doors that open out as well as in, to which we have our own, rightful keys.

Thinking about the privatized lives of so many as well as the public lives of the few about which we were taught for so long also opens to view the private lives of those few. This seriously transgresses boundaries that have long been fiercely defended. Here, too, we are challenged to rethink what that does and should ask of us. When the lives of girls and women are no longer closed out of the public, men's public lives and stories become highly vulnerable. Men can no longer safely close the doors on their private lives and count on other men to join them in this mutual protection pact. A similar breaching of barriers has taken place with the emergence of invidiously racialized people into public life: public careers can now be shattered as stories told by the long privatized are told for all to hear. What should be protected as "privacy" has thus become a question in a vivid, complex way made all the more so by modern communication technologies. Where, how, for whom, and within what new limits are we to protect private lives? It is both ironic and unavoidable that such serious issues arise in significant part because more of us, having achieved some public rights and standing, can also now claim protections for our private lives. However, perhaps this irony, like so many related to our ongoing efforts to undo old systems of domination, suggests new and more equal grounds for rethinking what is needed for all and not just a privileged few of us.

As critical scholars continue to reveal, the coherence in many of the stories we have inherited was manufactured after the fact to make sense of characters, events, and motivations that had been removed from their real, privatized contexts. We were given heroes who took on the aura of being good men in a moral sense without adequate examination of how they actually treated most other people. The acts and qualities of character their stories offered us were thus thin, selective, mystified. They could appear "larger than life" precisely because their actual lives had been left out of account. Those who admired them were thereby set up to model themselves on lives no one actually did or perhaps even could lead, and then to become cynical as they unavoidably realized that for them and for others, the public story was actually a complete sham at worst, a partial version at best. I believe it was Oscar Wild who said that hypocrisy is the tribute that vice pays to virtue. It is our ongoing challenge to retrieve and create less partial understandings of the virtues: we have had enough of hypocrisy and its corollary, cynicism.

Surely we can redefine heroism so it becomes a quality of character developed through a whole life, coherently realized through all sorts of relations, actions, and works, including those too long privatized.

We can now hear and tell the stories of "the conquest of the West" in the United States without suppressing the stories of the non–Indian women who also, and also differently, suffered hardships, built communities, were heroic in childbirth, and were too often abused by men from whom they had no protection.[25] We can now hear and tell the stories of Indian women and men as well as of "Indian fighters," of the heroic struggles of those whose lands were taken, and lives destroyed. Furthermore, struggles over slavery were not only basic to stories of the Southeast, unrelated to the histories of Native Americans there and in the West and North.[26] These are finally becoming public stories: without them, we can have only falsified, partial histories of this land and its many peoples.

Too many secrets have been kept for too long. Until we breach unjust, inequitable, dominance-serving barriers between public and privatized lives, we will not find truer stories of the sort that, like all good stories, are replete with tragedy as well as heroism. Truer stories offer both, along with the essential ground of real, actual daily lives that give both context and coherence for meanings on which we may all more safely rely.

There are statues in public squares of some 'kinds' of men who killed and died in wars; to my knowledge, there are no statues of women who gave birth, continued life. But humans are natal as well as mortal, and it is dangerous to privatize one and glorify the other. When we remember women, with all our differences, dominant cultural stories and their interpretations change and become much more complex; context and community re-enter; the exigencies and heroism of everyday lives become visible.

Examples continue to multiply of how we can come to think differently and thereby begin to transform knowledge when we see the obvious. Let us just note here the basic point: the shaping assumptions on which influential knowledge continues to be based are influential not despite but because of the fact that most people are unaware of them. Awareness can, then, become quite literally world-changing—consciousness-raising on a grand scale.

## Philosophical Cultural Analysis;
## Psychotic Cultural Systems

I now sometimes call efforts to discern and critique divisive, inegalitarian, unjust systems and meanings—and knowledges that have grown from and legitimated them—*philosophical cultural analyses.* Like that of individual-centered psychoanalysis (but on a far broader scale), the purpose of such analyses is to haul old, locked-in, distorting conceptualizations into the present so we can see and unfreeze them to disentangle ourselves from them. As with such work on the individual level, philosophical, or conceptual, cultural analysis is sometimes relatively easy. We encounter a way of thinking/feeling that is dysfunctional in the present because its source and referent are in some particularly marking experience we had in the past, when we were still learning about the world and had few resources with which to counter it. Re-encountering it consciously in the here and now, we recognize its limitations, its skew, and its hold on us dissolves. For example, we might remember that a man who scared us when we were three had an accent other adults around us did not; that we internalized a sense of unease associated with that accent; and that the prejudices of our informing culture subsequently exaggerated our fears. When we recognize these prejudices as just that, and remember our childhood experiences in the context of others that should have contradicted them, we can reopen ourselves to real other people with all their individual differences. We can thus undo conceptual errors, and move on.

But sometimes the prejudices of an entire culture are worked so deeply into its everyday fabric—so thoroughly reinforced by that culture's prevalent codes, signs, symbols, turns of speech, jokes, arts, knowledge, laws, and religions—that they do not simply skew some corners of our experience of reality; they *replace* reality. All encounters are then filtered through an elaborate interpretive network of schema—a network that protects us from any disruption of its logic, its meanings, its emotive hold. Anything or anyone that challenges that mad interpretive process is then ignored, marginalized, silenced, declared "insane," locked up, expelled, lynched.

Sexualized, gendered racisms can become culturally psychotic systems. It is because of their totalizing logics, which distort and defy realities, reshaping them in the closed terms of the system, that I refer to them as culturally "psychotic." We can become aware of the deadly absurdity of these closed logics, these reality-redefining meaning systems; however, releasing ourselves individually and collectively from their hold takes more than moments of awareness, however acute, moving, and convincing those moments are. Changing such systems requires actions, and even when we undertake those actions, and even when we are supported by others in those actions, we must continue to engage in conceptual critique. Acting against deep-rooted and massively prejudicial systems is no guarantee that we will liberate ourselves from, rather than just replace, them. They have the capacity to grow again if not ongoingly uprooted. Histories of revolutionary struggles that have replicated and reinstated sex/gender and racial/ethnic hierarchies should remind us that even successful actions offer no quick fix of these systems. Yet we can keep analyzing, critiquing, thinking and rethinking them until, bit by bit, we do track down all of their roots and recurrent manifestations. Transforming ourselves and the systems that live also in us is an ongoing philosophical, psychological, political project.

When we succeed in thinking ourselves free—even if only from one set of prejudicial assumptions, one aspect of an internalized system—learning can begin again in ways that are both enlivening and interesting. We are thinking creatures; locking up our minds is as much a punishment as locking up our bodies, and it takes even more ongoing work on the part of all concerned. We have better things to do with our energy than collude with prejudices that require constant tending to keep from collapsing in the face of the contrary evidence reality stubbornly persists in producing.

I do not have and do not seek any one replacement for closed dominant ideologies or for their recurrent expressions. Because thinking both entails and realizes freedom, insofar as we are free to enjoy it there will be many meanings at play, just as we are many and ourselves always changing. The point is not to be once and for all right. The point is to become more fully alive, responsive to and responsible for changing, contradictory, complex worlds that exceed and transcend any and all of us.

# III

# Conceptual Approaches

## *Thinking Through*

### Conceptual Errors: The Root Problem

We begin our critical, reflexive thinking again, now circling toward the central root problem, discovering it, circling out to see it differently, returning to reconsider it. Throughout what follows, I will continue to follow that kind of spiraling logic of exploration (which I call a *peri logos, peri* being Greek for "around," "about," "beyond"). I take this approach because my thinking has from the beginning been in conversation with many people, and I want to continue trying to open as many doors as possible. I do not want to argue anyone into agreement; that kind of agreement is entirely unstable, and rightly so. Argument by certain prevailing rules of logic is a kind of force; a good argument "compels" agreement. I do not wish to compel agreement. I wish to invite it, and I would like the reasons for agreement to belong genuinely to each of those with whom I think. The whole point of this exploration is to try to think ourselves free—to free our own thinking.

The *root problem,* as I saw it when my philosophical fieldwork focused on the exclusion and misinterpretation of women, reappears in different guises in all fields and throughout dominant traditions. It is, simply, that while the majority of humankind was excluded from education and the making of what has been called knowledge, *the dominant few defined themselves not only as the inclusive kind of human but also as the norm and the ideal.* A few privileged men defined themselves as constituting mankind/humankind; at the same time, they saw themselves alone as exemplars of what mankind/humankind ought to be. Removing women, nonprivileged men within their own culture, and those who belonged to other cultures from full membership in 'proper' "mankind," they justified that exclusion on the grounds that the excluded were by nature and by culture 'lesser' people (to the extent that they even thought of the others as having 'cultures'). Thus, their notion of who was properly human was both exclusive and hierarchical with respect to those whom they took to be properly subject to them: women in all roles, men who worked with their hands, male servants and slaves, women and men of many other cultures.

Such root definitions of what it means to be human, with the concepts and theories that flowed from and reinforced those definitions, made it difficult to think well about, or in the mode of, anyone else, just as they made it difficult to think honestly about the defining few.

"Know thyself," said the few ancient Greek men who enjoyed the leisure to explore "the life of the mind" and the privilege of living the "free life of the citizen"—and who are still mistakenly (those basic errors again) called "the Greeks" as if they were *all* the Greeks. Thus, they also created—and not for the first or only time in human histories—a haunting not-self that was essential to the admitted, recognized, claimed self. Their not-self—women, slaves, men who worked with their hands, "barbarians" (which originally meant non–Greek-speakers)—surrounded the self they sought to know, setting its boundaries by constituting some activities, some feelings, some human functions, some deep desires as forbidden while projecting them onto others. Those boundaries, of course, also constituted boundaries prescribed and enforced for those lesser others whom they then desired, feared, and felt it essential to control. This deep construction of a self—whether in Western (or individualistic) terms or in terms of roles and social relations—was inextricably tied to a devalued, threatening not-self. Much later, "Man's" feminized not-self was brilliantly characterized by Simone de Beauvoir in her concept of Woman as the Other. *The Other/othering* captures an existential reality as well as a conceptual move that remains at the very heart of many traditions in a way that is especially potent because it is far too often unrecognized. Yet it seems profoundly familiar once introduced:

In actuality the relation of the two sexes is not quite like that of two electrical poles, for man represents both the positive and the neutral, as is indicated by the common use of *man* to designate human beings in general; whereas woman represents only the negative, defined by limiting criteria, without reciprocity. She is defined and differentiated with reference to man and not he with reference to her; she is the incidental, the inessential as opposed to the essential. He is the Subject, he is the Absolute—she is the Other.[1]

The concept of the Other is a clue to the difficult conceptual knots we must untangle. It is very strange to maintain that one small group of people is simultaneously the essence, the inclusive term, the norm, and the ideal for all. Yet that is what we hear: "'man' is a generic term," but at the same time, "*vive la différence*," which positively celebrates the notion that "men and women are by no means the same." What, then, are we to do about the differences used to mark women as not-men? If "man" is generic, those differences must be the marks of non-humans. Women then become beasts or gods (whores or virgins in the sexualized construction imposed on women in many cultures) and/or non-entities, non-selves.

We hit absurdity fairly quickly here. Consider the famous syllogism, "Man is mortal. Socrates is a man. Therefore, Socrates is mortal." Try it with a woman: "Man is mortal. Alice is ___ ..." what? A man? No one says that, not even philosophers. "Man," the supposedly generic term, does not allow us to say, "Alice is a man." So we say, "Alice is a woman." Then what are we to deduce? "Therefore, Alice is ___ ..." what? It is *man*, a supposedly universal category that is simultaneously neutral and masculine but *not* feminine ("masculine" is defined in contradistinction to "feminine"), who "is "mortal." Is Alice, who is female and thus not in a category that is either neutral or masculine, then *immortal?* Is she mortal insofar as, for the purposes of such reasoning, she can be subsumed under the category *man* but not insofar as she is, specifically, female? Are we women, then, immortal insofar as we are female? Alice ends up in the peculiar position of being a somewhat mortal, somewhat immortal, creature. Or, we must admit, we cannot thus reason about Alice while thinking of her as female at all. We can think of Socrates as a man without derailing the syllogism; we cannot think of Alice as a woman. Reason flounders; the center holds, with Man in it, but it is an exclusive center, not a universal one. Alice disappears through the looking glass.

The fact is that "inclusive" or "generic" *man* does not include (or "embrace," as witty grammarians used to say) women or all humans, any more than qualities derived from man as he has been understood represent either the norm or the ideal for all humankind. That a handful of males have been thereby constituted as normative as well as generic humans is similarly both nonsensical and cruel. So is how they got that way. In her book about "freaks" in nineteenth-century America and Europe, Rosemarie Garland Thomson observes that "the constructed freak occupies the alarming and chaotic space at the borders that delimit the 'average man,' a concept formulated by the Belgian statistician Adolphe Quetelet in 1842.... The freak show's prevalence after about 1840 can be seen ... as serving to consolidate a version of American selfhood that was capable, rational, and normative, but that strove toward an ontological sameness."[2] "Normal" female bodies, being nonrepresentative of 'generic' man, were already not "average" and could hardly be normative for 'proper' man, of course—so female "freaks" marked several boundaries, including racial. The "Hottentot Venus," Sartje Baartman, was widely exhibited in London and Paris between 1810 and 1815 as both a violation of what man should be and a perverse confirmation of the fascination of woman cast as "Venus" and "Hottentot"—'higher' and/or 'lower' than Man, and so neither the same as he nor his equal.[3]

## Dividing by 'Kind'

Encountering such vicious nonsense not among a few individuals but across whole cultures presses us to realize that *there is a foundational tangle of errors that precedes even as it also repeatedly emerges from the error of taking a particular few to be the inclusive, normative, and ideal 'kind.'* That error entails turning some particular, socially selected *distinctions* into *divisions*; giving some of those divisions the ontological and epistemological status of *facts of Nature* and/or of *Nature's God*; and thereby allying historically, economically, and politically shaped observations of human differences with putative knowledge of both religious and supposedly natural classificatory systems. Human variation—which is a given of human being, of our plurality, historicity, physiology, mode of reproduction, minds, hearts, and cultures—is then frozen into divisions fraught with significance and signification; these divisions are then taken to be explanatory rather than themselves crying out for demystifying critique.

Such knowledge constructions dangerously prepare for and can be used to legitimate culturally psychotic complexes that are impervious to counterexperience—complexes on a mad, grand, and deadly scale that break out like plagues over and over: sexualized violence, anti-Semitism, witch burnings, ethnic cleansing, enslavement, genocide, homophobia, the creation of "freaks," racializations locked into racisms. Theodore W. Allen writes about the "howling absurdities" of continuing efforts to regulate "the [supposedly natural] races":

> Historically, "racial dissimilarities" have not only been artificially used, they are themselves artificial. In colonial Hispanic America, it was possible for a person, regardless of phenotype (physical appearance), to become "white" by purchasing a royal certificate of "whiteness." With less formality, but equal success, one may move from one "racial category" to another in today's Brazil where, it is said, "money whitens.". . . In 1890, a Portuguese emigrant settling in Guyana (British Guiana) would learn that he/she was not "white." But a sibling of that same person arriving in the United States that same year would learn that by a sea-change he/she had become "white."

Having shown the absurdity of explaining race systems as natural, Allen looks instead for "the operative element, namely 'oppression,'" to find "the organic interconnection of racial, class, national, and gender oppression."[4]

Such strikingly apparent violations of the consistency that conceptual logics are supposed to provide should alert us to the presence of other kinds of reasoning—the tortuous kinds that work with and for constructions of *women* defined as always and necessarily inferior to men, as well as and along with gendered, sexualized constructions of *races, freaks, queers, primitives.* All sorts of intellectual, legal, religious, cultural nonsense has had to be created to prop up such artificial figures. For example, our son reports that the male sushi chef at a Japanese restaurant reacted to hearing about the woman who presides at our favorite place by shaking his head vehemently. "Impossible," he said. "No, no, *no!*" "Why not?" asked our son. "Women can't make sushi. Their hands are too little and too hot." Not trivial, that. Systems whose deforming errors were to be found only in dramatically unjust instances would not last: "common sense" has to support them, make them seem "normal" so that we become not only inured to them but daily implicated with them.

But *human being* too often remains radically divided and ranked from 'higher' to 'lower' in all too many traditions and eras, and so also in too many versions of knowledge. This is not to say that principled intellectual, religious, moral, and political positions are not to be found opposing the injustices supported by fallacious hierarchies, and sometimes hierarchical thinking itself. But entrenched, culturally valued traditions of thinking are highly vulnerable to misuse, and we have many examples of just that. For example, writing to introduce Confucianism to the West, Ch'u Chai and Winberg Chai find it necessary to say:

> High in Heaven and below on earth, all things are scattered and diverse in kinds. In accordance with this pattern, *li* is instituted. . . . In ethics, Confucianism upholds the five "constant virtues." . . . These Confucian principles and values . . . could readily lead to the modern concepts of human rights and political democracy. However, in the course of time, they suffered much pandering in the hands of politicians and emperors, who gave prominence to that aspect of Confucianism which supports the autocratic rule. Thus for two thousand years Confucianism had been closely affiliated with the imperial system . . . as an ideological tool of imperial rulers.[5]

Something similar, *mutatis mutandis,* can be said of instances of Western science and humanism, Christianity, Islam, Judaism. One way to judge whether these traditions and systems serve equality or various kinds of autocratic "top down" rule involves observing whether *diversity of 'kinds'* is locked in as *division by 'kind,'* and then whether those divisions are ranked from 'higher' to 'lower' or held in egalitarian relation with each other. Where there are no useful, flexible distinctions but instead 'kinds' named, defined, and taught as real and significant across a whole culture, contrary experiences are set up to be denied, rendered illegitimate, and rejected as "out of order" and "destabilizing." It is significant that the book on Confucianism I cited uses "man" (in English) for humankind and has no index entries at all for women. Thus, ontological/moral/theological systems become political, and vice versa, and epistemologies and knowledges emerge that, through education and cultural spread, can sustain them even when scholars really do intend otherwise.

# Some Examples from the Curriculum

To begin to explore effects of such conceptual errors—some of which come together and lock in at culturally psychotic levels—let us consider the following examples (which I have made up but are based on a large collection of syllabi gathered from around the country and on my work at many campuses).[6] They contain clues to basic conceptual errors that make a change to more inclusive thinking improbable, if not impossible, as long as they remain unrecognized and unquestioned.

- An introductory course in art history requires one basic text. In that long text, *The History of Art* (not, you will notice, "*A* History of Art"), the works of only four women are discussed. There are few references in the text or in other materials to the art of cultures other than those that trace their origins to Greece. "Asian" art, for example, is 'covered' in a short unit at the end of the text. The art of nonprivileged peoples of all sorts is not mentioned, except in one or two short sections subheaded 'folk' and/or 'primitive' art.

- An introductory music course addresses the work of twenty male composers who worked within and/or created a specific set of musical forms. These men wrote music for certain groups, places, eras, and for particular social classes. All other kinds of music are, if not entirely ignored, presented as less "serious" than that of these twenty men. Students are told that the music of others is properly considered only under some subhead such as ethnomusicology, a specialty that is interesting but less serious than "classical" music. Jazz, today increasingly not only studied but glorified as the achievement mostly of Black males, is introduced in a special session or two. Native American music is relegated to ethnomusicology or left to Native American studies.

- Students in a history course are taught that Europe had an Enlightenment and a Renaissance. These terms—"Enlightenment" and "Renaissance"—focus attention on the activities, creations, and meanings important for a particular group of men, whom professional historians later studied. In this way, in students' minds, the Renaissance and the Enlightenment become things/events that contain/were an era's most significant and interesting realities. That most people—women and significant groups of men in Europe, in the colonies, and else-where—experienced and understood these times in radically differ-ent ways even when powerfully affected by them is not considered worthy of much discussion. Nothing is done to undercut the con-gratulatory tone of the eras' names.

• In an economics course, no mention is made of the role of racial-ized gender in economic systems, nor is there any effort to consider or discuss the implications of the unpaid and underpaid labor (pro-ductive and reproductive) on which paid labor (not to mention the whole society) so intricately and intimately depends. Thus, the degree to which gender, intertwined with race, class, ethnicity, immigration status, categories of disabilities, has provided workers persistently locked into particular kinds of jobs (overwhelmingly the lowest-paid jobs) never surfaces for attention. Students are left with the impres-sion that such things do not matter, are not real—or are, perhaps, mere aberrations in an otherwise 'rational' system or, worse, the fault of those who are trapped in dead-end, low-paid jobs.

• In a physics class, no mention is made of the history and politics of the development of the currently prevalent knowledge or of variations in other cultures and times. Western science, like and with Man, has cast itself as the thing-itself such that variations are moved out of its category and down a scale of worth and significance (Man is to "prim-itive" people/"natives" as science is to "primitive" knowledge/"folk-lore"). Great physicists who made recognized and influential discov-eries are mentioned, but none among them is female; Lise Meitner, who had the insight that ultimately made it possible to release atomic energy, is not mentioned, although Otto Hahn, her (non–Jewish male) research partner, is.[7] Furthermore, students in this class are led to believe that 'real' science is ahistorical and apolitical. Thus, some become able to contemplate with equanimity employment in labora-tories funded by corporations or the military, no matter what effects this control will have on open communication among scholars, no matter what the actual purposes to which their research contributes. These are matters for others to worry about; they "just want to do good science"—a phrase that reveals how narrow and protectively cir-cular the prevailing definition of science remains.

We have been, and on some campuses still are, so familiar with such examples that it is easy either not to see anything questionable about them or, at the other extreme, to write them off as outdated. But all courses have not changed, and thinking through such examples provides practice in locating the underlying errors that are by no means gone. One technique for doing so is to think in terms of groups we are not used to thinking of either as inclusive *or* as subject to prejudice. Imagine a course on the art of North Carolina called, simply, "Introduction to Art," in which any other art (if mentioned at all) is carefully prefixed or marked—for example, "New York art," "Florentine art." These, because they are a marked 'kind' or "school" and not Art-itself, would then be evaluated against the standard of (North Carolinian) Art. Unprefixed art history would then also exclude what was going on in the United States (of which North Carolina is one state) or elsewhere except insofar as it could be seen as having influenced or been influenced by (North Carolinian) Art. If North Carolinian artists were ignorant of these traditions, or believed it right and proper to borrow from without crediting them, these traditions would not appear in (North Carolinian) Art History texts. And that would be explained, perhaps sadly, by saying to anyone who protested, "Those people just haven't yet produced anything worthy of inclusion."

Ridiculous. Yet if the profession of art history had developed in North Carolina, that might be what art historians taught. And "ridiculous" is indeed a reaction that those who would teach about women have heard. Why? At a basic level, because *dominant professionalized traditions have prepared us to consider it absurd to claim the status of art, literature, religion, culture for any instances of these human phenomena except those long enshrined at the defining center of fields.* That which does not carry a prefix seems to be, and is assumed to be, universal: literature as it has been taught by professional scholars is the thing-itself, whereas women's literature is a kind of literature. Black women's literature is a still more narrow kind, and Third World Black women's literature is even further removed from generality and definitional centrality. The more prefixes, the further from the real, the significant, the best. One can map a culture's stratification systems by noticing that.

In speaking about our experiences in our communities, many of us also still do not say, "my American heterosexual able-bodied white male Christian banker," or lawyer, or doctor. These markers go against the grain of what is supposed to be noticed. Why? Because they are not commonly used to mark 'kinds' of people or works. A picture of a white male physician will be called "a picture of a doctor" by most U.S. Americans; a picture of a Black female physician will be identified with particularizing markers. Profound and some-times terrible histories lurk within the most persistent of these common usages. "Jewish" before "banker" can still evoke generations of European racism: it is not just a specification as, say, "Episcopalian banker" might be. (Have you ever heard a greedy, crooked banker or CEO called "a Christian banker/CEO"?) "Christian" and "Muslim" are rarely used before the phrase "slave trader" despite the active participation of Christians and Muslims in that egregious business (although "Arab slave traders" was used by the British and Europeans when they wanted to distance themselves from their own histories).[8] It is of concern on several counts that the phrase "Jewish slave traders/owners"—but not "Christian slave traders/owners"—has been appearing in recent years in the United States. It serves to hide Christian and Muslim participation by invoking a historically denigrated Other such that "slave trader" and "Jewish" conflate and can both be cast out, leaving a false sense of purity and inno-cence for those whose 'kind' remains unmarked.

It is, in fact, very easy to locate key instances of false universalization in dominant meaning systems. One need only note where prefixes, or markers, are not used *and would be startling if they were*: "the white male philosopher Kant," "a heterosexual marriage," "the two-handed pianist."

When we do not say "white men's literature" but do say "Black women's literature," we are reflecting and perpetuating a kind of knowledge in which the literature of one dominant tradition is seen as literature-itself, the inclu-sive term, the norm, and the ideal. When we do not say "Christian bombers" but do say "Muslim bombers," "Muslim" is being used as an evocation of both a historical and particular identity and of fearful Otherness, whereas "Chris-tian" is retained primarily as a normative ideal ("That would be the Christian thing to do") rather than as the particular historical identity it also is. Here, too, utter absurdity results, which highlights the deep skew that results when one 'kind' is entrenched as the ideal as well as the norm for all. In "Israelis and Palestinians: What Went Wrong?" Amos Elon reports that, at a crucial moment in "the UN Security Council, the American delegate, Warren Austin, pounded the table, saying the American government believed that it was high time for the Jews and the Arabs to get together and finally resolve their problems in a truly Christian spirit."[9]

Other literatures, other religions, and other traditions are then being cat-egorized as 'kinds' and relegated to subcategories, or if they are brought into the 'mainstream,' they are made vulnerable to inappropriate judgments inso-far as they are evaluated by standards appropriate to contexts and discourses that did not originally include them or that were founded by people who thought they *ought* to be excluded. For far too long, only the works and lives of the few have been regularly discussed in the curricular canon *within their own contexts,* such that their own meanings can be discerned. This statement does not threaten to "collapse us into relativism"; rather, it is a call for sound and sensibly appropriate comparisons and judgments. Does it make sense to taste-test a mango to see whether it is a good apple? That is just what we would do if we had conflated apples with fruit-ness, with fruit-itself. Things, people, works from other traditions, from other discourses, when submitted to the terms of falsely narrowed systems, cannot make much sense, cannot seem very good. Removed from their own conversations and forced into someone else's, they can only fall silent, or stammer, or imitate rather poorly those in whose company they have suddenly been dropped. Or, if they do speak up, they may seem distastefully defiant or ignorant when in fact all they are is different and quite understandably uncomfortable. Good judgment and notions of excellence, not to mention effective diplomacy, are then hardly well served.

## A Traditional Story

Ronald Takaki writes:

> Seeking to know how they fit into America, many young people have become listeners; they are eager to learn about the hardships and humiliations experienced by their parents and grandparents. They want to hear their stories, unwilling to remain ignorant or ashamed of their identity and past.

Native-American novelist Leslie Marmon Silko cautioned:

> *I will tell you something about stories . . .*
> *They aren't just entertainment.*
> *Don't be fooled.*[10]

In speaking of the development of the disciplines that dominate our curricula, of the knowledge we teach within them, we have been speaking of a very particular tradition, a particular if multivoiced discourse—the one long taught in "Western Civ" courses. Those educated in the United States are familiar with the content of that course, which tells a story that pivots around the birth of Jesus (history marked as "A.D." or "B.C.") but actually opens (rather mysteriously) in Greece before moving to Rome, spreading through Europe and Great Britain, and then arriving in North America, which is depicted as a "virgin land," a blank and empty space inviting Europeans to possess it. Knowing this story well has been considered the mark of one who had a 'sound' liberal arts education. We can now return to it, watching this time for how the few achieved and maintained not just their dominance but also their defining and standard-setting centrality. We can step outside that story and follow it from the perspectives of male "pagans," Africans, Indians, any 'kind' of women—or, as Foucault did in *Madness and Civilization,* from the perspective of processes that removed varying groups from "civilized," "sane" enclaves. This fascinating, transforming work has now been well begun— for example, in Ronald Takaki's book, cited earlier; *The Black Woman Cross-Culturally,* edited by Filomina Chioma Steady; Gerda Lerner's *Creation of Patriarchy;* Martin Bernal's *Black Athena;* Simi Linton's *Disability Studies;* Valentin Mudimbe's *Creation of Africa;* Vincent Harding's *There Is A River: The Black Struggle for Freedom in American;* Russell Means's *Where White Men Fear to Tread;* the novels of Linda Hogan; Dick Teresi's *The Ancient Roots of Modern Science—From the Babylonians to the Maya;* Gwyn Kirk and Margo Okazawa-Rey's *Women's Lives: Multicultural Perspectives;* and many others (a few of which I will cite elsewhere, although not sufficiently to introduce their extraordinary richness). These have been controversial works because they threaten the interpretive control of any one group's cultural stories.

## Paideia

*Paideia: The Ideals of Greek Culture* was at one time a highly influential book that gave educators "classical" ideals with which to conjure. In *Paideia,* Werner Jaeger writes: "The formative influence of the community on its members is most constantly active in its deliberate endeavour to educate each new generation of individuals so as to make them in its own image. . . . Therefore, education in any human community . . . is the direct expression of its active awareness of a *standard.*"[11] Note that this passage does not locate the "community" that is deciding which standards to use in educating new generations into its own image. We know, of course, since Jaeger is focusing on "the Greeks," that the exemplary community that was making these decisions did not include women, slaves, barbarians, or men who worked with their hands. "The [unmarked, unspecified] community" was the few who held power, the few who had relegated all the work that provided for their freedom to those they considered less fully human than themselves.

Such education, Jaeger continues, "starts from the ideal, not from the individual. Above man as a member of the horde, and man as a supposedly independent personality, stands man as an ideal ... the universally valid model of humanity which all individuals are bound to imitate."[12] "Man" is not to be considered as a member of the community—now called "the horde," and so perhaps including all the excluded others—or as an individual, but as "an ideal." And that ideal, developed, as Jaeger has said, with a view to perpetuating the values, knowledge, and ethics of those who take themselves to *be* "the community," is then to be taken cast as a "universally valid model of humanity." This, precisely, is the basic tangle of conceptual errors we are trying to unknot.

Such exclusivity, mystified and raised to the highest power through universalization, was not a temporary aberration on the part of a few Greeks. It was present also in the European medieval universities, not only in their exclusion of all but the few who qualified as those-to-be-educated, but also in their distinction between the liberal and the servile arts. The liberal arts were for those who could indulge in study of the 'higher' things; the servile arts were for those whose knowledge would be put to some direct use. The old privileged male Athenian notion remained, informing the idea that that which is an end in itself and so 'useless' is higher than anything that is involved intimately with the maintenance of life, with the nature above which Man is supposed to rise. And as in Athens, that hierarchy of value was applied to people, not just to ideas or works. Liberal arts were for "the free man," by which was meant not he who had political freedom but, rather, he whose thoughts could be occupied with things other than the necessities of life. Those who made that freedom possible—women, male slaves, servants—were held to be conditions for the existence of the proper, genuine, and ideal man, out of whose 'kind' they had been defined long before "modern science" produced its own classificatory schemes.

In the Italian male Renaissance, formalized education continued to separate the privileged few males from all others. The teaching of Latin was taken more, not less, seriously as Latin was superseded by Italian. Privileged boys left their homes to learn a language that few women or uneducated males learned. By acquiring Latin, they marked themselves as grown up—meaning, grown both 'above' and away from the home and those whose work was restricted to it. The educated man was he who need not lower himself to the pursuit of useful knowledge, to the work of caring for others, or even to taking care of himself.[13] Liberal arts education often still struggles against its own roots to make a case for its usefulness—even as it has persisted in keeping itself separate from its "applied" and practice-oriented branchings.

## Novus Ordo Seclorum: Ideals and Practices in the "New World"

That peculiar hierarchy, in which the dominance of the few reflected and helped perpetuate faultily abstracted philosophical schemes of worth, carried over into the so-called New World. In the United States, it was not until the mid-1800s that women, men of color, and the children of those who worked with their hands were allowed into 'higher' education. Oberlin College's motto, "To work and to learn," and its early admission of the historic outsiders—Black and white women and Black men—constituted a radical break in the tradition that is still being resisted.

Despite the persistent influence of the root problem, education in the United States has meant something different from education in continental Europe, Great Britain, and the countries they colonized (which had their own complex brews of hierarchies). Invoking the ideal of *paideia* even while attempting to alter its meaning, Lawrence Cremin has suggested that the United States has developed a "national *paideia*" that unites "the symbols of Protestantism, the values of the New Testament, *Poor Richard's Almanac*, and the *Federalist Papers*, and the aspirations asserted on the Great Seal."[14] Different, then, but by no means entirely open or adequately democratic for many of differing faiths, cultures, tribal and other social, political experiences.

Walt Whitman, in his 1871 essay "Democratic Vistas," wrote that his country would continue to fail its own noble vision "until it founds and luxuriantly grows its own forms of art, poems, schools, theology, displacing all that exists or that has been produced anywhere in the past, under opposite influence."[15] Whitman envisioned "a programme of culture, drawn out, not for a single class alone, or for the parlors or lecture rooms, but with an eye to practical life, the west, the workingmen, the facts of farms and jackplanes and engineers, and of the broad range of women also."[16] Whitman, like other visionary educator–philosophers such as Anna Julia Cooper, Mary McLeod Bethune, W.E.B. DuBois, John Dewey, Jane Addams, Carter Woodson, Maria Montessori, Alexander Meiklejohn, recognized the need for change in the hierarchical systems of supposedly egalitarian America. Tellingly, that need had also been enunciated by Frederick Douglass, who observed that "the day of rejoicing for a white majority celebrating independence constituted a time of mourning for the blacks they oppressed."[17] Others could say the same.

The histories of many people—those who established the land-grant universities; those who early supported women's formal education and founded such schools as Mount Holyoke, Bennett, Bryn Mawr, Spellman, Vassar; those who founded "historically Black colleges and universities"; those who campaigned for Indian-run schools at all levels; those who called for federally mandated provisions for access for people with disabilities; those whose schools offered night classes for working adults; those whose unions sponsored programs for workers, sometimes offering them at the job site—all of these speak eloquently to the continuing vitality of an "American vision of *paideia*" that transcends in many ways (but by no means all) not only the privileged male Athenian concept caught so well in Jaeger's description but also that of early America as described by Cremin.

About fifty years ago, Gunnar Myrdal spoke of the tension between ideals and realities that so profoundly characterizes the experience of education in the United States. He noted that America has "the *most explicitly* expressed system of general ideals in reference to human interrelationships. This body of ideals is more widely understood and appreciated than similar ideals are anywhere else.... To be sure, the Creed ... is not very satisfactorily effectuated in actual social life. But as principles which *ought* to rule, the Creed has been made conscious to everyone in American society."[18] It was also Myrdal who famously named "the American dilemma"—'race'—and thereby highlighted a stubbornly failed promise of the Creed. Failures of ideals and ideologies are of course common: socialist, communist, and theocratic creeds, which, once in power, reveal their own implication with the errors that legitimate dividing and ranking us, too often also fail their own ideals to deadly effect.

Surely, where ideals persist and yet persistently fail, we need more than renewed invocation of that to which we all supposedly aspire. Many superb works have been dedicated to helping us understand what is wrong not only with "us" and "our times," but also with the ways ideals are conceived and comprehended. Here, I am concerned primarily with the conceptual knots, the basic errors, that keep us from thinking clearly within—and about—ideals and practices of meaning systems that persist in being deformed by ways of thinking that serve dominance even when defined against it.

We cannot, of course, finally, once and for all times and all peoples, untie or cut through the conceptual knots that keep us from understanding exclusions that reflect and reinforce all complex power hierarchies. However, locating and clarifying root problems and some of the key conceptual errors they produce can help us and coming generations of thinker–activists think more effectively, as we must. Good hearts, passionate convictions, and dreams of reform or revolution do not, I fear, suffice (as history sadly proves). Critical thinking is required, lest even the most radical changes fail to deal with the deep conceptual rooting of dominant systems.

So, we now turn to four specific, and particularly potent, widespread manifestations of the conceptual tangle arising from the root problem of taking a dominant few to be the inclusive group, the norm, and the ideal—an error that results from turning some distinctions into divisions by 'kind.' The forms of the basic cultural complex I will discuss are tightly interwoven. In what follows, I distinguish among them so we can see them more readily and because the root problem appears in sharper relief in some areas and at some times in one or the other of its guises.

# IV

# Errors Basic to
# Dominant Traditions

TO START, here are the errors captured in historical relation to Empire:

The conception of a world imperial base, generating enlightenment and technology and laced with a certain amount of Christianity which constituted the "white man's burden", was perfectly in keeping with the late eighteenth-century notions of empire. *If the empires of the nineteenth century . . . were, as Marx and others supposed, merely the necessary expression of a certain kind of economic system, this was, in part at least, because their ideological groundwork had already been laid out.* The older providentialist languages of imperialism had been transformed into a pretence to enlightened rationalism. . . . Inevitably, however [in the earlier Romans' imperialist thinking], there existed a tension between a strong sense of inclusiveness in the *civitas* conflated with *Imperium* and the consequent belief that "So long . . . as you were outside it, a barbarian or a provincial [or a woman], you were in some sense less than human." . . . *It was, as Theodore Mommsen in his great history of Roman public law put it, "a familiar concept to the Romans that they were not only the first power on earth, they were also in a sense, the only one."*[1]

Four basic kinds of errors derive from and lock in the root problem of turning *distinctions* among groupings of particular people into abstract, hierarchical *divisions* by 'kind' such that a particular few emerge as the imperially inclusive 'kind' or term, the norm, and the ideal for all. They are:

1. Faulty generalizations and universalization;
2. Circular reasoning;
3. Mystified concepts, which feed and result from faulty generalizations/universalization and circular reasoning; and
4. Partial knowledge that serves the dominant order and is produced and perpetuated by the previous three kinds of errors.

Together, these errors, their causes, and their continuing effects reinforce conceptual complexes that to varying degrees render us impervious to the counterexperiences that could startle us into fresh, free thinking. In what follows, I will introduce these errors briefly, then explore different ways of approaching and thinking about them, selecting examples both of the errors and of some correctives as well as reflecting about some of their consequences. I will also think about the thinking we need to free ourselves from continuing vulnerability to collaboration with dominance.

Throughout such conceptual cultural analysis it is crucial to watch our language. Sometimes it seems possible to locate an error in thinking and/or its expression in speech and/or a particular institutional practice and then simply to change it. For example, in the United States it is by now quite rare to hear an adult Black man referred to as "boy" or to hear "Kaffir boy" in South Africa, although such belittling terms—reflecting disordered time in defining present-day adults as "earlier"/primitive and/or developmentally stuck in youth—were common in white speech until recently. But the errors that produced such usage are so deeply rooted within systems that they cannot finally be undone without fundamental redesign and rethinking of both broad systems and everyday conventions. Similarly, where we find sectors in economies that are dependent on underpaid labor that has been defined as "women's work" (such as "pink-collar" workers, secretaries, nurses, day-care workers, maids), change will depend on a lot more than renouncing "girl" as appropriate for grown women. "Girl" for adult women is, strikingly, a usage that is proving harder even than "boy" to change, perhaps because white people are more frightened of Black men's anger than men in general are of women's. This blithe resistance is related to definitions of femininity that entail being

enticing, pleasing, and receptive to males—definitions both exploited and perpetuated by highly lucrative businesses such as advertising, fashion, cosmetic
surgery. Assumptions that it is appropriate for women to be available to sat-
isfy the physical needs of others have in fact delimited and shaped "women's
work," a categorization that is no longer used in job listings in the United
States but that still reveals realities of interlocking dominance systems. Black
and immigrant women, for example, are found disproportionately in physical caretaking work that remains very badly underpaid. "Women's work" also
makes women—and those they care and provide for—particularly vulnerable to contemporary "structural-adjustment programs":

> Cuts in social services and health care, often already woefully inadequate,
> have increased women's responsibilities for child care, health, and fam-
> ily welfare. Cuts in government subsidies for food and other basic items
> and devaluation of local currencies have reduced women's wages and
> doubly reduced their buying power. Women's wages fell by as much as
> 50 percent in many countries during the 1980's.... The emphasis on
> cash crops at the expense of subsistence crops has devastating environ-
> mental consequences and makes subsistence agriculture—very often the
> responsibility of women—much more difficult.[2]

Thus, because the four errors listed earlier are entrenched in so many different forms—from words and phrases in common usage to economic and
other systems—the discussion of each that follows is long and sometimes
rather intricate. Once the errors are seen, however, I believe they will be obvious (although they can raise complex philosophical questions that are also
important and that I will occasionally address). I want the errors to be obvious and, most of all, to make sense on a useful level. Having located and
become used to working with them, we can proceed to uncover and undo
assumptions and practices that otherwise continue to shape our thought,
knowledge, feelings, and actions such that we do not always see our collusion
even with systems we judge to be unjust.

Perhaps I should also note (having heard mutterings among faculty
schooled in postmodernism when I speak of "foundational, or root, errors")
that, like changing language usage so we do not call contemporary adults
"boy," "girl," or "primitive," making "foundation" a taboo term does not suffice. It is more helpful to proliferate than to prohibit terminology. For example, Foucault writes that he seeks "isomorphisms" (among what I call meaning

systems) for "epistemological spaces" that he uncovers while studying "a positive unconscious of knowledge" through an "archaeological" method focused on "polymorphous techniques of power." I find these methods and terms useful for characterizing, but not for delimiting, fieldwork philosophizing in the service of cultural analysis—which in some ways is also isomorphic with psychoanalytical methods.[3]

What we are looking for is, in a sense, a collection of touchstones, not one theory or methodology. As many different examples and issues as I have raised here, I could have raised many more. The coherence of the discussion that follows does not depend on comprehensiveness. Neither does it derive from an undergirding theory. It reflects how stunningly common the root problem is. Tracing its manifestations and effects on our *perilogos* journey takes us all over the place, across all sorts of boundaries.

Here, then, is a kind of field guide to what we are looking for as we explore the kinds of errors that derive from and reinforce the root error:

1. The FAULTY GENERALIZATIONS and universalization that are of concern to us here are the result of processes of abstraction guided by distinctions that are already culturally shaped, taken to be obvious, and/or naturally based. Such abstractions lead to humans of a particular 'kind' being mis-taken as the only ones who are significant, the only ones who can represent or set the standard for all humans (who are also in some cultures radically divided from and elevated above nature). For example, it is faulty generalization to conclude from studies of white, middle-class U.S. "housewives" living in suburbia in a particular era that women in general suffer from a sense of meaninglessness, frustration, and boredom. Similarly, it is faulty generalization when traits observed in a few members of an oppressed group by someone of a privileged group are generalized to all members of that 'kind.' As Memmi wrote, "From the greed of one Jew the anti-Semite concludes that all Jews are greedy."[4]

   This error can usually be revealed simply by varying the sample from which a generalization has been made. For example, it would be startling in a culture in which being a Methodist is accepted as a distinction rather than a division by 'kind' to hear someone move from an observation that a Methodist neighbor is greedy to "Methodists are greedy," "shrewd," or "pushy." Varying the sample also helps us see how faulty generalization works both to continue prejudicial stereotypes and to keep the supposedly normative few at the defining center. It holds the dominant few in their role as representative of and for all by taking them to be the only ones worth generalizing from. Take, for example, the sentence: "Man demonstrates his superiority to the beasts by developing ever more sophisticated technologies." Generalizing to all from the few who actually develop and control sophisticated technologies leaves individuals and cultures that have not done so (by choice or otherwise) outside the category of "mankind," moving them down the scale toward the "beasts" and backward in evolutionary and developmental time. At the same time, faulty generalization about devalued groups reduces individuals to no more than examples of their 'kind' and of its supposed traits. For example, varying Memmi's example: "From the laziness of one Chicano, the Anglo concludes that all Chicanos are lazy." This is a faulty generalization used to re-prove an assumption that has already been made (circular reasoning). In technical terms, this is also the error of drawing conclusions from an inadequate and/or inappropriate sample and of drawing conclusions unsupported by the data.

2. CIRCULAR REASONING often works with faulty generalizations, as we have seen. Reasoning is "circular" when what is concluded is actually what was already assumed, often as that is enshrined in definitions. For example, when notions of what makes music "good" are derived from close study of a very particular tradition of music, and then those notions are cited as neutral grounds of judgment appropriate for the evaluation of all music, circular reasoning is in play. Indian ragas were not well known outside of Asia when the criteria for 'good' music were being derived from English and European classical music by scholars in those cultures. As a result, U.S. 'experts' judged ragas not as different but as less good when they first heard them. Similarly, it is circular reasoning when a history professor who is working with a definition of what is historically significant (whether said to be for "mankind" or "humankind") that is in fact based on what a few males have done uses that criterion to select what should be covered in a course. When asked to be more inclusive, the professor might respond: "I'd be glad to add a section on indigenous peoples to my world history course, but, you know, I have so much *basic* history to cover, I'm not at all sure

we can get to it." Particular past judgments of significance that are not recognized as such become so enshrined in definitions of a field that, in circular fashion, they turn around to justify continuing the old exclusions. Thus, old exclusions are not only continued but also hidden, mystified. We do not see the functioning of complex processes of dominance at work and our blindness ineluctably further falsifies the histories we can tell and reduces possibilities for change.

3. MYSTIFIED CONCEPTS both precede and emerge from the first two errors. In this context, they are ideas, notions, categories that are so deeply familiar that they are rarely questioned. Hence, we start generalizing from them without first critiquing how they may have preselected a too narrow and/or inappropriate sample for us. Then, through subsequent reasoning, we return to 'prove' what they already contained. Such conceptualizations can even lead us to think and act against our own interests and commitments, without being able to see why or how we got so tangled up. For example, the dominant U.S. idea of *individualism* carries a positive valuation of 'rugged' independence expressed as a radical lack of mutual interdependence with other people, with traditions, with nature. It sees the "individual" as standing out and standing alone, "like a real man." The concept can thus make many Euro-American women, and the people of some other cultures, seem inadequately 'individualized,' which can then lead us to seek help in being "more assertive" and/or to think of feminism as a movement solely for equal individual rights—which, in some instances, are rights established to protect privileged white men rather than for all. Feminism, however, is also a transformative movement that rejects or revalues old, imposed group identities; undoes forced dependencies; and works for equalized interdependence that is protected by new as well as some established rights and opportunities. It is only sensible that equalizing groups that were categorically denied their rights *as groups,* and precisely not as individuals, may require categorical rather than individual rights, but this idea remains shocking to those locked into old, mystified understandings of "individual."

Mystified notions of individualism can also poison impulses of sympathy and empathy. More than one dominant-culture U.S. citizen, observing news reports of suffering in "Third World" countries torn by war or devastated by drought, has said: "It *is* tragic, but fortunately those people don't care about the individual the way we do"—as if caring about others as elders or members of one's age cohort or animal clan or lineage precludes deep, specific love or is less heartfelt and so makes death less painful. "Individual" is mystified here. It fails to reveal even as it devastatingly reflects its cultural specificity, its history as a concept, its unanalyzed norma-tivity—its limitations. We conjure with such terms, invoking rather than thinking about them.

4. PARTIAL KNOWLEDGE emerges when we pose and resolve ques-tions within traditions in which reasoning is limited by the first three errors. It is partial in both sense of the term—that is, it is about, and therefore tends strongly to work for, a part and not the whole. For example, knowledge about "Western Civilization" has tended to be partial insofar as it has excluded, devalued, wrongly explained peoples it appears to cover but does not. It has thereby also falsi-fied stories of the included. Excluding and misinterpreting women, with all our differences, while hiding the exclusion and misinter-pretation through the conflation of male with man, and both with humans, cannot but produce partial knowledge. Similarly, telling the story of "Western Civ" without exploring formative influences from other civilizations and peoples (for example, Asian Indian, indigenous, African, Semitic) truncates and skews that story. Con-sider the curiosity of beginning the main line of the story of "West-ern Civilization" in ancient Greece while ignoring that seafaring and imperial culture's many mutually influential experiences with peoples from around the Mediterranean (removed from the story, one suspects, because they were "dark," or Semitic).

# FAULTY GENERALIZATION AND
# HIERARCHICALLY INVIDIOUS MONISM

THE ERROR OF FAULTY GENERALIZATION, or noninclusive universalization, results from abstraction from an inadequate, inappropriately
partial sample that is taken to be the proper ground on which to base statements about many (or all, if universalized).

It is important to remember that in the span of human history, the inclusion of the majority of humankind in any—let alone "higher"—education is
a very recent event. In what has been called the "Western tradition," women
were long denied learning, and our exclusion from every aspect of study,
including its subject matter, was considered right and proper. That is worth
emphasizing, because it reminds us that, however mystifying language can be,
the majority of humankind was not left out either inadvertently or unconsciously. *The establishment of the definitions and values of the few entailed generalizing purposefully exclusive notions.* We deal here not with the currently popular postmodern attack on universals per se, then, but with a critique of
generalizations derived from exclusions mystified by hierarchies of wrongly
ascribed significance, worth, reality.

What developed through such faulty generalizations can then be characterized as *hierarchically invidious monism* (yes, the acronym is HIM), a system
in which one category is taken to be not literally all there is, but the highest,
most significant, most valuable, and, critically, *most real* category. This hierarchical monism turns all relevant others into failures, or lesser forms, of the
one 'kind.' Eventually, that one category/kind comes to function as if it were
the *only* kind, because it occupies the defining center. Thus, some men became
Man, and out went all women and large groups of men from the category of
'real' significant Man, descending a very slippery slope of human worth, at the
foot of which was the division between Man and animal/Nature.

This slippery slope that Man fears going down, and rarely 'allows' others
to come up, is not, then, only or primarily a dualism (despite all the characterizations of Western thinking as harmfully "dualistic"). A true dualism posits
equal opposites, as in Good and Evil, life and death, something and nothing.
Although there certainly are influential strains of dualism in some dominant

traditions, I believe hierarchical monism is more deeply embedded, even in the Western tradition. What is important is not to choose one characterization, though. It is to watch for where our thinking blurs, because there are errors and consequent cruel absurdities.

Here is an example of influential hierarchically invidious monism: Augustine (one of the Christian "Church Fathers") broke out of the dualism of Manicheanism that was seriously problematical to a monotheistic faith by using the Neo-Platonic definition of "evil" as the absence, not the opposite, of "good." That solution was satisfactory to him, and to many after him, in particular because it established that evil has no being, and hence no power, of its own. Plato, whose work influenced Augustine via the Neo-Platonists, not only drew a line (his famous "divided line" in *The Republic*) between the realm of Being and the realm of Appearance, or Becoming (which by itself might suggest a true dualism) but also held that the lower realm was both less real than the higher realm and imperfectly reflected it. In such a hierarchical monism, true/ false, real/unreal are not dualisms, because "false" and "unreal" indicate degrees of lack of "truth" and "reality," which set the terms—as Man has for Woman; as in some cultures "white" has for racialized groups; as the self-designated "world religions" have for other faiths.

In dualisms of the equal-but-opposite sort, it is possible to achieve a non-hierarchical view of mutually complementary opposites, such as yin and yang. Some dualisms, that is, may open the possibility of conceiving social and political equality in which there is indeed separation, but neither pole is disadvantaged or devalued thereby. In the United States, claims used to be made that this is the kind of equality appropriate for differing 'races' and sex/genders, but that has been found to be untenable, in large part because a hierarchical monism preceded and undercut it. To be separated from the defining, real, normative, ideal 'kind' is by definition—and in systems predicated on such definitions, in practice—to be not only unequal but unequalizable. Some feminist anthropologists debate whether societies that construct two distinct and radically different sex/genders can nevertheless properly be called "egalitarian," because difference is not ranked invidiously (that is, by worth).[1] But in the West, as Simone de Beauvoir noted, the terms "woman" and "man" are neither parallel nor equal. Man is what it means to be human; woman is his Other (as, in different but related ways, slave is Other to master, and the 'primitive' is Other to 'civilized man').

In the meaning systems we are primarily considering, but that are suggestive for others, there were at the beginning (a beginning marked as such by a dominant story) the few privileged men who generalized from themselves to Man, thus privileging certain of their qualities that, they asserted, distinguished them from Woman as well as from "the horde." From then on, differences from those few were seen as marks of inferiority. And Woman already was, as we see in the profoundly influential works of Aristotle, defined not as the equal opposite of man but as a failed version of the supposedly defining type—higher than animals, but lower than men. This meant that, whereas the qualities picked out to be defining of men's humanity were taken to be universally human, women's qualities as defined by men were particularities, not to be generalized about or abstracted from in the quest for knowledge about humankind.

Thus, "feminine" adds something to the idea of woman but detracts from the idea of Man. It tells us that a woman enacts her gender in approved ways, while a "feminine" man is wrongly enacting what a human should be. So crucial are these gender-prescribed qualities to social hierarchies that they have sometimes been taken to be universalized principles, as when some Jungians speak of the "feminine principle" and the "masculine principle"—the *anima* and the *animus*. This can reflect an effort to establish a complementary dualism, but it cannot do so as long as "man" and "human" remain conflated.

It is no wonder that the whole issue of differences has become so central to feminist thought, even where French theorists' important and complex work with *differance* has not been adopted. It is extremely hard to think coherently or act consistently within a system based on faulty generalizations that have created hierarchically invidious monisms falsely presented as equal dualisms.

Thus, when people animated by several of this age's movements, such as women's rights, civil rights, disabled peoples' rights began again to struggle to gain access to the institutions, systems, and curricula that excluded us, many of us wanted to be included in the universal Man. Our differences having been marked as inferiorities, we thought we had to be the same as men to become their equals. Others among us, however, claimed instead an egalitarian dualism: women are different from *and* equal to men; Black people are different from *and* equal to white people; "handicapped" people are not 'dis'-abled but "differently abled." Still others went for superiority: "We" are different, and better. Today, some start with acceptance of the idea that the devalued Other—Woman, "freak," "queer," "gypsy"—has been constructed as Other (that is, as radically lacking in positive, real identity) and then proceed to use precisely that lack of meaning to de-center the dominant system. This view embraces what many have seen as the problem, claiming that as women (or another devalued group identity) we can crack the hegemonic logos, the ruling system, precisely because by its terms women exist as a problem and an ongoing threat, as well as a boundary marker and transgressor. Thus, if and as we speak ourselves, what was established itself becomes problematized and particularized and reveals its instability.

Each of these approaches[2] brings to the surface some important questions and considerations, and suggests strategies (always better to have those in the plural). But we can, and I think should, remain critically aware of how faulty generalizations and noninclusive universals may be skewing our thinking in each of them, lest we remain no more than reactive within (or think ourselves safely outside of) fallacious systems.

## Useful Universals?
### Distinguishing Thinking from Knowing

Despite having lost faith in some claimed-to-be generalizations and universals because they contradict themselves by being in fact partial, and because we have seen the harm they can do in covering over, justifying, and so perpetuating injustices, we may not want to do away with the idea of universals. As an idea, *universality* reminds us that we are capable not only of *knowing*—achieving specific answers to questions that can then be taught and learned in ways that shape cultures and so human worlds—but of *thinking about* what we know, and so also *thinking beyond* knowledge. Plato, the dramatist turned philosopher, tells us stories about Socrates haunting the public spaces of Athens, pouncing on all sorts of passers-by to engage them in questioning that never "gets anywhere" or "produces" anything but that does have a crucial effect. The questioning dissolves certainties, beliefs people hold as knowledge (conventional or formal), thereby reopening minds, reawakening curiosity, and, not incidentally, drawing people back into discussion with each other that equalizes them as lovers of wisdom none of them possesses. He mistrusted the sophists, the knowers who taught, did Socrates. The story tells us that he accepted the label of wisest person in Athens only after he had defined it to mean that he knew better than others that he did not know. Thus, the story suggests that in thinking about what we hold as knowledge, we not only lessen its hold on us but also become able to aim higher—to fall in love with wisdom, as Plato often said.

Much later, Hannah Arendt credited Immanuel Kant with making "the distinction between thinking and knowing, between reason, the urge to think and to understand, and the intellect, which desires and is capable of certain, verifiable knowledge." Further, "The ability and the need to think are by no means restricted to any specific subject matter," and thinking "leaves nothing . . . tangible behind, nor can it be stilled by allegedly definite insights of 'wise men.' The need to think can be satisfied only through thinking, and the thoughts which I had yesterday will be satisfying this need today only to the extent that I can think them anew."[3] She thus turned even wisdom, beyond any specific knowledge, into something about which we can think. But for both Plato/Socrates and Arendt, it seemed crucial to hold something before our minds that transcends anything we can actually come to know.

The idea of universality, when we think about it, can similarly remind us that there is always a 'more,' an outside of or horizon beyond knowledge. Thus, when we fall into believing that we *know* a universal, we set ourselves up to be collapsed into confusion when those pesky questions start up again. What can confirm a statement cast as a universal—say, that all humans are earth dwellers? Do we *know* there are no humans elsewhere in the universe? No, but perhaps we will find out someday. Will we? How will we *know* that some other being, able to live where we could not, is "human"? Ah, you say, shifting ground: but this is not an empirical question. It is a matter of definition. We define humans as earth dwellers, so all humans *are* earth dwellers. But how do we know the definition is not just ignorant or arbitrary? We don't, so we might say that, ultimately, such huge statements always are just definitional. But who is then to keep someone else from putting forward a different definition? And if she or he did, how would we judge which is right and truly universal? Perhaps we want to say that there is a universal guarantee for some such knowledge— a god, maybe. But how can we mere mortals know what a god knows? And, as Descartes asked in his quest for absolute certainty, how do we know that such a deity is not fooling us? We don't. Descartes solved this dilemma by deciding that even if he was being fooled, he must be thinking in order to be thus misled. "I think," he famously said, "therefore, I am." This is questionable too, though. He may have discovered a primacy of thinking, but he did not prove that *he* exists—only that thinking (or, anyway, fool-ability) exists. And on and on. The point is that claims to *know* universals immediately raise questions. Philosophy in all cultures is full of them, leading to different conclusions rather than to certainty. That is what set Descartes off on his quest: a fit of pique that knowledge is not settled, certain, stable, agreed on. And it is what has turned others to religion to claim that we *believe* precisely because reasoning cannot settle such issues.

There are no universals, then, we might be willing to think, or if there are, we cannot know them (even if we can choose to believe in them, against reason). But here we are, thinking, recalling the free powers of thought that can illuminate, play around with, make permeable, and raise questions about what is outside the defining boundaries of knowledges. But does not thinking "too much" lead to nihilism, skepticism, cynicism? Not necessarily. Reopening to questioning seems a failure only to those who believe that certainty is a good, and that its only alternative is chaos of mind, of morals, of society.

But that takes us back to our starting point. We have had experience of certainties that are wrong and that do violence when acted on. So we could think it necessary to renounce any and all certainties, especially those that have been set up as universals—those that give their believers license to hold them to be true not just about, but for, all others, anywhere, anytime (turning deviation and difference into error, heresy, evil). But we can also both embrace the reawakening of thinking, as Socrates did (and jesters, riddling sages, and the trickster do), and use the idea of universality that cannot be known but can be thought as inspiration. A universal idea of humankind seems to me useful, for example, perhaps particularly on a moral level, as long as we remember that no content it has yet had is adequately inclusive, and that even much more inclusive thinking cannot fill it in entirely or settle its meaning once and for all. A universal can then be thought of as an idea that is inspirational, regulative, evocative, that raises rather than answers questions and so always retreats to a horizon that eludes even as it calls us. Such an idea of *humankind* can call us to remain open to what it may mean so that we are both drawn into equalizing discussions with as many others as possible and kept from settling for any of the generalizations we and others will make en route. Might we then despair because we do not get somewhere, produce anything, find certainty and thus a stopping place? Why? It sounds like great fun to me, a real adventure—and one that puts us at less risk of doing violence when we are not properly open to all that appears to us in its strangeness as well as its familiarity. As Kant said, we need to go traveling—and as Maria Lugones added, not only in first class.[4]

In thinking around and about and beyond what we can know, we hold open a space of freedom for ourselves. Realizing our freedom, we are less likely simply to trot out and apply what we have been taught, as if we had no choice or responsibility. Instead, we question, and choose how to respond. We thus accept our responsibility for what we choose to know and how we choose to be with it, to act in its light. We heighten our response-ability: we accept responsibility to meet others and all that we encounter not only on our terms but on theirs, recognizing that such encounters can and will startle us back into thinking because they will at times bring us face to face with the unexpected, the not yet or differently categorized that must matter to us on our quest under the aegis of universality. That is, thinking can prepare us to encounter the particular, the individual, the unique more freely than we could if we were locked into generalizations. Thinking moves us into a more poetic mode in which we can delight in searching for analogies, tropes, figures of speech that suggest without pinning down a special kind of encounter. I do not think that we can open ourselves to or return from such encounters with 'raw' phenomena that can make sense to, be integrated by, ourselves and others (except perhaps in some extreme situations and states, about which we then say, "I cannot describe it at all," as mystics do when trying to evoke their visions, or sufferers of atrocities struggling to speak the "incomprehensible" do). But I do think we can loosen the hold prior conceptualizations have on us, and that we can locate and remove some conceptual lenses created by and for specific knowledges, when we begin to see them as harmful because of their effects and because we have reflected on them from outside *as if* we could get to universals.

We can practice this *as if*, this *peri*logical thinking that is less located, by using what Kant called "the enlarged mentality," our ability to think in the place of others. For example, someone who has grown up and been educated within the terms of Euro-Anglo-U.S. dominant cultures can now go to the Museum of African art in Washington, D.C. That's a start right there. "African art" would have seemed an oxymoron in this tradition not so long ago. The art the museum displays may jar Euro-American aesthetic sensibilities at first, perhaps delighting, perhaps shocking, perhaps being troublingly elusive and so evoking confusing feelings and thoughts. Some of the artworks show the Euro-American how some African people to whom *they* were startling, jarring, looked back at them. And once our blinders have been taken off, we do not just see 'my' way plus 'their' way. The experience of 'seeing' has itself changed. We are more likely to "look around," remembering that there are other angles of visions. We can then *imagine* a universal standpoint, a vision that could take in all perspectives at once. If we can avoid the arrogance of claiming to have achieved that god-like view, it can keep us from forgetting something that human perspectives do have in common: that each is itself particular and not definitive.

Or try this: imagine that you are a dog trying to teach her pet human to read scents. How frustratingly dumb the human would seem, limited in the most important kind of intelligence and barely trainable. Generalizations about intelligence that omit how the nose knows are then revealed as terminally human-centric. We can become, through such journeys (of which daily life offers a surfeit, though we may rarely accept their invitation), expatriates from our own 'kind' at least momentarily.

Thinking critically, reflexively, imaginatively, we can perform such thought experiments, bringing to the surface and varying what had been buried so deeply as to be invisible, 'unpacking' familiar generalizations, questioning universals that, the minute they are formulated, become limited and thus essentially self-contradictory or paradoxical. Thus, we can also begin to rethink what generalizations and universals are *for*. As we do so, we prepare ourselves to think better about the differences that do indeed characterize us as individuals in our groups, our times, and our cultures without unthinkingly ranking them along a sliding scale that moves downward from the defining 'kind.' Turning the divisions among us back into distinctions and then considering whether or how those distinctions are useful—and to whom they have been and are useful, whose purposes they serve—frees us from having to be suspicious of distinctions per se. We are then invited to make new distinctions with more care, modesty, and responsibility.

Along these lines, Marjorie Pryse, thinking about women's studies and interdisciplinarity, has proposed "a transversal feminist methodology" to enable us to deal theoretically with multiple differences without falling either into chaos or faulty universals. I am not sure that changing from "universal" to "transversal" saves us from the dangers of singularity, of mono-vision. (Why do we so crave *one* methodology?) But as an ideal rather than "a common methodological language" that could then shut out others, what Pryse proposes is useful. She writes: "The lattice-work produced by the intersection of vectors of oppression with interdisciplinary epistemologies—a transversal methodology—creates a conceptual structure strong enough to be suspended across the gaps between us rather than built on anyone's back. . . . [T]he term *method* signals a 'going after,' a pursuit that derives from *met(a)-*, after, and *hodos,* journey."[5] Here, an ideal of universality is recast as engagement across differences with what is *trans*—that is, transitive/among and transitive/beyond.

# Articulating the Hierarchy:
## Sex/Gender, Class, Racialization

That sex/gender, class, and race are mutually implicating stratification systems is almost a truism today. Although focusing on them is not sufficient, it can help us see how the basic categories of 'kinds' of human beings that cultures establish to mark us off from other beings (animals, vegetables, minerals; gods, devils, spirits, angels; ancestors; totems; golems) and from each other not only lock in within cultures but do so in ways that differ across time and place. The *kinds of relations* that such classificatory systems reflect and perpetuate between and among 'kinds' also both lock in and differ. There are, for example, relations of hierarchy; of opposition; of mutual interdependence; of unification under the aegis of ideals or by making the claim that we are all made of the same substance, however much our attributes vary. How and why we believe we *become* the 'kind' we supposedly *are* varies, too. For example, I am what I am now because of how I lived my previous life; because of the spirit that chose to be reborn with/as me; because of what my mother saw, did, dreamed, or was frightened by while carrying me; because complex chemical interactions that are internally coded and externally enabled, or disrupted, took place; because eternal ideas inform material reality; because God made me. These and many more stories are told about how we became *what* we are, and each story carries within it possibilities for and limitations on present and future relations among us.

I will explore in a preliminary way how the historical divisions by sex/gender, race, and class of the U.S. dominant culture look when we reflect on each *as a figure that would not be as it is without the ground of the others.* I suggest this way of thinking, and will practice it here with you, to explore one possibility among others, but also because I believe that it works somewhat better than some other approaches. For one thing, it does not assume, and so does not reinscribe, the notion that sex/gender and race, for example, are external to each other and thus can only be added to each other or intersect with each other. Instead, it suggests that racializations both entail and shape genderings, and vice versa.

## Sex/Gendering

In the hierarchical invidious monism that can arise from faulty generalization, the sex/gender order that is central is not simply a dualism of Man and Woman (or Man versus Woman in the old "battle of the sexes" construction).

A wrongly universalized particular group of males has been established as the inclusive and ideal term for humans. As a result, all women and some 'kinds' of men have been rendered both marginal and lesser, leaving Man as the 'kind' of human who ought to be dominant. His dominance has been supported intellectually, politically, economically, culturally, socially to such an extent that men's superiority to women seems obvious, natural, unavoidable. This 'superiority' has been attributed not only to men of the defining group generally, but to each particular man. In this kind of dominant culture, boys grow up thinking that, to achieve manhood, they each *ought* to be smarter, stronger, faster, taller, wealthier, more responsible than any female. More than one boy child has been told that, in the temporary or permanent absence of a father, he is to be "the man of the house," meaning that he is to be responsible for and to protect the females, however much older and obviously more capable the females may be. Males in devalued groups also suffer from such patriarchal prescriptions: how are they to become 'real men' if they cannot protect and provide for 'their' females? They can then come to feel "unmanned," shamed before both males and females. And where "being a *man*" means being a powerful *somebody,* feeling "unmanned" can provoke self- and other-destructive rage. Perhaps this is one reason why in the United States today, it is not only rare to hear an adult Black man called "boy," but the age at which boys start being called "men" seems to be getting younger all the time. Not so incidentally, while males can be *unmanned,* women cannot be *unwomanned.* No such term or notion exists. This suggests—does it not?—that as females, we have no significant status to lose.

In heterosexual couples, the male is still often expected to be older, more highly educated, more highly paid. This has been changing, but a big fuss is still being made over "househusbands" and "stay-at-home dads," who are evidently seen as not quite 'normal.' That the male sometimes is not, and may not have any chance to be, 'more' in all these ways than the female has not broken through the cultural psychosis. It has forced couples to find ways between themselves and in public to explain or otherwise compensate for their 'abnormality.' They might respond by proclaiming their commitment to feminist values, but this is hardly a safe haven, as it puts them at risk of being attacked for "political correctness" or "destroying family values." Saying, "She got the best-paying job, so I stay home with the kids," is still not quite sufficient. And it is not just heterosexual couples but whole populations in which females are just as likely, or even more likely, to receive higher education or jobs (as in some Black communities) that bear the burden of analyses from the dominant culture that depict them as 'dysfunctional.' "Single mothers," perhaps especially, are worried about all the way to the White House but to very little effect other than to problematize *single* in relation to *mother*. Left unremarked are the cruelties of economic and social systems that turn caring for children into "women's work" that is so socially and economically unsupported that those who do it are forced into insecure dependence.

Thus, the dominant culture in the United States (and increasingly elsewhere) maintains the unequal, heterosexual, male-headed nuclear (which always makes me think "explosive") family in a capitalist economy as both the norm and the ideal. Other kinds of families may be increasingly recognized, and that is helpful, but still they remain 'other,' lesser, oddities. Tolerance is better than scorn, but, as has been said, it does not put bread on the table or provide secure, reliable community support.

Class and racialization are evidently always also at work, affecting the ways in which gendered identities and roles are lived on various levels of hierarchies. In Europe and elsewhere there were noblewomen who were considered 'higher' than peasant women *and* peasant men, just as the wives of slave-owning men in the antebellum United States were considerably 'higher' than slave men as well as women, and "ladies" were 'higher' than other women. (It is not only amusing that the signs on public bathrooms for women in the United States often still read "Ladies," while men's bathrooms are labeled "Men's." Is "women" felt to be too raunchy?) Similarly, Brahmin women were 'higher' than Kshatriya women, and the castes 'descended' to "untouchable" women and men in India. The czarina of Russia was 'higher' than all other women and men who were serfs. Some power over and some status above men as well as other women has thus been available to some women even while they remained 'lower' than men within their own rank.

Thus, different sorts of questions need to be raised to sort out the tangled systems of sex/gendering as they work within other hierarchies across cultures. However, "Who controls women's sexuality, and how is that control effected?"— as the pioneering feminist historians Joan Kelly, Gerda Lerner, and Linda Gordon, and now many others, have asked—remains a necessary complement to such familiar questions as, "Who controls the means of production?" or, simply, "Who holds power over whom?" The question pulls forward configurations of sex, sexuality, gender that too often remain unexamined in relation to power, thereby perpetuating old traditions in which these were said to be private matters. Actually, they were *privatized*: women were made available for use by men who had public rights allocated only to the few. For example, until quite recently no such category as "marital rape" existed in the United States. A husband had a right to 'take' the woman who 'belonged' to him. Similarly, the medicalization of "deviant" sexualities entailed denial of public rights and created vulnerabilities that had not existed in the same way before. Thus, only the dominant few, self-defined as ideal and normative, remained public, rights-protected citizens. Their sexuality, like and with their gendering, established them as 'proper' humans, while the sexualities and gendering of all others marked them as improper humans and so properly less powerful or even entirely powerless.

Analyses of constructions of sex/gender and sexualities do more than supplement other analyses of hierarchies of power. Struggles for equality that do not undertake such analyses will continue to fail, leaving "power" itself a masculinized term and locking it, and us, into old formations. How many revolutions and movements carried out in the name of justice and equality have contradicted and undercut themselves by failing to become genuinely egalitarian for women and for "deviant" men? There are also movements, some of them aspiring to be revolutions, that have undertaken to reassert the 'proper' order of patriarchies. Women rarely reliably benefit from masculinized revolutions and wars. It is more than a little unnerving, and instructive, to observe that, in its "war on terrorism" declared after September 11, 2001, the United States has also invoked the cause of equality for women to justify its takeover of Afghanistan and Iraq, even though the United States supported both the Taliban and the Baathists in Iraq for years, with no apparent concern for what was happening to women. At the same time, we hear that one of the rotten things about the West against which good Muslims should struggle is that it does not properly protect its women, that women in the West are sex objects in the most demeaning and violating ways. Does this suggest that all of these men care deeply about the equality of women? Hardly (although some may). It suggests that men find fighting over women to be a manly—that is, good and legitimate—thing to do. We cannot comprehend war without facing up to the realities (from the physical to the symbolic) of how men make use of women during conflicts and how that reveals and exacerbates the masculinization of power, dominance, violence. Even though men's sexualities have also been used and controlled (also in and for wars), men have rarely been controlled under the terms of or by methods set by woman-run, or nonmasculinist, systems.

Sexual abuse, sexualized violence, and ongoing daily harassment affect all women. They are a threat all the time; they are actuality with stunning frequency. As Susan Brownmiller, Catharine MacKinnon, Andrea Dworkin, and others have pointed out, rape *is* violent, but it is not explained by saying that it is a violent act (as distinct from a sexual act) or by considering it the act of an aberrant male. Sexual harassment and sexualized violence and abuse express specificities of and constantly reinforce gender hierarchies in many ways, as exploitation and the powerlessness of poverty do for class, and as de facto and de jure segregation do for race. Each creates as well as compounds the purchase and effects of the others.

Sexual abuses of males by males, of males by females, and of females by females also take place, although these are much less common than male–female sexual abuse. The pain of these rarer situations is compounded by their 'abnormality,' which brings its own kind of shame and can lead to silencing. The pain of male abuse of females is compounded by its exaggerated 'normality,' which has too often resulted in victims' being told to "get over it," to "forgive and forget," that they must have "asked for it" or failed to "take proper precautions"—and even that they should avoid "ruining" the abuser's life by bringing charges against him (yes, rape victims have told me this was said to them). Bring race and class forward and the truly devastating effects of sex/gender hierarchies also become evident. White lynchings of Black males in the United States were commonly cast as defenses of "white womanhood." Poor women working in homes and factories have been vulnerable to sexual demands from bosses. Occupying armies have been 'supplied' with girls and women forced (sometimes sold by their parents) into prostitution because of desperate poverty.

Simultaneously, hierarchy confers privileges on those who abide by the sex/gender system in its particularized forms, although those privileges are double-edged and costly. Any woman (whatever her race or class) who has sexual relations with women becomes vulnerable to losing some gender privilege, regardless of what other privilege she may have. (Such losses, however, may be cushioned by wealth, which can provide privacy as well as reasons for some people to continue to defer to her.) Women who affiliate with men, accepting the terms of the sex/gender heterosexual hierarchy, can find themselves treated significantly better in some ways than they would be if they 'belonged' to no one man or if they 'intruded' on no male-defined group or profession. And some female-specific privileges are built into gender systems, primarily in the form of rights to 'protection.' I have a hard time describing these as "privileges," however. Such 'privileges' granted within patriarchies of differing sorts are the result of a protection racket. Against whom, and from whose systems, do women need protecting, after all? And what is being protected? Remember, for example, that we used to be 'protected' from better-paying jobs that involved perfectly manageable physical labor. And what, or who, is actually being protected from what, and whom, when our "purity" is guarded through the imposition of all sorts of restrictions not on those who threaten to "take" our "purity" from us, but on us? Men are dangerous to women. So why is it not men who are restricted, held accountable, punished most rigorously, kept from walking freely on the streets, subjected to violence if they go out alone at night or in packs, required to wear restrictive clothing?

As Adrienne Rich puts it, "The lesbian trapped in the 'closet,' the woman imprisoned in prescriptive ideas of the 'normal,' share the pain of blocked options, broken connections, lost access to self-definition freely and powerfully assumed."[6] So, in differing ways, do gay men and heterosexual men constrained by prescriptive ideas of the gendered 'normal.' Common grounds can indeed be found and claimed here, but they do not obliterate the hierarchical differences that privilege men over women, and they do not make relations between us any less twisted and complex. As Eve Sedgwick writes regarding the strange inclusion/exclusion of men's relations with other men:

> "Homosocial" is a word occasionally used in history and the social sciences, where it describes social bonds between persons of the same sex; it is a neologism, obviously formed by analogy with "homosexual," and just as obviously meant to be distinguished from "homosexual." In fact, it is applied to such activities as "male bonding," which may, as in our society, be characterized by intense homophobia, fear and hatred of homosexuality. To draw the "homosocial" back into the orbit of "desire," of the potentially erotic, then, is to hypothesize the potential unbrokenness of a continuum between homosocial and homosexual—a continuum whose visibility, for men, in our society, is radically disrupted.[7]

Homosexual men in this period of the dominant history of the United States have been cast out of the falsely generalized category Man, but the male "homosocial/homosexual" continuum is not the same as the "woman/lesbian" continuum. For one thing, the continuum of men includes those who are dominant in our culture, polity, and economy even though it also includes those who are subjected to extremes of hatred and violence for enacting sexually the bonding that maintains the system.

Today, many gender studies scholars claim that sexualities are constructions and enactments of genderings (rather than vice versa, the earlier view).[8]

In any case, while we continue to struggle with this enormously fraught and complex set of issues, it is helpful to use the term "sex/gender" to refer to what is a primary power, identity, and meaning system of many—if not all—cultures. And I do mean that "primary." I fear that a kind of generalized acceptance of feminism among some contemporary scholars and in the mainstream has sometimes led not to serious work on this figuring of power/identity/knowledge but, instead, to the tacking on of "and women," "and gender," "and feminism" to analyses that are not themselves subjected to feminist critique and are thus still exclusive. However well intentioned such tacked-on recognitions are (and they are better than analyses that disregard sex/gendering systems entirely), I fear that they threaten once again to reduce desperately needed local unto international women's movements into mere adjuncts of other causes taken to be more real, more pressing, primary, prior.

## Class

*Class* is invoked in many of the works, courses, discussions, and movements with which we are concerned. In this context, the term "class" refers to stratification systems based on relations to wealth and the means of producing and controlling it (for example, owners, laborers). Class also involves the privileges and status that societies make available to those with more wealth—and hence, with more power—although in some societies and eras, power and status and their privileges can be (or, before globalizing capitalism, could be) obtained without significant wealth. For example, England and other European countries have had impoverished aristocrats; India has had Brahmins who are not wealthy and *saddhus*, holy people, who live as beggars; and in some cultures, teachers and professors, artists and writers, and some government office holders have had relatively high status and some power, regardless of their personal wealth. When we analyze by class, then, we focus primarily on significant differentials of power in relation to the deployment of more or less scarce goods that are primarily, but not exclusively, defined in relation to wealth. Wealth has been defined in terms other than money—for example, as possession of cattle—but as capitalism spreads globally, "worth" tends to be reduced to "cash value."

It can be, and has been, argued that this reduction to cash, or exchange, value is in some senses liberating. A male child of a poor laborer who becomes rich can thereby 'rise' in a class hierarchy and take on the status and privileges once precluded for his 'kind.' A wealthy man of color in some South American cultures can break through skin-color–coded racial hierarchies. A rich woman can achieve power otherwise denied her sex/gender, and so on. Of course, this 'liberation' by money simultaneously recognizes that those who are not wealthy are "low class" as well as marked and disempowered racially and by sex/gender. It also does not always recognize the ways in which racialized sex/gender systems persist even among the wealthiest of those who have 'risen' in the hierarchy, shaping their experiences daily, reminding them that their privilege is more vulnerable than that of the 'highest,' 'proper' 'kind' of person. A rich man of color in Britain who loses his fortune is not as likely to remain an "aristocrat" as a white man from a "good family" in identical circumstances—although if the man of color were to return home to a formerly colonized country with a British education and fluency in 'good English,' he might find himself "high-class" there.

So we can focus on class to pull forward ways in which wealth functions as its own kind of hierarchical monism—that is, as a system in which all are reduced to one attribute or kind of possession; some few are defined by it as better and higher than all others; and the 'lesser' others are (differentially) shoved down an invidious scale toward the animals and inanimate nature. The very lowest—the poorest of the poor, especially when also racialized as 'naturally inferior'—have been cast as creatures that can be owned, exploited, bred, killed without moral qualms. But we have already encountered complications here—other systems that work both with and, to varying degrees, against that hierarchical monism. These systems include sex/gender, race, nation, history (for example, of colonialism), religion, and various potent mixtures of these and others, such as physical abilities and the lack thereof.

It is where all these systems come together that we see the most entrenched systems of dominance expressed as and backed up by a complex hierarchical monism. Think, for example, of an able-bodied, middle-aged, heterosexual male of the dominant racial and religious group who is wealthy and occupies a position of political power that also confers status and respect in his culture. In the United States, where a mystified notion of the "individual" is still very potent, such a man, astoundingly, is commonly thought of as having "made it" because of his own abilities and hard work. The sense, and real possession, of entitlement he has been given through all those systems is rarely seen as the result of a massive engine of affirmative action for his 'kind.' This is the core instance of how the root error, so entrenched and systemically articulated as to have become culturally psychotic, continues to have its effects. Varying the scenario brings this into sharp focus: a Black woman from a poor family does well in lousy schools against all odds and is accepted into a good college. She has individually broken through systems heavily freighted against her at every turn, yet she is the one who is *seen* as having been admitted not as an individual but because of "affirmative action—that is, primarily on the basis of her 'kind.' Her 'kind' is taken to be significant at every turn.

Things complicate again, and radically, when we see class on the ground of sex/gender. Women's 'places' in class hierarchies have been mediated through relations to men, but men's relations to material conditions and to each other have rarely been mediated through women—although, as always, there are variations (for example, in some matrifocal cultures). On a hierarchy chart, each stratum of men may have not one but two appended, lower groups of women. One of these groups is in critical, if not all-inclusive, ways 'dependent'; its members achieve their place through relation to a man, but their situation is nevertheless not parallel and equal to that of similarly placed male groups. These are women as men have defined and delimited us in a sex/gender system, which far too often turns us into dependents, hanging from or onto a man's class, status, power. The second group consists of women who, by choice, chance, or necessity, have lived independent of men and so lost a major route of access to direct participation in defining material conditions.

Women can also be recognized as a major socioeconomic category, albeit not in the same way as men. The idea that women as a whole constitute in some senses a class has been widely debated (and is today hard to maintain when the very term "women" is challenged), but I believe it has real usefulness in revealing the different ways in which women and men are (re)created as potent categories of 'kinds' by economic systems. That "woman" is an economic and class category with its own varying levels (for example, by race, ethnicity, religion) is starkly revealed in any study or chart of categories of work and pay. Women are still found overwhelmingly in a very few job categories. In the United States, they are concentrated in service professions, primary-school teaching, secretarial and word-processing, nursing—and, to mention the unmentionable but omnipresent, a wide array of "sex work."

Those categories have consistently been poorly paid. It is noteworthy that, historically, the change of a male-dominated profession into one with a majority of women marks the point at which power, status, and money decrease—when teaching became "women's work," for instance, and when women became doctors in the former Soviet Union. Conversely, pay and status have increased when men have taken over a job or profession—except, again, in cultures such as some Native American in which women have been powerful and respected.

That *woman* for so long was not seen as a class-related category and "women's work" was not studied as such by economists reveal yet again the errors that can lock into psychotic conceptualizations. Consider "Economic Man," that abstract creation of theorists who were supposedly thinking about all economic actors but were actually including only those who had already been created by dominance systems as significant and properly 'rational' decision makers (itself a highly partial, mystified concept that is finally being rethought even by mainstream economists). Economic Man, whatever else can be said about him, was not involved in what Marxist and socialist feminists call "reproductive labor"; nor did he make his decisions based on the necessities and values of prescribed women's lives. Left out of the generalizations about this already abstract creation, the "women's work" that required putting care for others above self-interest has long posed quandaries for "rational man" as constructed in several areas, including, embarrassingly enough, ethics in some Western philosophies—wherein altruism has stubbornly seemed anomalous. Without analysis of women's work of all kinds, underpaid and unpaid, productive and reproductive, adequate analyses of economic systems cannot be carried out. The availability of cheap female labor—cheap because female and more so if also immigrant, or Black, or migrant—has underwritten much more than has ever been acknowledged. Consider the community volunteer work carried out by women of all groups and the home work of many that made it possible for men to work outside the home without renouncing the possibility of home and family (a wrenching 'choice' that women still disproportionately face). Think as well of the paid domestic work that has allowed privileged women to pass their prescribed function 'down' to other women. Computing the essential economic value—not just the 'replacement cost' figured by insurance companies—of homemakers, houseworkers, and volunteers brings to the surface the socioeconomic centrality of "women's work" and of all women who work for (so often less) pay. It also shows how both have been ignored in (faultily generalized) studies of economies. That we still have few good tools to carry out such computations indicates the degree to which entire fields, and their 'neutral' research methods, have produced partial knowledge as a result of the other errors.

As always and everywhere, women have challenged and, in some instances, changed aspects of these systems. In doing so, we have also revealed their workings in ways that ought to be studied far more than they have been. Actions for

equity, for example, cause systems premised on denying it to reassert themselves or to readjust around the changes with as little disruption—or real
change—as possible. As they do so, we can see more clearly than usual what is
really being served, what is protected by the systems, what is most central to
them, what is peripheral. As Alice Kessler-Harris writes about U.S. women:

> As it turned out, moving toward, even achieving, equality at work proved
> to be the beginning, not the end, of the battle. Each step on the road to
> equality—equal pay, an end to discrimination in hiring and training,
> access to promotion—exposed a deeply rooted set of social attitudes that
> tried to preserve women's attachment to the home. To work freely, women
> required control over their own reproduction and sexuality. They felt
> entitled to sexual gratification, as men had always been, and to access to
> birth control and to abortion if necessary. Economic independence
> encouraged freer life styles, reducing the dependence of women on men
> and permitting a genuine choice of life partners—male or female. Women
> who earned adequate incomes could choose not to have children or
> among a variety of child-care arrangements if they had them. Freedom
> for women to live without men, to live with them without benefit of legal
> marriage, to create two-career families, or to live without families at all
> posed staggering challenges to traditional [dominant culture] values.[9]

Indeed. Women entering class hierarchies premised on a faultily generalized but idealized norm of dominance by men produce tremors and cracks
through all the articulated systems.

## Race

Something particularly curious has been happening to *race* in this age of movements around the globe. While there are those who question that the reality of
gender is physiological (*gender* having been specifically distinguished from *sex*),
sex, gender, and sexuality are still recognized as significant in human lives and
systems. Similarly, even in the United States, where class remains a suspect and
almost taboo category of analysis, few deny that differential relations to wealth
and status do exist and have real effects, however clearly artificial all their social
prescriptions. But the growing consensus among scientists, and more recently
among the general public, is that there is no sound, reliable, consistent biological
basis for categorizations by race, and as a result, the reality of race is increas-

ingly in question. Indeed, those who now insist that race is real although not 'natural' can face the charge that they are the racists. Some denials of the reality of race can lead to denigrations of efforts to describe, study, report on, and act against the ongoing effects of racializing systems: those who persist in studying race are then told that they are actually creating what they are trying to dismantle. Stop using the category "race," we are told, because it is not real (that is, it is not a scientifically sound biological division), and race, with all the injustices from which it derived and that it has so long served, will cease to exist.

This curious, ahistorical notion was invoked by proponents of Proposition 54 in California. Had it passed (it was defeated when brought to a vote in 2003), the proposition would have made it illegal even to report on racialized patterns of health, wealth, education, and so on. But ignoring them obviously would not have made such patterns disappear. It would simply have erased them from the public records on which public policy and informed actions can be based.

However odd and irresponsible such a shoot-the-messenger view may be, it has been widespread enough even among scholars that the American Sociological Association felt it necessary to issue a statement in 2002 asserting the continuing relevance of studies of race for efforts to understand social orders and their stratifications. That this has needed to be said reveals precisely what is denied by those who want to "move beyond race"—the depth and stubbornness of the belief that race is essentially, primarily, and significantly a physiological reality. Since defining race as 'natural' removes responsibility from those who use it for their benefit, it is not surprising that it is not willingly relinquished or that those so long used by it can have come to believe not only that discrediting its scientific basis is important, which it is, but that it suffices. Unfortunately, neither faulty conceptualizations of race nor racist systems that created and are, in circular fashion, legitimated by them disappears when its scientific formulation and imprimatur are withdrawn.

The 1995 "Revised UNESCO Statement on Race," produced by prominent scientists in fields from biology to physical anthropology, concludes that "the same scientific groups that developed the biological concept [of race] over the last century have now concluded that its use for characterizing human populations is so flawed that it is no longer a scientifically valid concept. In fact, the statement makes clear that the biological concept of race as applied to humans has no legitimate place in biological science."[10] Well and good, we say. Surely this is progress in undoing the virulence of racial prejudice underwritten by Western science at least since the great classifiers (whom we

met in the Introduction) ranked humankind down from the ideally normative North European Man, from and about whom knowledge of "mankind"
was wrongly generalized. However, we then confront the need to recognize
that race *never was* a natural reality, and so we must still figure out, and face
up to, what it really has been and is. We have not solved the "problem of race."
We have cleared away errors that still have to be accounted for if we are to
arrive at more adequate understandings. That work has now begun.

The sociologist Troy Duster calls race "a stratifying practice . . . [with] very
complex, inter-active feedback loops between biology and culture and social
stratification."[11] Stuart Hall calls it a "floating signifier," not 'naturally' real but
extremely potent in its use—through many permutations and combinations
in many cultures—to encode prescriptive inferiorities.

George M. Fredrickson, a major historian of race and racism, suggests: "Like
the modern scientific racism that is one expression of it, [race] has a historical trajectory and is mainly, if not exclusively, a product of the West. . . . [I]t
originated in the fourteenth and fifteenth centuries . . . and was originally
articulated in the idioms of religion more than in those of natural science."
Racism, in his view, "is not merely an attitude or set of beliefs; it also expresses
itself in the practices, institutions, and structures that a sense of deep difference justifies or validates. . . . It either directly sustains or proposes to establish *a racial order,* a permanent group hierarchy that is believed to reflect the
laws of nature or the decrees of God."[12] Further: "Race," wrote Howard Winant
in 1994, the year before the UNESCO statement quoted earlier was issued,
"shows no sign of declining significance. Quite the contrary: in a range of manifestations wider and wilder than the most fertile imaginations could have
dreamed up, race continues to operate as a fundamental factor in political and
cultural life all around the world."[13]

So, rather than asking, What (essentially, universally, transhistorically) is
race? we ask, What is going on here? Winant suggests that, despite all the
'proofs' that race is not real, despite the ending of past imperialisms that made
bald use of race to put some 'kinds' of people on top of imposed orders, despite
the defeat in World War II of fascistic systems based explicitly on race and
"blood" rankings of humankind, despite the U.S. Civil Rights Movement, "race
remains a fundamental organizing principle . . . in those *milieux* where, historically, race has been foundational—that is, in most if not all human societies . . . even after the original reasons for invoking it have disappeared [because
it is] . . . deeply fused with the power, order, and indeed the meaning systems
of every society in which it operates."[14]

In the terms I am using to get at precisely those meaning systems, all of these analyses of race reveal it to be a prime case of the basic error of defining a few as the inclusive, ideal, normative 'kind' and then generalizing what it means to be 'properly' human from and for them so that all other people come to be seen not just as different, but as deviant, lesser, degenerate, impure. Hence, some 'kinds' of people are defined not only as unequal but as unequalizable. Despite the obvious errors in the reasoning on which the legitimation of such a conceptualization of *race* has been based, *race* in all sorts of forms has been planted so deeply into the meaning systems that sustain, and are sustained by, economic, political, and other systems that it has usually proved impermeable to counterevidence, to experiences that should confound and refute it, to radically changed circumstances. When one of its supports collapses, others adjust themselves to compensate, keeping the racist system intact even as it reconfigures. Even when meaning systems change, economic systems continue to produce racialized differences; even when economic systems become less racially entrenched, meaning systems shift around to keep prejudices in place. Thus, racialized systems—along with "raciology," as Paul Gilroy calls the "lore" of race[15]—make it humanly real, even though it is evidently neither natural nor just, and even though intellectually it is not a theory but an ideology— a 'logic' so designed to maintain itself that it becomes culturally psychotic.

The fact that race, racism, and raciologies are real *and* run the gamut from nonsensical to virulently mad has hardly gone unnoticed. In 1942, more than fifty years before the UNESCO statement, Brewton Berry observed in "A Southerner Learns About Race" that "hardly two [scientists] agree as to the number and compositions of the races. . . . Huxley gives us four; Krocker, three; Goldenweiser, five; and Boas inclines to two, while . . . Linton says there are twelve or fifteen. Even my dullest students," Berry says, "sometimes note this apparent contradiction."[16] We are thinking creatures, if far too infrequently and unreliably so; we are startled into reflection by evident absurdities. But while that can start a process of thinking ourselves free so that we can act far more effectively and thus remain morally and politically responsible, it can also activate protective evasions and ideological elaborations masked as theorizing and research. Writings of scholars and scientists, no less than popular beliefs, display both possibilities.

This deadly muddle is compounded by the reality that race does not stand alone any more than sex/gender and class do. We see the effects of these mutually constructing systems in statistics on the distribution of wealth, on health, on education, and on marriages and complicated designations for "mixed breed," "mulatto," or "mixed-race" children. Behind the statistics and labels, of course, are stories that show how they are reproduced on the ground. I was once driven through a poor Black community in Florida on an outing planned, as I found out, by a white, barely middle-class mother so she could explain to her daughter (and to me) why white girls must not be friends with Black boys. "See?" said the mother, gesturing toward the inadequate housing in the segregated area. "It's not because he has Black skin. It's because they're different from us in more important ways. Look how they live! Your father and I wouldn't want you to marry someone who would make you live like that." The daughter, then about seven years old but already gendered to believe that her future depended on marrying right, got it. Meanwhile, we can surmise, with unfortunate odds of being correct, that the seven-year-old Black boy who had been friendly with this white girl was being warned away from her by parents who rightly feared for his safety, possibly even his life.

Sex/gender is also always present as a ground for the figuring, and reconfiguring, of racialized class relations among girls and women. As Angela Davis observes, "The condition of white women workers is often tied to the oppressive predicament of women of color. Thus the wages received by white women domestics have always been fixed by the racist criteria used to calculate the wages of Black women servants."[17] We are locked together; we are pitted against each other. It is hard to think yourself out of situations in which interests, identities, status, jobs, power, and sex are so intimately entangled. Too many people trying to survive in such systems remain vulnerably befuddled, if not fearful or defensively angry.

Gendered race enthralls even freedom fighters, who all too readily claim the "rights of a MAN!" How can one not do so when "man" and "human" have been conflated for so long? How can one not do so when being powerless before other men "unmans" males in their own and in the dominant culture? In both, to be out of power is to be "like a woman"—a shaming insult. When "manhood" is defined by the few men in power, who generalize from themselves as they prescribe what it means to be a "real man," the men who have been excluded are rendered "impotent" in several senses.

This masculinization of power and rights puts women in an absurd position. It is still necessary, and makes international headlines, to proclaim, as Hillary Rodham Clinton did at the United Nations Fourth World Conference on Women in Beijing in September 1995, that "Women's rights are human rights!"[18] That is a patent absurdity. What kind of rights would women have, if not human? Inhuman rights? Semihuman rights? And if "human" rights do not cover more than half of humankind, how can they be claimed to be, as they have been, *human* rights? No one has proclaimed that "Men's rights are human rights!" That would sound ridiculous—except to men defined not as "man" but as a 'kind' of men. Thus, during the Civil Rights Movement, Black men defiantly carried signs that said: "I AM A MAN!" What were Black women, so active in and crucial to the movement, to do with that? What were white women allies to do? Could a woman, any woman, carry such a sign without feeling ridiculous and highly vulnerable to being put back in her gendered place by both white and Black men? One male Civil Rights leader famously characterized the position of women in this and other movements as "prone." (The story is perhaps apocryphal, but it clearly touched an exposed nerve.) And homophobia would come into play, too. A woman carrying the "I AM A MAN!" sign would be seen not as claiming her human rights but as revealing a deviant identity and sexuality.

As long as power can be taken and held through the invocation of hierarchies of human 'kinds' legitimated by erroneous conceptualizations such as those we are exploring—whether underwritten by nature, religion, ancestors, science, spirits, lineage, blood, nation, tribe, or any other source of authority—too many of us will collude in keeping the systems going, even, tragically, when our intention is to stand against some aspect of them. The systems have given us no place to stand simultaneously as who we are individually, the 'kind' we supposedly are, and the equal human beings we should be.

Nevertheless, despite the difficulty of taking a stand on unrecognized ground, clear views from inside and outside, which are so necessary to sanity on all levels, can always be found, often among the nondominant. This is one among many reasons we should all have the benefits of a truly inclusive education. W. E. B. DuBois saw "the problem . . . of the color-line" in the United States a hundred years ago. Anna Julia Cooper, his contemporary, went further. She thought about how that 'problem' was entangled with "the woman question" and spent her life as an educator challenging both.[19] Such examples of inside–outside clarity are invaluable in reminding us that, however firm a system, it is indeed possible to think freely, to retrieve knowledge that actually included many more critical dissident voices than made it into the 'canonical' dominant stories.

Invaluable, too, are histories and examples of systems that are inside/outside, scrambling as they do what 'we' thought 'we' knew. Consider the history of the Seminole in Florida. George Walton writes about the Seminole Indian War of 1835–42, which was fought because some tribes refused to "migrate"—

a euphemism for forcible removal to another part of the country ordered by
the U.S. government. That order was given in large part because the Seminole
were providing sanctuary for escaped Black slaves and refused to stop doing
so. Still, they were not entirely outside the system. Walton also tells us:

> The Seminole held slaves, both Indian and Negro, but the institution was
> unlike that under both the English and the Spanish. More vassal than slave,
> the Negro, or on occasion a captured Indian, was permitted considerable
> freedom.... The Negro slaves of the Seminole were permitted to marry
> and raise families. On rare occasion, they married Indians and were
> immediately given their freedom and went to live in a Seminole village.[20]

The Seminole example also scrambles dominant gender system models.
Chieftainship was hereditary and male-only, but it descended through the
female line and moved to another line if a family failed to provide good chief
material. This system may not be perfect or without conceptual and systemic
errors, but it is interestingly different from the more closed dominant systems
that could not abide the Seminoles' independent differences.

The constructs most basic to systems reveal themselves starkly even when
the challenge is not radical, and certainly when it is. Consider the general agi-
tation, reactionary electoral effects, and violence precipitated by the Civil
Rights Movement's press for voter registration, access to equal educational and
economic opportunity, and fair housing in the United States. There is still
organized backlash against these unarguably "American" promises, but the
backlash is now defined by its spokespeople not as a racist agenda but as
premised on the civil rights belief in non-discrimination. This claim makes it
evident that discrimination has too often been defined and understood in
terms of ahistorical, faultily abstracted and generalized notions of the individual enshrined by the men who established slavery even as they declared that
"all men are created equal." Thus, the pretense that "color-blindness" is all that
is needed. Consider, too, the disruptions that followed "guest workers'" claims
to social services and efforts to achieve decent pay in Germany; efforts by the
Roma to get even a basic education in Eastern Europe; the opening of jobs
that were once taboo for "untouchables" in India; land-rights claims by indigenous peoples in South America. Nation, religion, culture are all in play here,
making use of and used by gendered raciologies to protect the dominance of
the few over those defined and stratified as less than they.

Meanwhile, scholars and social commentators of various stripes continue to try to illuminate "social problems," and public-policy offices use their findings. Unfortunately, too many conceptualizations, methods, theories remain uncritiqued and locked into the partial knowledge created by faulty generalization and the other errors. As a result, crucial knowledge is missed; faulty conclusions are drawn; and policies shaped thereby fail to help and sometimes even harm. For example, for years, studies of the "Black family" in the United States have 'shown' that it is "dysfunctional." Note the singular "family," which should alert us to the possibility that one cultural construct of *family* may erroneously have been taken to be the norm and ideal. That this is the case is vividly marked by the choice of "matriarchal" by some scholars as a descriptor for what is most egregiously "aberrant" about families riven by racialized, gendered poverty, prejudice, and the violence and despair these can breed. "Patriarchal" was not used as the descriptor for 'real,' 'proper,' 'normal' families, just as "white" was not marked. Both thus worked all the more effectively to mystify the dominant few as the only real and proper exemplar of 'normal,' 'proper,' 'good' people and families.

Kinship, a crucial ordering system that takes different forms in many cultures, has thus been left out of adequate interpretative account. It has been hidden by the error of faulty generalization. As Carol Stack notes in her classic study of U.S. Black families, "Much of the controversial and misleading characterizations of kinship and domestic life can be attributed . . . to the lack of ethnographic data that interprets the meaning people give to the chain of parent–child connections within a particular folk culture."[21]

Since in the dominant tradition in the United States the white people who have defined things have taken themselves to be the real kind of people, the norm, and the ideal, the U.S. *concept* of race, like and always with sex/gender and class, does continue to need very careful reconsideration. It also needs (and is increasingly receiving) analyses that both distinguish it from and locate its deep roots in concepts of race from Europe and around the globe, where race has been both home-grown and imposed (not only, though importantly) by European imperial powers. In the United States, some immigrants were both liberated from the strife and oppression of variously racialized struggles and painfully stripped of their ethnicities, traditions, languages, and, very often, their European-bred class-consciousness in order to "become white"—that is, to become "American." (See, for example, studies by David Roediger.) The power of race has been enhanced, not undercut, by the contradictions, complexities, and confusions created by this American brew, in which citizenship required a "whiteness" of its own creation. The very lack of clarity of the concept of race seems to have made 'race' available to be used to mark 'lower' status for many 'kinds' of people and to pit 'them' against each other in shifting ways as immigration patterns have changed.

The entrenched role and fluidity of the definition of race are evident in the history of legislation through which determined U.S. judges re-created racial categories that suited the class and gender prescriptions of their times. Marital status was an element in decisions about a woman's citizenship status, and the specter of "interbreeding" hovered always. In their findings, the judges openly invoked views of "the common man" (itself a mystified, faulty racialized, gendered abstraction) as grounds for their often truly weird but potent decisions. For example, *United States v. Bhagat Singh Thind* (261 U.S. 204 [1923]) held that "the words of familiar speech, which were used by the original framers of the law, were intended to include only the type of man whom they knew as white.... [I]t cannot be doubted that the children born in this country of Hindu parents would retain indefinitely the clear evidence of their ancestry" (as others of "European" origin, the finding observes, will not). "It is very far from our thought," the justices then say, "to suggest the slightest question of racial superiority or inferiority. What we suggest is merely racial difference ... of such character and extent that the great body of our people instinctively recognize it and reject the thought of assimilation."[22] "Interracial sex," "inter-breeding," stood uncontested as the unavoidable result of social "assimilation" that "the common man" naturally ("instinctively") rejects. Odd, that, on many counts. Were it truly the case that "the common man"—which is to say, lots of 'ordinary' males—"instinctively" recoils from "inter-racial" sex, why should there be any need to make laws against it?

Whatever else it is, race is always and everywhere a highly sexualized construction, as well as a complexly and vehemently gendered construction. 'Lower' racialized males are *not* to be allowed any chance to "breed" with the female 'stock' of the 'higher' males, and the fear that they will do so has led to all sorts of horrific efforts to make that impossible. Such efforts have always failed, but that has not refuted claims that it is "interbreeding," not the laws against it, that is "unnatural." It has led instead to still more mad efforts to control and even to remake nature, from segregation to avoid "assimilation" to expulsion, castration, lynchings, genocides. Faced with such histories, it is hard not to see race as also, and basically, an excuse to reinforce constructions of sex/gender that establish male dominance over females to limit competition and preserve "blood lines." Class stratifications and all their elaborated significations and prescriptions, by which the few privileged, dominant males defend their control of the "means of production" *and* reproduction from other groups of males, have also been 'protected' and backed up by laws related to breeding, such as inheritance. Some religions, too, have proscribed "intermarriage" even as they preach the universality of their creed's route to goodness, salvation, liberation.

We surely need to keep asking, What is going on when people kill in the name of a just, loving, merciful god? When governments founded on the principle that all (supposedly generic) men are equal are also founded on slavery and the denial of citizenship to all females? When science inscribes culture-specific prejudices into supposedly universal classificatory schemes? That all these systems can be seen as *evidently* erroneous at root—and, to those who refuse to stop thinking, as contradictory in significant ways as well as downright ludicrous—should long since have constituted an evident call on scholars *as scholars* as well as citizens and would-be decent people to locate, analyze, and refuse them in all fields. Their fallaciousness is hardly hard to discern. Racist systems are absurd and deadly and manifest as both where they are in power. Troy Duster tells us this:

> At the height of the apartheid regime [in South Africa], the official color classification was enforced by the state and provided [or denied one] access to employment. In Capetown, being "colored" permitted one to have a pass to work on some jobs. Some Africans classified as "black" wanted to be reclassified as "colored" so that they could claim these jobs. The whites devised a "pencil test" to determine which of the blacks could be reclassified. It was not a paper and pencil test. Rather, a pencil was inserted into the hair of the African applicant. If (s)he shook their head and the pencil fell out, that person could be reclassified as "colored" because the hair texture of the blacks would, it was assumed, retain the pencil.[23]

Forcing reality into nonsensical, counterfactual forms that serve man-made dominance hierarchies takes fertile imaginations and the scary willingness among many people to act in ways that range from the foolish and petty to the monstrously violent for extended periods of time. History, I fear, makes it evident that it does not take monsters to perpetuate large-scale monstrous acts. It takes ordinary people living within skewed systems without questioning them. The October 26, 2003, edition of the *New York Times* reports that J. K. Banthia, the commissioner for the census in India, "estimates that several million fetuses have been aborted in India in the last two decades because they were female." Further, "Interpreting census figures of the last century showing widening divergences in the ratio of females to males, he estimates that as many as 25 million female fetuses and babies have been killed before, during or after birth in India." This is not a horror caused by, nor will it be stopped by ending, the availability of abortion. It is continuous with millennia of exposures of babies unwanted specifically because they are of the 'wrong kind.'

Too many examples of conventional people and prestigious scholars and leaders determinedly pursuing the distorted knowledge that legitimates great harm are available. The eugenics movement is a prime case. In studies, records, and continuing traces of this movement, we see racializations from Europe in U.S. form: upper classes determined to control challenges to privileging systems; the misuse of Western science to legitimate constructions of race that foreclosed options (such as they were) of assimilation or conversion; the active support of highly prestigious academic, public, and philanthropic institutions; and the evident linking of racializations and class with breeding, and thus with sex/gender systems that maintain privileged male dominance using means that range from parceling out privilege to segregation, incarceration, sterilization, all the way to mass slaughter.

In *War Against the Weak: Eugenics and America's Campaign to Create a Master Race,* Edwin Black writes about the development in England and the United States of scientific research based on early genetics and evolutionary theory that supported projects aimed at sorting out the "fit" from the "unfit" (including the use of "intelligence quotient" tests) and keeping the "unfit" from breeding by any means necessary. I will cobble together a long quotation from Black's carefully researched book to suggest just how prolonged and intricate the story of eugenics—the 'science' of "good breeding"—is:

> It didn't matter that the underlying science was a fiction, that the intelligence measures were fallacious, that the Constitutionality was tenuous.... None of that mattered because [the highly prestigious scientists, public figures, and philanthropists involved] were not interested in furthering a democracy—they were creating a supremacy.... During the [World War I] years, eugenic organizations proliferated in America. Like-minded citizens found ethnic solace and even self-vindication in the idea of biological superiority.... In 1914, Dr. Kellogg organized the First Race

Betterment Conference.... The conference's purpose was to lay the foundations for the creation of a super race.... "We have wonderful new races of horses, cows, and pigs," argued Dr. Kellogg. "Why should we not have a new and improved race of men?" ... [The] white races of Europe [for which the Nordic race, in particular, was taken to be exemplary] ... [should] seek to establish a Race of Human Thoroughbreds." At the Second Race Betterment Conference ... a Yale University economist was equally blunt. "Gentlemen and ladies.... You have not any idea unless you have studied this subject mathematically, how rapidly we could exterminate this contamination [of the "germ plasm" of 'inferior,' 'dark' immigrants; "Negroes"; Jews; epileptics; "the feeble-minded"; "loose women"; and the poor, whose poverty 'proved' their "unfitness"] if we really got at it, or how rapidly the contamination goes on if we do not get at it." ... During [the Nazi] Reich's first ten years, eugenicists across America welcomed Hitler's plans as the logical fulfillment of their own decades of research and effort.... Ten years after Virginia passed its 1924 sterilization act, Joseph DeJarnette, superintendent of Virginia's Western State Hospital, complained in the *Richmond Times-Dispatch,* "The Germans are beating us at our own game."[24]

That eugenics was not science but, rather, a determinedly closed ideology in service of gender, racialized class hierarchies is obvious, so some people today conclude that the undoing of pseudo-science can uproot prejudices. However, the same story reveals that the culpable 'science' was itself a product of older, deeper systems that can and do send up new, virulent formations if they are not radically disrupted. For example, there is here a contradiction that has to do with understandings of nature. Fredrickson concludes *Racism: A Short History* with this: "To attempt a short formulation, we might say that racism exists when one ethnic group or historical collectivity dominates, excludes, or seeks to eliminate another on the basis of differences that it believes are hereditary and unalterable."[25] But even Fredrickson passes over the contradiction between "hereditary" and "*un*alterable." Life, by definition, is "alterable," and heredity via the mixing of genes through sexual reproduction is one of the enhancements of that essential quality. Shrinking gene pools by elimination of 'different' carriers can constitute a threat to, not an enhancement of, functional continuity via heredity.

The eugenicists knew that. They marked "in-bred" groups as targets for their "improve-the-race" sterilization and segregation projects. But they twisted their science around to *justify* inbreeding for the 'superior' few. Racism that locates its absolutizing warrant in nature while determinedly pitting its own prescriptions against natural processes thus reveals that its agenda is not to follow, or to perfect, but to *replace* nature's creativity with that of men determined to remake humans in their own image. Racists' obsession with breeding, and so with sex and so with gender, is not an additional madness. It is the extension of a logic with which they have replaced observation of and respect for the real, natural, human world that refuses to conform to their dominance systems.

## "Reverse Discrimination"

In systemically hierarchical systems, we need to be careful about charges of "reverse discrimination." They tend to imply that what is wrong for some is necessarily wrong always and in the same ways for all. But human, humane justice is a historical and contextual matter that requires free judgment. It is not strictly logical. To argue that act "x" is wrong in the same way and to the same degree no matter who does it, no matter what the circumstances in which it is done, is to choose abstract, absolutized principles over concrete, complex, changing human realities. Such choices, history tells us, can lead to the same violations, and violence, that efforts to perfect and purify humans so often have.

We do not act in our real worlds for all time; we always act in the here and now. We may hold "for all time" as a regulative or horizontal test for our ideals but it is safer to do so without presuming to think we know definitively what those ideals ask of us. In this real, plural, changing world, justice does not require the imposition of absolutized rules: who would make them? Who knows enough, is good enough? Rather, justice requires constant efforts at ad-*just*-ment in light of horizontal ideals, themselves always open to reflection and possible change.

It is not unreasonable, in this view, to hold that quotas used against a 'lower' 'kind' of people (as they were used against women of all groups, Jews, sometimes Catholics, Black people not so long ago) violate principles of individual rights, but that quotas used to open access to groups that were long judged not as individuals but as instances of their constructed categorical 'kind' are needed (we hope, temporarily) to produce the conditions that will allow all to claim those individual rights.

Remembering histories and contexts also suggests that we take into account the fact that many colleges and universities have persistently used more than a few 'special' categories when making admissions decisions. Some of these are held consciously and acted on purposefully; others function less directly. A flute player, for example, has a better chance of admission than a football player if a school prides itself on its orchestra and not on its sports teams. But a white flute player who has had expensive training may get in more easily than a Black flute player whose application lists no such training. Geographical diversity has long been uncontested as an institutional interest in admissions. But a wealthy applicant from South Dakota may have a better chance to get into an elite Northeastern school than a poor applicant from another underrepresented area.

And, as we all know, "legacy" candidates—children of alumnae/ni, particularly those who are big donors—almost always have an advantage over children of non-alums. Here, too, we encounter other, less admitted criteria. Few schools will *say* that rich, well-connected alums' children should be preferentially admitted. Fewer still will say that, in privileging "legacy" applicants, they want to perpetuate privilege. However, the group of those denied admission because there were not enough places left after the legacy admits is likely to include candidates whose parents could not go to that college (or perhaps any college) because of prejudice, quotas limiting their 'kind,' poverty, physical disability. Discrimination in favor of privilege is then passed on, hidden behind loyalty to alums.

None of this is unknown. Why, then, are universalized, abstract principles that purport to value "individual merit only" believed to be operative across the board? And why is "individual merit only" thought to be so particularly—and shockingly—perverted only by admissions categories designed to undo "legacies" of *dis*advantage? Why is it acceptable for a school to select students to strengthen its reputation for a fine computer program but not to make every effort to serve education's purpose of preparing all—and not disproportionately some groups of—citizens to be informed, reflective, and empowered? Schools are perfectly free to decide to change from privileging regional applicants to seeking more national applicants, and vice versa; to accept fewer would-be writers when the writing program is declining and the economics program, say, is gaining strength; to take more football players when a few winning seasons have brought in larger donations from pleased alum sports fans. All such choices mean there will be fewer slots for some qualified applicants. But we hear no outcry about "reverse discrimination" against the non–flute player, the would-be writer, the local or regional student bumped in favor of one who will expand the catalog's list of states from which students come. We do hear just that, though, when white people, rich people, children of power-ful parents find themselves competing for slots against applicants whose legacy disadvantages are neutralized (to some extent) by efforts to act affirmatively to counter that legacy.

Some bad faith is at work here, even among those who do not wish to col-lude with old injustices and their continuing effects. The old errors are at work confusing equality with sameness by way of establishing the defining few as those to whom others must become similar to achieve equality. To this mind set, efforts to achieve equality by diversifying criteria can only seem self-contradictory. Wait a minute, the privileged are likely to say: I thought equal-ity meant that you wanted to be just like me. Being a generous soul, I agreed that I would compete on the same field and by the same rules as you—not that there might be more than one field, more than one set of rules, and cer-tainly not that my field and rules might be changed.

Equality is needed, however, precisely because we are not, cannot, and should not aspire to be the same. Humans are not singular abstractions. We are each a unique configuration of all sorts of discernible similarities and dif-ferences that go far beyond those picked out in differing cultures and polities as significant, whether for good or for ill. If the gifts and potential of each and all of us are to have the chance to develop and enrich the meanings of human being, we need protections that will prevent our many differences from being sorted out in ways that categorically, inappropriately, and persistently disad-vantage some 'kinds' of us.

Yet equality, which keeps differences from disadvantaging us, does not mean that our differences are always irrelevant. If I am claustrophobic, it is not wrong to exempt me from the cave exploration my gym class is going on; if I am tone deaf, it is not wrong to choose someone else to sing the solo; if I am poor at arithmetic, I should not be hired to keep accounts. Proper, as distinct from inap-propriate, discrimination based on our differences requires ongoing efforts to sort out which are relevant and which are not with regard to clear, sensible cri-teria that themselves are assessed against overarching principles of fairness that keep both rules and principles responsive to real situations.

Categories that have been used to oppress people must be dismantled because they make relative, appropriate, fair discrimination impossible with regard to some 'kinds' of people. If I prejudge someone's intellectual abilities because I believe I already know that "his kind" is by nature less bright than mine, I have not just discriminated—I have, specifically, failed to discriminate appropriately. Gross, sloppy thinking is the problem, not the fine art of discriminating judgment. What keeps us from seeing prejudice—in its sloppy thinking form—as such is centuries of skewed thinking by people who have persisted in trying to prove that their assumptions are true instead of being open to having them proved false.

Prejudicial exclusions are pre-judicial—they are based on judgments made before, not in relation to, the facts. They must therefore be undone as assumptions, and the ramifications of centuries of actions based on those assumptions must also be traced and rectified. Making an exception for some individuals, or providing tacked-on provisions for a few of the excluded 'kind,' while leaving intact the assumptions and systems premised on them cannot work. When women were excluded from Harvard, they were not then provided either with the same education as, or an equal education to, men admitted to the university when some professors did the women the favor of teaching them separately from the 'real' students. Nor are Black students given the same education as, or an equal education to, white people—even if they sit in classrooms together—as long as what is taught, how it is taught, and who does the teaching continues just as it was when all education was designed by and for an exclusive few who were wrongly taken to be the inclusive, ideal, and normative 'kind.'

It is no more possible than it is right or desirable to rectify systemic exclusions person by person, individual by individual. Imagine what would happen if every individual who has been wrongly treated because of what she or he has been prejudicially identified as (Black; female; disabled; non-heterosexual; old; fat; a midget, dwarf, or giant; an Indian; Jewish; a racialized ethnic group) were to bring an individual suit to claim individual rights. Not only would all of the courts be so swamped they could no longer function, but the systems that produce the injustices would go right on producing potential new cases. Even if they could and would take histories of prejudicial categorizations and their effects into account, the courts are not adequate to address the full range of changes needed. But they can contribute, as we know, through rulings that make it clear that laws still explicitly based on those old errors cannot justly be applied. They thereby return such issues to the social and political realm where they have had such powerful purchase, and where we can act to press legislatures to devise and pass better laws.

We cannot fix all systems, cannot make them entirely just. That is beyond us, and who could be sure in any case what "entirely just" means for us all?

What we can do is recognize that problems require solutions that are appropriate to them, and that any such solutions may in future become problems themselves, not because they were initially wrong, but because situations are always complex and do change. After all, when we try out a solution to a problem, we need not claim, or be taken to be claiming, that the solution is in and of itself a good. Few corrections, and fewer punishments, are right and good in and of themselves. Affirmative action, civil-rights legislation, the equal-rights amendment, the Americans with Disabilities Act—these ought not to have been necessary in the first place. We did not work for them for their own sake; we worked for them because they were needed. We are not reversing injustices through them. We are interrupting injustices on a scale that is not adequate to their full reach but is closer than any individual action, remedy, or change of heart can be.

However, it is also rightly of concern that, with any major adjustment to long-prevalent systems, there will be some people who may suffer difficulties, and we will all find ourselves, at the least, off-balance for a while. Such situations can and should keep us thinking as creatively as we can about many ways to effect ongoing changes, instead of refusing even to try or becoming wedded to the most obvious but not most promisingly creative solution. (This may be what quotas are: not ethically wrong, inherently contradictory, or prima facie unjust but unimaginative.) So even as we do need to think in categorical terms to deal effectively with old categorical injustices, we also need to remember how complex social systems always are. Not all women have been denied all privileges, for example; neither has privilege or victimization been the same for, or defining of, all women who have experienced it.[26] None of the old categories of 'kinds' are internally consistent. They have complex, shifting meanings and an extraordinarily varied range of uses. No one attentively studying even a somewhat transformed history that tells the stories of a few more of us will fall into the error of thinking that the category *white male* functions the same way as that of *Filipina female* just because, abstractly considered, both encode racialized sex/gender. Actions designed to limit entitlements of white males are by no means really the same as or merely reversals of actions designed to empower Filipina females except on that abstract level, and we do not live there.

Adjustments made for the sake of equality and full recognition of those variously excluded and devalued and privatized do indeed require limitations on and disruptions of "business as usual." Such adjustments are not "reverse" but "anti-inappropriate" discriminations. If we do the work it takes to clear spaces in which to see and judge each other appropriately and creatively, holding ourselves always open to learning more about the real complexities involved, that process itself will be transforming.

## Taking the Few to Represent All

Political representation cannot but have differing meanings when only one 'kind' has long been seen as the real, normative, and simultaneously inclusive human. That is a kind of imperialism of human representativeness. For privileged males in would-be democracies, this has meant having someone like them exercising power on their behalf (whether for good or ill)—a recognition of their right-fullness. For the rest of us, it has meant, at best, having someone unlike us do for us what we cannot do for ourselves. It was not our power they exercised but theirs. For a motley lot of us, being represented has in reality been a lot closer to being ruled. We are to be grateful for favors, not entitled to our rights.

In systems of representative governance run by rules (overt and implicit) developed during times in which exclusions were considered right and proper, being an effective representative tends to require skill in certain practices and devotion to interests that were enshrined long ago as definitionally basic, central. Consequently, even in a polity defined as inclusive in principle (such as that of the United States), those who were privatized in practice through denial of citizenship and its rights continued for a long time to be seen as, and were literally made to be, "out of place" in public. Thus they/we were perforce unrepresentative of an exclusively—faultily—abstracted "American people." It is still the case that an elected representative who works for child care, for comparable worth, or for any other provision necessary to the full inclusion of women, or for labor, or for racial equality, or for Indians or any other 'kind' of people(s) will quickly be labeled, and encapsulated, as an advocate of "special interests," as "out of step," "uncooperative," "too ideological"—in short, as not "one of the guys." He or she might also be branded "politically correct." Yet a lawmaker who pushes for tax breaks that disproportionately benefit the rich or for exemptions from environmental strictures for global corporations is not often said to be acting in the service of "special interests" or charged with being "ideological," although these positions are far more literally "politically correct" according to the prevailing systems.

Meanwhile, a well-meant public-service ad representing a man holding a child announces, "Breast cancer doesn't just affect women." Thus, it is strongly suggested that if it did 'just' affect our half of humankind, this cancer would have less claim on public action, public monies. I have yet to see an announcement depicting a man with prostate cancer that says, "Prostate cancer doesn't just affect men." Similarly, some HIV/AIDS public-education materials stress that it is not 'just' a "gay disease," again reminding us which populations are, and which are not, expected to represent "us" all. Have you ever seen a public-health ad that says, "Sexually transmitted diseases are not just the problem of heterosexuals"?

It is also considered a mark of worthy literature that it "speak to all of us," that it speak "universally." In at least some respects, some of the "great literature" we still study may do so (if anything can). But so may literature by and about, say, a Roma woman that disrupts generations of stereotypical appropriations of the "Gypsy Woman." It remains the case that a girl from a non-dominant group is less likely to be featured in a story chosen to represent growing up, coming of age, than is a dominant-group boy (or a boy who overcomes obstacles to join the dominant male group). Literature about those who are considered representative not of all but merely of their 'kind' is far more likely to be taught, as today it might be, to help "us" understand "them" rather than for its universal meaning. A teacher who includes literature from and about 'other' people(s) may also say she or he does so because, "Really, we are all alike"—a gesture toward the possibility of universality. Unfortunately, the tolerant "We are all alike" is simultaneously so reductive and partial— which similarities are to be picked out, which differences scraped off, to leave only likeness that one's students will recognize as such?—that it is almost certain to undercut itself. Instead of being challenged by getting to know different people(s), students may well learn only to refuse to see those troubling differences that mark their own limits. Then who, or what, are they actually 'seeing'? And what have they learned? *Adding on* stories from and about multiple cultures helps, but it hardly suffices. In courses as in governing bodies, decentering the normative few requires more than display of tokens of 'our' tolerance, of more or less 'exotic' alternatives.

Another example: as Carol Gilligan has pointed out, the people whose moral development was taken to be representative of 'normal' moral development were for a long time male. The consequence of generalizing from them to all was, first, that females were not studied at all. Hence, it was false to claim that "moral growth and development" itself, rather than white, privileged, twentieth-century, urban North American male growth and development, was being studied. This is the error of faulty generalization. Second, as girls came to be studied within the theoretical framework abstracted and then generalized from the study of (some few, only supposedly representative) boys, girls as a group tended to appear less developed morally than boys. This, as we shall see, is circular reasoning, the next category of errors we will consider.

Some such errors can be, and are being, disrupted. A *New York Times* article on the PBS documentary *Free to Dance* says that the film "shows how black dance artists honor their heritage and transform their responses to society into glorious dancing that challenges the conventional wisdom that modern dance was a creation of white choreographers."[27] These artists have achieved a transforming breakthrough of no small proportions—perhaps not so much for themselves as for those critics and audiences invited by their work to rethink conventional dominant circular reasoning they had unwittingly accepted.

Defining whole peoples—like defining whole fields and art forms—by drawing on faulty generalizations derived from only some materials, peoples, or issues impoverishes our imaginations, constricts the reach of empathy, falsifies history, and so skews representations of many kinds. In work by the long influential white male European philosopher Immanuel Kant, we can see just how hard it has been for representatives of the privileged few in the dominant culture to 'read' representations of and from devalued traditions. Kant, who sometimes and importantly knew better, nevertheless slid into characterizing, and judging, other cultures based on how they measured up against standards of "man" and "reason" that are evidently the product of faulty generalization. He simply could not see how males from other cultures (and females from his own) might represent humankind. They remained, for him, a particular, curious, and lesser 'kind': "If we cast a fleeting glance over the other parts of the world, we find the Arab the noblest man in the Orient, yet of a feeling that degenerates very much into the adventurous. He is hospitable, generous, and truthful; yet his narrative and history and on the whole his feeling are always interwoven with some wonderful thing. His inflamed imagination presents things to him in unnatural and distorted images."[28]

Of females in general, Kant wrote: "The virtue of a woman is a *beautiful virtue*. That of the male sex should be a *noble virtue*. Women will avoid the wicked not because it is unright, but because it is ugly; and virtuous actions mean to them such as are morally beautiful. . . . Woman is intolerant of all commands and morose constraint. They do something only because it pleases them. . . . I hardly believe that the fair sex is capable of principles."[29]

The point is not to collect absurdities uttered by European American male philosophers. It is to note that the same mind that believed these absurdities also gave us the critiques of "pure reason" and "judgment" that remain central to the field of philosophy as it is still taught. How can we assume that Kant's treatment of reason was not skewed? Knowing that he excluded and devalued modes of thought and feeling he considered characteristic of the "fair sex" and the Arab man, we should surely hesitate before we assume that his notions of pure reason can be universal. He has taken the few to be the norm, and from, as well as for, them he has sought the ideal. He has generalized too far from too few, drawing on and then re-creating representations that were already prescriptive, not descriptive, for the included and the excluded. This is how prescriptions on a cultural level are absorbed into, and become formative of, philosophical prescriptions that claim (and desire) to derive their warrant from 'pure' reason alone.

In its false generalizations, what Kant says of the Arab man and of women is strikingly like what Thomas Jefferson says of the African writer Ignatius Sancho, who published his epistles in 1782 in London. Jefferson, writing about a particular person and work, used a standard of 'real' and 'sound' reason to see in Sancho not difference but inferiority, deviance. Clearly, nothing in Jefferson's background and education prepared him to read Sancho in terms that might have been appropriate to Sancho himself and to a culture his thinking did represent. Sancho's epistles may have been excellent or they may have been poor examples of their own kind; we cannot tell what they represent from Jefferson's comments, because Jefferson can see only how Sancho fails to be what Jefferson thinks he ought to be: "His imagination is wild and extravagant, escapes incessantly from every restraint of reason and taste, and, in the course of its vagaries, leaves a track of thought as incoherent and eccentric, as is the course of a meteor through the sky. His subjects should have led him to a process of sober reasoning: yet we find him always substituting sentiment for demonstration."[30] Just like a woman, as Kant might observe. And we should note that males 'othered' by dominant traditions are frequently feminized as well, which unfortunately has not tended to encourage those men to make common cause with women but, instead, has caused outrage over such a demeaning association.

"Rational man," as we have been taught to think of him in the Euro-American dominant tradition, is a gendered, racialized construct, a partial prescription of and for a particular few. "Rational man" is not only not representative but potentially dangerous when idealized. The capacity for 'adequate' rationality has been enshrined as a criterion for moral agency and so also for political rights. As women's and men's multiple traditions, modes, works are retrieved, revivified, published, and studied around the globe, philosophy can only benefit from such rich evidence of the achievements of human minds. We will still select representatives of what we wish to aspire to as "the best," but it is to be hoped that our selection process will proceed less prejudicially by moving to idealization after, not before, appropriate judgments are rendered.

## Markers of Particularity

One way to see so we can overcome the limitations generated by these errors, as I have already suggested, is to notice who and what is marked as particular and who and what is not. A curious thing about "Rational Man" is that, while "Man" is conflated with "human," it lends its mystifying definitional imperialism to "rational" so that "rational" does not particularize "Man" but instead becomes ideally coextensive with him. Other modes of rationality then slide down the scale with the 'lesser' beings who are not 'properly' Man. The hunger with which contemporary scholarship claiming empirically to have located and named other kinds of "intelligence" has been taken up shows how painful it has been, and for how many, to be defined not as differently rational but as less so—as 'stupid.'

Thinking about markers, or prefixes, also reveals that students in too many cultures and countries have learned not about philosophies, or literatures, or histories, or psychologies, or arts, but about one exclusive tradition's versions of those subjects. Because students cannot tell from the un-prefixed titles of courses and works that one tradition (and a partial one at that) is all they are learning, they internalize the notion that everything else—the lives and works and psyches and stories and theories of all others—is at best a subset of the type they have learned. Sometimes they learn that variants are heresies to be avoided, scorned, repressed, and that any adherents to them are to be converted or combatted. When faultily abstracted basic definitions are then represented in forms that particularize them, embody them, tell stories about them, prescribe ritual practices to evoke them, they simultaneously make their actual historical, cultural limitations evident—and lift those limitations to a level at which they conflate with supposedly nonlimited principles, truths. Sojourner Truth's oft-quoted statement in response to a white preacher shows us the kind of harm this erroneous thinking can do and how we can refuse that harm:

> The Akron [women's rights] convention [in 1851] was marked by the presence of many men of the cloth, most of whom apparently were opposed to the granting of freedom to women. One based his argument in favor of male privilege on man's greater intellect; another on the manhood of Christ; another on the sin of Eve.... [S]lowly from her seat in the corner rose Sojourner Truth to say, "Well, children, where there is so much racket there must be something out of kilter. I think that 'twixt the negroes of the South and the women of the North, all talking about rights, the white men will be in a fix pretty soon.... That man over there says that women need to be helped into carriages, and lifted over ditches.... Nobody ever helps me into carriages, or over mud-puddles.... And ain't I a woman? ... I have borne thirteen children, and seen them most all sold off to slavery.... And ain't I a woman? ... Then that little man in black there, he says women can't have as much rights as men, 'cause Christ wasn't a woman! Where did your Christ come from? Where did your Christ come from? From God and a woman! Man had nothing to do with Him."[31]

An interesting example of reframing, is it not? And out-reasoning, too, done by that supposedly doubly less rational creature, a Black woman. No wonder posters bearing those words hung in almost every tiny, basement office of almost every tiny, still largely subterranean women's studies office I visited in the early days of that field's development. Sojourner Truth gave us a radically different representation that we badly needed.

## Invisibility

Those who are not represented are made invisible, and that invisibility itself teaches something. It is not just an absence. Students who never hear of or see a woman philosopher have trouble believing in such a creature. On a deep level, the level on which we learn cultural presuppositions of the most basic sort,[32] it comes to seem wrong to them for a woman to be a philosopher. The two categories *philosopher* and *woman* exist for them as mutually exclusive. Women have more than once said to me after I gave a public lecture, "I loved just watching you—a woman, right up there, philosophizing!" *Presenting Women Philosophers,* the title of a collection of essays edited by Sara Ebenreck and Cecile Tougas about women who have philosophized, nicely speaks to the need to see ourselves where we were so long rendered invisible.

Since the curriculum for too long excluded works by and about women, it is not at all surprising that students taking a course in philosophy that at the most includes two or three works by women come to feel that the course is "ideological." They see the men represented and discussed in their courses not *as men* but, rather, as philosophers, writers, painters, significant historical figures, important composers. But they do see the women *as women* because they have learned from the use of prefixes in course titles and the omissions in their courses that women are oddities in the dominant tradition, that women are always a 'kind' of human, a 'kind' of writer or whatever, and never the thing itself. They do not notice when a course concerns only men, yet they often feel at first that a course that mentions women more than a couple of times "overemphasizes" women (and sometimes complain that their instructor is "obsessed with women"). Their discomfort is but one more indication that such courses are very badly needed. A case in point: not a single male signed up for a course titled "Thinking Women" that I once taught as a visiting distinguished professor, a course that should have been seen as 'legitimate,' given my fancy title. Even more revealing, no men, but significantly more women, signed up for my offering the following semester, "Women Thinking about Violence." This course threatened to (and, I hope, did) make publicly visible the costs of privatization and invisibility for so many females for so long. Those costs, and the responsibility for them, are not subjects many males are yet willing to allow fully into their consciousness, let alone to think openly about with women.

Learning takes place at many levels. It not only affects what we hold consciously as knowledge; it also establishes habits of association and expectation. It is part of the constant process of identity definition and development. While it can be useful to make a distinction between psychological growth and development and intellectual training, it is disastrous to assume that psyche and mind are literally separated. Changes in what is taught, how it is taught, and who teaches it produce such strong reactions that we should know better. The violation of what is expected, what is familiar, can startle or evoke anxiety and even anger among students, as any teacher knows who does not "look like a professor" and/or has tried to work in the classroom in ways that deviate from students' long-established and now preconscious—and so all the more influential—expectations.[33] White male and any other dominant-group students, asked seriously to open themselves to an understanding of those with whom they have never been encouraged to identify, can become troubled and angry. So can privileged female students who identify strongly with those who have been in power. So can we all, in fact: it is not easy to shift or make less rigid one's sense of identification, to see what has been rendered invisible where that has been virtually taboo, to open to voices one has never been encouraged to hear, even when that voice is one's own.

Those who have taught women's studies and transformed courses in other disciplines have experienced how quickly males begin to feel left out, threatened, upset, when a course does not focus almost exclusively on their kind. Women of all groups, and men from those groups excluded from the curriculum, have spent all the years of their schooling in precisely that situation, but until relatively recently they have rarely expressed discomfort, let alone anger. In fact, as noted earlier, many of us did not even notice that we were left out. Women and unprivileged men fought long and hard to gain access to 'real' education, to the 'best' education—and that meant education into the dominant tradition. It is emblematic that Anna Julia Cooper, a great fighter for Black and women's education at the turn of the twentieth century, earned her Ph.D. (in her sixties) from the Sorbonne—in Latin.

To change the curriculum is by no means to change only what we think about. It is to begin to change who and how we are in the world we share, to learn how to represent ourselves and others publicly, to refuse privatizing invisibility of all sorts. Teachers who join in this effort become part of an educational project that recalls Plato's dramatic sketch of the cave in *The Republic*. There, Socrates makes it clear how well he knows that people do not find it easy to stop watching the same old representations reflected on the cave wall; they do not want to stand up, turn around, and begin the difficult journey toward a more complete and real knowledge. He also notes that one who has made the journey and then returned to teach about a fuller reality will be in danger from all those who have built competitive and identity-establishing careers on their mastery of the one-dimensional images on the cave wall from which all that passes for knowledge—and reality itself—has been derived.

But if we never startle our students or any of those with whom we share our work, our life, and our world; if they never feel any anxiety; are never roused to anger or to sudden, intense, personal engagement by what we say, we surely ought to be concerned. Such comfort can indicate that the learning in which we are engaged is not touching the old errors so deeply embedded in dominant cultures. It is significant, I believe, that although many teachers and scholars profess to admire and try to emulate the Socratic method of teaching, most of them conveniently forget that Socrates was put to death for "corrupting the youth of Athens." One who questions not as an intellectual game, not as a kind of conceptual muscle building, but to make evident and open to serious public reconsideration the deepest presuppositions and behaviors of the culture and the state is going to arouse discomfort and anger.

Alfred North Whitehead suggests: "When you are criticizing the philosophy of an epoch, do not chiefly direct your attention to those intellectual positions which its exponents feel it necessary explicitly to defend. There will be some fundamental assumptions which adherents of all the various systems within the epoch unconsciously presuppose. Such assumptions appear so obvious that people do not know what they are assuming because no other way of putting things has ever occurred to them."[34]

*Reality* is one of the most complex of all concepts, one with an ever shifting, never finally knowable, or even definitively specifiable, set of referents. The point is not to attempt now to know reality correctly and finally; the point is to undo those errors in our thinking that clearly have consequences of which we no longer approve. It is not right conceptually, morally, or politically to construct, and mark, 'kinds' of humans in a way that leaves only one such kind in the centrally defining, norm-setting, idealized, unprefixed position.

The new insurgent scholarships, like the political rebellions of "conscious pariahs," are making publicly visible, audible, palpable, thinkable, and speakable that and those who were long privatized—domesticated, sequestered, closeted, veiled, housebound—and thus publicly invisible and unrepresented. Rosemarie Garland Thomson writes: "Focusing on cultural representations of disability reveals a politics of appearance in which some traits, configurations, and functions become the stigmata of a vividly embodied inferiority or deviance, while others fade into a neutral, disembodied, universalized norm." She sees what I have been calling the articulated hierarchy of invidious monisms at work therein: "Such readings of the body are the coordinates of a taxonomical system that distributes status, privilege, and material goods according to a hierarchy anchored by visible human physical variation."[35]

# CIRCULAR REASONING

CONNECTIONS AMONG the ways we think and the ways we perceive, feel, imagine, empathize, and act continue to become evident as we consider the next conceptual error: circular reasoning. Our reasoning is circular when we end up where we began without recognizing or admitting that that is what we have done. Circling back to beginnings can be a part of profound learning, as when we return and "know it for the first time" (T. S. Eliot). But circular reasoning is quite different from such returns. It is an error to start from an assertion and then 'prove' its truth by referring back to it, defining anything that might disprove it as irrelevant or out of order because, by the assertion that is supposed to be proven, that contrary evidence cannot be considered. "Girls are not good at arithmetic." "Females are more intuitive than rational." ""Blacks have rhythm." "Asians are good at mathematics." "Native Americans drink." "Gypsies are thieves." These are examples of such assertions. They are revealed as circular when we point to counterexamples, only to be met with, "But they are exceptions"—which does nothing but protect against disproof.

Such assertions are not open to contradiction because, it turns out, they are not what they appear to be—*descriptive* statements, empirical generalizations. Instead, they are *prescriptive*. They state not what 'we' or 'they' are but how the 'kind' to which we have been assigned is supposed to be and, by implication, is supposed *not* to be. Another way to get at this kind of error is to say that what appeared to be an empirical statement is actually a definition. "Girls are not good at arithmetic" seems to be a summary statement made after observation, a statement of fact. But when contrary observations or facts are suggested, the speaker changes ground, saying, in effect: "It is a defining quality of girls not to be good at arithmetic. A girl who appears to be good at arithmetic is, then, not really, entirely, or properly a girl."

We are not after logical precision here; we are simply trying to undo quite obvious blocks to sensible thinking. However necessary it is to start somewhere, to have some principles or propositions or definitions or axioms that are not open to proof or disproof because they themselves set the terms for proof, it is not right to elevate to that position statements or beliefs that have resulted from the fundamental error of taking the few who occupy the taken-to-be-representative 'kind' to be the inclusive term, the norm, the ideal. Faulty generalizations taken up into abstract concepts should not be used to justify their own continuing centrality so that we spin around and around in our cages, not only failing to advance ongoing quests for knowledge as for justice, but locking ourselves into harmful, often dangerous old ways of perceiving, feeling, judging, acting.

In a rather benign but telling example of this error, William James wrote: "He whom we have once called an equestrian is thereafter rendered forever unable to walk on his own feet." James links the making of such errors (which he calls "vicious intellectualism") with their unfortunate real effects, to "monism" rather than dualism, as have I, and sees it at work in "the treating of a name as excluding from the fact named what the name's definition fails positively to include."[1] At this level, the danger consists of contracting horizonal possibilities by limiting our perspectives only to those prescribed by an established definition. We have encountered that concern already. Our focus here, however, is on the particularly vicious effects of conflating knowledge, opinions, faith derived through faulty generalizing with impartial knowledge, and then reasoning in ways that can only prove, and never correct, the original assumptions.

## Faulty Standards

In dominant cultures, much is made of the need to have young people study the "the best" of the tradition—as if learning about what has been established as "the best" were a straightforward matter. But study of the best is not a neutral, purely intellectual matter. Those who are educated formally and informally into their cultures learn that they are supposed to admire, even to love, it. And that means that "the best" is supposed to motivate them, to draw and inspire them, on a personal as well as intellectual level. Consider the study of art history. The "masterpieces" shown in slides in lecture halls are supposed to call forth the students' admiration in a way that responds to the respect the teacher shows these works. *These* paintings, the teacher says or implies, are awe-inspiring. In them, genius is at work; greatness is made manifest. This mode of relating to art is by no means morally neutral. A student who rarely responds on a personal level to the works discussed in an introductory art history course or hung on mansion, palace, government, corporate walls, or a new citizen who visits an art gallery and does not respond to the unfamiliar "masterpieces"

there, can feel that she or he is in some serious way inadequate. Good people—
*finer* people—admire and enjoy such "great art." Those who do not like what
the tradition enshrines as art are seen as 'lower,' "less refined," than those who
do. This scale of refined taste, from the 'cultivated' to the 'crass,' 'insensitive,' and/or
"unhip" (particularly when 'high' art and 'popular' cultures are being simultaneously bridged and mutually challenged) is compounded oddly of established
definitions and moral and class-based judgments and is often circular at base.
'Finer' as well as 'cooler' people have keener sensibilities—that is, they like what
the dominant culture has selected as great or the "coming thing." People who
do not like the music, drama, literature, paintings that constitute 'higher' culture or the 'in thing' are devalued by these putative failures of "good taste."

This is a fascinating and complex subject in itself, revealing the class- as
well as culture-related nature of much of what is taught in our schools, particularly in arts and humanities courses, as well as what we learn from the cultural establishments of states, cities, and communities. The point here, however, is that whole traditions of creative works have been excluded from the
collection of Great and Significant Works we are taught to admire. Such exclusions not only make other works and creators seem odd, startling, out of place,
should they ever be mentioned; they mark them and the cultures from which
they come as less worthy of being loved, valued, admired, studied. A faultily
generalized study of art leads to the circularity of accredited tastes, which are
then used to 'prove' not just one's 'good' education but one's worthiness to be
a member of a specific level of a specific culture—the one that has had a cor-
ner on defining, cultivating, and protecting "good taste" (which is often confused with expensive taste).

Circularity extends the error of generalizing too far from too few into the
standards by which the hierarchy is maintained to such an extent that the few
reappear, tellingly, as *the ideal.* Consider that the creation of literature as a field
in most cultures that have such a category was carried out by particular people in particular places at particular times and took as its focus particular
kinds of works and some few kinds of writers. The *objects* of this thought, the
*sources* of notions of what is good (or great) writing, and early *theoretical conceptualizations* of literature then lost their specificity as they were taken up
into ever grander theories. But those sources did not always or entirely disappear, were not genuinely transcended. Had they been, the application of principles of selection, judgment, and taste derived from them would have resulted
over time in still more varied texts, anthologies, play productions, novels,
poetry by a far more inclusive group of people.

Thus, circular reasoning recapitulates and perpetuates faulty generalizations by making them immune to calls to include differing works, and particularly works and creators that were originally excluded. Some academic and cultural discourses then become not coherent, delimited conversations, but hegemonic, closed, circular constructs.

As some studies of levels of intelligence derived from a small, homogeneous sample of elite children turned around and became prescriptions for the attainment of 'higher' levels of intellectual abilities for all, Janson's and Norton's original criteria for inclusion in Western art-history texts turned around and became prescriptions for what Art should be. That, of course, is circularity, although it is often defended as "maintaining standards." It is as if redheads first defined red hair as an essential quality of humanity, and then—lo and behold—'proved' that red hair is necessary to anyone claiming inclusion in the category *human* by appealing to their own definition.

In the same way, a few Europeans made whiteness—scientized as "Caucasian"—the prescriptive norm and ideal for humankind in ways that reflected and exacerbated prejudices among Europeans as well as European fears of Others, including the anti-Semitism that showed its true colors in the Holocaust. In *On the Natural Varieties of Mankind* (1775), Johann Friedrich Blumenbach wrote that "[Caucasian-variety] stock displays . . . the most beautiful form of the skull. . . . Besides, it is white in color." (I have to ask it: What color could the other skulls have been? Did he actually *see* them as "colored"?) Thomas Henry Huxley responded in "Methods and Results of Ethnology" (1868): "A Georgian woman's skull was the handsomest in [Blumenbach's] collection. Hence it became his model exemplar of human skulls, from which all others might be regarded as deviations. . . . [Hence] the notion that the Caucasian man is the prototypic 'Adamic' man.'"[2] Huxley did not note, but we can, the anomaly of a woman's skull being taken to be "the prototypic 'Adamic' man." This anomaly did not derail 'scientific' discussions about the inferiority of Woman, but then neither did Huxley's critique derail the use of "Caucasian" for white people, let alone the hierarchical monism he saw so clearly.

We must beware of taking inherited standards of what is good, significant, beautiful, meaningful to be more than they are. They may work quite well when applied to the works or cultures (always riskier) from which they were derived, or to others that are akin to them, when they are not as patently absurd as the derivations of "Caucasian." (Absurdity, as we have observed, can be a mark of virulence. It results from tortuous efforts to avoid changing assumptions in the face of obvious evidence of their fallaciousness.) But inherited standards do not work at all well when applied to that which was excluded in the first place, in part because the standards were formulated to explain and justify some of those very exclusions. One cannot define art, or morality, or heroism, or reason in a way that excludes the art, morality, heroism, reason of particular groups of people and then turn around and use the standards based on that definition as if they were appropriate to the excluded. As any child might say, That isn't fair. Circular reasoning is a prime example of unfairness: "You said you were going to pick the best hitters for the team after tryouts, and I hit the ball farther than anyone." "Yes, but you're a girl." Untangle that, and you find the sort of circular reasoning that concerns us from the local to the global level.

## False Claims to Neutrality

In philosophy, the claim is often made that we are more concerned with ways of reasoning than with subject matter. Teachers may tell students that philosophy has no subject matter: it takes all subject matters, and the very idea of subject matter, as its purview. But the particular modes of thought considered to be properly philosophical were selected within particular traditions that had long since relegated the intellectual activities assigned to women and 'lower' men and 'exotic' cultures to some different category. We saw such effects at work in Kant and Jefferson, and I encountered it in some students' reactions to Yoruba philosophy, which they assumed was too 'primitive' to belong in a philosophy course. The criteria for a 'sound argument' or 'good reasoning,' which are used to judge not just students' work but all works that might have some claim to be included in philosophy courses, are turned around to justify not just their own soundness, not just past inclusions and exclusions, but also the *neutrality* of prevailing definitions.

Michael Q. Patton, a scholar and practitioner of evaluation methodology, notes: "In effect, identifying objectivity as the major virtue of the dominant paradigm is an ideological statement the function of which is to legitimize, preserve, and protect the dominance of a single . . . methodology."[3] Objectivity and neutrality are not quite the same, but both, attributed to a paradigm, method, theory, or attitude, give it a privileged, superior status in the dominant culture of the West. It is significant that, in hierarchical monisms, "objective" and "subjective" are often used in ways that indicate a lack of parallelism similar to that between Man and Woman. For example, the charge that something is "merely subjective," which is often still leveled at works refused entrance into curricula, is not reversible: one rarely if ever hears that some work or theory is "merely objective." And although we do hear that women's studies or other critical scholarships are "too political," we rarely hear that mainstream scholarship is "too apolitical"—or, for that matter, "too antipolitical." The category of subjective scholarship, like the categories of woman and "the primitive," has had little to no positive content of its own; these have been used most often as an indication of 'lack' measured on a scale calibrated in relation to the categories that exclude them. I might also observe that as the "subjective voice" (curiously and unhelpfully singularized) gains legitimacy along with the new insurgent scholarships, it still arguably remains largely defined in relation to objectivity. Some scholars now "admit" their "bias," thus claiming their particularity but, unfortunately, only by claiming a negative, justifying that odd move on the ground that *all* approaches are biased. But if all views are biased, none are: "bias" loses all meaning. Neither epistemological stance helps us undo either monistic or dualistic framings that keep us from thinking through what *objective* and *subjective, neutral* and *biased* might more usefully mean if freed from the old, closed, self-validating circles.

I am not taking on the question here of whether, reconceived, these attributes could help us describe what we mean by "sound scholarship." I am simply observing that one function of *claiming*—or, equally categorically, *denying*—mystified notions of objectivity and neutrality for scholars and works that speak from, of, and for falsely generalized (even universalized) perspectives is to hide yet again the root partialities that feed dominant traditions. And one effect of that hiding is to lock us into circular reasoning. As with the referee, the umpire, the judge, the "blind review," that which is supposedly neutral and objective is placed both outside and at the center of knowledge making and evaluating. It is outside insofar as we are not to question the meaning or merit of that which makes it 'objective' or the appropriateness of objectivity itself. It is at the center because, as established knowledge or virtuous quality, it continues to justify itself in a way that marginalizes whatever differs from it. For example, one is not allowed to protest a "blind review" "subjectively," whatever one's reasons, because subjectivity has been conflated with emotions, and emotions are defined as nonrational. (It is not irrelevant here that emotions have long been assigned to females in ways that mark them and us as 'less' worthy and far less reliable than Rational Man, and that this has also been used to privatize us as dependents of a "head" of family.) "Subjective" objections to "objective" judgments are then not evaluated to see whether they are right or wrong. They are dismissed as out of order.

In the early days of feminist scholarship, it became evident that established scholars judging by established criteria effectively continued the exclusion of scholarship of, by, and about women. For the judgment process to have the old exclusionary result, it was not necessary for the judges to be purposefully or consciously exclusive. All they needed to do was to apply in a 'neutral'— that is, *not* reflexively critical as well as *not* 'biased'—fashion notions of 'soundness' derived from already exclusionary scholarship. Fault and failure judged as such by standards of, by, and for exclusive scholarship thus became neatly attributable to that which was judged. There was no way to judge swans in a world of ducks; the young swan was quite clearly, if regrettably, an ugly duckling. (Interesting, that. Those who do not "measure up" are often labeled "ugly," even if the scale at issue has nothing overtly to do with beauty—perhaps because they are not acceptable and so not 'pleasing.' Feminists, like ducks in a world that favors swans, are also rather expected to be "ugly.")

## Closet Platonism

To move still further into the question of how circularity works, we can turn to one of Wittgenstein's famous de-essentializing examples. He observed that the only meter that is not a meter is the standard meter. The standard meter is not a meter because it cannot be judged to be or not to be one, being itself the source and only warrant of what it means to be a meter. When feminist scholars suggested that Man is not defined with reference to an essential Idea of Human that can truly serve as "the measure of all things," they threw dominant systems into terrible confusion. By what, then, are we to justify our measurements? If that which is established is to be seen as 'merely' conventional, what is to tell us what is significant, what is good, what matters, even what is real in ways that can coerce assent? The loss of (faulty) warrants for fundamental cultural constructs has led faculty members, scholars, conservatives, and fundamentalists to claim that everything is being "reduced to relativism" just because their own assumptions are put in question. If the meter itself, if Man himself, if the "Caucasian variety" itself, if any one religion's creed can be seen as the result of unnecessary *choices* of what and whom to measure by, and critics then refuse to abide by (faulty) traditional or conventional choices, what is to keep *everyone* from choosing to measure as she or he pleases? Chaos—or, at least, a failure of authority—threatens. But, of course, *maintaining* the meter, or man-the-measure, or a patriarchal religious ordering in an absolutized authoritative position does not save us from having to make choices in our real, changing, particular, plural world—unless we go on dangerously nonresponsive autopilot. A devoutly Christian friend of mine, tired of such closed minds, has posted a sign in his workplace that reads: "Jesus came to take away your sins, not your mind." Efforts to perpetuate uncritically the choices made by others in earlier and different times can pervert culturally dominant belief into something all too like psychoses.

Few academics are actually closet essentialists, or Platonists, or intellectual fundamentalists, but many sound as if they are when one questions the founding definitions and assumptions and standards that, as Whitehead noted, they may not even be aware of holding. Thus, they stay within the circle, within the set defined for them by the creators of their fields, even while priding themselves on being critical thinkers and working hard to liberate students from *their* unacknowledged assumptions. Thus, they can create particularly painful dilemmas for students from differing backgrounds, of differing turns of mind, whose identities and loyalties are cast as liabilities from which they should liberate themselves.

Feminist scholarship that is not just additive, that does not simply find what women have done that is as close as possible to what (the right 'kind' of) men have done, necessarily breaks the closed circles of admitted and unadmitted essentialisms and of conservative conventionalisms. It makes available to thought and to revisioning that which had been unquestioned. As Joan Kelly notes, for example, women's history has made "problematical three of the basic concerns of historical thought: (1) periodization, (2) the categories of social analysis, and (3) theories of social change."[4] Studies that put women, with our many differences, at the center force open questions about what is 'normal,' 'significant,' 'good,' leading to reconsiderations of the basic conceptual tools of all previous studies.

As Kelly notes, the problem of circularity is evident in the abstract idea of a European "Renaissance," an abstraction derived from study of the lives of a particular group of men presented as gender neutral. But women may not have had a Renaissance in Europe at the same time or in the same ways that (some) men did—and whether they did or not cannot be answered without careful gender analyses. Until such analyses have been done, it is almost unnecessary to say "women did not have a Renaissance" for the same reasons we have not needed to say that women did not belong to fraternities. As long as the exclusively defined concepts that are central to fields remain untransformed, research shaped by them will tend very strongly to 'prove' only its own prior assumptions.

These are not just trivial or curious instances of circular reasoning. They matter, and deeply. When tools of analysis, methods, concepts based on unquestioned assumptions are claimed to be neutral, we yield too much power to those who developed them. If we care about truth, meaning, and justice, we cannot afford to yield such power to an exclusive past and its major beneficiaries. Nor, it is important to note again, should we fail to discern where and how old prejudicial errors *were* seen and rejected by those who preceded us. We are not without teachers in our efforts. None of them is perfect, as we certainly are not, but some did break out of the closed circles of their times.

## Circular Definitions of Fields

Some years ago, when Peggy McIntosh and I were engaged in an early study of curriculum-transformation projects, we stumbled on one of those naive questions that prove in suggestive ways to be difficult to answer. I asked an art historian, "What is the subject of your field?" After a pause, she said, "I'm not sure. That's a hard question. I've never asked myself that." I asked, "Is it art?" "Yes," she said, "and no, of course. There is also history." "What is the subject of history, then?'" The conversation sputtered into silence. A little later, we asked some historians the same question: What is the subject of history? "The past,'" one of them said quickly. Then there was an awkward pause. "Well, not really," another said. "I mean, what is the past?" Someone else said, "We study records of and artifacts from the past." In neither conversation were any of us comfortable implying that the subject of a field has some kind of separate, essential existence 'out there.' Nevertheless, some of the same faculty felt licensed to exclude scholarship then emerging from feminists on the ground that "it isn't history, literature, philosophy." They could not define it, but they did think they could recognize it.

We also asked, "Where is the art in works of art? Is it in the work? How? Is it in the artist? In the viewer? Is it in some interaction between artist, work, and viewer? Is it in cultural notions of and provisions for art?" Such questions are (to some of us, at least) fascinating in any context, but the point in raising them here is to observe that, for the most part, they are rarely discussed in graduate or undergraduate courses. When most faculty members decide what they will teach under the label of history, literature, philosophy, they often consult a *sense* that they know what the subject matter 'really' is and should be rather than a firm definition or an open, critical investigation of it. But when one compares syllabi from around the country and from all kinds of academic institutions, it becomes readily apparent that, in a real sense, history, classics, art history, and the rest are what teachers of those fields teach—as "intelligence" is functionally defined as "what intelligence tests test." And that, of course, leaves us stuck within circular reasoning.

Philosophy teachers claim to be teaching a subject that is primarily about reasoning itself. In fact, they are "covering" certain texts and the problems the texts' authors are treating—which are, of course, the problems those authors already assumed to be 'proper' philosophical problems. Thus, the texts lock in definitions of philosophy-itself. Even a philosophy text organized around modes of reasoning rather than around texts or problems will almost certainly introduce, or be correlated to, a reading list of the same familiar texts, now introduced as *examples* of the various sorts of reasoning rather than their *sources*. That, too, is circular—an error defined within, but seldom used to critique, the dominant philosophical tradition.

If academic fields were held responsible for addressing the complex and fascinating, continuing, and evolving question of what their subject matter has been, is elsewhere among others, and could be taken to be (and do not assume that "a hegemonic discourse" is the only possible right answer), we would surely see more variation in what is taught than any national study of syllabi reveals. In those fields that have proved most open to feminist, antiracist, multicultural and multinational, postcolonial, and other scholarships, questions about the fields themselves are more common and more seriously discussed than they are in those fields that have resisted. In the "hard" sciences, for example, alternative notions of what constitutes *science* are almost inadmissible. Students learn what science is by learning what professional scientists in the United States, who increasingly work internationally but within the same tradition, have agreed is 'good' and 'real' science. Thus, some scientists say with confidence, "I can see how studying women in science might have something to do with the history of science, but *real* science has nothing to do with who does it, or why." And when it is suggested that perhaps science has been defined in an extremely narrow way if it excludes all historical, political, economic, professional, and moral considerations, and that this may not only falsify but become dangerous, they are often flummoxed or outraged. They repeat, "Those are interesting considerations, and they should be taught as history of science, ethics, or economics of science, but they aren't *science*." Reiterating a definition does not justify it; it merely invokes the definition's authority to stop questions. The new field of science studies has been one result: the questioners have had to move outside, because they are unwelcome within.

At this point I admit to feeling a tremor of fear and sometimes anger. I think of scientists working in germ-warfare laboratories, on nuclear weapons, on chemical defoliants for military use, in university laboratories increasingly funded and controlled by profit-driven corporate "partners," all the while saying, "I just do good science. It is no business of mine what others do with it." Narrow definitions of realms of knowledge that define as out of order all considerations of context and consequences serve our human capacity to compartmentalize, to avoid thinking about what we are doing, and so to wash our hands of responsibility. I have the same problem with business people and politicians who say that ethics should be considered, of course, but "the bottom line is the bottom line" and other such silly, self- and system-protecting circular clichés. It does no more good to tack a separate course in ethics onto business-, public-policy–, science-, or law-school requirements than it does to tack on a single course that 'covers' women or a single "multicultural" requirement. The questions that need to be raised are intrinsic, not extrinsic, to what we are teaching, learning, practicing. Adducing circular arguments to justify the continuing marginality of all that has been excluded for too long does nothing more, or less, than protect the same old inner circle.

In fields such as literature, where almost every once central notion has recently been put in question, feminist scholarship has been included much more readily. If what is meant by "text" is open for discussion, then works that would have been excluded not long ago by circular reasoning can indeed be considered. If what is meant by "author" is a serious question, then definitions of authors derived from and circling back to justify a list of pre-established, accepted writers can no longer function in the old, exclusive fashion. If delimitations of subject matter are recognized and loosened, fascinatingly transgressive reflections can emerge.[5] Of course, if the old conceptualizations are dissolved *entirely*, we risk throwing the baby out with the bathwater, leaving ourselves with no option but to replace one totalizing framework with another from which we can continue to prescribe what is and is not significant.

These are errors akin to the one in a famous philosophical example. "'All swans are white,'" said European and British scientists who had seen only white swans, and philosophers took that to be an example of a definition derived from empirical findings—one that proved so constant as to have revealed an essential, not accidental or even secondary, attribute of "swan-ness."

Then black swans were 'discovered' in Australia (obviously not by Australians, who knew of them all along but were not consulted). What to do? If white is an essential, defining quality of swan-ness, then the black swans could not be seen as swans at all. If white is not a quality of swan-ness, then what had appeared to be a definitional (even a tautologous) statement had to be recast. Women's studies has challenged the definitional limits of all fields and, in doing so, has produced the same problem for those who took faulty generalizations as captured essences. Many have found it hard to say, "Oh, right. Then what we have been teaching is not history-itself but certain men's constructions of history." Like the European and British philosophers and scientists who were so troubled by black swans that they were tempted to decide that such odd birds could not be swans at all, some faculty members have preferred to act (and teach) as if women's music is not really music; as if girls cannot do arithmetic; as if a Black man is essentially aberrant; as if multiculturalism is perforce radical relativism—as if, in short, "*our* tradition's" universalized essences are the only *really* universal ones.

As I noted earlier, my U.S. students had difficulty recognizing Yoruba thought as anything other than "primitive" and aphilosophical. Given their notions of philosophy, different sorts of thinking (and ways of sharing thinking—orally, for example, rather than in a particular kind of written text, or ritually rather than in a particular form designated "rational") had to be not-philosophy. They had, through their formal and informal schooling, come to mistake particular philosophy books and courses for philosophy-itself. They were more open to Zen Buddhism and to Jaina logic, but there, too, they had a hard time considering these highly sophisticated intellectual systems as properly, normatively rational (although in these cases, that is part of what they liked; they scented freedom). Works that were nontraditional (in the dominant culture of the United States) remained alien, of interest not for their merits but for their exoticism and for what was misperceived as their non- or even anti-rationalism. That is, some U.S. readers of other philosophizing traditions embrace them as a way to counter rather than reconfigure what they do see and object to as narrow rationalism in their own tradition. Thus is Native American wisdom appropriated by alienated Euro-Americans as more natural, more emotional, more spiritual than "philosophy" (which does nothing to change the prevailing narrow notion of rationality). Meanwhile, "philosophy" continues to exclude Native American wisdom, refuses to learn from it, and effectively denies that "Indians" can and do have sophisticated intellectual traditions developed from their own *philo sophia* (love of wisdom).

I fear it may also be the case that some who have been educated in the United States find Japanese and Chinese, Hindu and Muslim philosophies easier to take seriously than African or "native" philosophies because both "Black" and "native" have for so long been used as markers of 'primitiveness.' Philosophy from the "Dark Continent" cannot be philosophy, just as black swans cannot be swans. A romanticized embracing of what was excluded can also derive from circular reasoning—in this case, however, done inside-out in such a way that those things still defined as essentially different are simply revalued from "lesser" to "better" without rethinking the flipped-over standards.

We cannot afford to forget that, when we deal with thought and knowledge, with conceptual matters, we are also dealing with preconscious cultural assumptions and habits that can reflect not only the ignorance but the systemically created and reinforced prejudices of dominant cultures. None of this helps us think responsively. On the contrary: it keeps the circles closed.

# Prejudice

Prejudice—pre-judgment—can itself be defined as circular reasoning: it rests on judgments made before the fact that are not open to reconsideration in light of new or particular experience or evidence. When notions thus made impermeable lock together in systems, theories, methods, beliefs, psychotic cultural complexes can emerge that must thereafter be forced on a stubbornly resistant world of particularities. And, sadly, even those who are willing to be called back into thought are often ignorant of much that could transform our closed systems. Far too few of us, in all lands, know enough about other cultures not to assume, as in Frank Newman's example, that "to be Bulgarian [or whatever people one does not know] is to suffer from a moral flaw."[6] Trapped in circular justifications of hierarchical monisms, we continue to believe that it is a moral flaw to be other than the defining few—to be female, to be poor, to be differently abled, to be nonheterosexual, to be a "resident alien." That such beliefs can be internalized by those they rob of independent identity and human worth makes the situation all the more tragic. The works of those who have analyzed the effects of colonialism on the psyches, spirits, minds, and hearts as well as the political and economic systems of the colonized—for example, Fanon, Memmi, Cabral—remain telling and helpful.

Before they enter our classes, our students are strongly inclined to believe what far too many teachers, however unintentionally, confirm for them: those who have been excluded from the curriculum *ought* to have been excluded. This (usually unstated) judgment cannot but compound the errors that created and, if uncritiqued, will continue to create prejudices that we may wholly disavow when we encounter them elsewhere. We need to move beyond operational definitions that restrict fields to what has been taught and to the ways it has been taught. As the authors of *The Humanities and the American Promise,* a report for the National Endowment for the Humanities, write: "We think it is misleading to regard the humanities basically as a set of academic disciplines or, even more restricting, as a set of 'great books.' We identify them, rather, with certain ways of thinking—of inquiring, evaluating, judging, finding and articulating meaning."[7] Having broken out of the circular notion that humanities are what humanists have taught, they continue: "A citizenry that is humanistically aware is a citizenry that is capable of confronting diversity, ambiguity, and conflict, overcoming prejudice and self-interest, enlarging its sympathies, tackling tough public issues, and envisioning possibilities beyond the limits of circumstance."[8]

## From Classroom to Country

If the people of the United States had continued to abide by early prescriptions of who is and ought to be a citizen, African Americans, Native Americans, Asian Americans, white women, those who do not own property, those who cannot pass inappropriate "literacy" tests still would not be enfranchised. If citizens and those refused full citizenship had continued to accept prevailing laws as fully expressive, even defining, of justice itself, instead of calling on horizonal ideals of justice *not* derived from and locked in circular fashion into old exclusionary laws, all women still would not be allowed to vote (or even to wear trousers); miscegenation ("cross-breeding," "mixed marriages") would still be illegal; legally enforced segregation would still stigmatize the United States, as apartheid did South Africa; people with disabilities would still be "shut-ins" because access would not have to be provided for them; "out-castes," "untouchables" would still be treated legally like the "night soil" they were forced to carry away—just as "same-sex" couples are still not allowed to marry in almost all states and countries.

In considerations of knowledge, as in considerations of justice, there are horizonal ideas and principles that transcend, rather than simply repeat, particular examples—ideas and principles such as *humanity, justice, truth,* and *meaning.* We need not locate such transcendent ideals and principles in some essential, unchanging realm to think them. We can simply hold, as I have been suggesting (with Kant, William James, and Arendt, among others), that humans are capable of thinking ideas that they cannot know. We know perfectly well that we have dreams of justice and of truth that are not limited to knowledge of particular sets of laws or systems of knowledge. It is the restlessness of mind and spirit kept alive and productive by our ability to be imaginative, to think reflexively, to critique and re-form what we know, and to learn to think in the place of others and to empathize with them that make democracy a real, if not actualized, possibility. Horizons can and do hold us; we will not fall off a flattened globe if we dissolve the rigidly closed circles that we have substituted for them.

# MYSTIFIED CONCEPTS

THE MEANING of any concept is extremely difficult to state unambiguously, let alone definitively, as is the meaning of *concept* itself—not to mention the meaning of *meaning*. I will not now attempt to develop (or even consistently borrow) a single philosophic stance with regard to these intriguing issues. What I do want to do is explore some of the particular concepts that have emerged as having particular significance during my years of work with faculty members and community groups to make knowledge and thinking more inclusive. Somewhat hesitantly, I call these concepts "mystified concepts." I do not use the term "mystified" in quite the same sense as Marcuse, for example, but I do want to imply that that which is mystified is simultaneously confusing and, because its opacity keeps us from seeing clearly how it reflects and serves powerful systemic interests, efficacious. That is, mystified concepts are also mystifying: they *do* something to us.

It is not the effort to uncover or establish 'true' meanings for the concepts that interests me, although I will suggest ways of understanding them that can be reclaimed so that we do not lose what is useful about them when we see through and peel off the distortions. What interests me is the way these concepts function, while still mystified, to lock in old forms of thought, old hierarchies, and old errors within the academy and dominant cultures even as they appear neutral and above the fray. For example, in a *New York Times* report, "Colleges Find Diversity Is Not Just Numbers," a Dartmouth student from Singapore is quoted as saying: "This racial diversity, which has been an obsession of the administration, has been misguided. My opinion is that Dartmouth should be focusing on intellectual diversity."[1] *Of course* "racial diversity" is "not just about numbers," although the numbers reflect what racial diversity *is* about: seeing that something has been very wrong and recognizing that something must be done to keep it from continuing. "Intellectual diversity" for each, as for all, of us is not possible as long as the profound effects of millennia of prejudices continue to deform what we think we know and how we think and feel, and so limit our capacity to think *with* others as the differing creatures we are. Purposefully changing "the numbers" to counter old prejudices that are still working in mystified fashion in practices that are not really neutral is not an absurd "obsession" with the insignificant. It is like changing the numbers in a budget to reflect and enable reordered institutional priorities, as is done in any responsible planning process.

In this section, we will explore a few of the mystified concepts that could lead a smart, well-meaning young man—along with many others—to miss the point as the quoted Dartmouth student did. We will reflect on *excellence, judgment, equality, rationality/intelligence, liberal arts, woman, sex, man, war,* and *gender* (and with them, a number of related concepts). I hope to ameliorate somewhat the frustration of an at best suggestive discussion by suggesting some of the richness of available thinking and resources. What is important to me is to make the very familiar begin to seem strange and worthy of a great deal more serious thought and conversation and reading, and to inspire searches for further source materials. The words, the concepts, we are about to consider tend to be mind-numbing because they have been worn smooth into platitudes (as in pious invocations of excellence) or because they are fraught with emotion and taboos (sex, war). I want us to *think* about them for precisely those reasons: platitudes and taboos are two sides of the same barrier to thinking.

## Excellence

A prime example of a misused and mystifying concept is *excellence.* It is invoked frequently and solemnly in discussions of the mission of higher education, particularly when such discussions are provoked by considerations of possible changes. Allan Bloom, an academic believer in the necessary conflation of excellence with elitism, called efforts to make the curriculum more equitable and responsive to the needs and interests of more students "an unprecedented assault on reason."[2] This is an absurd statement. Bloom knew history better than that: the creation of new fields of scholarship based on today's critiques are hardly in the category of "assaults on reason" such as Socrates's death at the hands of the Athenians; the destruction of the great library at Alexandria; the Inquisition; Gaileo and other early European scientists' trials; Savanorola's book burning; McCarthyism; the Cultural Revolution in China; and so on. It is those who believe that their state, their rule, their religious control is threatened who have carried out "assaults on reason," not the vulnerable few who question. In the United States, there were book burnings in a few communities when textbooks revised to be more inclusive were sent to schools. The authors of those updated textbooks did not burn the old ones; they worked with them as they tried to make them better.

Few among those in higher education who call on us to defend excellence (which in educational discussions is almost always evocative, in particular, of "high standards") reveal their prejudices so crudely. But then, they need not be. The prejudices are woven so deeply into the dominant tradition that our most inspiring concepts have become mystified in ways that keep doing the old work of exclusion. Allan Bloom's *The Closing of the American Mind* became a bestseller even though what he opposed was *opening* "the American Mind"— undoing that odd singularity, and so refusing unanimity, that old enemy of active reasoning by plural minds.

Excellence, as it is called on in the academy, can almost be said to take its meaning from the sentiment of *loyalty.* If someone feels it is necessary to invoke excellence in a discussion, it is usually the case that the speaker intends to remind others of their commitment to the calling of higher education, to the reasons such education not only exists but ought to exist. But that solidarity in loyalty—which is strongly recommended if one wishes to retain credibility within the academy—is entirely vague in its content. Or so it seems. In fact, there are so many possible meanings for excellence that a loyal adherence to it necessarily means, in practice, a loyal adherence to the measures as well as to the exemplars of excellence that valorize a dominant tradition. And that throws us right back to the root problem and its consequences: generalizing too far from too few and then, in circular fashion, abstracting apparently neutral standards for inclusion, significance, and quality from those few. That which has already been judged to be excellent within the dominant tradition is taken to embody the standards for anything else that might claim such high status.

Calls for a new inclusiveness, particularly when they are couched in terms of equity, are therefore heard as threatening excellence-itself. Of course, such calls are not attacking excellence, any more than new laws, rules, and regulations necessarily threaten overarching ideals of justice that particular laws and codes are meant to serve. What such reactions reveal is the lack of any idea of *excellence* that does not conflate it with *exclusivity.* It is exclusivity, not excellence, that is undone by equality. Excellence, to shine forth, requires openness so 'the best' can appear and be so judged; exclusivity requires the closing and guarding of doors.

All judgments of excellence require some exclusions: if everything were excellent, nothing would be. But the two terms should no longer be confused.

The exclusivity of excellence is a byproduct, not a goal. The best teachers try very hard to help all students do their best work, and they know perfectly well that the persistence of less than excellent work is an ongoing challenge to teach better rather than proof of their loyalty to "high standards." However, the failing of students by "strict" teachers is all too often used as just such 'proof,' a self-serving, protective move that is still available because the old constructions of education persist in sorting out "the best from the rest," in gatekeeping. When the goal really is excellence, exclusion is a regrettable byproduct, not a point of pride.

Some country clubs and private men's clubs are exclusive, but that by no means makes them excellent. It simply means that they refuse membership to some categories of people. Although doing so may make members feel special, it does not make them better. If we want to make institutions as central to democracy as education and government less like the old white male Christian clubs, we have to be very careful about the exclusions that persist as extensions of exclusive choices made, requirements established, practices followed.

One test of whether excellence is being confused with exclusivity can be found in how consequences are interpreted. Take as an example a set of tests established to sort out who is and who is not prepared to work at the levels at which excellence is approached. If those tests produced scores showing more women than men, more Latino/a people than Euro-Americans, more Black than white people doing poorly, they would today tend to produce anxiety about "diversity fairness" and might lead to revisions. But not long ago, that would not have happened, and some people still persist in believing that such results prove lower-scoring groups' inability to "measure up" rather than the tests' inadequacy. Under that interpretation, efforts to revise the test will perforce be seen as inappropriate, explainable only as something like "political correctness." But this overlooks a different kind of "political correctness" that is mystified, and so invisible. For a very long time, new tests that in early trials resulted in notably, consistently lower scores among privileged white males were revised because they were seen as evidently "skewed." Imagine a test of quantitative ability on which girls consistently did better than boys. That would so violate established "findings" that it would cast serious doubts on the new test—though the pattern of girls' doing less well than boys on the old tests did not.

A "Great Books" list that includes almost no books written by those who have been long excluded is, on its face, simply reinforcement of faulty generalization and circular reasoning. It perpetuates the dominance of those who defined the terms of excellence to fit their own favored works in the first place.

This does not mean that some of those "Great Books" are not excellent; it means that we cannot be sure that they are, because we have not judged them against adequately derived standards. (Similarly, we cannot be sure that boys are proportionately better than girls at math, or that girls are better than boys on verbal tests, until or unless we use adequately developed assessment methods.)

Equity—that is, a commitment to inclusive, unbiased, appropriate consideration of significance and merit—is a prerequisite for adequate judgments of excellence. Without equity, how are we to know enough, to have considered enough, to trust that the standards by which we judge are adequate for any but a particular group or kind? Consider a dog show. The pinnacle of achievement is to win the "best in show" ribbon. How would the dogs' owners feel if the judge for that final contest were an expert only on French poodles; chose a French poodle as "best in show"; and justified the choice of a French poodle as a neutral judgment of excellence for all dogs? What those judges actually do is look for the dog that is a better example of its breed than the others are of their breeds. This effort recognizes standards without denying that they have been derived for some (prescriptively bred) grouping and should not then be extended to all as if they were universal. An excellent Pomeranian is not an excellent mastiff, but that makes it no less superb. (It also makes it no less an example of human efforts to conform nature to our own criteria.)

But I have often heard U.S. faculty members who are ignorant of African philosophies, of early women's novels from multiple cultures, of East Indian gamelan music—of any work other than that which is similar to what they were taught in graduate school—say, in response to invitations to include some such works: "But surely we should not teach work that is less than the best? Surely we should not lower our standards just to be inclusive." We are not asking them to lower their standards when we ask them to refrain from applying particular standards as if they were universal and to take the time to learn something about new materials before rushing to judge them by inappropriate standards.

Defenses of past and present curricula that are characterized as struggles to "maintain [a mystified notion of] excellence" can, I believe, be traced in part to flight from the uncertainties that are necessarily present in any act of judgment, and particularly so when horizons are expanding and old forms are being reconfigured. To become able to make reasonable judgments of excellence— whether excellence of kind or excellence in a moral sense (which also tend to be conflated where the few considered their 'kind' to be the best in all regards)— we require a broad and deep acquaintance with more than any single group or any one tradition, however abstracted and universalized, can offer. If we are to make any sense of excellence that will make the concept useful as more than a call for loyalty to the exclusivities of the past, we need to consider also what *judgment* has meant and can mean.

# Judgment

Let us begin by considering *judgment* in a legal sense, in which to judge something is to bring it, in all of its particularity, before a set of laws, principles, or standards in such a way that both the particularity of that which is to be judged and the generality of the principle, law, or standard is honored. Even this apparently straightforward and familiar act—applying a law or principle to a particular—cannot be certain (for example, stealing is illegal; a child takes a cookie she has not been given; is her act illegal?). Judgment is not the result of straightforward deductive reasoning, a fact that is recognized through the institution of judges: if we believed that rules could be applied to individuals and individual cases directly, we would have no judges, only law books and enforcers. We have judges because we know that no law book imaginable could include, before the fact, everything that could possibly be done by anyone under any circumstances, and the books certainly could not tell us what we need to know to judge each individual's actions fairly in every possible case. Laws, like principles, are abstractions and general; they not only do not, but cannot, contain within themselves the requisite specificity to allow a direct match with all possible particular, real, concrete people, acts, and situations. We have history to remind us that efforts to apply the law, whether secular or sacred, as if it were adequate unto itself for all instances of human action and behavior result in terrible cruelties, as well as in absurdities. We recognize that a two-year-old taking a cookie from another child is not the same, and should not be treated the same, as an adult stealing a car.

In a different realm, we know that it takes more than knowledge to judge art. We speak of people with a "good eye," a fine "feeling" for art. We need someone who knows a great deal about art in general but who also has skill in seeing and understanding unique works. The pedant who knows only prevalent theories about what makes for 'great' art in any tradition is by no means necessarily a good judge of contemporary art or of art inspired by different traditions. Faced with genuinely original works, such people may be rendered helpless simply because the works to be judged are unfamiliar. Stories of failures of judgment are familiar to art historians. Rembrandt was by no means the first or only artist to see his work greeted initially with the judgment, "*That is not art*"—a classic expression of circular reasoning that uses, and reinscribes, a mystified conceptualization of *art*.

It is difficult, but by no means impossible, not to be mystified, however. A story I heard once but have never tracked down makes this point in a different and intriguing way: When the furor surrounding the Impressionists finally died down, and the works of some had come to be greatly admired, it turned out that Peggy Guggenheim owned examples of precisely those artists who were now seen as 'the best.' Since the Impressionists had purposefully broken most of the standing rules, even those who had liked their works had not been able to judge among them. Guggenheim was asked how on earth she had done so. She replied, "I bought the works that most infuriated me."

The art connoisseur—like effective political leaders, sages, healers in their realms—has long been a fascinating figure precisely because what she or he is able to do is mysterious. It cannot be written down as so many laws, ready for application, and it is outside "common knowledge." Secure, accepted mastery of what experts in a field know can even be a hindrance in some cases. This is not to say, of course, that ignorance is preferable to extensive knowledge of principles and of that which is to be judged. It is simply to recognize that judgment (particularly as it shades into something as elusive as taste, as Kant's *Critique of Judgment* suggests), is not the direct result of knowledge. We find ourselves saying things like, "He has exquisite taste," "She is a good judge because she has compassion," "She is an uncannily good diagnostician." With such statements, we recognize that the kind of mental and emotional engagement involved in judging what is good, important, significant needs to be more like thinking than knowing, more like taste than deductive reasoning.

The ability to move from the conceptual to the physically apparent, to connect the established with the innovative, to see in an individual case what is general and how the general illuminates the individual case is required in good judges of any sort, from those in law courts, village squares, or kitchens to teachers assessing individual students' progress. However, the dominance of the deductive model (and the appeal of its greater certainty, which lessens responsibility) tends to push us away from focusing on the individual toward focusing on standardized measures, rules, principles. In schools, standardization too often takes the place of standards, requiring that individuals be treated as if they were entirely the same except as measured against the same, usually quantified, criteria—as if all that is relevant is whether they scored a 100 or

85 or 50 percent on a test. (Why this is not seen as a violation of education, as distinct from mass-production of goods that should be as identical as possible, is beyond me. But as we have noted, absurdity does not often enough disqualify or undercut the most entrenched if violative notions.) However much we recognize that no certainty is available to judges, however much we value compassion as a judicial virtue, there is always pressure on the courts to reduce judicial latitude. Such flights from the necessarily free act of judgment subvert our efforts to hear those whose realities continue to be excluded because of faultily abstracted, circular assumptions, mystified definitions, standards, rules.[3]

As Kant observed in *The Critique of Judgment,* both taste and judgment can be developed but not taught, demonstrated but not proved. (He makes the same point in the first Critique, A133B172.) That does not make taste and judgment any less valuable than deductive reasoning. On the contrary: uncertainty, which is the necessary result of openness to what is unique, individual, particular, new, is a virtue that reflects an open and enlarged mind, a capacity for empathy. The opposite of such uncertainty is not knowledge as we would have it be but dogma and pedantry, which John Dewey describes in *Quest for Certainty* as characteristic of the dominant Western tradition, specifically insofar as it carries antidemocratic tendencies from the past within it.

It is worth remembering that the clichéd idea (often announced as if it were fresh and radical) that knowledge gives us power over the object of our knowledge, or over other people, is not a necessary idea. It was almost certainly alien to Socrates, for example, who was willing to accept the label "wisest man in Athens" as long as everyone understood that his wisdom lay in knowing that he did not know. His struggle with the Sophists—at least, as Plato depicts it for us—can be understood in part as a conflict between one who thought of teaching as an effort to remove too-empowering certainties from the mind of anyone who would converse with him and those who sought to teach people how to win arguments and so gain power. The violent way that Thrasymachus enters the opening discussion in Plato's *Republic* is intended, I believe, to dramatize the differences between Socrates's efforts to find grounds for genuine harmony among different people and a brash younger man's desire to establish and justify his own dominance. With Socrates's death for "corrupting the youths of Athens," Thrasymachus, we might say, triumphed. But still and elsewhere, there are other traditions in which the way of knowing is one of renunciation, of gentleness, of acceptance and not at all of "mastery."

That many of us fear to be judged even more than we fear judging in a world run by "masters" is perfectly sensible: we fear being mis-taken, being marked as inferior rather than simply different, and we understand that someone is trying to control us by submitting us to such (faulty, but very powerful) judgments. This is a fear born of experience. As the authors of *The Humanities and the American Promise* suggest, too few have realized that "a large dose of humility is the first requisite for the humanist contemplating material for which old terms and standards do not necessarily suffice."[4] I agree, and all the more so when I consider that dominant traditions have judged not just academic material but people, even whole peoples, using principles that enshrine errors in the service of lust for mastery and thus have done terrible harm. But when I have suggested, in workshops with faculty members, that it is absurd to judge works such as quilts made by women for use in the home by prevailing standards for 'art'—standards that were developed by those who defined creations such as quilts as non-art—I have been asked, "But then how are we to judge at all?" The response seems to me to be twofold. First, if there really are no people who have the requisite level of general knowledge and particular experience to judge a newly considered category of works, we should be willing to dwell with those works long enough, attentively enough, and with enough commitment and care to let them develop in us the ability to respond well and truly. In doing so, we honor the advice of many writers and artists through the ages. T. S. Eliot wrote that his poems had to teach people how to read them, and Susan Van Dyne, working with faculty members on how to teach women's poetry, has suggested that "the poem in refusing to answer old questions can teach us what new questions to ask!"[5] And second, there is never complete ignorance even about what seem to denizens of the traditional academy to be new categories of works. There may be no, or few, art critics trained and practicing in the academy who know enough about quilts to be able to judge them, but many quilters can do so. Academic training is not the only kind of training, and academic and Western standards are not the only standards in the world.

The problem with including new kinds of works in the curriculum is not, then, that there is no way to judge them. It is, at least in part, that those who are qualified to judge may not be academics at all. That is hard for many academics to swallow, but it needs to be recognized. Efforts to make the curriculum more inclusive are indeed part of the effort to make whole societies more equitable and hence better able to choose what to value, whom to admire, whom to elect, even what to enjoy. There are experts of all sorts out there with whom those in the academy can enjoy mutual learning.

If we are to honor excellence and not merely exclusivity, and if we are to learn to make sensitive, appropriate judgments and not merely apply pre-existing rules, we cannot remain within closed circles. Judgments and the ways we make them need to be reflexively considered within a context of commitment to respectful openness and caring. The tradition I know best offers guidance in this quest. I have drawn on Plato's Socrates and Kant, along with John Dewey. I could also have quoted Jane Addams, Hannah Arendt, Katie Cannon, William James, and others, including Walt Whitman, the equality-besotted poet of democracy, and the Nobel Prize–winning Wislawa Szymborska, a poet dedicated to protecting the particular from the abstract (as so many poets are). Remembering the basic errors and the ways they are insinuated throughout the fabric of our lives is crucial. We must think ourselves free for ourselves although we do so with many, many others.

Even when we follow the contemporary shift toward valorizing narrative as well as deduction to move closer to genuine respect for individuals and particulars and/or turn to tales from other times and peoples, we find that some stories come to be paradigmatic, canonical, exemplary. Societies that did their teaching primarily through stories and examples in most cases were not less exclusive than those espousing more supposedly rational and abstract systems. There are few consistently helpful alternatives to dominant traditions; we are going to have to create weaves of our own from strands we can indeed find—not as completed utopian visions or tightly systemic ideologies, but as open processes of active engagement in thinking together. Fortunately, we can do that kind of thinking, and we do have many pasts to do it within our own presents. Our relationships with sources and resources can be ours to negotiate as respectful, thinking friends. Arendt, whose final work, unfinished when she died, was on judgment, wrote:

> This thinking, fed by the present, [may work] with the "thought fragments" it can wrest from the past and gather about itself. Like a pearl diver who descends to the bottom of the sea, not to excavate the bottom and bring it to light but to pry loose the rich and the strange, the pearls and the coral in the depths, and to carry them to the surface, this thinking delves into the depths of the past—but not to resuscitate it the way it was and to contribute to the renewal of extinct ages. What guides this thinking is the conviction that although the living is subject to the ruin of time, the process of decay is at the same time a process of crystallization, that in the depth of the sea, into which sinks and dissolves what once was alive, some things 'suffer a sea change' . . . as though they waited only for the pearl diver.[6]

# Equality

A curiously distorted notion of *equality* prevails in the dominant U.S. culture and works its way through our efforts to think well about "excellence and equity" in the curriculum, as well as political, social, and economic arenas. I have come to believe that, without a transformed understanding of equality and commitment to actualizing it, neither excellence nor judgment can be well comprehended.

Equality, one of the basic political principles and promises of the United States, has long been confused with sameness. To gain a hearing or achieve any recognition from the dominant few (and sometimes even from ourselves), women of all sorts, Black and Native American/Indian men, and others excluded from the "American promise" from the beginning have had to struggle first to prove that we are 'as good as'—in the sense of being the same as—those who excluded us. That political as well as intellectual distortion is one of the most glaring instances we have of the basic conceptual errors inherent in dividing humans from nature, and then by ranked 'kind' from each other, while simultaneously taking the few to be the inclusive term, the norm, and the ideal for all. It is that complex that forces the absurd choice between being the same as those who have excluded us and being different from them in a tradition in which the very differences at issue have been marked as deviance and deficiency.

We do not want to be the same *or* different: those are wrongly polarized abstract notions. None of us can actually be the same as anyone else, nor are any of us entirely different. The notion of equality exists precisely because humans are always both similar to and different from each other in infinitely complex ways and yet, at times, wish to speak and act together on intellectually, professionally, politically equalized grounds. We establish provisions and protections for equality (laws that protect free speech and the franchise for all citizens; procedural rules to which all are subject) precisely so we do not have to be the same before we can act and speak together, precisely so that whatever differences we have do not always and necessarily divide and wrongly rank us. Equality is specific: it is established externally and on purpose so that we may say, for example, "Before the law, all citizens are equal." That does not mean that all citizens are the same. That is so clearly untrue as to be absurd. What it does mean is that all that has been taken to mark us as the same or different can be held irrelevant for some purpose, with regard to some provision or standard or act or protection or intellectual inquiry. Very different works and voices can be given equal respect and attention in a class. They need not—and we precisely do not want them to be—all the same.

Provisions for equality allow us to make distinctions that are not pre-set or prejudicial but that are relevant and appropriate to a particular situation or set of considerations or principles. What equality means, what kind of distinctions it allows and disallows, differs according to the kind of situation for which we attempt to establish it. When we say, "We are all equal before death," we mean that death is such an imposing human reality that it can force us to disregard all other distinctions among us. When we say, "We want equal rights in the marketplace," we mean that we wish only *appropriate* discriminations to be made—perhaps those between people clearly possessing or not possessing essential skills for particular jobs, or between people able or not able to pay for a product—regardless of other differences, such as racialized gender. As a goal, then, "equal rights" does not ask us to disregard all distinctions—quite the contrary. To establish equality, and to protect it, we need to ascertain very carefully which distinctions must be recognized in order to be neutralized; which can be ruled entirely out of order; which may need to be privileged (if only temporarily) to allow all to start on an even footing (like giving racehorses different weights to carry). Equal rights is an enormously complex and changing goal; we simply frustrate and mislead ourselves when we assume that it has to do with absolute sameness, with blindness to all distinctions.[7]

To say, "Women should receive an education equal to that received by men," is therefore precisely not to say that women should receive either the same education as, or a different education from, the education men receive. It is to raise the question that has vexed the history of education in most cultures from the beginning—the question of which distinctions are and which are not relevant. It is not an equal education for women when we study a curriculum that excludes or devalues us, although such a curriculum is the same as that long studied by men. Black people, Indians, aboriginal peoples, disabled people entering institutions previously closed to them may have achieved access to the same education as that given to dominant-group people, but that did and does not make the education equal. Nor were we receiving an equal education when our curricula were different from those established for the 'right' kind of people. Then we were taught what some educators thought we should know to fulfill roles prescribed for us by a society premised on our continuing inequality, or what they thought we needed to know to become the same as those who were devaluing and excluding us. In neither case was the education designed to be equal to that provided for the dominant few. As in racialized societies, it gave us only the 'choice' of being pariahs or parvenus.

As Jane Roland Martin has pointed out, the philosophy of education has not demystified such 'equality.' Instead, it has taken these deformations into itself so that education-itself has been defined solely in masculinist terms. Either we see Rousseau's Sophie (or her equivalent in other cultures where women are defined by and for males and their use of us) educated in coquetry and guile in order to please (and manipulate) men, or we do not see her at all. (Rousseau's book is titled *Emile,* not *Emile and Sophie.*) Should we then *add* what Rousseau and his peers elsewhere prescribed for girls and women to the male curriculum? Hardly. Martin writes:

> When the educational realm embodies only male norms, it is inevitable that any women participating in it will be forced into a masculine mold. The question of whether such a mold is desirable for females needs to be asked, but it cannot be asked so long as philosophers of education assume that gender is a difference which makes no difference. The question of whether the mold is desirable for males also needs to be asked; yet when our educational concepts and ideals are defined in male terms, we do not think to inquire into their validity for males themselves.[8]

Only as we particularize what has been faultily universalized will we be able to make adequate judgments about what is and what is not appropriate for setting the terms for equality in differing realms. We can do so with the help of 'pearls' from the past that have "suffered a sea change." Plato, exploring through dialogue what might be needed to prepare for philosophical leaders, declared that sex is not a relevant criterion, even though he knew this statement would invite the "greatest wave [of opposition, of incredulous laughter] of all." We need not cast Plato as a champion of women's rights to be impressed with his care in making distinctions appropriately—distinctions that allowed him to avoid being trapped by some erroneous divisions by 'kind.'

Taking excellence to mean exclusivity and equality to mean sameness are related errors, and both serve to fend off the need to exercise responsibly appropriate, never certain, judgment. The persistence of such errors indicates that they work well within—and mystify—systems of meaning that take the few to be the whole, the norm, and the ideal so that the rest of humankind cannot be adequately comprehended. Arendt liked to say that our commonality as natal creatures (that is, that we are not only mortal, subject to death,

but natal, born to live) is that we are each unique and capable of new beginnings. Education, like politics, that tries to make us the same rather than equal
betrays that "paradoxical commonality" and the freedom for which it is a condition and of which it is a realization.

## Rationality, Intelligence—and Good Papers

I once suggested to students in one of my philosophy classes that they find whatever way they wanted to show me they had understood the text on which we
were working (Plato's *Republic*). I told them they could write a paper of the
kind with which they were already familiar or, alternatively, draw a diagram
showing how the central concepts in Plato's philosophy relate to each other;
write a short story about someone coming to Plato's Republic and trying to fit
in; make a list of what seemed clear to them and what did not; come and talk
with me about the text; prepare a short play presenting the important ideas;
or discuss with me other ways they would like to work. I received diagrams,
letters to friends about the book, regular papers, journal-type entries, and lists
of thoughts and questions. I also had several conversations with students who
were more comfortable talking. When I had discussed each student's presentation with her, we talked in class about translating the different modes of
expression into the conceptual form and language of the usual academic paper.
I then asked all of the students to write such a paper, drawing on their own,
more comfortable ways of thinking about the subject to help them through it.

The papers were significantly better than any I had received before. Had
I shown some of my colleagues the same students' earlier papers and the
papers written after the experiment, with names removed, I believe they
would have judged the second set of papers to be the products of "more intelligent" students. My experiment was designed to help me, and the students,
see how they really tended to understand, and then to help them work in the
one way for which they were most likely to be rewarded in higher education.
I believe one reason they did better on the second papers was that they felt
more confident simply because I had recognized that the academic paper
form is only one of many ways of achieving, expressing, and communicating fully 'rational' understanding.[9]

*Rationality* is a mystified concept (as was suggested earlier via Kant's and
Jefferson's judgments of the 'irrationality' of those whose mode of understanding differed from the one they recognized and valued). It has so many

meanings that even (or, perhaps, particularly) among philosophers, it is difficult to pin down, yet it has enormous prescriptive force. Students are supposed to be learning to be "more rational" through education, and that is understood to mean that they are becoming better citizens, even better people. To be labeled "irrational" is to be discredited. But, as the experience in my course indicates, there are many modes of thought and expression that are not irrational but simply different from the primary modes of expression of rationality valorized (usually in circular fashion) in schools.

I have worked with students and thinking friends whose strongest mode is one, some, or many of these and more: analytical, synthetic, factual, imaginative, holistic, atomistic, relational, argumentative, suggestive, symbolic, juxtapositional, oppositional, deductive, inductive, narrative, poetic, concrete, intuitive, abstract, totalizing, particularizing, dramatic. Each is capable, when working from her or his own strengths, of excellent, rational work. We pay a high price collectively as well as individually for 'training' so many wonderful minds into too few modes.

In the dominant culture of the West, a narrow view of what is rational has created educational systems that can make many of us feel inadequate and inept because our ways of thinking, of making sense, are not met, recognized, given external form, clarified, and returned to us refined and strengthened. Instead, too many people are made to feel "stupid." Their minds, their beliefs, their own most comfortable mode of expression tend to work differently from those defined as right and proper in school—even when they are common in other spheres. I have worked a great deal with older students returning to higher education. Time and again, I have heard painful stories of early experiences. And often, after I have given a philosophical talk, women (students, faculty members, members of the community) have said, "I always thought I would like philosophy, but when I took it as an undergraduate, I felt like a real failure." When we discuss what happened in those unfortunate classes, I hear that the professor intimidated students, argued with them, or seemed to delight in "putting [them] down," and that the students who did well were those who flourished in what these women felt to be a very unpleasant, combative arena. I always think of these stories when I notice yet again how often academics speak of good papers as "presenting a good argument"—the best of which establish an "impregnable" position. Is this militarized, masculinized picture really preferable to one of pregnable, fruitful thinking?

Especially in the so-called hard sciences, which stand at the pinnacle of intellectual respect, the more distanced the knower is from the known, the more 'pure' the knowledge produced is supposed to be. This is not the place for another critique of the currently dominant mode of science, but it is important to recognize that the liberal arts, as well as the dominant culture in general, are by no means free of the tradition that led not only to the development of modern science but to its near-apotheosis as the exemplar of human rationality. Every field shows recurrent indications of a craving for the apparent certainty, the "tough-mindedness,"of the sciences in contrast to the "soft" humanities, gendering attributions on which I am sure I do not need to comment. Many fields today suffer from hard-science envy.

Gayatri Spivak, Toril Moi, Monique Wittig, Nancy Miller, Alice Jardine, Chandra Talpade Mohanty, and others have joined the critique of a masculinized, colonial logos and done effective analyses of such "phallocentric reason" (a term that is offensive, or laughable, to some who do not even hear themselves saying "impregnable argument," "tough-minded," "penetrating analysis"). Feminist critiques also have other sources of support and inspiration. For example, in his introduction to *Philosophy Born of Struggle: Anthology of Afro-American Philosophy from 1917*, Leonard Harris reminds us that "philosophic texts, if products of social groups doggedly fighting to survive, are texts born of struggle. They must cut through the jungle of oppressive deeds to the accompanying labyrinth of words masking the nature of the deeds. Fraught with controversial intuitions that reflect the coming accepted beliefs of the new world, such texts challenge prevailing ways of viewing the world."[10] Those "controversial intuitions" are the product of active intelligences honed through 'book learning,' community conversations, and conflict, and they are invaluable in helping to demystify prevailing notions of rationality as well as other hegemonic definitions. The "intuitive," like the "irrational," has been defined in contradistinction to narrowly constructed notions of the "rational." But intuitive reason may also be open to less simplistic consideration. The ways we have of comprehending are many; why continue to restrict ourselves to so few?

Daniel del Castillo, choosing not to be thus restricted, has written of a project that transforms old divisive hierarchies into complementary resources:

> Before the French colonization of Mali in the 19th century, traditional medicine was the only type of treatment available. But during the colonial era it was officially banned, and healers moved underground to avoid detection and persecution.... Today ... Madani Traore, whose visage and manner convey a spiritual quality not evident among the academics, [works with teachers of Western medicine to train new healer/

doctors].... Mr. Diallo and his staff evaluate patients after their treatment and compare those results with statistics from patients treated with
Western medicine. "What we're finding is that there are diseases that traditional medicine is better at," he says. "Liver diseases, for example. We've
seen that plants often work better than commercial products. And psychiatric disorders as well; village healers are very effective at bringing the
community together for therapy. It's not just a matter of giving drugs."

According to Mr. Diallo, traditional healers play an extremely important role in Malian society, not the least through their ability to cure people who have crossed paths with evil.[11]

Not long ago, such a report written so respectfully would have been almost
unimaginable in a Western educational publication. The notion of "rational
scientific medicine" that underwrote *not* testing and comparing differing
spheres and kinds of healing but, rather, banning them and persecuting their
practitioners would have precluded it. Western rationality is not yet, but is
becoming more, pregnable.

However, *intelligence,* as the naturalized capacity for 'rationality,' is still often
narrowly understood to be what the IQ test tests, and the results of that test
have been used to mark entire groups not as different, but as inferior. There
is "extreme danger nested within seemingly scientific genetic explanations of
social inequality,"[12] danger of which we should be acutely aware, given the history of scientistic 'explanations' of the 'natural' inferiority of some 'kinds' of
people. Eugenics (the 'science' of human 'breeding' directed at "improving the
race") makes sharply evident that such constructions are compounded—
as gendered racializations always are—by hypersexualization of 'animalistic
inferiors' and consequent concern over their "prolific breeding." Both threaten
interpsychic and systemic control of sex/gendering exercised by dominant
males over "their" women, "those men," and their own 'lower' drives. That these
tangled old roots continue to have vitality was evident when Arthur Jensen,
Richard Herrnstein, and Hans Eysenck's works on genetics and intelligence
were published and received wide publicity in the 1970s: "Jensen, Herrnstein,
Eysenck and others have been trying, quite successfully, to resanctify the I.Q.
and intelligence testing as a measure of 'merit' and as a predictor of social and
economic success."[13]

But relatively few are aware of this history, entangled as it is with the
deadly eugenics movement that was interwoven in the United States with
anti-immigrant fears, ongoing racialization, scorn for and anxiety aroused

by people branded physically and mentally "abnormal" and "degenerate." Eugenics found its apotheosis in Hitler's Germany, where it provided 'scientific' justification for the elimination of "degenerate" people(s) and for Dr. Mengele's infamous 'experiments.' William Ryan writes:

> Historians of intelligence testing rarely give a very accurate view of the early years of the I.Q. movement, led by such now-canonized psychologists as Lewis Terman, Robert Yerkes, and Henry Goddard. At the time the intelligence test was translated from Binet's humanitarian and vehemently anti-genetic views of intellectual processes. The leaders of the American testing movement were also among the leaders of the Eugenics movement. They were, at the time, terribly agitated about the "immigration problem," which meant, to them, a flooding into the country of genetically inferior "races" (the term they used for national and ethnic groups) who would pollute and degrade the American "breeding stock" (they really did talk that way, as if they were the proprietors of a herd of cattle), hitherto made up largely of the descendants of the obviously "genetically superior races" of Northern Protestant Europe.... Terman [1916] suggested that children of these genetically inferior "races," ... "should be segregated in special classes.... They cannot master abstractions, but they can often be made efficient workers.... There is no possibility at present of convincing society that they should not be allowed to reproduce, although, from a eugenic point of view they constitute a grave problem because of their unusually prolific breeding....
>
> The restrictive immigration laws of the 1920's were a direct result of the I.Q. movement and were the direct cause, fifteen years later, of the shameful refusal of the United States to admit hundreds of thousands of Jewish refugees from Hitler.
>
> What began as pseudoscientific research into the genetic determination of I.Q. scores—in what passed for laboratories in Stanford, Harvard, and other famous American universities—was ultimately played out in the gas chambers and cremation ovens of Auschwitz, Dachau, and Belsen.[14]

In its less evidently deadly uses, definition of intelligence by scores on the IQ test also impoverishes everyone's understanding of intelligence. Children grow up knowing about IQ tests (and ACT tests, SATs, and so on). It is almost impossible to convince them that these products simply assess their ability to take a particular kind of test, that they cover only particular skills that have been isolated as having to do with a particular kind of success in particular kinds of institutions. People of all ages believe that their intelligence is being tested when they take IQ tests—as if we know all that intelligence might be. Thanks to work by Howard Gardner and others, Western educators are now trying to be more open to differing kinds of intelligence, but we have a long way to go before the full range of human capacities and the kinds of knowledge they create have been mapped (if they can be, which I do not believe: minds are infinitely complex, capable of thinking even about themselves and thereby remaining free).

Mystification of the moral as well as of the intellectual consequences of apparently neutral systems of definition and explanation has kept us from such explorations. In the United States, great civilizations such as those of the Yoruba and the Jaina, among many others, have been seen as 'primitive'—meaning illogical, less than fully rational—and their people as less intelligent. Of course, not only are there other systems of logic in the world—in the sense of systematized descriptive and prescriptive sets of statements about how reason works—but they deserve our serious attention. Consider an example in which I have found students to be profoundly interested once they get past their initial skepticism. Jaina thinkers—who have a seven-pointed logic, not the two-point logic with its law of excluded middle that characterizes the Western tradition—had their greatest influence in Gujarat, the area in India from which Gandhi came. It is not surprising that Gandhi was able to develop his philosophy and practice of non-violence by bringing many different Indian traditions together with what he learned of the West. He was nurtured in a culture that prepared him to think syncretistically, not exclusively.

In the Jaina system, as A. L. Basham describes it, "there were not merely the two possibilities of existence and non-existence, but seven." The seven are derived by bringing into the place of the Western excluded middle (in this context, "something either is or is not") a third possibility: that in one aspect something is, but in another it is not. That possibility allows us to recognize that existence has—or, in any case, has for us humans—aspects, and that those aspects do not need to be scraped off, as it were, to obtain significant knowledge about it. Another possibility is that something exists, "but its nature is otherwise indescribable."[15] There is, then, also a recognition of limitations on human knowledge; it cannot encompass all. We need not go into the technicalities of various logics to see why this one is appealing. As I understand it, the familiar story of the blind people describing an elephant is of Jaina origin.

The lesson of the story is that the one who, feeling the tail, thinks an elephant is like a rope is not wrong unless she or he thinks she or he is right and that that is all the elephant is. The one who, feeling the leg, thinks the elephant is like a tree is not wrong unless she or he thinks that is all the elephant is. And so on. This is not a story that promotes relativism. The point is not that each of the blind people is right, nor is it that all are wrong, and so there is no knowledge of the elephant on which they can or must agree. The point is (I believe) that knowledge requires multiple perspectives, and that even apparently incompatible models or metaphors can provide part of the picture—if we can give up the notion that only one paradigm can or must rule.

Along these lines, it may and may not be true that women learn, understand, relate differently from men, as works such as those by Carol Gilligan, Mary Field Belenky and her colleagues, and Nell Noddings suggest, although these authors are careful not to claim that modes of knowing and responding are either sex-determined or consistent across historical, contextualized genderings. It seems likely that many humans think well and effectively in ways that differ in some aspects from ways that are established as normative and/or ideal but are not necessarily or entirely *less* rather than *differently* "rational." Again, this need not collapse us into a relativism that allows for no judgment about, no guidance for, better reasoning. One of the reasons for the stunning popularity of works that suggest differing 'voices,' differing ways of being 'intelligent' is no doubt that they strike a powerfully resonant chord among people whose minds have not been judged or nurtured in the light of nuanced descriptions that make recognizing and evaluating differing aspects of complex human minds possible. These books are widely popular and frequently cited in part, I think, because of their courageous efforts to ask the question: What does reason, what does intelligence, look like when we put women or differing cultural traditions at the center, as feminists and multiculturalists suggest? What would we learn about alternative ways humans have now, and always have had, of being rational, of learning, of understanding, relating, being moral?

It has been suggested that any effort to say what women, or whole other cultures, are like risks perpetuating the old errors that result from faulty universalization (or essentialism). Women are by no means all alike, not only across but within cultures and subcultures. That is one problem. Another is that the ways of reasoning, of knowing, of judging depicted in these books, precisely insofar as they may be general (if not universal), may derive from the general oppression of women. That is, what we find by studying "the

woman's voice" *now* may not only not be *the* woman's voice; it may specifically not be *the,* or *a,* voice that we would be hearing had women not been
oppressed so systematically for so long. The debate about these works is complex and important, but here I will note only that their popularity in and of
itself may be significant, because it tells us that many of us are deeply hungry
for public recognition of ways of thought different from the few that have been
in the ascendancy. I will also note that, as Sara Ruddick shows in *Maternal
Thinking: Toward a Politics of Peace,* we may indeed need to find the suppressed voices not just to make ourselves feel better, or to change education,
or even to enrich our understanding of 'rationality,' but to make the peace we
must have if we are to survive on this earth.[16] For that essential effort, differing generalizations drawn from differing populations are surely useful. They
provide alternatives where we have had too few, whether we are thinking for
ourselves or seeking help in comprehending and thinking with differing others. Horizonal universals that we glimpse beyond many such generalizations
may also be helpful—again, not as things we can *know,* but as ideas we can
think, as we can think of an aspirational ideal of justice that is not and can
never be realized in any particular set of laws, institutions, or practices.[17]

Circular, self-referential, and self-justifying meanings of reason need to be
particularized if we are to think afresh and more freely about thinking, about
knowing. But, as we have seen, many respond to the effort to particularize as
if Reason Itself were under attack. It is not. What is put in question is the insistence that any one historical definition of and set of 'laws' for Reason-Itself
should be taken to be the inclusive kind, the norm, and the ideal for that infinitely rich gift in its many aspects. Among those aspects is the reflexive turn
that makes it possible to think about any conclusions from 'outside,' thereby
holding open the space of freedom to go on thinking.

But here we should recall that we are exploring *mystified* concepts, which
raises particular kinds of questions. In this vein, I suggest that the narrow view
of reason we find functioning in (rather than consciously held by) many academics (among others) has served some purposes in the world, whatever its
merit or lack thereof to epistemologists and logicians. Among other things, a
tightly prescriptive, narrow definition has worked effectively to allow the dominant few in the Western tradition to brand others "irrational." In a tradition
that has taken rationality to be *the* characteristic of the truly, fully human—
and, in influential schools of thought such as the Kantian, also of the possibility of being ethical, or a "moral subject" or "citizen"[18]—this move has had
very serious consequences. As Aristotle said, slaves and, in different ways, 'free'

women, being less rational than free men, *need* to be ruled—and, the European colonial tradition added, the "Dark Continent" *needs* to have 'enlightened' rule imposed. Conquest, rule, mastery are all well served by a notion of reason that is both narrow and absolutized. When one has said, "That's an irrational idea," one has exempted oneself not only from asking whether it is true, but also from considering whether it is personally, socially, politically, morally meaningful; expressive of a significant, sharable experience; or indicative of someone's good-faith effort to remedy a situation. One need not ask, for example, when thus defended, whether that which now seems "irrational" is perhaps born of an "intuition" of a "new world."[19] The irrational, judged as such against a particular definition of "rational," is not the same as the *anti*-rational— although it may be *anti* an imposed status ordering of 'kinds' of people.

## Liberal Arts

In practice, the liberal arts tend to be defined by a list of standing disciplines which these days includes some of the new interdisciplinary fields. In both the particular fields and in the liberal arts generally, that kind of operational definition serves to encapsulate, to protect what is against questioning. Conceptions of the liberal arts that tend to hide the old errors that perpetuate the articulated hierarchy from which they sprang can thereby be mystified.

In liberal-arts institutions, studio courses—*doing* courses of any kind— are still barely recognized. Or, if they are recognized, they often are not given full liberal-arts standing (despite the increasing emphasis on 'practicality,' "engaged scholarship," and "preparing for the workforce"). Technical schools are considered, if not openly called, intellectually inferior. Those divisions reflect histories of upper-class/caste privileges. In the West, they perpetuate the privileged, male, Greek (largely Athenian) division between those who use reason and lead a life devoted to it and to public life, and those who work with their hands or are otherwise privatized. Elsewhere, the higher reaches of education (and sometimes all education) have been restricted, for example, to mandarin males, to upper-caste Hindu males. That self-justifying division (self-justifying in both theory and practice: those who are denied education because of their 'kind' are then 'shown' to be "less rational" or "intelligent" than those who received it) has more or less persisted through colonialism, "modernization," and revolutions.

Rey Chow notes, for example, that "as one of the most oppressed sections of Chinese society, [women] get short shrift on both ends [of struggles for national liberation]: Whenever there is a political crisis, they stop being woman" for the sake of a 'larger' solidarity. But "when the crisis is over and the culture rebuilds itself, they resume their more traditional roles as wives and mothers as part of the concerted effort to restore order."[20] And, as Martin puts it, even the division between liberal-arts and technical schools (in many countries now) is only between kinds of "productive" knowledge; neither takes into account the "reproductive" knowledge that has long been considered appropriate only to women.[21] It is as if we still believe that "those who do, do not think, and those who think, do not do." An updated version of this bizarre division is familiar: "Those who can, do; those who can't, teach." (A still more recent addition has it that "those who can do neither, consult.") Then many profess to worry about the ethics of professionals and of citizens, They claim to be—and often are—bewildered that teaching people about something does not seem to make them good at it, in the technical *or* the ethical, political sense of "good."

Professional graduate schools in business, law, and medicine tend to combine practice with theory in ways that are rarely encountered in the less openly professional, liberal-arts Ph.D.-granting schools that prepare researchers, who most likely will be employed as professors. But it is in nursing schools that one finds serious attention paid to the care of human beings, and it is in the training of elementary-school teachers that one is likely to find open admission of the fact that teachers need to be able to practice their art with and for the benefit of students (rather than doing their most important work primarily for the 'community of scholars' or for those who pay for it). The 'higher' the profession in the articulated hierarchy, the less emphasis it places on practice *or* care—and the smaller the proportion in it of women and men who have traditionally been 'lower' in the hierarchy of power.

In the United States, a subtradition of educational thought has long struggled to undo the curious separations that derive from old class/caste. gendered, racialized/ethnicized hierarchies. Oberlin College's motto, "To Learn and to Work," stands as a striking reminder of that subtradition, as does the continuing, if sadly no longer very influential. progressive education tradition. John Dewey, Carter G. Woodson, Alexander Meiklejohn, W.E.B. DuBois, Maria Montessori, Anna Julia Cooper, Sylvia Ashton-Warner, Paulo Freire, Ivan Illich, and others still inspire some to try to bridge the gap in education between knowing and doing, and between the liberal and the civic arts. Feminist educators are attempting to undo the gender mystifications built into even some progressive views.

But most educators involved in higher education continue to hold a peculiar notion of the liberal arts. It is assumed that the liberal arts liberate; that they counter human limitations and enrich human abilities. But can they do so while we retain the old, monistic hierarchy, which, despite the pairing of terms, does not create mind and body, knowledge and action, theory and practice as equal (even if 'separate')? They certainly cannot do so as long as those paired terms continue to reflect the errors we have been exploring—errors in which the 'lower' human activities and functions are defined as appropriate to women and lower-caste men and thus as 'improper' for the educated 'free man' (at least until a skill has become highly profitable, as, for example, 'technical' knowledge of computers has). To help liberate humankind from past prejudices and beliefs that derived from and justified the assignment of physical and daily maintenance work to lower-caste people, we need to know much more about all that truly makes life possible and humane, from mothering[22] to community building, surviving with imagination and dignity intact in deprivation and poverty, and working with our hands with art and integrity.

The "liberal" in liberal arts was never intended to mean "liberating" except insofar as the arts that were taught 'liberated' some men from concern for mundane, useful, caretaking concerns—which is also to say, from their implication with women and men who labored with their bodies, as well as from their 'othered' natural self—ostensibly so they could give their full attention to 'higher' things. The history of the liberal-arts curriculum in America is one of struggle between such 'higher,' 'classical,' and (originally) theologically oriented learning designed to preserve the past and prepare ministers, teachers, scholars for the future, and pressures exerted on it to educate men for the professions and according to the "new learning" emerging from the European 'Enlightenment.' Throughout, however, higher education continued in its role of preparing those who were preselected as the right 'kind' to hold positions of power. As Frederick Rudolph writes of one period of some change:

> By the time this course of study had moved out of the medieval university, passed through the universities of Renaissance and Reformation England, and landed in the American forest, much had happened. A broadened view of letters and language, knowledge appropriate to the

responsible use of leisure, and an interest in Greece and the Greeks before
they fell into Latin translation entered. . . . What had been a curriculum
for theologians now carried the burden of training a governing class of
gentlemen and men of action.[23]

Over and over again through this history we see the proponents of the liberal arts trying to ward off subjects and concerns that would, they thought,
lower that 'high' calling by making the course of study suspiciously useful for
any other kind of life or inclusive of troubling new views (let alone new people). Mathematics, for example, was long considered "a slight remnant of the
ancient quadrivium," and therefore teachable, but nevertheless "of use to
mechanics but of no value to gentlemen, scholars, and men of affairs."[24] Yet
it was in these schools and programs that attention was to be paid to questions of meaning, of worth and character, in ways neither required nor expected
of those designed specifically to teach skills to men who could expect to have
no leisure for the scholarly life, the life of the gentleman, or civic leadership.
The liberal arts that descended from the education of gentlemen still carry
within them the errors that exclusiveness and snobbishness built into them.
Yet it is to the liberal arts that we turn today to show and promote concern
for the "enduring questions" of human life and meaning.

The problem is not that no one in the liberal arts cares about either the
enduring questions or the questions that press so hard on us today. They/we
do, and despite the persistence of the old errors, there is, of course, great richness within traditions of 'higher' education in the liberal arts. The problem is
that those who teach 'useful' skills are neither prepared for nor expected to be
concerned with anything other than the technical training they offer, while
those whom we expect to do more often are too narrowly 'trained' in our disciplines. Professionalization has entered the liberal arts, too. Undergraduates
are basically offered entrance-level training to the academic disciplines in the
devout hope that they will continue through graduate school (thereby becoming qualified to become professional professors). At the same time, too little
is being done to bring into all curricula the new learning of this age, which
raises anew, and differently, fundamental questions about what it means and
ought to mean to be human. These are issues that should press us all beyond
concern for "training" any kind of professionals—including professionals in
the new fields themselves.

A transforming education is surely one that does more than 'train' professionals of any stripe; more than "prepare an educated workforce" (even one

in a "global marketplace"); more even than "lay the groundwork for lifelong learning," at least while 'learning' is in so many senses narrowly understood and so often conflated with "mastery." As we open to more and different wisdom traditions, more ways of thinking, perhaps we can find horizonal visions that help us hold all knowledges in perspective as contributions to ongoing quests for meaningful lives for all people and peoples.

## Woman

Mystified meanings of *woman* are deeply related to almost all central expressions of dominant cultures. Constructed meanings of woman, thought through, can thus reveal articulated power hierarchies not only in their broad outlines but also in their most intimate expressions, because women—and/or tropes, signs, and significations of the female/feminine—are found in almost all groups and activities of cultures and polities. Where women are not to be found, prohibitions against women/females/the feminine are, revealing that the exclusive group, the masculinized activity, depends on sex/gender exclusion for its own meaning. Think of highly sexualized depictions of women in male-only or male-dominated barracks and camps, dormitories, workplaces; the female muse inspiring male artists when women could not be artists; "Lady Liberty" holding her torch at the entrance to New York Harbor; depictions of females meant to inspire male revolutionaries; the female figure holding the scales that depicts justice. Yet we live in a world in which it must still be proclaimed that "Women's rights are human rights." This discrepancy reveals starkly that Man and Human have been conflated, pushing Woman out and down the slippery slope of human worth and power.

Women were not the subject matter or central issue of any academic field before women's studies, but women have indeed been thought about. All that I have said about the exclusion of women, physically and conceptually, as valued contributors to the human story does not mean that nothing has been thought or written about Woman by the men who defined and maintained dominant cultures and institutions. On the contrary: Woman has been used as the delimiting boundary for meanings of Man and so has been present even when apparently absent. As Spinoza noted, everything is what it is by not being something else (technically phrased as "all determination is negation").[25] Stunningly often, Woman has been that "something else," that which almost everything and everyone defined as dominant is not to be.[26]

The now familiar problem is that that which pertained to Woman was thought about within systems and in terms that made it impossible to think well, let alone accurately, adequately, and in ways appropriate to women rather than to a few men's prescriptive conceptions of us. Woman has been Man's Other. Because of the ways in which he was defined, Woman had to be mystified as that from which Man issued; that for which he continued to yearn and came to desire; that from which he had to distinguish himself; that which he denied in himself; that through which he symbolized origins (the Earth goddess, Mother of god[s], fertility goddesses). Woman thus figured for him yearnings and desires to be satisfied, life forces (female figures with cornucopias, pornography), and their obverse of renunciation, 'purity,' annihilation (virginal religious and culture figures; Kali, goddess of destruction and creation in India). Woman also figured the forbidden (veiled, sequestered women; women 'marked' as 'belonging' to 'higher' males—for example "ladies"). Woman had no meaning of her own, no real and positive identity or subjectivity in dominant systems, and this ongoing negation was perpetuated through physical enforcement and conceptual, symbolic mystifications.

Keeping women lumped together under the concept *woman* kept us, in all our extraordinary diversity, available to be the Other for the faultily abstracted, singular, universal Man. Thus, the singularity and universality implied by "Woman" (unlike that implied by "Man") did not fill the concept with relevant meaning; it meant that it was empty of meaning, only negative. V. Y. Mudimbe notes a similar (I would say isomorphic—that is, similar in form/formation) phenomenon in European men's constructions of "the African" and "Africa." "From Herodotus on, the West's self-representations have always included images of people situated outside of its cultural and imaginary frontiers," Mudimbe writes, outsiders who were "nonetheless imagined and rejected as the intimate and other side of the European-thinking subject." To be dominant Man's Other is to be, with and like Woman, available for mystified "paternalistic" abuse.[27]

At the same time (and again, not unlike Africa as imagined by European men), Woman was thereby defined as "for Man" as well as "not Man," and that complicated matters. The men creating and working within gendered meaning systems held that Woman referred directly back to biology, to nature. She was not Man and yet was properly available for the satisfaction of his 'natural' needs. *A Feminist Dictionary* notes: "The word *woman,* and its etymological companion, *wife,* have together received from the English etymologists an astonishing number of interpretations, most of them based on the presumed sexual or domestic function of women."[28] Thus, women are turned into the empty, singular, universal Woman, who is not Man, and then are reattached to men through sexual/reproductive and related domestic functions. It is worth remembering that "husband" is a verb as well as a noun and that it means to cultivate, to manage, to administer. Men can *husband* their resources; women cannot *wife* theirs, because, of course, as women/wives we are that which is cultivated, managed, administered (along with men's animals and fields, the other primary objects of "husbandry"). Sherri Ortner's early article "Is Woman to Nature as Man Is to Culture?" explored some of the meanings of this lack of parallelism between Man and Woman, husband and wife, and culture and nature.[29]

Woman is alien to Man, Other than Man, and yet—and so—essential to men on all levels, from the intellectual to the physical; the political to the privatized domestic; the imaginary erotic to the actually procreative. Man needs her, yet he cannot acknowledge mutual implication with her. Is it any wonder that misogyny and homophobia are so often expressions of dominant cultures—are, indeed, the intimately related obverse of prescriptive, mystifyingly romanticized heterosexuality?

In strongly masculinist societies that are informed by and depend on mystifications of Woman, it is obviously risky for males to see, think about, and take into moral account real women as individuals, or even as a familiar group. It is no mere coincidence that thinking about the moral standing of devalued males and animals has posed similar risks. Moral standing has been restricted to those who are of the defining 'kind.' This has led to a surfeit of troubled consciences that, too often, has brought about not change on the systemic level (of institutions or conceptualizations) but, rather, more guilt and/or shame. A dominant group member who "went soft," who "went Native," who opposed animal vivisection because of real experiences with and attachment to 'lesser' beings revealed his untrustworthiness and was written off as "unsound." His 'failure' stood as a warning to others.

When the 'obviousness' of sex differences is adduced to explain hierarchical gender constructs (or even to revalue them, as in works by Julia Kristeva), it is worth remembering that humans differ physically in a great many ways. There are all sorts of variations within and across any selected category of differentiation (skin color, shape of features, height, hair color and texture). Physical attributes also change through time. We may be particularly interested in reproduction, evolutionary processes being as they are, but reproduce is hardly all that we do, and the desire to reproduce is not solely, or even often, the determinant of whether, when, where, how, with whom, to what result we copulate. Desire always exceeds possibilities and complex codings of acceptability in human cultures. It cannot be real physical differences that account for—as distinguished from figuring, symbolizing, signifying—cultural and political inequalities; nor is being an egg bearer or sperm bearer sufficient to explain the division of humans into two kinds that are considered fundamental from birth to death (and beyond—even the deceased, who are hardly able to reproduce, are still said to be either male or female). In all cultures, a prior move ("prior" conceptually and historically) has selected from among human characteristics those that are to be focused on to establish and justify the prescribed—rather than given—physical markers used in the service of inequalities.[30] In short, however important physiological sexual differentiations are, they are not 'by nature' always the same; always equally evident; always relevant; always functional; always significant. It does not require that we pretend they do not exist or matter at all to refuse to give them self-evident, 'natural' priority over so many other differentiations. Demystifying them enables us to sort out and retrieve what is indeed useful.

Once the quest for 'natural' warrants for a two-sex social construction focused on appearance; today it seeks its warrant from invisible genes and biochemistry. But searching for something that proves "we just are naturally male and female" is pointless. Millennia of gender hierarchies can hardly be explained by something (like genes) that only contemporary, technology-assisted scientists can 'see' and have knowledge about. However, in pushing women down on his monistic scale of real, significant humanity, man has created the need for some fierce dualisms to mystify what is going on. For man-who-is-not-woman, significant personhood and physical being were split apart, leaving men with various versions of the infamous mind–body problem to think about in the studies and schools from which women were excluded, lest the thinker be distracted from his 'higher' cogitations.

At present, the category *human* is filled with notions derived from the privileged few males who have defined their cultures over time. Once those notions have been honestly particularized, the category may reveal itself as empty (a suggestion Foucault also famously made, albeit on different grounds). It will then become the exciting work of new generations to begin to rethink it. But we cannot, I believe, *know* what it is to be human. That would require that we know ourselves as objects, a knowledge contradicted from the very beginning by the fact that it is we who are subjects of our own knowledge, as well as by the surely obvious observation that, in knowing ourselves, we thereby change the knower and the known. What we know when we know ourselves is, at best, what has been, not what is at the moment and what is always coming to be. But that does not mean that we cannot *think* about meanings of Woman/women, Man/men, along with other ways of human being that have always refused that divisive hierarchy, watching out for dangerous mystifications of particular meanings every step of the way.

# Sex

Analyses of meanings of *sex, sexuality, reproduction,* and *gender* have moved far beyond the crucial early feminist distinction between sex (as a biological given) and gender (as a sociocultural prescriptions, earlier called "sex roles"). Sexualities, now in the plural, are not taken to be the same as, or to be fully contained within or expressed by, sex, and reproductive capacities and experiences can be distinguished from both. We face a complex tangle of meanings, desires, actions, experiences, values here, and each and all can also be analyzed as being prescribed and regulated in ways that differ across histories and cultures, within and across class and caste and ethnic and racialized groups. And, of course, prescribed sex/genderings can be transgressed in ways that challenge but can also reinscribe the rules.

So how is sex mystified? Could we count the ways? Certainly not in their particular forms, which range from association with just about everything human to fiercely marking the boundaries of meanings of *human.* Is sex a mark of our "fallen" nature such that, if we are not strong enough to renounce it, we must at least radically contain it? Is it a human experience of transcendence of self through love and union with another, perhaps prefiguring a sacred love and union? Is it the animal in us that we are called to 'humanize' lest we become "no better than the dumb beasts"? Or whatever we think and feel sex to be, is it really no more than evidence of the workings of evolution via "selfish genes" that "select" bearers of other genes to use for their own continuation?

Cultures, religions, sciences tell us authoritatively (albeit variously) what we are and are not and relate those prescriptive definitions to more openly prescriptive codes concerning what we should and should not do. They do this work with striking inventiveness when it comes to sex. Rites and rituals; arts and sciences; mores, morals, ethics; regulations and laws; celebrations and punishments—sex has been and is one of the prime subjects and objects of them all. So much attention should suggest that, however 'natural' sex is, we are dealing with human constructs that carry very high stakes indeed.

Fascinating. It would be a lifetime's work to decode even some of that. However, since our concern now is with conceptualizations that reflect, reinforce, and perpetuate unjust systems of dominance, our question actually is not, What is (or are) the meaning(s) of sex? It is, rather, How does all this (hard not to say "fevered") generation of meanings that reflect and reinforce many systems do the work of dividing and ranking us? How is dominance of the few mystified by all this elaborate, fierce attention to sex?

Here is one sort of inquiry that those questions suggests. Kathy Peiss, who focuses on feminist analysis of class, writes:

> Reformers, social workers, and journalists viewed working-class women's sexuality through middle-class lenses, invoking sexual standards that set "respectability" against "promiscuity." . . . Chastity was the measure of young women's respectability, and those who engaged in premarital intercourse, or, more importantly, dressed and acted as though they had, were classed as promiscuous or prostitutes. Thus labor investigations of the late nineteenth century [in the United States] not only surveyed women's wages and working conditions, but delved into the issue of their sexual virtue, hoping to resolve scientifically the question of working women's respectability.[31]

Dominance in its many formations has been backed up by notions of *respectability*, a term that strikingly bridges the supposedly private, intimate act of sex and the public realm where friends and strangers relate to each other and, in doing so over time, create reputations. When we pause to reflect on what they are and what work they do, we realize that reputations provide some semblance of control via stories that suggest continuities. They are a kind of story that allows others among whom we have been acting to take into consideration what and who we revealed ourselves to be in the past when they need to understand or evaluate us in the present. This is useful, even essential, in making the uncertain decisions that we face in public life. If I know that a very persuasive speaker has a reputation for lying, for serving the interests of groups to which I am opposed, for being determined to retain power rather than follow principles, I can assess what is said by that person better. In some cultures and subcultures, deals are made "with no more than a promise and a handshake," which tells us just how strong and functional their concern for reputations is.

Well and good. But while none of us can entirely control the stories told by observers that establish our reputations, some of us have far less scope of action in the first place, far less leeway even within the imposed limits, and very few, if any, opportunities to undo the reputations that more powerful others give us. Other people set the terms and judge us by those terms, and can therefore "ruin" our reputations, to disastrous effect. In 2003, U.S. news reports on the reopening of schools for girls in Afghanistan often included statements that daughters' reputations were at risk if they attended. Since their families' reputations, as well as the lives of the girls, were at risk, many of them were kept at home. Those who have been privatized, as females so persistently have in many eras and cultures, must not even appear in public. This means that we literally cannot be seen as individuals, that we are subjected to a collective identity that we must not breach by any act that "draws attention" to who we might really be.

When women went "out to work" in the United States, they became subjected to a constant need to protect their reputations for "chastity." Men, the 'proper' denizens of the public realm, did not have such worries about their reputations. But women's imposed, prescriptive identities had to do with their sex, and their sexuality, reproductive and nurturant capacities were defined in relation to the men who made use of them. Women could and did lose their reputations for "respectability" not only on the basis of acts that were forbidden to "good women," but because of how they "looked," how they appeared as judged by others applying prejudicial, inadequate categories in circular fashion. Loss of "respectability" carried a high price. It made those denied it still more vulnerable to what we now call sexual harassment in school and at work and, if they tried to say no, to loss of jobs. Being given a "bad reputation," then, left women unable to support themselves—and, in a double-whammy, unable to wed men who would support them. So it needs to be said that women could be forced to become the "loose women" and prostitutes they were already called, a prime case of mystified circular reasoning that is taken, perversely, to prove its own premises. Thus does sex, mystified as a criterion for respectability, keep females dependent on and available to dominant males.

Race, as always, compounds the situation. White men have sexually violated women whose racialization made it impossible for them to be seen as "respectable" by the dominant few, no matter what they did or did not do. Black women's struggles to lay any claim to "virtue" have been essential to liberation efforts (as seen in works by DuBois and Anna Julia Cooper). The history of slavery in the United States is a history of sexual violation that starkly reveals the old, ranked divisions between "man and animal" that mystify sexualized racisms. Barbara Omolade writes: "The racial patriarchy of the white man enabled him to enact his culture's separation between the goodness, purity, innocence, and frailty of woman with the sinful, evil strength and carnal knowledge of woman by having sex with white women who came to embody the former and black women who came to embody the latter."[32]

Poor "white" women have also been seen by those who exploited them as more sexual than privileged women, who were then blamed for being 'asexual' or "cold" and for 'driving' privileged men to turn to those 'lower' women. It is stunning how consistently those who have been *most exploited* have also been defined as *most sexual* by their exploiters. When intimacy is so distorted by public systems, it can hardly remain unaffected. It is hard here not to think of "obscenities" that dot common speech—for instance, "Fuck you!" which reveals the linking of sex and violative submission, shaming, tainting. Consider, too, all the insulting swear words that refer to female genitalia.

From another angle—that of psychoanalysis—Jessica Benjamin writes about "the violence of erotic domination . . . the strange union of rationality and violence that is made in the secret heart of our culture and sometimes enacted in the body." She continues: "This union has inspired some of the holiest imagery of religious transcendence and now comes to light at the porno newsstands, [where it is evident that] the slave of love is not always a woman, nor always a heterosexual; the fantasy of erotic domination permeates all sexual imagery in our culture. This rational violence mingles love with issues of control and submission."[33] The most taboo acts and subjects come together with the most reverential reaches for transcendence; both have been revelatory of human desires so informed and deformed by mystified but commonplace injustices that it is impossible to know what, and how, human psyches and spirits and bodies might otherwise desire.

Another approach: Simone de Beauvoir, considering what it has meant to become a woman, "the second sex," famously observed that, while Man could and did seek transcendence, Woman was locked into immanence. This is the same hierarchical scheme we keep encountering in which mind/spirit/Man is both ranked above and pitted against body/matter/Woman. Superiority is then related to dominance, and dominance becomes invested with both desire for transcendence and repugnance for the material, the real, the immanent in a recipe for violation, for violence.

A *New York Times* reporter tells a story about a man who runs rehabilitative sessions for men charged with violence against their partners: "At the end of one 26-week class, one of [the] men asked if he could hug [the group leader, who was] taken aback. He doesn't really do hugging. He asked the man why. The man told him that he had never before met a powerful man who wasn't abusive. [The group leader] hugged him."[34] It is a touching and promising story but perhaps risky in its familiar suggestion that public policy should be directed toward providing more rehabilitation programs for individuals rather than also undertaking to change the systems that have so betrayed us all.

Nurturing care obviously needs to be retrieved as a valued human quality. To do so will require releasing it from assignment only to the weak, the dependent, the privatized—the feminized.[35] Knowledge of humans that leaves out of consideration the essential activities that sustain life is historically congruent with all those imposed strictures on women's "respectability." So women acting to claim public rights also carry the complex and dangerous burden of demystifying sex in all its implications with power.[36]

For other analysts—those who 'read' the world's realities as texts in which meanings are always already encoded and complexly inter-referential—change is taken to require better interpretations. Eve Sedgwick writes: "Before we can fully achieve and use our intuitive grasp of the leverage that sexual relations seem to offer on the relations of oppression we need more . . . daring and prehensile applications of our present understanding of what it may mean for one thing to signify another."[37] For her and those working along similar lines, sexuality *is* signification. This is obviously a long way from taking sex to be a physiological, natural given that, though it seems so simple, may be the most mystified meaning of all.

Along those lines, Judith Butler writes approvingly that "the loss of gender norms [that create] the 'real' and the 'sexually factic' . . . would have the effect of proliferating gender configurations, destabilizing substantive identity, and depriving the naturalizing narratives of compulsory heterosexuality of their central protagonists: 'man' and 'woman.'"[38] Whether or how such a project is desirable or to be feared is hard to say, given how deep, various, and widespread the evidence is that human societies found themselves on their own narratives of sex. Nevertheless, for far too many people who are known as women; for far too many people who are known as deviants, perverts, unnatural; and for all those who have been sexually vulnerable and violated in established systems of dominance, the older ways can hardly be considered 'safe,' 'realistic,' or desirable, either. Demystifying normalized sex insofar as it is evidently serving eroticized dominance seems essential, and devastatingly overdue.

# Man

Central to what I have been saying is, of course, that *Man* has been a mysti-fied concept that entangles us in all of these, and many other, ways. How odd it is, when we think about it, that in some dominant traditions it can be very difficult to think about men *qua* males, even though women are always thought of as females. This evening, on the news, I saw film footage of an angry anti-U.S. demonstration in a largely Muslim country. The commentator reported the number of people in the streets; mentioned their religion; gave some back-ground about their history—and never once observed that the "people" shown were apparently all men and boys. Had thousands of girls and women been in the streets, that would have been central to the news. They would not have been seen as and referred to solely as "people." That is the result of the basic error: if the 'kind' Man is also to be used as the inclusive term for humankind, then Man cannot be admitted to be male in any real, particular—that is, lim-ited and precisely *not* all-inclusive—sense.

If Man's particularity as male, which is at once so fiercely defended and equally fiercely 'overlooked,' were fully recognized and thought through, the daily, the public, and the shadow meaning and power systems of cultures and epochs would also be startlingly demystified. Where too much is denied, too much is also permitted: who, and what, kept women from joining, opposing, or being interviewed about that protest on the news? Whose interests are served by utterly ignoring—not even seeing—their absence? Perhaps every woman who was not there chose freely not to participate; if so, we should know that, just as we should know whether they did not dare or were refused the right to participate. How else are we to comprehend what an inclusive "peo-ple" are trying to say through protests and other expressions?

As long as Man and Mankind are not just falsely universalized but *singu-lar* terms, it also remains difficult to think well about plurality, diversity, dif-ferences. To be inclusive of many *and* singular, concepts must be on a level of abstraction at which we do not *picture* what they mean, because as soon as we do, they take on particular, necessarily exclusive content. (Try it: picture one 'human' that is neither male nor female; neither old nor young; that wears no clothing linked to gender or nationality; that has no skin tone, no 'type' of facial features; that is neither tall nor short, fat nor thin. . . .) The use of singular abstractions is of specific concern when their most commonly 'pictured' con-tent—which we do attach to them, wittingly or not—derives from typologies that reinforce hierarchies. For example, "the student" pictured as a young,

white, privileged male has long led teachers, other students, funders, legislators to think of returning adult women as less 'real' students, just as night classes
designed for working adults have been considered a sideline to the 'real,' pres-
tige-conferring work of schools. Provisions for those students were tacked on
to 'real' curricula, 'real' schedules, and so on, if they were made at all. All those
'other' students, those less 'real' ones, became widely imaginable as "the student" only when educational economics recast them as saviors of schools that
were losing the students they were designed to serve (and bill).

Analyzing another often singularized term, "the enemy," J. Glenn Gray
observes that "always, the definite article is used with the noun, not *an* enemy
or *our* enemy. The implication easily drawn is that the opponent is mankind's
enemy as well as ours, and also that this enemy is a specific, though undiffer-
entiated group, an implication that is only pseudo-concrete. That is, by reference to *the* enemy we seem to mean a unified, concrete universal. . . . By des-
ignating him with the definite article, it is made to appear that he is single and
his reality consists in hostility to us."[39] Right. And something stranger still happens when we do not use any article at all with a "unified, concrete universal"—not *the* Man, or *a* man, or *our* man, but *man,* both specified and unlim-
ited. This is common in usages of "man." For example: "Reason of the highest
sort belongs to man alone." This is rather like usages of "God," which is one
reason I often capitalize Man. Some say "a god," "the god," "our god," but when
we are trying to invoke a universally transcendent meaning of the kind that
defines the monotheistic faiths, many say "God," without delimiting articles.

Such conceptualizations and usages may be necessary and good in some
contexts. Universals are useful, perhaps even essential, for truly inclusive thinking by which we reach beyond concrete limitations for ideals. But when particular content sneaks into them, the consequent self-contradictions can be
dangerously mystifying. If "reason of the highest sort belongs to man alone,"
but "man" is not really inclusive of all humans, then some 'kinds' of humans
are moved out and down a scale, which has significant consequences. It would
be more honest, if no more just, to say, "Reason of the highest sort belongs to
the man alone." The trouble is that this kind of statement, which was made
often enough not so long ago, is far more likely to provoke disagreement—
that is, it is not as mystified. Sometimes, we should note, efforts to appear more
'tolerant' can lead to more, not less, mystification. Horizontal ideals, which do
not have specific content, are not the same as vacuous pieties, nor are they the
same as concretized universals that are abstracted from, but still carry with
them, exclusive exemplars.

Thus, when people stumble over the "she or he" of inclusive language, I often suggest that it is not only easier but helpful to try switching to a plural subject. Saying "the students" makes it much more likely that we will remember their plurality and differences in the proposition that follows. And if we were to say "men" rather than "man," and "the men" rather than "men," we would not so readily 'overlook' women and some 'kinds' of males. Of course, the next necessary step is to add other qualifiers that indicate who it is that we are actually thinking about. "The men who are rational," even without further specification, is quite different from, "Man, who is rational," and "The educated white men who are rational" is a different ballgame altogether.

As we challenge the deeply inscribed meanings of the defining few that are expressed and reinforced by singular terms, commonality and community may seem to be disappearing—not to mention ease of unselfconscious speech and writing. Of course, what we are really doing is clearing the ground so that it can open to, accommodate, and be common equally to all, so that speech and writing and signing can flow easily, without self-erasure, from the mouths and pens and signing hands and keyboards of us all. What cries out to be created is a community of understandings that would allow "all members to rejoice," as Anna Julia Cooper hoped we could, in the uniqueness that characterizes all human being. As Hannah Arendt put it, "Human plurality is the paradoxical plurality of unique beings."[40]

# War

No doubt you noticed, when I quoted from *The Warriors: Reflections on Men in Battle,* that Gray uses—and was not startled into thought by the usage of—"man" and "he," even though he was writing specifically about the dangers of singular, concretized universals ("the enemy").[41] Gray, like so many others, did not stumble over "the Warrior" as a profoundly significant figuration of Man/he because the Warrior has been simultaneously a male; a man; a hyper-masculinized figure; and an idealized expression of Man-as-Human. Whether some aspects of warriordom have been construed as failings ascribed to "human nature" or as marks of man's/humankind's nobility, the Warrior is at the core of Man's meanings, from his "bestiality" and "evil" to his dreams of glory and even transcendence.

We are once again in highly fraught territory. Men have killed, suffered greatly, done great harm, died, been permanently scarred physically and psychologically, overcome greatly, succumbed to horrors beyond bearing, failed, and transcended themselves and their causes in the crucible of war. Where so much has been asked, gained, lost, distorted, won, much has also been mythologized, denied, repressed, celebrated—transmuted in ways that are understandably highly resistant to questioning, let alone critique. But this is also the case with memories and living experiences of the other phenomena we have tried to face up to and think through to keep transforming knowledges, to keep trying to make sense so that we do not remain entrapped in, rather than empowered by, pasts that are always still with us. Where thinking is hardest and least welcome—that is where there is a desperate need, as Arendt said, to think what we are doing.

Men are not alone in having done and suffered so much in wars. We cannot read the lessons of war while women remain invisible. It *matters* that, in stories and histories of the Warrior, Woman is a symbol of the home he fights for, an excuse for fighting, a comfort giver and healer when he is in pain, a goad to stay and fight so he can be a 'man' ("Come home with your shield or on it"), an opiate when he needs to forget, a diversion when he needs to relax, an aid in bonding with other men (in part because she masks the eroticism of the intense homosocial relations that are among the mystified gifts that veterans treasure). While Woman is used to raise the spirits of the Warrior, to justify what he does, to care for his body, to relieve his desires, there is no room for—is, indeed, for him great risk in—recognition of the particular personhood of the women thus used. Real women are subsumed into Woman as virgin, girlfriend, wife, mother, daughter, figure of home–country–cause, and the obverse of these—whore, temptress, trophy to be 'taken' and, once used, thrown away, dismembered, killed, enslaved. But it is the real women who survive the violation who are believed to have been "shamed," and the children born of assault who have been scorned, not the Warrior. This is insane, psychotic; this has been 'normal' "in times of war." What should that tell us about wars and the systems that not only legitimate but glorify them?

It is a marker of significant change that rape by "warriors" can now be seen as a war crime as well as an act with genocidal intent. In addition, the provision of prostitutes—or "comfort girls," as Korean women 'provided' for Japanese troops were called—has finally been declared culpable and grounds for reparations. Such realizations, and actions premised on them, may slowly lead to significant changes. That some countries' armies now have female troops (including the U.S. army) will also, over time, have effects that are hard to foretell.

We would not have seen such changes had women's movements and feminist scholarship not begun to make it evident that, in the way war has been practiced and represented by dominant traditions, we can see almost all—if not, indeed, all—of the uses and abuses to which traditions have made women vulnerable and how deeply implicated these are in Man's meanings and men's actions. Because of such work, we have also begun to see that, although Woman has been created by and for warriors in these dangerous ways, the real women who have suffered have not only been victims. Women have also been part of and actively opposed to war throughout the ages and across cultures. Women have fought; women have tried to stop the fighting; women have been on the front lines as suppliers, nurses, spies, and have worked behind the lines as cooks, secretaries, seamstresses, drivers, translators. To keep the country going, women have moved into positions vacated by men going to war, and women have been forced out of their jobs when the men returned. Without women, the historian Gerda Lerner has said, no war could have been fought.[42]

Unprivileged men who had no part in making wars have also been used, and that use has been 'justified' in terms that reveal how they, too, have been defined primarily as physical beings and therefore expendable as substitutes for privileged men, as "cannon fodder." As always, we see here not only mutually constructing sexualized/gendered class/caste divisions and associated racializations, but also how gendering works to maintain the male use of females in most groups. "The enemy's" use of women has more than once been called "abuse" (as it is being called today), and "saving women" from him has been used to justify war. At the same time, male soldiers from all groups have used those very same women, just as warriors always have.

On a different but intricately related level, we remember the centrality that dominant cultures have given to mortality as a defining characteristic of Man and the deep silence surrounding natality. But women have remembered both, and some have raged against war in the name of natality. Maria Bigoszewska, a contemporary Polish poet who has seen too much violence and domination, writes about her ancient subject: "What then are the rights of women / half stifled / by blood / which flows out of their heavy hearts / if even children / become men / and leave for another / war."[43]

What sense does it make, and what does it cost, to focus so much on death, to betray the miracle of birth? To focus on endings, forgetting beginnings? To emphasize the aloneness or the solidarity of dying unbalanced by the complex relationality of birth? A self defined under the shadow of "all men are mortal" feels itself threatened and alone. But we do not begin our lives alone or threatened; we begin protected by the womb, connected to another. Being defined as those who are mortal but not natal cannot help but make those so defined identify with death and, too often, with killing, an act that seems to return to men their agency in the face of mortality. Natality has been treated as Other to mortality, as woman has to man, as dependence has to independence, as emotion has to intellect, as home has to public life ... as peace has to war.[44]

Historical meanings of peace are stunningly similar to historical meanings of Woman. That similarity is no accident. Peace is often symbolized as a woman and is considered to be feminine and feminizing in direct relation to the rampant machismo of war. Male pacifists have always been taunted by being called effeminate. The initial, remarkably intense opposition to women in the military reflects these constructs, as, particularly, does continuing opposition to women in combat. It *frightens* men to think of women being "in the trenches" with them. They assume women are always and everywhere 'soft' in ways that admit no contrary evidence; they think that, to be men, they will have to take more risks to 'protect' female soldiers; they cannot imagine taking an order from a woman; they worry about having to watch their language and avoid using women as occasions and excuses for eroticized male bonding (although they do not object in those terms, needless to say). Think about that fear; listen to those who express it. Much, if not all, of what we have been discussing will become almost glaringly evident. The most dangerous, deep, and pervasive mystifications are by no means subtle, and they tend to be strongly emotionally defended even as the defenses are publicly put forward as dispassionately 'rational.'

I was told by a mother with a son in the military that she—a publicly successful woman who has no doubts at all about her own equality with the men in her public-policy work—did not want her son's life "put at risk because of some feminist social experiment." I said I didn't either and am hardly a great advocate for women becoming warriors. I would prefer to end wars. But, I said, females as well as males should have the chance to prove that they have the abilities required for any role or job. They should not be *categorically* excluded or included without the necessary preparation.[45] If her son is to fight beside female soldiers, they should of course be qualified, just as any soldier should be. Not all males make good soldiers, either. The woman repeated with real fury that she did not want her son dependent for his life on any woman. I do not discredit her fears or her protective love. I honor them. I do question the direction of her attack. As a soldier, her son is indeed at very serious risk, but that is hardly the fault of those who seek equal rights to equal opportunities. If what we really want is to be able to select the best for each task by the most appropriate criteria, we are contradicting our own stated purposes when we prejudicially exclude possibly excellent candidates on the basis of differences that are not necessarily relevant. We need also to consider that some people link war with "becoming a Man" in ways that can be dangerous to us all, because they emphasize defiance of death rather than sustaining of life. No mother's son or daughter should depend in battle on this sort of hyper-masculinity.

If we wish to think about peace as well as war, and to do so without the old mystifications that so often direct our fears and doubts away from the real causes and perpetrators of what concerns us, we need to *recognize* that peace, like women, has been strikingly absent from curricula and courses through which cultures perpetuate themselves. Courses are not infrequently organized around wars—"America from 1776 to 1865," "Europe Between the Wars," "Japan after the Russo-Japanese War"—but never around 'peaces.'[46] Peace in history is unnamed in its own right (except when secured through a treaty so that it can be marked by reference to a war—as women are 'marked' by reference to the men who 'make history'). We do not even have a plural for peace that is parallel to "wars." Because we do not speak of "peaces," we render peace ahistorical and turn it into a hopelessly 'unrealistic' ideal. Thus, pacifists have been labeled "idealists" (or even "traitors") and war planners have been called "realists," without regard for the kinds of analysis each actually does.

'Realism' by no means adequately or accurately captures—and frequently actually mystifies—the orientation of those who advocate, make, or write about war. The war correspondent Chris Hedges, reflecting on his near-obsession with war (in order finally to renounce it), writes: "The enduring fascination of war is this: Even with its destruction and carnage it can give us what we long for in life. It can give us purpose, meaning, a reason for living. Only when we are in the midst of conflict does the shallowness and vapidness of much of our lives become apparent. . . . [W]ar is an enticing elixir. It gives us resolve, a cause. It allows us to be noble."[47] This, like the rest of his remarkably honest on-the-ground reporting, allows us to consider that clear-eyed realism may indeed be more, not less, common among pacifists and antimilitarists who are not fleeing their lives but, instead, are struggling to preserve and protect life for all.

Many people around the globe are stuck in lives so meaningless, so grindingly difficult and hopeless, that they are vulnerable to idealistic calls to war, to self-sacrifice for a cause, to a quick and "glorious" death. These include, as

Hedges also writes, those who feel that their lives are meaningless even though they are economically secure. Tragically, there is no question about that. But there are many other questions. In our context, surely one of them is why it is *war* that offers the only apparently 'noble' escape. It takes massive mystification to make "noble" organized killing and all that makes it possible, sustains it, and attends it—including training designed to turn thinking individuals into reflexively obedient units; grinding boredom; rigidly enforced inequality; physical deprivation and exhaustion; and sights and experiences of suffering, dismemberment, and real and messy death. Whether or not wars are sometimes necessary, how are the horrors that define their realities transmuted into "a reason for *living*"? That I might kill someone whom I could not otherwise stop from killing or raping is not a glorious, noble thing; it does not justify my life or give it meaning. On the contrary. In such a moment, all that makes life with and among others possible and valuable is being violated. I would not emerge from such a killing ennobled. I would survive it, if I did, permanently scarred, with faith, hope, trust, love violated, and with the knowledge that I, too, have killed. That I might then need to transmute the horror and the irreparable losses, and suppress the memories, by finding something to believe in absolutely enough to keep silencing what haunts me is humanly tragic; it is not ennobling.

I remember, from the Vietnam war era, a returned marine saying on television: "If you want us to go and kill, at least do so honestly. Do not ask me to lie to you about what I have seen, and what I have really done, in your name. I live with it; so should you." My memory of his words may be wrong, of course, but what I took in when he spoke remains vividly with me. This man was a marine, and not a pacifist. He was, in fact, going to return to fight some more. He asked of us 'simply' that we not require him to lie, to suffer his nightmares, to feel his pride in what he had been trained to do and did well (he told us this) alone or only among the friends who survived. He was determined that we should not privatize him and so many others, not lock them away from us to protect systems we do not want to risk, or bother, assessing, even though we ask others to die and kill in their name. He asked us for a demystified realism that is neither romanticized nor protectively abstract.

War is neither romantic nor abstract, although it reveals what Hegel called "the fury of abstraction." In reality, war is always about someone's real torn flesh—even if we fail so terribly at being able to remember, to imagine, to feel that embodied reality when we are far away, when we are thinking in terms of numbers too great to allow us to picture each individual, when planning strategically, when waving our flags. There may be—there always are—acts of individual nobility in such times, but those acts move us because they stand in stark contrast to (rather than ennoble) the purposeful carnage that surrounds them. There may be—there have been—causes for going to war, but the failures on all sides that fed and led to them, and the failures on all sides to find less catastrophic responses, to break out of the vicious escalations that violence always provokes, should surely keep us from celebrating what has gone so very wrong.

In *War, Politics, and Power,* Karl von Clausewitz (1780–1831) wrote of war that it is "*an act of force to compel our adversary to do our will*" (the italics are his). This obviously admits that war, whatever its causes (or claimed cause, usually in the singular to press us into unanimity), is a struggle for dominance. "Victory" means that one side has been reduced to submission. Less obvious, until Clausewitz insists we see and admit it, is that "the ruthless user of force must gain an advantage if his opponent does not do the same. Thus each drives the other to extremes which are limited only by the adversary's strength of resistance." So "the use of force is theoretically without limits," and "*an* act of force" can and usually does result in the unleashing of force from most, if not all, restraints. The actors themselves are subjected to the escalation of what they intended only as a means. Von Clausewitz does not flinch: "It is a waste of effort to ignore the element of brutality because of its repugnance. . . . So we repeat: War is an act of force, and there is no limit to the application of that force."[48] Again we encounter a kind of realism that should call us all—from pacifists to warriors—to recognize not only that war is not a noble end in itself but that it is also not a mere means that can remain safely under control.

But von Clausewitz, who knew that so well, did not oppose war. On the contrary. He concludes by writing: "Boldness, that noble virtue through which the human soul rises above the most menacing dangers . . . come[s] into its own . . . in struggle. . . . In our times, struggle, and, specifically, an audacious conduct of war are practically the only means to develop a people's spirit of daring. Only courageous leadership can counter the softness of spirit and the love of comfort which pull down commercial peoples enjoying rising living standards."[49] So here we are again. There have always been other purposes for war, and they have openly included 'overcoming' "softness," "love of comfort," the meaningless privilege awarded some "commercial peoples" even as others are reduced to a struggle for mere existence. It is better, in this view, when thus tempted from or rendered incapable of hard boldness, to overcome "repugnance" for "brutality" and let loose the uncontrollable dynamic of force—to seek at all cost to dominate, to make others submit. This is no longer realism; it is the romanticism of a hyper-masculinized aristocracy. But those old roots are still feeding wars waged by democracies. How do we, in the United States, want our president to appear in his role as commander in chief? What aspects of the dominant culture do we want him—and could 'he,' figured as warrior in chief, acceptably be a woman?—to represent and call forth from us?

The British historian John Keegan, author of *The Face of Battle*, writes about war as few have. In concrete detail, he discusses historical instances of generals who avoided battles at all cost; the number of soldiers who drink or use drugs to function under duress; the percentages of troops who break in the first, second, third. and consequent months. He also writes about how soldiers have been educated in military academies. He speaks of "the sensations and emotions with which the participants are grappling, though they relate to a situation which lies in a distant and perhaps never-to-be-realized future." These feelings, "after all, are the product of some of man's deepest fears: fear of wounds, fear of death, fear of putting into danger the lives of those for whose well-being one is responsible ... They touch too upon some of man's most violent passions; hatred, rage and the urge to kill." Then, after describing the "serenely parklike, ornamentally watered and planted and landscaped" grounds of the British military academy Sandhurst, which is blatantly "not conducive to a realistic treatment of war," Keegan, who taught at Sandhurst, observes that "one detects in one's own attitudes, and in those of one's colleagues, in those who know and those who don't, in the tough-minded almost as much as in the tender-hearted, an implicit agreement to preserve [the cadets'] ignorance, to shield the cadets from the worst that war can bring." About this "desensitized treatment of war" that characterizes instruction at all of the military academies about which Keegan has knowledge, he observes that it is so common because any more realistic, honest approach "will seriously hinder, if not indeed altogether defeat, the aim of officer-training. That aim ... is to reduce the conduct of war to a set of rules and a system of procedures—and thereby to make orderly and rational what is essentially chaotic and instinctive." Thus, officers-to-be learn "a corporate standard and a common form" for everything, including "'military writing' and 'voice procedure' which teach [them] to describe events and situations in terms of an instantly recognizable and universally comprehensible vocabulary, and to arrange what [they have] to say about them in a highly formalized sequence of 'observations,' 'conclusions,' and 'intentions.'" But this is not language that is "universally comprehensible." It is not everyday language. It is "highly formalized." It moves us out of our real lives into imagination-numbing, mind-stopping jargon with its own self-referential and legitimating 'logic.'

Keegan is not criticizing this training in reality-defying standardized abstractions; this is what he teaches. What he is doing is being honest.[50] Abstraction allows us to kill, and despite the desired avoidance of emotions it serves, it is fraught with passions. Those passions—both those to be mystified, hidden, repressed, by abstractions and those with which 'rational' strategic logics thereby become invested—are deeply shaped by gender.

In *War Machine: The Rationalization of Slaughter in the Modern Age* (a study of "illustrious writers" on war), Daniel Pick, who has clearly been informed by feminist analyses, observes that "sexualised imagery and argument run like a conspicuous thread through the pages that follow. The nation is itself often gendered as female; yet women apparently count little. . . . War is the fault of women. War is born from the womb of the state. War is the testing ground of virility but it disturbingly produces 'feminine' hysteria amongst the men." Then we finally hear from a woman. Pick quotes Virginia Woolf's, "Scarcely a human being in the course of history has fallen to a woman's rifle," and then observes—as we have by now in so many contexts, "It seems that the rationales for military conflict, as for private property and male exclusivity, have to be ceaselessly and wearyingly undone." Woolf, too, had written: "It seems as if there were no progress in the human race, but only repetition."[51]

What would happen if cultures, through informal as well as formal education, told the true, full stories of wars, including their deep and profoundly gendered roots? What would happen if, instead of especially celebrating heroic soldiers, cultures also told the stories of heroic activists who struggle to make life better and so hearten people to be brave enough to try to change what causes injustice and grinds the meaning out of lives at home, rather than flee into deadly "adventures" elsewhere? There is danger aplenty at home for those who challenge dominance. There is bonding among friends working for a cause. There is self-transcendence. What if "we, the people" were to honor our activists while they are still living rather than waiting until they are safely dead and no longer a threat to dominant orders—or our settled lives and uneasy consciences? What would happen if boys and men had other meanings of "manhood" to fire their imaginations, inform their games, speak to their desires, release their frustrations—to give lives meaning in 'peaces' rather than wars? What if we all saw wars as so many girls and women have? What if it were not shameful for boys and men to empathize with children, girls, women; to imagine themselves as one of them; to comprehend as also their own these human stories?

Attachment to masculinized war—which is not restricted to males and always has its "women's auxiliaries"—is old and deep, psychological and mythic, as well as economic and political. It is profoundly related to Man's need both to possess and to distinguish himself from the dreaded "effeminacy," the privatized domesticity, the realism discredited as soft "idealism" so long projected onto, prescribed for, and carried like a contagion by Woman. Natality, nurturance, love, peace—these, too, need to be let out of the closet, deprivatized, given equal public standing. They will not "unman" us. They are necessary to humanize us so that, even if it seems we have no recourse but to meet force with force, we can do so honestly, struggling to hold what we do within limits rather than romanticizing what violence, once unleashed, does to us all.

A growing body of works by feminists can now be consulted for such demystifying thinking, for a very different kind of realism. I commend these works to you with the deepest respect for their authors' clarity and their courage. My list is too short, but it may be a start: Virginia Woolf, Simone Weil, Helen Caldicott, Cynthia Enloe, Sara Ruddick, Bat Ami Bar-On, Jean Bethke Elshtain, Anuradha M. Chenoy, Sybil Oldfield, Carol Cohn, Rhonda Copelon, Seungsook Moon, Leila J. Rupp, Gwyn Kirk and Margo Okazawa-Rey, Rita Arditti, Vesna Nikolic-Ristanovic.[52]

Sara Ruddick reflects with such thinkers on the complex relations of feminists and feminisms to pacifism and nonpacifist antimilitarism (the latter being the position with which she allies herself). She suggests that ongoing revisions of the 'figure' of "a woman of peace" pose questions "feminists will answer collectively and contentiously as they continue to respond in individual situations from their particular endangered or safe, embedded to distant, relation to violence." Fully acknowledging that we will, and should, differ, she then suggests "some directions they (we) will take." First, she says, "peacemaking is only one identity of a woman of peace." It does not define her or prescribe only one position for all situations. Second, "a peacemaker could continue to abjure moral language, ... preferring instead the driest descriptions of deplorable, temporary tactics for stopping violence." And third, "even if she endorsed a particular and limited use of violence, even if she petitioned for it, a peacemaker could keep her mind focused on the 'postviolent' peace that violence is meant to provide."[53] All, some, or none of this may speak to you, in your situation and with your commitments, but it surely bears thinking through, thinking with, as a practice of demystification of the old meanings that have kept us stuck within wrongly universalized, pur-

posefully abstract, too often romanticized, gendered systems that keep submitting us to the struggles for dominance that have set the terms for human
histories for so long.

## Gender

In 1715, Elizabeth Elstob wrote this about the grammatical meaning of
"gender":

> In Anglo-Saxon grammar: "The Substantive and the Adjective, must not
> only agree in Number, but they must accord in Gender, or Sex, and in
> Case, or Termination: for the Adjective being a proper Attendant upon
> the Substantive, it hath been thought decent that it should not only be
> of the same Sex, that is, a Male to wait upon a Male, and a Female upon
> a Female, but likewise to appear in a Dress, or Habit, by which it may
> easily be discern'd to which Sex they belong. The first of these Answers,
> the Grammatical Term of Gender, the other, of Case."[54]

With its courtly figuring of grammatical terms, Elstob's definition now
sounds quaint at best. Why bother with it today, when most of us are aware
of the early "second wave"[55] feminist distinction between physiological sex and
social constructions of gender, not to mention transforming 'transgressions'
of sex/gendering codes that are ever more evident in scholarship, the media,
political actions? But we are searching for deep formations that continue to
do the work of creating 'kinds' and "orderly arangement[s]"[56] among them,
and "orderly arrangement of parts" is what "syntax" means. The syntax within
which Elstob wrote reveals a tangle of root meanings worth our attention on
many levels.

First, we can observe that, although both of the words/concepts "sex" and
"gender" were available to Elstob, they were also conflated ("Gender, or Sex").
It was *case* that was figured as a code by which sex was to be socially signalled
("by which it may easily be discern'd to which Sex they belong"). Gender/sex,
then, was *what* was to be signaled; case concerned *how* that signaling was to be
done. Elstob was aware that *how* mattered but shows less awareness of the complexity of the *what*. This should be familiar to us. "Sex" has long been assumed
to be 'naturally' given, leaving "gender" (now as an analytic analog to Elstob's
grammatical "case") to carry the freight of complex meanings and signalings.

Nature, then, is as so often being used as the unquestionable warrantee of the real and unchangeable. Just how perverse that is we will see again later.

Second, we can see the seeds of complexities later analyzed implicit in Elstob's *case,* the *how.* To communicate, social signals must already be codified. A signal others are to read cannot be idiosyncratic. It must be conventional enough to convey the intended meaning. And, of course, we must already know which of many sharable meanings has been defined as belonging to that which we wish to signal. This social location of sex should let us know that it is not just there to be indicated; it is already infused with social meanings. If it were not, we would not know which of the legion of available social signals to use for it.

Third, we can observe that the conventional code to signal sex/gender was of a particular sort. It was not, for example, a code for signaling an intended meaning about a personality or, more generally, a self. Elstob does not mention anything about *who* one is; rather, she mentions a specific sort of *what* one is. And that *what* does not, as one might think (given supposedly baseline, natural meanings of "sex") refer directly to reproduction via copulation. The display of case is likened by Elstob to "a Dress, or Habit, by which it may easily be discern'd to which Sex they belong," but it evidently is not, like animal sexual 'displays' (the peacock's spread tail; the changes in the vulva of the female chimpanzee in estrus) a display of actual sexual readiness for the reproductive act. What Elstob evokes as social syntax for the signaling of sex is, on the contrary, conventions concerned with regulating sex by preserving propriety, respectability (as we saw in discussing gendered class), "decency." So much for reading the case of gender as expressing nature as distinct from anti-nature social formations.

Fourth, and not surprising, what is "decent" is also not simple or straightforward. Case, as Elstob has it, is to signal sex within conventional codes concerning maintenance of 'decency' in two immediately evident ways: as 1) a clear discrimination of sex into one of two forms (female or male); so that 2) male and female can be properly separated, and precisely *not* so they can come together to copulate. Thus, "it hath been thought decent [that] a Male wait upon a Male, and a Female upon a Female." The prescribed "decency" then simultaneously insists on and is to control hetero-reproductive sex.

In sum, sex is conflated with gender within a social system premised on two 'kinds' of humans whose relations must be prescriptively regulated rather than simply indicated. "Animal" displays of our reproductive readiness—or, signals of what the function of sex usually is said naturally to be—would

clearly be judged the very opposite of "decent." "Decency" requires our separation, not our union. Nevertheless, Elstob's females and males were to dress
in ways 'proper' to their reproductive role in such union: presumed egg bearers were not to dress as if they were potential inseminators. Clearly, this social
syntax is fraught with anxiety. Sex/gender is to be made "decent" so it will not
take, even as it is defined by, its "natural course." Slips, mistakes, and tricks
and transgressions are obviously known to be possible. (It's hard not to think
of Shakespeare here, of course.)

In defining "gender" as *distinct* from physiological provisions for reproductive sex, later feminists were in tune with the social/linguistic grammar and
syntax within which Elstob did her work. But although "gender" in one sense
simply took on the role of "case" (or was more clearly seen at work between
sex/what and case/how), the feminist distinction was put to use to reveal, to
critique, and potentially to change what Elstob's grammar simply (well, complexly, but as if it were simple) adduced.

By now, the continuing use of sex/gender as an analytical, critical, demystifying concept for those concerned with both truths and justice has extended
beyond questioning supposedly natural, but actually highly codified and prescriptively regulating, constructions of male and female. But there is more. It
turns out that if we pursue the etymology of "gender" still further, we find
connections of "gender" to the very idea of discerning 'kinds'—any kinds at
all, not just "female" and "male." Then we find that, just as the categories of
female and male are precisely *not* to relate as "nature intended," so, by this dominant system, must other categories or 'kinds' also be "properly," "decently"
related. It is not just odd, then, that so many languages have "genders" that
apparently have nothing to do with "sex"

The *Oxford English Dictionary,* which traces changes in meanings, tells us
that an early meaning of "gender," which developed from both Latin and Greek
(the root is *gen,* 'to produce'), as well as Sanskrit (*janas*) brought together 1)
"to produce; cf. Kin"; and 2) "Kind, sort, class."[57] With regard to "2), kind,"
meanings are given for "gender" from the 1300s to the 1700s in English that
include, as two examples, "Diseases of this gender [that is, this kind of illness]
are for the most part incurable," and "Supplie it with one gender of Hearbes,
or distract it with many."[58] "Gender," then, concerned discriminating sorts of
things *in general,* even as that discrimination itself related to producing, to
generating, and not just to observing.

With regard to "1), to produce," the *OED* gives us also *Gens,* which comes
from a different root meaning "to beget . . . to be born." These two—to produce

and to be born—come together, for example, in meanings for fictive kin in the form of "clan or sept; a number of families united by the ties of a supposed common origin, a common name, and common religious rites."[59] We note, too, that "genus," which means "race" and "stock," developed within this braid of meanings. Thus, as things and animals, including humans, were classified linguistically, conceptually, socially by 'kind' through comparison and contrast with other things and animals, they were also being classified in terms of their engendering—their production and reproduction. Their 'kind' had to do with their *breeding*. Here is the root of notions that some 'kinds' of people are "well bred" and some are not; that "a people" or "a nation" have "the same blood"; that there are "races" that are of different "stock" and so must not be "mixed"' that there is "pure" and "impure" "blood"—that nature, left to "her" own devices, can and will breed "degenerate" as well as 'proper' 'kinds.' "Kinds," or "genders" in its early meaning, having been discriminated from nature are then held to be of nature—to be 'true,' 'real,' and not arbitrary. But they are also to be regulated so that nature will not reclaim and mess them up. Man's neat, hierarchically arranged divisions have thus been ascribed also to deities to elevate them safely above nature ("By God, that is unnatural!")

Sexual reproduction clearly informs these meanings, but (as we saw in Elstob's definition) it is equally clear that social meanings inform them just as tellingly. We remember, to think this through, that copulation need not and cannot, except at some times for some people, always produce offspring; nor has it always and everywhere been understood as the cause or even the occasion of impregnation. So to define human sex solely as nature's provision for reproduction is to define it with regard to a rather dicey effect rather than a much broader range of experiences. Definition always limits, but that tells us that it is always illuminating to pay attention to which limits have been imposed—and to where and how they are relaxed. Here, we notice that "kin" is a more extensive notion than begotten offspring, so definitions by 'kind'/ "gender" that supposedly have to do with "bloodlines" also allow for other sorts of relations that could, and did, extend also to fictive kin of various sorts, including those added by (the social institution of) marriage and other social or legal rituals.

Most languages have two or three grammatical genders (masculine, feminine, sometimes also neuter), but it is by no means obvious or easy to relate gendered substantives to anything that actually concerns physiological sex *except* as gender/'kind' on a general level. Reproductive copulating, however, remains a primal figure lurking (and arousing anxiety) in the background, a threat to neatly divisive orderings that put, and keep, everything and every-one in their 'proper' places. The linguistic "copula" and "copulate" correspond: "Copula: part of a proposition connecting subject and predicate, spec. the verb 'to be'; . . . tie, connection, linking of words . . . fasten. . . . So, copulate, couple; unite sexually."[60] Right. But don't "unite sexually" "indecently" with the wrong 'kind,' and do not breed meanings or people that violate our ordered social syntax. (Poets, too, have been thrown out of Republics for being unre-spectable.)

But what about the issue of sex/gender *inequalities* in all these relatings? The *OED* cites an example of a 1784 usage that reveals without recognizing an already established hierarchy of sex/gendering inequality: "I . . . am a man of importance, a public man, Sir; of the patriotic gender."[61] Here we have "a man of importance" who is—as no woman and some 'kinds' of men could not then have been—a "public man." Exclusive, but also hierarchical, mean-ings of "man" and of "public" are in play, but that is hidden, mystified. The "patriotic gender," which supposedly meant the patriotic-kind-itself, is there-fore also exclusive. Those who were not men or the 'right' 'kind' of males—that is, those who were not allowed public lives—could perhaps have been patri-otic, but they could not have been of the common or general 'kind' of patriots. Their 'kind' was, *as a 'kind,'* not of the 'proper' 'kind(s)' of Man/human. It was disabled, disempowered, without that even needing to be said.

The inequalities were there, mystified by the root error we have been trac-ing: discrimination of 'kinds' that are claimed to include all similar, related sorts of things/people but that do not actually do so. "Sameness" has thus become hierarchically monistic. It is used to cover over the fact that a 'proper,' 'real' example of humankind is actually on the top of a scale that moves down-ward toward the (dreaded even as it is adduced as warrantee for 'reality' and 'truth') nature that knowledge and some religions are to help Man rise above and master. George Orwell's *Animal Farm* comes to mind: ALL PIGS ARE EQUAL, BUT SOME PIGS ARE MORE EQUAL THAN OTHERS.

I cannot resist noting that, in her 1972 study *Mother Camp: Female Imper-sonators in America,* Esther Newton "found that drag queens of the mid-1960's consciously thought of themselves as lacking 'Americanism.' They saw their alienation from mainstream society not as a deliberate rebellion but as a bun-dle of stigmas that inevitably flowed from their femininity."[62] Well, right; "feminine" was then stigmatized, and its stigmata were coded as signs war-ranting privatization, denial of public rights, responsibilities, and freedoms in the dominant meaning and political system. While Man was conflated with human, women were gendered (discriminated as a 'kind') and required in all sorts of ways to signal that we were not his "fellow Americans" or "of the public gender."

By uncovering the tangled but deep roots of the word "gender," then, we have found the roots also of "kind." Together, they have meant "birth, descent; nature; manner; race, kin; class, genus, species . . . natural; lawful."[63] This is a contradictory confluence indeed. Thus, class, caste, racializations are genders/kinds in the form of projects that entail control of actual but also of figurative and fictive breeding (mixing). They are prescriptive, not descriptive; thus, they require regulation of reproductive and other social engenderings through complex codes, conventions, rules, laws.

"Not of our kind" thus does not mean simply "distinguishable from us." It means "should not breed with 'us'"—or even "should not breed at all," as we see in laws enforcing sterilization of some 'kinds' that were justified in the name of the 'science' of eugenics (*eu*, 'good'; *genics*, 'generation,' production, birth). As we saw in Elstob's definition, separation must be maintained if relations are to be 'proper.' That distinctions separate is not the problem, of course, nor is it necessarily a problem that relations are regulated to sustain useful distinctions. We "make sense" together and by all sorts of more and less evident prior agreements. But problems do arise when distinctions are wrongly made, rigidified, and enforced in the service of unjust inequalities. With this in mind, it is both startling and illuminating also to encounter definitions of "kind" as "showing benevolence" or gentleness, as well as "well-born, well-bred."

So engenderings of race, class, genus, species—as of kin and clan and nation and all sorts of other social projects that require discriminations among and maintenance of 'kinds'—have long been related internally and to each other by deeper syntaxes that are found within and regulate languages, social orders, knowledges, faiths. All of these are ways of being human, or projects of human be-ing, as the creatures and creators of meanings that we so variously are. Today's critiques of knowledges reveal our cultural syntaxes; so do etymologies that illuminate the definitions, usages, grammars that set the terms for what can 'properly' be said by scholars and in everyday talk. But we are not trapped by all that informs us and regulates our interactions. We can see what is going on and thus know ourselves to be capable of more, and other than, our inheritances. A more inclusive education offers us differing locations within and about which to think.

The *OED* entry for "gender" also cites "the North American Indian languages," which "are said to have two 'genders,' animate and inanimate.'" And, "with still greater departure from the original [whose?] sense, 'genders' has been applied to the many syntactically discriminated classes of [substantives] in certain South African [languages]."[64] That is, these languages divide by 'kind'/gender differently from the Anglo-Saxon (and some other) languages: there are always differences, other realities. And still, gender as we think about it today clearly not only *has* but *is* a taproot of social orderings, of the very notion of 'kinds,' of categorizations that are not only useful within but informing of whole meaning systems that circle out from sex-as-breeding relations through exclusively defined public life to knowledge and faith traditions and back to the most intimate 'unions.'

So what about knowledge? In *A Feminist Dictionary*, we also find a 1981 definition that makes more explicit what was so densely packed into Elstob's earlier one: "Our ideology and practice of sex roles construct, out of what are only tendencies toward genital dimorphism, two mutually exclusive categories, that is, genders. The dress and behavior codes of our culture try to hide the full range of diversity in order to create an appearance of dimorphism."[65] We could say, in light of contemporary knowledges, that both sex and gender have been demystified by being pluralized, denaturalized, and so also descientized. What is 'given' by nature, the knowledge domain most firmly controlled by scientists in the Western world, is no longer taken to be what is most real and basically determining—a matter of 'hard' fact rather than social, moral, political creation and responsibility. Even the claim that science deals with facts, not values, is taken by significant strands of contemporary critical scholarship (for example, science studies, "post-Positivist" scholarships) to be socially, morally, politically informed. Such analyses take claims to value-neutral scientific factuality to constitute both a renunciation of responsibility for judgment and an assumption of coercive authority. But one can still hear modern popularizations of uncritiqued scientistic moves in arguments that women, or racialized, or "disabled" groups of women and men "just are different: you can't change nature," however sad that may be. Thus are social prejudices, and the related lack of material provisions that turn some physical differences into "handicaps" (for example, building steps rather than ramps), reproduced.

Questioning scientific 'fact' is not uncomplicated; it is not a simple matter of rejection or acceptance of fact or value, scientific or social, or the old nature versus nurture. Dualistic either–or framings can all too readily entail no more than reversals that remain within prevailing systems. Taking gender, race, and/or disability to be 'nothing but' a social construction can lead to seeing them as not 'real' after all, as we saw when we considered *race*. That error, which remystifies as 'only social' what had been mystified as 'natural,' leads us to vastly underrate the bedrock reality of social constructs for humans while we also rather weirdly ignore the fact that embodied social humans are within and of nature. (The old divide between Man/humans and Nature at work again.) To question social, political, moral, economic formations that have been naturalized, it is not necessary to deny that we are natural creatures at all.

Women's studies, gender studies, queer studies, critical race theory, science studies, disability studies, and more (including anthropology, sociology, American studies, and other 'mainstream' disciplines such as biology and physiology as they are engaged with the new scholarships and fields) continue to work on these crucial and difficult issues. Such scholarship is demystifying old conceptualizations of gender precisely by using the still complicating *critical* concept of gender/genderings. But the old systems, as we have seen again and again, have a way of contorting themselves rather elaborately to neutralize critiques that challenge them. It is important to keep trying to catch the cultural syntaxes within and by which we live even as they thus shape-shift. We return, then, from the broadest, deepest meanings of "gender" to their narrower shoots—those with which we are more familiar.

*Gender* has become a popular, almost conventional, term, and it usually has a kind of feminist aura around it. But when *gender* appears in the media, in common speech, and in nonfeminist scholarship, it often still does so as a mystifying substitute for *sex*. One hears, for example, "the female gender" rather than "the female sex." I rather suspect that "gender" is less embarrassing to say than "sex," and that is one reason it has caught on (although the *Oxford English Dictionary* gives an example from 1709 in which a woman writes that she is glad to be of her gender because it means she doesn't have to marry—to live and have sex with—a woman). With this usage of gender we are still within an apparently dualistic, bimorphic construction of what it means to be human, the same construction that masks the great complexities of sex and sexualities; the variations in cultural prescriptions across times and regions; the invidious monism that works behind the apparent dualism so that females are defined not as equal 'opposites' but as lesser humans; and the use of 'nature' to provide a warrant for all of these enforced constructions and for branding variations as 'deviation' that is "unnatural." The popular usage of gender does not mean that systemic gender critique has become commonly accepted. On the contrary. It too often means that it has once again been domesticated.

Another contemporary confusion: among some who see themselves as defending the cause of women against wrong-headed radical feminists, *gender equality* is used in two ways. Sometimes it is used as a substitute for "equality of the sexes," but it also appears as a term for the position being opposed. These antifeminist feminists thus remain within the old naturalized, hierarchical systems, although—by no means trivially—they want those systems to become more equitable. What makes that desire troubling, and entangles it in contradictions that keep undermining it, is that it tends to remain premised on naturalized, prescriptively hierarchical constructions of bimorphic sex. This allows "equal rights" feminists to appeal to women and men who want change for individuals but not change of the systems that have denied us such rights.

Characteristically, the proponents of extending untransformed individual rights to women seek a "fair field with no favors,"[66] as Christine Hoff Sommers puts it. Invoking this 'classic' liberal trope, Sommers says she wants the "gender feminist," a figure she attacks in her book (full disclosure: among others', my work is invoked) to "divest herself of the sex/gender lens through which she now views social reality and join the equity feminist mainstream," a "mainstream" that demands "for women the same rights before the law that men enjoyed."[67] The problem with this position is not only that the "sex/gender lens" is hardly the creation of, or maintained by, those who have created sex/gender *critiques*. Elstob and the woman who did not want to marry a person of her own gender clearly had a sex/gender lens. The problem is also not that feminists scorn *equalized* rights. Quite the contrary. The problem is that, without gender critique, we cannot see why and how "the *same* rights that men enjoyed" cannot reliably or generally be simply extended to women.

As a key example: on a "field" for a 'game' defined by and for masculinized individual men/Man, there are no provisions for what have been feminized mothers' activities, arts, functions, concerns. Nor are there adequately publicly recognized and validated extensions of those concerns to a world in which women and children bear the brunt of so much (notably, poverty, war, illiteracy, sexual violation). But Sommers wants "a fair field *with no favors*"— that is, one on which those who have carried responsibility for children, for home life, for all that sustains life, must become the *same* as those whose sphere has been defined in contradistinction from, and superior to, theirs. Sameness, we must repeat, is not equality. Had we been the same as men, or had we been allowed to live as if we were, we would not need to be equalized. And if we were to become the same, what would happen to the care assigned to mothering, among other things? Fathering by the old systems entailed inseminating, 'protecting,' and providing material sustenance, but not the essential, minute-by-minute work—and gift—of ongoing nurturance. Like *human* in societies divided and ranked by sex/gender, *parent* has no meaning of its own. Put it this way: while sex/gendering systems divide and rank us as two different, oppositionally constructed, 'kinds,' one 'kind' cannot become "the same" as the other without the loss to all of us of what was assigned to and made possible for it by the systems that Sommers and others do not want to change.

For example, that feminism has not made it possible for women to "fit their new gains at work and in the public world into some version of the story of marriage and the family they have inherited from their mothers" does not, as Elizabeth Fox-Genovese asserts, prove the failure of feminism. It is not feminists who created and have enforced inequitable versions of "the story of marriage and the family" that privatized it, leaving "work and . . . the public world" free of any need to take family life into account equally and equitably for all. The lives that women in gender-hierarchical systems "have inherited from their mothers,"[68] remain very difficult indeed for women, or men, to add to work lives premised on full-time, child-care–free workers.

The old mystifications thus continue to turn systemic divisions and inequalities into ongoing occasion for judgments of individual failure. *You* cannot balance full-time work with motherhood? Something is wrong with you. *Your* desires do not follow the bimorphic heterosexual script in our culture's highly specified forms? Something is unnatural about you. *You* wish to be equal to the men alongside whom you are struggling for freedom, for justice? You are disloyal to the Cause. Shoot the feminist messenger, take up your 'proper' role again, and we will all get along so much better. Thus is the inequality written into the old, dominant gendering scripts and systems protected against—and its hierarchical divisiveness projected onto—individuals and causes that challenge them.

As we have seen, those grammars of sex/gender are far broader and deeper than most realize. As the feminist philosopher Sandra Harding writes: "The genes of the sex/gender system now can be detected in most of the social interactions which have ever occurred between humans of any sex, age, class, race, culture."[69] In her work on the "Indian Woman Problem" in Trinidad and Tobago, Rhoda Reddock found that "it was the historical conflation of interests between migrant Indian men, struggling to improve their socio-economic and caste position within a new and hostile environment, colonial capital, and the state's desire for a stable . . . self-reproducing and cheap labor force [that, as M. Jacqui Alexander concludes] worked to generate ideologies aimed at curtailing women's autonomy."[70] Sex/gendering is always also at work producing/reproducing 'kinds'; it is the copula that connects them as regulatory systems specify.

Such analyses are telling and very useful in planning actions for change. However, they need not, and should not, be allowed to mystify realities yet again by casting those who have suffered injustices primarily, let alone only, as victims. That, too, would mean we were generalizing wrongly, leaving out crucial differences, mystifying real lives. People have created qualities, experiences, values, works, systems of thought and culture that we (differing *we*'s) may wish to affirm, to revalue, not to dismantle. The Indian women Reddock and Alexander write about were not only victims (as these authors fully recognize). Like many others, they have their own critical analyses and theorizations and their own ways of working within, against the grain of, and sometimes in open opposition to the systems that multiply affect their lives.

And differing situations invite differing analyses and choices. The Polish writer Malgorzata Hillar introduces her 1995 volume of poems by claiming her own kind of feminism: "I am a feminist. Of course, not a fighting one, since . . . I have long ago eliminated the word—fight—from my vocabulary. I am a woman–feminist, fully aware of my femininity and accepting this femininity. . . . I cultivate my otherness, being aware at the same time of the evident discrimination against women."[71] Regina Grol, Hillar's English translator, rightly reminds us that such choices among Polish, as among all, women reflect judgments made in light of their own local, national, historical realities. In this instance, Grol writes, some Polish women who are choosing "conventional roles of mothers and housewives" do so *not* because they are embracing mystified versions of earlier women's lives, but "to reclaim the private realm and distance themselves from the corrupt public domain in which they were forced to participate under Communist rule."[72] Systemic political change is required to make the "public domain" liberating, as profound changes in the world of paid work are needed before entering it is actually liberating.

Theresa de Lauretis writes: "Representing the [actual, historically/systemically shaped] conditions of existence of those subjects who are muted, elided, or unrepresentable in dominant discourse, this new understanding of the nature of identity actually opens up the possibility to 'set about creating something else to be,' as Toni Morrison writes of her two heroines in *Sula*."[73] The invocation of Morrison reminds us that becoming conscious of what has been mystified, hidden, denied can indeed be agonizing and dangerous, even as it is liberating. Few capture the pain lived by those caught in the 'triple oppression' of sex/gendering, racialization, and class/caste categorical 'kinds' as brilliantly as Morrison. And even fewer catch also the strength, the love, the subversive and creative wisdom that call out to be recognized and affirmed.

Such subversive and creative wisdom can also be found in scholarships, fields, and movements that have used demystifications of sex/gendering systems to deprivatize "closeted" sexualities simultaneously locked 'in' and locked 'out' by binary, oppositional co-constructions of Man/Woman. As Diana Fuss writes, "The metaphysics of identity that has governed discussions of sexual behavior and libidinal object choice has, until now, depended on the structural symmetry [of 'heterosexual'–'homosexual,' and 'inside'–'outside'] . . . and the inevitability of a symbolic order based on a logic of limits, margins, borders, and boundaries."[74] Gender analyses working within lesbian, gay, bisexual, transsexual and transgender studies, and/or queer studies, as well as "gender bending" and other deprivatizations of gender "transgressions" more openly (but by no means without cost and complexities of many sorts), 'play' with—within, around, against, beyond—prescribed naturalized and symbolically inscribed definitions (*de finis*, 'having fixed limits'). Gender does not refer only to social roles 'properly' and "decently" displaying naturalized heterosexuality. It extended beyond, and moved differently within, heterosexual–homosexual divisions long ago. This is becoming more evident now, as the new scholarships and activisms develop. William L. Leap has said about transgendering and transsexualities: "Trans issues are not the same thing as lesbian or gay. You've got really good trans anthropology emerging. And it is not at all about the same issues of power or privilege or opportunity—or, for that matter, sexual identity or practice."[75]

However, as the limitations and controls legitimated and mystified by mystified conceptualizations and prescriptive systems are dissolved (but never entirely: cultures display many different more and less accepted escapes), they are not simply jettisoned. They mark what is to be challenged and reconfigured and are in varying ways also reappropriated and revalued. Their older meanings remain with us as our individual and cultural pasts always do. What can change is our relations with, within, around and about, and against them. A return to mystification, however, remains an ever present possibility, even in the most radical analyses and challenging actions. Fuss recognizes that "breaks" with established meanings that she (with others) seeks "inevitably seem to reassert what they sought to supersede." She suggests, however, that "one can, by using these contested words, use them up, exhaust them, transform them into the historical concepts they are and have always been."[76] Or, as I have put it, one can haul their old roots into the present and thus reduce the power they retained while they informed the present but were still hidden, repressed, denied.

Genderings reveal extraordinary complexities, reopening whole areas of definition and social syntax that both enabled us and closed us in all sorts of ways into 'kinds.' Critiquing them is intellectually and emotionally liberating, and it works with efforts to deprivatize, to come out into public lives that entail also rights to protected private lives. But it is not easy to live, love, act with such consciousness, or—to narrow our focus to teaching—to respond to changed consciousnesses in students that can emerge (always differently) when intimately fraught mystifications of 'kinds' and all their regulated relations crack open. Needing *some* way to continue categorizing (without which we cannot even speak, let alone know anything), some teachers and students fall back into mystifications such as absolutized victimization or romanticizing the oppressed, as if the opposite of the falsely negative categorical generalizations of prejudices can only be equally falsely positive generalizations. Some neatly continue to avoid engagement with the complexities of pluralizing, changing identities and other ways of sorting things and people by leaping from supposedly apolitical, universalized principles ("I teach the best literature") directly into an equally thoughtless acceptance of divisive identities ("I could teach Black lesbian women's writings, but I am not one of 'them,' so that would be wrong"). Some avoid the mess of personally felt confusion by holding discussion tightly within the elaborate language of highly sophisticated theorizations of identities/'kinds.'

These are not our only choices. Dismantling the errors that derive from and perpetuate the distortions of oppressions and victimizations is crucial to honest intellectual work. But the horizons of possibilities for, and the real, multivoiced stories of humans everywhere and always, remain available to help us rebuild, guided but not confined by the best theories we can find. We seek finer, subtler, more complex, and more inclusive ways of knowing and being, not crude reversals, the substitution of new ideologies for the old, or new mystifications that protect us from having to keep thinking.[77]

In *West Side Story*, a teenage gang member sings defiantly but cheerfully, in a spirit that recognizes as it mocks the ways he has been explained in systems not of his own making, "I'm depraved on account of I'm deprived." That knowing, defiant spirit is familiar to feminist scholar–teachers and our students, as well as to others who renounce the deadening effort of refusing to see all that has been hidden in mystified meaning systems, even when at first it seems that all we find is absence, devaluation, distortion, victimization—or decontextualized, romanticized resistance and heroism. It has taken far too much energy to keep our eyes and minds closed, whether in submission or in defiance. The release of that energy is enlivening, empowering in and of itself. It is repressed and wrongly directed anger, hurt we have not yet dared to feel fully, only reactive rebellion that fears thinking lest it lose its nerve that are always serious.

It is not surprising (although it flies in the face of stereotypes of 'unattractive,' 'humorless' activists) that movements that involve ongoing demystifications are also characterized by humor. Prejudices really are absurd, as are all those codes and conventions that require us always to be properly clothed so we do not offend 'decency.' *Mercy, It's the Revolution and I'm in My Bathrobe*, the feminist cartoonist Nicole Hollander titles one of her books. Remarkably broad audiences laugh, cheer, cringe, cry, and learn at the same time during performances of Eve Ensler's *Vagina Monologues*. Postmodern political activists further develop some of the humor of the 1960s. Some perform gender bending in public to the startled delight, and shock, of people "disarmed" by the outrageousness of it all, as some soldiers were "disarmed" when flowers were carefully placed in the barrels of their guns by 1960s antiwar protestors. It is also true, as the political cartoonist Doug Marlette says about the furious reactions his editorial cartoons sometimes evoke, that "where people are all caught up in reverence, they take irreverence, which is what humor is, to be hostility."[78] Humor is to reverence as thinking is to knowledge. Both, like the gadfly to which Socrates likened himself, sting us awake.

Jane Wagner wrote the following lines for Trudy, the "bag lady" Lily Tomlin portrays in her one-woman show *The Search for Signs of Intelligent Life in the Universe*:

> I got the kind of madness Socrates talked about,
> "A divine release of the soul from the yoke of
> custom and conventions." I refuse to be intimidated by
> reality anymore.
> After all, what is reality anyway? Nothin' but a
> Collective hunch. My space chums think reality was once a
> Primitive method of crowd control that got out of hand.
> In my view, it's absurdity dressed up
> In a three-piece business suit.
>
> I made some studies, and
> Reality is the leading cause of stress amongst those in
> Touch with it. I can take it in small doses, but as a lifestyle

*I found it too confining.*
*It was just too needful;*
*It expected me to be there for it* all *the time, and with all*
*I have to do—I had to let something go.*[79]

Tomlin's character, a "bag lady," is a figure written against the syntax of 'decency' and 'proper' ordering of dominant systems—a 'failed' woman, right out there on the streets, evoking all too many of the anxieties that attend fierce but also contradictory, elusive, unstable prescriptions concerned with *what* and *how,* rather than *who,* we are. We avert our eyes and hurry past. Trudy, aware of her appearance in her own way, says about the pantyhose rolled so far down her ankles that she can hardly walk: "Hey, it's a look!"

In this spirit, but at the other end of the sex/gendering continuum where opposites reveal their relation, we might put RuPaul, who has made a career and a life as a drag queen. In his/her autobiography, *Lettin It All Hang Out,* RuPaul gives us a list of "Things You Need to Be a Drag Queen." It includes thirty-five items. Trudy has the first and last items—but none of those in between. The list begins with "Flawless, fierce attitude" and ends with "Positive love energy"; in between it includes "disposable razors. . . . Full coverage pancake makeup in light, medium, and dark. . . . Eyelash curler. . . . Tweezers. . . . Panty hose [well, Trudy does have those]. . . . Corset. . . . Push-up bra. . . . High-heeled shoes. . . . Hotpants, mini-dress. . . . Gloves. . . . Press-on nails. . . . Wigs" and "A lot of time to get dressed."[80] A lot of time, some pain and ongoing discomfort, money, serious painterly skills, lots of consumer knowledge: the art of "being feminine" is a demanding one. RuPaul admires and appropriates it, making his/her own case of and for it. What he does, he says, is "really no different from when the little boy puts on a cowboy outfit for the first time and starts acting big and tough like John Wayne. You see, clothes aren't just things you wear—they bring out the flavor of the person, magnifying hidden areas of your personality that spend most of the time cooped up in the cellar of your consciousness. From time to time you need to take them for a walk around the block to stretch their legs."[81]

So much for Elstob's grammar. Here is its very nightmare, in our face, both as its perverse obverse (flipping over a still dualistic system) and as its scrambling (mixing, blending, shifting). He dresses as a woman; she also dresses as a man. "I want," s/he says, "to present a whole and complete picture—the yin, the yang; the black, the white; the boy, the girl; the sane, the insane. Because we are all Everyman [*sic?*]—a rainbow of different roles and different people. . . .

There is no such thing as normality—each and every one of us, if we dare to be whole, is a gorgeous peacock."[82]

Arguably, RuPaul remains within racialized gendering systems (as Fuss suggests those who defy them may) even as he transgresses, and revalues, their divisions by insisting on daring "to be whole." He is quite clear that he is "really" "a man," even as he claims the "illusion" that she is "a woman"—and that the illusion is "more real." Perhaps this is why he, and some other drag queens, tend to be crowd pleasers even as they lead dangerous lives very much "on the margin" and always extremely vulnerable to the all-too-empowered anxieties of others. We grant some, but not safe, freedom to those who, like artists and admitted performers, simultaneously play with and recognize constraints from which we crave, even as we may also fear, relief. But this is risky business. "Queens" take huge risks to "be feminine," to enact gendered prescriptions some of us desire just as passionately to be free of. And designated 'females' who know that they transgress what that is prescribed to mean and who seek to display and/or to embody "maleness" can be at even greater risk. The more powerful can 'play' a bit (note Harvard University's traditional Hasty Pudding drag performances), but the least powerful must not presume 'above' their "place." If the dangerous transgressive elements could be rendered less dangerous, who knows what *human being* might mean?

Well worth thinking through, these seriously irreverent figures that bring so many genderings together. Gendering, being so directly related to defining figurations of meanings, is powerfully illuminated, and reworked, in just such ways. That there are alternatives is crucial to know when so much is at stake. Suzanne Kessler and Wendy McKenna write: "People must be confronted with the reality of other possibilities, as well as the possibility of other realities." Such real, "other possibilities" are needed, they say—reminding us both of uses for and limitations on knowledge—because "whenever science has offered evidence of a biological continuum, but everyday members insist (because of the way reality is constructed) that there are discrete categories, there have been attempts to legislate against the continuum." Kessler and McKenna then discuss the kinds of legislatively definitional actions we saw when looking at *race,* as well as "rulings in sports . . . which legislate a person's gender."[83] They do not adduce (but could have) different languages, as well. They do discuss "the berdache"—a term for people who re-gender themselves and are in their cultures accepted—and note that, "although the term *berdache* is technically reserved for members of American Indian societies [the same that have lan-

guages in which 'gender' encodes not 'male/female' but "animate/inanimate"?],
berdache-like people have been found in Alaska, Siberia, Central and South
Asia, Oceania, Australia, Sudan, and the Amazon region."[84] Kessler and
McKenna call systems of reality construction "incorrigible" when they refuse
and insist on containing such "real possibilities" that challenge them. I have
sometimes called them "psychotic" for the same reason.

"Kinds" need not be established as divisions. They can be retrieved as distinctions and thus help us see the systems within which they were generated
so that we can more effectively, when we judge necessary, set about adjusting
our meanings and so also the relations and actions they inform and reproduce. Once it is demystified, gendering reveals itself to be a taproot of creativity that can simultaneously disrupt and renew our multifold relations.

# PARTIAL KNOWLEDGE

B Y "PARTIAL KNOWLEDGE" I do not mean a bit of knowledge that, like a piece of a jigsaw puzzle, has not yet been put in its proper place. Nor do I mean knowledge only of a subset of an entire body of work, such as knowledge of Kant's *Critique of Pure Reason* but not of the philosopher's work as a whole. I also do not mean something like knowledge of all of Tolstoy's writings but not of the field of literature. However, with the latter instances, in which the question of where to draw the circle defining the "whole" is at least somewhat problematic, we approach what I mean. Imagine an introductory course titled "U.S. History: 1800–1900" that listed on its syllabus only studies of New England. Its misleading title would sooner or later provoke questions, and the course would have to be retitled to add the requisite, "in New England," or the syllabus would have to be significantly changed. But that appears straightforward. The professor's colleagues and students would see and think they knew how to remedy the problem. This is not unlike a course supposedly about religion but actually only about Christianity that, in secular liberal-arts colleges, would have to be changed also to 'cover' the "world religions." But even that course would remain "partial," as I intend the term here, as long as it continued to exclude significantly different faith traditions against which monotheistic faiths have struggled for supremacy. The story of "religion" told from the perspective of those who see monotheism as more true, real, significant than other traditions is likely not to deal directly with the experiences of adherents of other faiths who were forced to convert; killed; driven into hiding or flight; or 'allowed' to persist in increasing isolation, subject always to prejudice and scorn, if not outright persecution. Thus, for example, we have had histories that tell of the "martyrs" who died for the faith that ultimately won, while the martyrs among those who lost have been called "heretics," "infidels," "unbelievers," "superstitious Natives." Even a study of "religion" that tells some of those other stories would remain partial if we hear only from the men and the variously systemically privileged on all sides.

A course that reflects and perpetuates the sort of partial knowledge that concerns me here is, then, 1) about only a part of its claimed subject; when 2) that subject matter itself is predefined in too narrow ways; but 3) presents its part of the narrowly defined subject *as if it were the whole*; and so 4) uses mystified definitions and preset norms related to ideals by which any other claimants for inclusion must be judged of the wrong 'kind,' or 'inferior,' or exotic, or no more than historical leftovers to be, at best, tacked on "if there is time when we have covered the basic material." Such a course thus remains within and perpetuates the notion that its partial knowledge is actually inclusive, general, and perhaps universal, of and for all proper knowledge of its subject. Such knowledge is "partial" in both senses of the term, then: it is both of and for (and, historically, has usually also been by) the part it maintains in its powerful definitional role. It is also not impartial in either sense of *impartial*. It is not 'above the fray' and disinterested, and it is not fair.

I do not mean to collapse all meanings of partial knowledge into any specific one, even the complex one with which I am primarily concerned. Life is complicated. More, and more flexible, distinctions are needed, not fewer and more rigid ones. The jigsaw-puzzle analogy has its uses, too. It reminds us that, when the point is to be able to re-create a picture of, say, the Taj Mahal as someone else has painted it, we can hardly want people inserting pieces from a puzzle depicting an aardvark. But if I were teaching about India, I can imagine having other purposes for depicting the Taj, and so wanting to put the building in contexts omitted when we look at it in isolation as a singular aesthetic object (while also valuing that). There are always choices to make about where to draw boundaries, about what our purposes and responsibilities are.

There is a business-school story along these lines. A streetcar manufacturer, faced with the proliferation of cars, buses, and subways, realizes that its real business is transportation, not streetcars, so it diversifies and reinvents itself. Another streetcar manufacturer, convinced that it is making the only real, true, right kind of transportation, soon folds—or so the business-school story goes. The second company, of course, could also have decided to reduce its size and specialize in producing historically accurate streetcars for devotees. By keeping streetcars from disappearing entirely, the second company would also have helped to keep the "successful" companies from convincing themselves and others that "transportation" can mean only those modes that prove more "fit" under the terms set by a profit-driven economy. Many kinds of partiality are falsely cast as the best, or even the only, way.

We could tell similar stories about fields of knowledge. Psychology, for example, now includes many more theories, clinical practices, subjects, and modes of research than it once did. Had it not reconfigured as the knowledge and societal expectations of its scholars and practitioners changed, it, too, might have folded—or become a tiny field only for specialists in the arcane.

But there is more to these stories of changes in fields, and our concern is with the kinds of violation—sometimes to the point of deadly violence—that partial, closed systems can entail. People who believed that children should not work in factories for ten to twelve hours a day and that workers had rights to safety provisions, to weekends off, to the eight-hour workday, to a living wage have been (and, where fair, equitable labor legislation has not been passed and enforced, too often still are) fired, blacklisted, beaten, shot. And while some scholars as well as bosses and politicians continued to claim that there were lesser humans who 'by nature' could do nothing but labor, who should not be educated or allowed free time lest they get "ideas above their station," such unjust actions were justified by what passed for knowledge. Enslaved people (defined by some scholars as 'primitive,' 'childlike') who tried to learn to read were beaten, sold, killed. Women who believed they had minds, could be educated, could do many kinds of work were met with 'scientific' studies that 'proved' that using their minds 'too much' would draw blood away from their wombs and render them both "hysterical" and infertile. 'Scientific' economic theories that take Western capitalism to be the norm and the ideal of "economic development" can cast the values of unfettered profit-seeking competition as the engines of any and all 'true' and 'real' "progress" and "freedom" without regard for the exploitation of the poorest and most desperate workers on the globe.

Knowledge of, by, and for a part that has been defined as the whole, as well as the right, true, significant thing-itself, is and has been associated with virtually every systemically legitimated injustice. Such knowledge provides the conceptual warrants that domination requires to become normalized and legitimate. Its warrantees may be rationalized philosophically and/or scientistically. They may also, in some cultures and eras, be cast in religious terms or as cultural narratives that sustain traditions. Cultures typically privilege some 'kinds' of people, activities, beliefs, relations over others, and they provide legitimation for doing so in differing conceptual modes. When these stratification systems come to be seen as unjust, and have been delegitimated through struggle, we become able to look back on the old partial knowledge so intimately related to them and see just how skewed, even bizarre, it was. Partial knowledges in all forms can be corrected, and that should be remembered, and honored.

However, if we leave out of the stories of the self-correction of knowledges over time all that people did, and suffered, to bring about those changes, we create yet another kind of partial knowledge, another set of self-congratulatory, exclusive narratives. We owe a great deal to feminist and other critical scholars and activists for breaking out of partial narratives of Heroic Knowledge. Established systems of any kind do not necessarily "correct themselves in time." Women were not "given the vote" in the United States or elsewhere, for example. They wrested it from the hands of those who resisted, just as they struggled to retrieve women's history.

The works that are remembered in dominant traditions themselves tend originally to have been the products of independent-minded people who set out to change and correct something others accepted. There are many stories in the West about the hero, Man Who Is Rational, doing just that. But some of these stories were nevertheless partial and became more so once they were established. The radical work of originators is famously codified and reduced to in-group expertise by followers, leading to sayings such as "Marx is not a Marxist" and "Freud is not a Freudian." Similar disclaimers are also found in prefaces written by Foucault, who tried to distinguish his meanings from those of others, who, he believed, mistook, distorted, and sometimes reduced his radical thinking to something more familiar: a new theory to be applied.

The deep roots of erroneous, unjust knowledge constructions have skewed even the terms in which critiques are carried out and the stories that are then told about them, leaving some manifestations of those errors still with us. So, when, for example, research retrieves the stories of women who participated fully in the work of a now famous male partner, as well as in the weaving of cultural meanings within which all such work is done, we learn more about how scholarship has actually been conducted and more about the thinking that really informed what we have inherited. As we then rethink what we thought we knew, we also learn more about its meaning, its scope and limitations, its uses and misuses.

Katie Geneva Cannon, a professor of Christian ethics, writes of her search for less partial knowledge:

> The method used in this study departs from most work in Christian and secular ethics. The body of data is drawn from less conventional sources and probes more intimate and private aspects of Black life. The Black women's literary tradition has not previously been used to interpret and explain the community's sociocultural patterns from which ethical values can be gleaned. I have found that this literary tradition is the nexus between the real-lived texture of Black life and the oral-aural cultural values implicitly passed on from one generation to the next.[1]

## Impartial, Objective Knowledge

In the dominant U.S. culture, both reason and impartiality—a key virtue long associated with reason—have been limited by some or all of the differing meanings of "partial" I sketched earlier. Yet they continue to be used prescriptively in a judgmental, moralized, coercive way. In a class I taught at a large university, I asked the students what someone was *doing* when she or he said, "Be reasonable." Remembering times they had been told to "be reasonable," the students said it meant: "Shut up and sit down," "Don't be so emotional," "Don't be so passionate," "I'm right; you're out of order," "I won't talk to you unless you play by my rules." Basically, they felt dismissed, discredited, and castigated for a failure to be what, or as, they should be. You can discredit this story by calling it "just an anecdote," of course, or by thinking that the students *should* have been put down because they undoubtedly were "too emotional" and not thinking 'clearly' or 'effectively.' But not all anecdotes are trivial, and not all people who feel put down when they are told to "be reasonable" are wrong in objecting to it. Not all 'emotional' thinking is "irrational" or wrong, and not all 'rational' thinking is emotion-free, either.

Impartiality has been moralized not in terms of its particular prescriptive content (like a code of moral behavior, of dos and don'ts) but as the quality and goal of a supposedly neutral judge. It is taken to set the terms for acceptable—which is not necessarily the same as sound—scholarship. Most of the time, when we speak of impartial knowledge, we actually mean 'real' knowledge, that which has not been distorted by bias, by partial, particular perspectives. That is, we mean that such knowledge is 'objective,' and by 'objective' we mean not 'subjective'—that is, not personalized, not tainted by emotion. The assumption is often lurking here that prejudice, a strong kind of bias, is emotional in essence and precisely not rational. An impartial, objective knower, we tend to think, is 'fair' in the sense that she or he will be persuaded only by 'sound' reasoning and 'hard' evidence, not by anything 'soft,' such as feeling, or 'nonrational,' such as anger, hatred, prejudice.

Impartial, objective knowledge, in dominant traditions that value those 'virtues,' has most often meant what one can know if one follows the 'right' way to the 'real' truth—that is, truth that can, and should, coerce the assent of anyone whose reason is "unclouded" by irrelevancies seen as such from the perspective of operative definitions of reason (in the tradition I am using as an example, perspectives other than those of highly abstract rules and methods for reasoning in ways that can coerce assent to properly drawn conclusions).

This is the "view from nowhere" of (against) which many feminist and other critical epistemologists have written. It is supposed to be knowledge from no standpoint or perspective, knowledge of the real, true object as it is—and/or as it is knowable by methods designed to control against the subjective (the 'merely' perspectival, the biased). But as Lorraine Code, who joins the critique of this view, writes: "Only God and his would-be successors can pretend to a God's-eye view. Those who are not sufficiently privileged to occupy such a position will always find that their position is constructed relative to it, and the old illusions and oppressions will remain firmly in place."[2] Good, logical reasoning can challenge faulty claims of a "god's-eye view," but it can also continue to 'prove' some of its assumptions when they have been established as true. It is an important method: it is not, in human hands, perfect.

Thus, we return to our beginning: *impartial*, as distinct from *partial*, does relate to knowledge of the whole, but it does so in a particular way, because what and who defines "the whole" is a decision, a choice (whatever its grounds, although obviously from any perspective there are better and worse grounds). *Impartial* has been used evaluatively to characterize a particular kind of knowledge (god's-eye, and thus moralized as 'good' in both senses) of what has been defined by some to be the whole—but that always also excludes some other knowledges and their ways of being in relation to the object of knowledge (that is, not from a god's-eye, unlocated, objective perspective). Knowledge of a part has thus been shifted to mean knowledge from a perspective, and knowing from a perspective has slid into meaning being 'only' personal, subjective, emotional, and these have collapsed into meaning being biased. That's a lot of stuff to put in the "bias" basket: knowledge of the wrong 'kind' of part; identified perspectives; located knowers; personal knowledge; emotions; and with these, the cultural assumptions that create them as 'problems.'

And then, "bias" is often used as a synonym for "prejudice": "You can't trust him; he's biased against (whatever)." Being impartial then re-emerges as meaning "not taking sides," being "above the fray"—having no (admitted) stake in any inquiry except that of finding "the truth, the whole truth, and nothing but the truth" and a related stake in doing so by using the 'proper' methods and procedures (which themselves have histories, of course). That is, there are things at stake for the impartial knower, but they, unlike other possible stakes, are claimed to be not only unbiased but the remedy for bias. That is a powerful position to be in, needless to say: to protest against it except in its own terms—which concedes definitional power from the get-go—is to render oneself dismissable. The case each of my students remembered she had wanted to make when she was told to "be reasonable" was not heard. The one who remembered crying while trying to say why cruelty to animals is wrong was told she was "too sensitive." Having been silenced again, she did not ask, ""Too sensitive for what, for whom, from what and whose perspective?"

But human beings (I want to add "and other animals," but we will get to that) think and make all sorts of judgments in many ways. We are indeed "swayed" by emotions; we use our imaginations; we are empathetic and sympathetic; we sense things without knowing how or why; we feel our realities, values, judgments in our bodies; we are convinced by what we know of a speaker's character, by gestural meanings, by the contexts in which arguments are made as well as by logical correctness considered in abstraction from all else. So how, and why, did "logic," as highly particular as it is, become the best, or even the only, legitimated way to achieve not only sound and good and real but fair and morally defensible (impartial, objective) knowledge? We could also ask, as we might need to in some cultures and eras and groups, how and why and to whose benefit traditional knowledge, religious knowledge—any authoritative, dominant, legitimated knowledge—became the only sound and good (again in both senses) knowledges.

Such dominance may suggest that logic's coercive qualities were needed because too many people were resisting what the few wanted them to accept (and to convince themselves of, as well). If a few people had wrongly defined themselves in contradistinction from and as superior to others, they would then have had to define "those people's" knowledges, and the human capacities and functions their knowledges derive from and speak for, not just as different, but as inferior. Rulers and bosses of many kinds are rarely comfortable with the idea that they are exercising power over their equals, let alone their possible superiors. Capacities and functions, along with knowledges, that were therefore cast as 'lesser' would then mark who, and what, was rightly to be controlled. But the 'superior' few (still human, after all) would also then have to keep the inferior capacities in themselves under control. They would have to display "self-mastery," to 'transcend' the 'lower' aspects of their own human being. And they would have to be sure that others, and not they, fulfilled the functions defined as inferior. Their stratification system and the definitions that back it up, then, would be prescriptively present in their preferred modes of reasoning.

When prescriptions are enforced, they can turn around and reappear in the form of descriptions—and research 'findings.' When some 'kinds' of people have been defined as less intelligent and, being less intelligent, as properly to be denied education, they are likely to appear thereafter really to be less intelligent. This is especially likely when ignorance is confused with stupidity, as it so often is, but it also follows when "intelligence" is only defined in terms of the abilities that are practiced and developed through education. That is pure circularity: defined as not able to do it; not allowed to learn to do it; 'proved' to be unable to do it.

Similarly, upper-class women denied physical exercise because of their supposedly natural, but actually prescribed, fragility are likely really to become fragile. People living in built settings designed on the assumption that everyone can do what, in fact, none of us can do all the time, at all ages, under all conditions, do sort out neatly into the pre-established categories of "healthy" and "normal" versus the disabled, the old, the infirm, the fat, the uncoordinated, the "dwarfs" and "midgets," the "giants," the "freaks" into which a world not built for them/us turns us/them. So again, knowledge that begins as partial but takes over as the very standard of impartiality can be kept closed to correction *because knowledge matters: worlds are built to conform to it, and those worlds then produce 'evidence' of the accuracy of their own original premises.* Were you or I to be locked up and treated as some "insane" or "criminal" people are, we would find it very hard indeed to prove a mistake had been made. Protesting "I don't belong here," anger at being treated this way, despair can be taken to prove that we do indeed belong there, just as the anger of those locked out by prejudicial systems has been taken to prove their emotional instability—that "they" are dangerous, that "they" must be kept under more, not less, control.

But again: there have always been voices questioning such systems. In her monumental *Mind: An Essay on Human Feeling,* the philosopher Susanne Langer has some subversive things to say:

> Logical conviction is such a pin-pointed feeling that it has, in itself, none of the widespread and involved character of emotion; it seems the very opposite of emotion, although all sorts of highly cathected ideas may gather around it, and make it a tiny firm center in a maelstrom of fantasies. . . . And, furthermore, it leads to the peculiar social circumstance that it is relatively easy to confront different individuals with the same challenge to feeling, unimpaired by the usual modifications due to personal context. This makes for a unanimity in logical convictions that has few if any parallels in the realm of human feeling, and gives to logical perception an air of 'objectivity.' . . . But there is much more to rational

thinking than the highly general form which may be projected in written symbols or in the functional design of a machine. Thinking employs almost every intuitive process, semantic and formal (logical), and passes from insight to insight not only by the recognized processes, but as often as not by short cuts and personal, incommunicable means.[3]

## Unanimity

As glad as some of us are to have feeling, emotion, intuition revalued as aspects of "rational thinking" and of "mind" (which helps revalue Woman as well as men of some groups and times), it is crucial not to overlook what Langer is also saying: that knowledge has been established as objective/impartial when it comes closest to *forcing unanimity*, "unimpaired by the usual modifications due to personal context." This should make every antenna we have go up. Such decontextualized unanimity threatens at the root what the philosopher Hilde Nelson calls "practices of personhood"—the ways we signal to others who (rather than what) we are and the equally crucial ways others read those signals, take them into account, and thereby relate with us.[4] Thus, we may co-create meaningful personhood as an existential reality. But when, instead, we adopt ways of thinking that require that our communication be "impartial," defined as "unimpaired by ... personal context," we are at very serious risk of violating our own and others' personhood—which is the experience my students had suffered and remembered so painfully.

Focusing on the political implications of unanimity, Hannah Arendt wrote: "Unanimity of opinion is a very ominous phenomenon, and one characteristic of our modern age. It destroys social and personal life, which is based on the fact that we are different by nature and by conviction. A unanimous public opinion tends to eliminate bodily those who differ, for mass unanimity is not the result of agreement.... In contrast to agreement, unanimity does not stop at certain well-defined objects, but spreads like an infection into every related issue."[5] Those who know Arendt's work will recognize a warning akin to the one she made about violence. Arendt was profoundly concerned about the use of violence, even when she thought it necessary and justified, because— as we saw in the very different writings of von Clausewitz—violence ("force" in von Clausewitz) so quickly and almost unavoidably takes over, sets the terms within which all then find themselves trapped. Soon we find ourselves not trying to stop some specific people from doing some specific, horrendous things, but trying to *eliminate* the Enemy. To support such an escalating effort that takes us far beyond the rationale with which we originally justified our own use of force, we come to require unanimity at home, and among allies. Differences then become grounds for action against "traitors."

Because in reality we differ, and because reality is always more than we are and changes, those who construe knowledge as necessarily and rightly singular, static, and properly coercive of assent by all can end up devising methods and systems and theories that are elegant, internally consistent—and incompatible with realities. When such elegant logical systems are then imposed on the world, they can become dangerous. But they do not always do so: good has been done by 'experts' in virtually all traditions; abstract conceptual schemes have proved useful in predicting observable phenomena; amazing devices and cures have been created that have saved and improved lives; devastating economic problems have been, if not solved, at least ameliorated for some. I am not forgetting all that. I am simply not celebrating it alone. That is amply done elsewhere, and if it is done partially, it can hide the more complex and painful stories that also need to be told.

There have always been warnings against taking a part, or a partial approach, to be the whole, or impartial. Those warnings have come from within as well as outside of dominant traditions. They are not always remembered, but there they are. Aristotle, for example, wrote that "we must not look for the same degree of accuracy in all subjects; we must be content in each class of subjects with accuracy of such a kind as the subject-matter allows, and to such an extent as is proper to the inquiry." The economist Andrew Kamarck uses that quote on the first page of his *Economics and the Real World*, a critique of his field. He also cites Goedel's proof that "no axiomatic system could be complete," and quantum mechanics' demonstration of "insuperable" limits to "know[ing] precisely both the exact position and the momentum of a simple elementary particle." Kamarck makes a crucial distinction between "accuracy" and "precision": "In common usage, the meanings often overlap—there is a predisposition to believe that the more precise a statement is, the more accurate it is." However, he says, this misleads economists, as it does many others, because it is not in fact truthful to be "precisely wrong" rather than "roughly accurate" when the latter is all that is possible in "the real world."

Further, Kamarck recalls that his field is itself partial and risks harming those it should help when it denies its partiality. He notes that "natural language can be more flexible in conveying meaning" than can mathematics, or

any field's technical vocabulary, and that "it is infinitely richer in vocabulary
... and can frequently be more accurate although less precise." Finally, he also
cites (to dismiss) a reason that is rarely publicly acknowledged for holding a
field within mathematical or other precise technical language: "We [econo-
mists] need the shelter of Mathematics to protect Economics from intruders."[6]

Similarly, Lynn Hankinson Nelson writes about her field that "traditional
philosophy of science has demanded and been granted rigid boundaries
between epistemology, metaphysics, science, methodology, and values—including political values and practices." Impartiality, recast to include responsible
recognition of multiple kinds of mutual implication as well as limitations, can
be retrieved from such protective, sometimes reality-defying, field-enclosing
partialities and their dangers. Nelson continues: "But in the last three
decades"—and further back, if we remember, for instance, aspects of U.S.
Pragmatism, as well as differing traditions elsewhere—"research into the
assumptions, theories, and practices of the sciences, and the social and political contexts in which science communities are located, has demonstrated
interrelationships between all of these activities the traditional [dominant] view
wanted to keep separate."[7] Impartiality can then be understood as a virtue that
can help us in, rather than keep us from, discriminating between accuracy and
precision. It can also thus serve fairness where fairness is understood as entail-
ing accurate, context-appropriate, personhood-recognizing judgments rather
than the application of abstract, universalized principles and methods without adjusting for (and maintaining openness to the possible need for correction in light of) real particularities.

## Emotions, Animals, Morality

We will not succeed in transforming these crucial meanings and the practices they reflect, legitimate, perpetuate any more than others have through
the generations if we do not remember what Langer underscored: that logics can provide a *feeling* of certainty in the midst of the usual "maelstrom" of
emotion. That is, despite their own claims, such logics are by no means 'purely'
rational. They do something gratifying for those who hold on to them. No
small part of what they do is protect individuals, professions, social orders
against loss of control. But the kind of control sought from logics (and ideologies, for that matter) corresponds all too well to domination. It is control

through coercive rules rather than persuasion that invites agreement. Modes of knowing informed by coercive logics or ideologies that are partial while claiming impartiality can reinforce prejudicially assigned inferiorities of other modes and traditions of reasoning, as of the people(s) defined as characterized by them.

Too many hierarchies of modes of knowing, and of knowers and subject matters, reflect the errors of the invidious monism discussed earlier. Masculinized 'hard' science, with its self-enclosing mathematical language and logics, reigns supreme in the dominant culture of the West over a hierarchy that slides downward to the 'soft' knowing of nonquantifiable fields. We approach the bottom when we reach the "intuition" attributed to women and the "instincts" of "primitive" people. The 'bottom,' of a scale of animate life, is reached when we cross the divide between Man and (other) Animals. But, I repeat, this hierarchy, which depends on wrongly taking a part to be neutral, the whole, and the best, is not necessary. Some cultures that have their own hierarchies do not rest on this one, and some Western thinkers are challenging it yet again. For example, the British philosopher Mary Midgeley has written against the long-dominant view that made anthropomorphism (defined as the wrongful projection of human capacities, feelings, motives onto animals) virtually a heresy:

> Whether, and how far, interspecies communication works for feelings and motives is an empirical question. On the whole, it does. *That* it does is not surprising, given our evolutionary relationship, and the fact that it could be quite dangerous to misconstrue the behavior of creatures outside of one's species, and quite convenient to read it.... Particular forms do vary, which is why you have to know a good deal about a species to read its gestures reliably. But then they vary in human life too; culture does what it can to confuse us. The skills we develop for penetrating the curtain of culture probably help us in dealing with other species also.[8]

Conversely, refusing to be blocked by the iron curtain between Man and Animal also helps those of us who have lived with it to deal better with other cultures. For one thing, lifting the curtain delegitimates the tendency to project *animal* qualities onto some 'kinds' of *humans* in ways that license treating them as shamefully as some people treat animals. And just as Man can have only limited knowledge of himself while he must *not* be akin to Woman, humans can have only limited knowledge of ourselves while we must *not* be akin to the other animals.

We are breaking out of the old partial knowledges that legitimated ranked divisions by 'kind' for so long. Some of us may even be approaching "practices of personhood" that extend to our relations with animals. (I am obviously focusing on dominant traditions that have, as others have not, constructed this radical division in the first place.) That would be a transformational achievement. When the need and knowledge-warranted support for defining humans in radical contradistinction from animals disappears, far better ways to think about all relationalities and the moralities that express and should protect them may be allowed back into view. Our own experiences and the cultures of others stand ready to provide alternatives once fierce defenses against admitting the legitimacy of those experiences are overcome.

Undoing the radical division between Rational Man and the Dumb Beasts also helps us think better about moral relations with people who, by prevailing partial standards, cannot be defined as "rational moral agents," such as infants and children, the "mentally ill," people with brain damage. Why, after all, must possession of a particular sort of rationality be taken as *the* marker of one who has a rightful claim to moral personhood? And why must we recognize such claims only from persons? If we recognize that all of these potent terms—"reason," "person," "moral"—may be limited, partial in every sense, we may make room for moral relations with the nature that implicates our being with itself and, thus reconnected, find that we are better prepared to think about many ways of being human.

We should also note that, however pre-eminent it is, reason is not the only discriminator when it comes to granting people moral worth and the right to empowerment. Under U.S. law, convicted felons and bankrupts have 'bundles of rights' unlike those of 'normal' citizens. Having been judged to have transgressed against property or failed in the competition for wealth, they have often also been categorically judged morally inferior (compare this with the 'kinds' of people the eugenicists proclaimed "unfit").[9] Where 'proper' relation to reason, to 'normal' embodiment, to property, to wealth variously but similarly entails rights or the denial of rights, and rights are supposedly premised on (even as they confer) recognized personhood, old hierarchies strongly tend to retain their power.[10] And animals, held across the firmest division of all, are kept available to justify them: "They're animals, no better than the beasts," those who wish to dominate other people(s) can continue to say.

## Undoing Partial Public Authority

Despite the persistence of circular, emotionally freighted partial knowledges, established thinkers of the past and present challenge its sway in many ways. Among the men who have done so, we might list Friedrich Nietzsche, Michel Foucault, Michael Polanyi, Thomas Kuhn, Peter Berger, Thomas Luckman, Edward T. Hall, Lewis Gordon, William James, Charles Sanders Pierce, Clifford Geertz, Michael Berube, Ronald Takaki, Jacques Lacan, Cornel West, Jacques Derrida, Richard Rorty, François Lyotard, Henry Louis Gates, Frederick Jameson. These critics, too, remind us not only that knowledge is a human construct, but that it also carries cross-references that simultaneously sustain it and continue to exclude those who have been privatized, silenced, dominated. Barbara Johnson, the translator of Jacques Derrida's *Dissemination,* observes: "The deconstruction of a text does not proceed by random doubt or generalized scepticism, but by the careful teasing out of warring forces of signification *within the text itself.*"[11] She holds, as I keep insisting, that this project is not about destruction; it is about undoing partial constructions that have themselves been destructive. "If anything is destroyed in a deconstructive reading," she says, "it is not meaning but the claim to unequivocal domination of one mode of signifying over another."[12] Disestablishment of the authority for such domination is mistaken for demolition only by those who choose to remain locked into the establishment, whether as insiders or as wannabes.

Some scholars working within established traditions, if less radically, are also disestablishing old, prejudicial conceptual errors of partial knowledges. For instance, the textbook *Race, Gender, and Sexuality: Philosophical Issues of Identity and Justice* draws on "critical thinking theory" premised on basic Western logic as it defines "*validity, truth,* and *soundness.*" It uses these standards and the methods associated with them to counter systemic prejudices. The textbook's introduction asserts: "In order for an argument to be good, it must do two things. First, the premises must logically support the conclusion. If they do, the argument is *valid.* Second, a valid argument must be made up of only true premises. If a valid argument has true premises, then the argument is *sound.*" Using this logic—the very one I have been critiquing when it is extended too far and becomes the sole arbiter of impartiality as both soundness and fairness— articles in the textbook demonstrate that, how, and to what distorting or illuminating effects "conceptions of race, gender, and sexual identity permeate

theoretical discussions of oppression and justice as well as discussions of specific social issues such as discriminatory harassment and pornography."[13]

Through such works, as well as contemporary critical scholarship, some
of the most familiar sources of authority for knowledge have been *problematized*. And, as Alice Jardine reminds us, by problematizing authority, those
works are also (wittingly or unwittingly) demystifying gender as the 'logic,' or
syntax, of control of all 'kinds':

> Over the past century, those master (European) narratives—history, phi-
> losophy, religion—which have determined our sense of legitimacy in the
> West have undergone a series of crises in legitimation. It is widely rec-
> ognized that legitimacy is part of that judicial domain which, historically,
> has determined the right to govern, the succession of kings, the link
> between father and son, the necessary paternal fiction, the ability to decide
> who is the father—in patriarchal culture. The crises experienced by the
> major Western narratives have not, therefore, been gender-neutral. They
> are crises in the narratives invented by men.[14]

Remembering gender with and against critics of "master narratives," we
again bring to the surface the social implications that inform and emerge from
authorized knowledge. Knowledge is not the kind of thing that lies around
waiting for us to 'discover' it. It emerges from encounters with what is taken
to be its object of a very particular sort. To engage yet another school of
thought, phenomenology: we know what we *intend* to know—and *what we
intend to know* is by no means only an individual matter. For something that
has been conceptualized to be construed as knowledge, it must be comprehended (*com*, 'brought together'; *prehended*, 'reached for, grasped, taken in')
by a human mind, and human minds are formed (not determined) within
reality-framing cultural languages that are not individual (that is, private; as
Wittgenstein pointed out, a private language is a contradiction in terms).

Further, what an individual has thus comprehended must then be con-
veyed 'properly' to, and must be accepted as knowledge by, others. The simple assertion "I know X" does not suffice to achieve acceptance for most of us.
Were I to say, "I know that economic decisions are not made by rational deduction by most people most of the time," lots of people would nod. (I have
observed this, having tried it many times over the years.) But I would not win
the Nobel Prize, as did those who 'proved' what you and I have always 'known'

but did so in legitimated, established ways that forced assent, however reluctant, from their professional peers. There is nothing necessarily wrong with this. Why should people grant me authority solely on the basis of my own "I know"? But it is nevertheless noteworthy that even an "I know" that is immediately recognized by many others has no standing as legitimate knowledge if it comes from someone not previously authorized, and/or finds agreement from other nonauthorized people.

But some individuals—those who are ranked above others socially, politically, theologically—can speak as 'proper' knowers, and sometime even beyond the sphere in which they have become legitimated. In both such cases, although more obviously in the latter, they may be so subsumed into their authoritative role that they and others 'overlook' what is actually authorizing their knowledge: not the usual rules for 'sound' knowledge but their socially enforced power. What Mao wrote in his Little Red Book was to be learned as knowledge. Stalin prescribed the rewriting of history to erase his opponents as "non-persons." Ayatollah Khomeini issued a *fatwa* against what he defined as Salman Rushdie's "heresies." The pope in Rome is believed to be infallible on some questions. Presidents of the United States have cast questioning of their decisions as disloyalty to the country rather than doubts about their own veracity and judgment. From these pinnacles of various sorts of power, the scale moves down to those whose assertions of knowledge carry no weight and have no authority, even if what they say is recognized as true and useful by many others.

We should remember, then, that authoritative knowledge of whatever stripe is public. An individual may 'have' it, but its warrant *as authoritative* is collective. I have no authority if I am not socially, politically, culturally licensed to speak for, or as, a publicly established legitimating source (for example, by holding the right academic degree); if I am not backed up by power to underwrite my knowledge; if there is no agreed-on method, itself backed up by an accepted methodology, by which I can 'prove' (that is, coerce assent to) its correctness. Authorized knowledge requires social forms such as roles, schools and degrees, professions, codes, rituals, edicts that are inhabited, used, issued by social figures such as sages, shamans, popes, rabbis, academics, imams, elders, *saddhus*, chiefs, dictators, presidents, heads of professional associations, licensed psychologists, certified "master" plumbers. Authoritative knowledge is also, and is therefore, created and expressed in 'insider,' esoteric, technical, community-based languages, some of which become established as 'higher' and more worthy than others. These hierarchies of communities of knowers and their languages reflect and perpetuate accepted modes of thought and views of reality. Together, they form the common stock of cultures that is transmitted to new generations. Thus, they reflect throughout the basic constructs of dominant cultures—and those cultures' stratification systems (by which other kinds of knowledge are also ranked). They are not neutral, disinterested, above the fray. Like the denizens of the castle in Kafka's novel by that name, they decide from the heights, using their own logics, who is to be admitted, who is not, and how all are to be treated.[15]

In short, behind and within any particular body of accepted knowledge are the definitions, the boundaries, the partialities established as central by those who have held power. To refuse them is to be shut out even from debate; to transgress them is to mark oneself as ignorant, unprofessional, stupid, biased—even, in some cases, as mad, heretical, dangerous to public life. The English insults "idiot" and "idiotic" derive from the Greek *idios,* meaning "personal," "peculiar," "separate." Those who have been privatized have thus been denied socially recognized authority of all kinds, including that of knowledge.

In some of these rankings and exclusions—those that have become closed and rigid—we encounter not only the necessary delimitation of definition, the marking of boundaries and noting of relational patterns that allow us to recognize things, categories, kinds, and to reason about them together, but also the mystifying errors of faulty generalization and circular reasoning. As Foucault observes in his study of the human sciences' constructions of *madness,* there are histories of "resemblance," of sameness to be discerned in histories of knowledge, and they produce (in our terms) circular reasoning that creates not just differences but excluded Otherness. Foucault writes:

> I am concerned ... with a history of resemblance: on what conditions was Classical thought able to reflect relations of similarity or equivalence between things, relations that would provide a foundation and a justification for their words, their classifications, their systems of exchange? ... The history of madness would be the history of the Other—of that which, for a given culture, is at once interior and foreign, therefore to be excluded (so as to exorcize the interior danger) but also by being shut away (in order to reduce its otherness); whereas the history of the order imposed on things would be the history of the Same.[16]

What Foucault says of madness applies, with little alteration, to the study of women, of lower-caste or 'primitive' males, of disabled people, and of various sexualities, as many contemporary scholars have explored. The 'kinds' that are cast out, and to what degree and effect, always varies by culture, regime, era, but the old errors may still be at work below those differences. A public "history of the Same" that was created by the root problem of ranking humans by 'kind' and then taking the few to be the inclusive term, the norm, and the ideal will always be partial and erroneous. Focusing on humans in our diverse relations with each other, to other animals, to nature, requires violating traditional, publicly empowered authorities insofar as they are more or less openly monist and hierarchical. And in some instances, it suggests locating *madness* not in individuals but in 'insane' social-psychotic constructions that have become coercively unanimous, such as those that 'normalize' witch burnings, lynchings, genocides, devastating exploitation of nature.

Henry Louis Gates Jr. also sees circular, mystified reasoning at work through old exclusions, although he does not name it as such. He asserts that "literary works configure into a tradition . . . because [published, authoritative] writers read other [published, authoritative] writers and *ground* their representations of experience in models of language provided largely by other writers *to whom they feel akin*. It is through this mode of literary revision, amply evident in the texts themselves—in formal echoes, recast metaphors, even in parody—that a 'tradition' emerges and defines itself. This is formal bonding, and it is only through formal bonding that we can know a literary tradition."[17] That is what "literary tradition" has meant, and it need not be cause for concern. But Gates is also reminding us that there is indeed such cause when traditions are founded on exclusions. He wrote what I quote here in his introduction to a series dedicated to retrieving the works of nineteenth-century Black women—the works of women whose 'kind' had long been vulnerable to many more modes of exclusion and violation than the literary by those who defined themselves as not "akin" and as superior to them. Literature, like and with stories and histories, informs our imaginations, and dominance-deformed imaginations can also be cruel and deadly.

What we have learned and what we teach require critique to reveal who and what these ongoing conversations first excluded and then could not include except as negativities—privatized, partialized Others. (See, for instance, Toni Morrison's telling *Dancing in the Dark: Whiteness and the Literary Tradition*.) Using such critical, 'archaeological' methods, we can see both power and authority at work *without having to look for any singular, purposeful intent either to include or to exclude. Such an intent may be present or absent: the point is not that it does not* matter, *but that it is not necessary.* That we know what we intend to know, as phenomenologists assert, is more than a personal matter. Systems, once established, inform our intentions—unless we think reflexively and critically about what we are doing.

Thinking critically about the radical privatization of women in and through traditions of literature and literary criticism, Gayatri Spivak suggests feminist disruptions of "public rigor" through the telling of "private" stories. She advocates against "the fiction of mainstream literary criticism—so generally 'masculist' that the adjective begins to lose all meaning, [another] view, coming from a mind-set that has been systematically marginalized . . . : that the production of public rigor bears the strategically repressed marks of the so-called 'private' at all levels. . . . This is especially the case with feminist alternative readings of the canon. . . . Women must tell each other's stories, not because they are simpleminded creatures, but because they must call into question the model of criticism as a neutral theorem or science."[18] We might say the same of other theorizations and sciences, including logics taught in critical thinking courses; some Marxist theoretical works; 'objective' social-science research; and much more. Methods and methodologies as public, professional, epistemological, interpretive bonding traditions created within 'masculist' and racialized—invidiously stratified—cultures cannot simply be extended to include that which, and those who, have been radically privatized. They can, however, become freshly useful if they are themselves submitted to ongoing critique.

It remains radical to move Woman into the public domain of authoritative knowledges (and authoritative critiques of knowledges). Jane Flax observes that "because historically women have been the caretakers as well as the bearers of children, they represent both the body and our first encounter with the sometimes terrifying, sometimes gratifying vicissitudes of social relations. They become the embodiments of the unconscious, just as men become the embodiment of reason and law (the ego and the superego)."[19] This brings us back to the "feeling" dimension of logic discerned by Langer, as well as our analysis thus far (neither of which derives, as Flax's analysis does, from psychoanalytic theory). The old roots of social prescriptions by 'kind' inform psyches in ways that can lock them within political, moral, religious and knowledge systems. We are by no means 'only' dealing with public, disinterested rationality here. Listen to the European cleric and philosopher Abelard, who wrote to the brilliant Heloise in the 1100s: "The more subtle [the tongue] is in you (*vobis*) and the more flexible because of the softness of your body, the more mobile and prone to words it is, and exhibits itself as the seedbed of all evil."[20] As long as Woman appears to Man as what he is not—he as separated, differentiated, individuated; she as the tempting, too fluid, Othered, subjective/subjected dimension of his always insecurely achieved masculinized separateness—we all remain partial, mystified, and dangerously unstable.

Robert Coles and others have suggested that similar dynamics are in play with regard to some whites' projections of their repressed fears and desires onto Black people, whom they are then fearfully drawn to and so feel the need to control, punish, reject—or even eliminate. This process of projection of forbidden aspects of the psyche/self onto others who have been defined, and forced to live, as 'lesser' 'kinds' is evident also in the hypersexualizing of some 'lower' class and ethnic groups by those who exploit them.[21] Authority systems fueled by such dynamics readily become mystified and so all the more powerful.

In philosophical language, Hegel has interesting things to say about the dialectical relation of such creations as 'subject' and 'object,' 'Master' and 'Slave.' He writes about the problem of an as-yet-unhealed partial self that craves that from which it has nevertheless separated itself. Claims that knowledge and reason ought to be solely or 'purely' objective betray what Hegel calls an "unhappy consciousness" in which the self is radically divided, alienated from itself. That alienation is found in, created by, expressed through modes of knowing and of relating to other people. In this view (found also in Heidegger, Sartre, and those they influenced), we can bridge "being for-itself" and "being for-another" through *recognition,* the achievement of healing mutual interdependence that overcomes the splitting of known from knower. Such recognition, the end (as Hegel saw it) of the dialectical process of development of the self as well as of human history, is possible only between people who are equals (although Hegel restricted that possibility to "the West," and only to some even there). In the development of knowledge, this is possible only when that which has been held to be utterly separate from the knower is re-cognized as in relation. Difference is thus maintained, but the oppositional, hierarchical division that requires as it suffers from relations of dominance is overcome.

Simone de Beauvoir was very familiar with Hegel and Sartre, but she also honored the publicly unrecognized knowing of women. She wrote *The Second Sex* to work through her realization that, and how, domination and its refusal of recognition implicates gender throughout. In *The Idea of Africa,*

V. Y. Mudimbe also uses gender analysis tellingly "to meditate on the complexity of the dialectic between inside and outside, domestic and foreign, civil and savage." He focuses on Herodotus's *Oiorpata*, "warlike women" or "Amazons" (Amazons: *a*, 'without'; *mastos*, 'breast'). "The fable" of the Amazons, Mudimbe observes, "seems to double . . . a silent disciplinary model. . . . [T]he gender division (in education, initiation, responsibilities) can be used as a key to an understanding of the general economy" based on an oppositional association of war (which turns boys into men) and marriage (girls into women)— or still more basically, we might say, of mortality/death and natality/birth.[22] Gender, which, as we have seen, *means* "kind" is always there, constructing and defending orders taken to be 'proper'—and doing so also by the use of "fables" that appear to challenge but also 'silently' "discipline" their audiences.

In her monumental work *The Anatomy of Prejudices*, the philosopher and psychoanalyst Elisabeth Young-Bruehl rethinks U.S. and European theorizations of *prejudice* in a way that is not dialectical in these ways but that is similarly attuned to subjective/objective tensions in human psyches and societies. She makes a highly suggestive case that we cannot understand prejudiced psyches as long as we construe them as distorted in any singular or privatized way. Interweaving psychoanalytic diagnostic categories with historicized political analyses of normalized and extraordinarily virulent prejudices, Young-Bruehl argues that socially conventional prejudices provide occasion for disturbed psyches to externalize their troubles and, sometimes, do so for massive numbers of people. (I have called the latter instances socially psychotic and also see them as on continua with 'ordinary' constructions of inferior 'kinds'.) Differentiating among sorts of troubled psyches, Young-Bruehl shows, for instance, how some are drawn to racialized prejudices, some to gendered prejudices, some to homophobias. What we can then see is how prejudices, which always place some—a part, a 'kind'—of humankind below others as threatening/threatened 'inferiors,' are by no means only individual aberrations or personal, privatized 'irrationalities.'

Thus, in conversation with many differing schools of thought, action, and practice, feminist antiracist, antihomophobic, and other critical scholarships are in opposition not to the quest for impartial authoritative knowledge per se but to the persistent failure of what it claims for itself. In a sense, feminist scholars are like civil-rights activists who call on the dominant tradition's best principles *as if* those principles were not tangled, partial, and self-contradictory: if "all men are created equal," and "men" is inclusive, then *we* are created equal, and you are, of course, in favor of our full inclusion. If the pursuit of knowledge is to be disinterested, nonpolitical, then it cannot mean to exclude us, and many others, so you will certainly welcome women's studies, multicultural studies, and the other critical 'special' studies into the center of all learning as necessary correctives rather than mere additives.

## Personal, Subjective, Located Knowledges: Relativism?

Although transforming knowledge may begin as the task of feminist scholars working with other scholar–activists, this is not, it is important to repeat, because rethinking traditions is impossible for those who are grounded in them. Paradigm shifts (to use the Kuhnian notion) may be repudiated by established orders at first, but when such shifts make better accounting for phenomena possible, they are indeed comprehensible—at least, to those who are not locked defensively into conceptual systems. Teaching rests on the faith that, although we differ and may have different stakes in learning and in what is available to be learned, we can nevertheless approach comprehension even of that which appears to be utterly outside our own experience. How else can we translate the past into terms accessible to newcomers, to students? How else can we study differing schools of thought, let alone cultures? Translation across such lines is possible, and the effort to achieve it rewards us not by giving us more of "the same," but by revealing mutually enriching differences along with discernible similarities. Good teachers and genuine scholars are not restricted to teaching their own perspectives, views, espoused theories, or cultures. They are, pre-eminently, creative translators. Maurice Merleau-Ponty thus valued cross-cultural understanding: "It is a way of thinking, the way *which imposes itself* when the object is 'different,' and requires us to transform ourselves. [When we] let ourselves be taught by another culture . . . a new organ of understanding is at our disposal—we have regained possession of that untamed region of ourselves, unincorporated in our culture, through which we communicate with other cultures."[23]

Proponents of "standpoint epistemology" and "identity politics" also seek to regain selves "unincorporated in our culture," but they do so from the personal/political 'subjective' stance of a knower who not only rejects the quest for some universal standpoint but positively affirms a particular one—one that is their own rather than that of an 'object' that is 'different.' By publicly claiming a political, historically located positional self that knows, and doing so without reifying even as we revalue that socially constructed identity, we can reground knowing in the real world where we are not only plural—in some regards, similar; in others, different—but each and every one unique.

One who seeks a free zone from dominant cultures in personal/political experience, identity, commitment does risk becoming incomprehensible to too many others or unknowingly perpetuating that culture because it is so deeply embedded in us. But that is not inevitable. As I noted earlier, we are neither trapped nor free; we are always in interaction with our culture, our times, our realities, and we are always able to think about as well as within them. It occurs to me here that Alcoholics Anonymous (AA) suggests something about the power of speech from and about who and what we are, even when that speech is utterly uninformed by political or historical or any other kind of analysis. In AA, as I understand it, people tell their own stories. Simply by doing so they begin a process of change that otherwise seemed almost impossible. Feminist work that seeks to ground knowledge in particular experience, claimed as such, has become much more sophisticated than the earlier discovery of consciousness-raising groups that "the personal is political" and that speaking the personal helps free us. But it is worth remembering, when we become embroiled in complex epistemological and political analyses, that there is something very powerful in the direct, nontheoretical turn to speaking oneself with others who really listen. Genuinely partial knowledge that is neither claimed as impartial nor restricted too fiercely to a particular group can, it seems, heal. Retrieval of our own uniqueness, and encountering that of others through their stories, provides 'outside' perspectives that enable reflexive thinking without the need for god-like objectivity.

To seek knowledge as who we are (our unique identity) and what we are (our social roles and 'kinds'), even when the 'what' has been imposed on us by oppressive systems, can free us even as we express ourselves. It is empowering to claim the identity that one was taught to hate; to explore its strengths, its resistances, its originality, its suffering, its personal and collective history as that story looks from the standpoint of those who have lived it. "Black Is Beautiful" is not just a statement of defiant opposition to racism. It is a statement of genuine discovery, of a moment of transforming knowledge. It reflects a move outside the standpoint of the partial, dominant few—a step out from behind the veil, as W.E.B. DuBois put it.

After all, we are each not only a mysterious and elusive and unique *who* that cannot be known as an object. We are also people who live in the real world, where *what* we are matters. We have been labeled, categorized, branded, but we have always also been much more than our labels. Chandra Talpade Mohanty is suspicious of women speaking *as* women, as she is of any assumption that the female is a direct line to the feminist. She writes nevertheless about the power of claiming our *multiple* personal, political, historical identities without forgetting who each of us uniquely is:

> In this country [the United States], I am, for instance, subject to a number of legal/political definitions: "third-world," "immigrant," "post-colonial." These definitions, while in no way comprehensive, do trace an analytic and political space from which I can insist on a temporality of struggle. Movement *between* cultures, languages, and complex configurations of meaning and power has always been the territory of the colonized.... The struggles I choose to engage in are then an intensification of these modes of knowing.... There is, quite simply, no transcendental location possible.[24]

But does that mean that "everything is relative" in the sense that no epistemological or moral claims on the assent of others are possible?

## The *Threat* of Relativism?

I do not share the fear that recognizing the personal, the privatized, the politically non-dominant in the quest for knowledge leads us ineluctably to the slippery slope of relativism. What it does, or can do, is open up space for the renewal of thinking that is compatible with diversities, plurality, particularities, change—and relationality. I confess that fearing the "relative" seems odd to me. Being in relation, being relative—rather like being a relative—seems to me just how we are and therefore a realistic source for relational moralities and epistemologies. People and things need not be viewed as singular atoms suddenly released by the destruction of a dominant, ordering tradition or Absolute to whirl, and collide, in a void. Shifting from static vertical orderings of separated entities ranked downward from (erroneously partial rather than horizontal) universals to *relations* enables us to see our world as an interdependent, changing, organically and internally—rather than mechanistically and externally—related nexus.[25] Thus, democratic, organic epistemologies can emerge to challenge monarchical, tyrannical, or totalitarian orderings.

We then see order not as rigid imposition, but as the working out of patternings within interrelations, as matrices rather than static typologies. As in ecology, we can see what we focus on as "nested" in a more or less supportive system on which it depends, and which depends on it. Ecological systems provide an intriguing alternative to rigidly schematic knowledge in which *transactional* relations cannot be seen as basic. We become open to serious consideration of narratives, as well as—and sometimes instead of—deductive arguments, and to exploration of the ethics of care as well as of rights.[26] In political terms, we can discern and propose epistemologies, logics, ethics, political philosophies that do not undermine democracy, however inadvertently, but that support and strengthen it through their recognition of plurality and change as givens rather than threats, as aspects of dynamic relatings rather than as deviations defined against static norms and ideals.[27]

Those who believe that the only alternative to the Old Order is radical, chaotic, and, hence, paralyzing relativism reveal the degree to which they are still seeing from the perspective of the few who have been taken to be the whole. The rest of us know very well that there are many ways to make distinctions, to discern and understand relations among differences—that imposing scales of descending worth is not the only way to avoid chaos.

I am reminded of students with whom I have worked in courses on political philosophy and ethics. Over and over, I have seen them retreat into a position of "relativism" when they fear that conflict is about to arise over moral positions. They say, "Well, that's your opinion," or "It's just a matter of semantics," or "I guess it's just how I was socialized." Or they trot out a phrase or two of postmodern antiessentialism. I have come to believe that such retreats from engagement with moral differences derive not from the relativism with which students are so often charged but, on the contrary, from the old roots of moral absolutism. Dominant traditions have not helped us learn how to converse together as equals about the most important values we hold. Instead, they have taught us that those values must be absolutely right or they are not values at all. So when students encounter serious differences, they are startled, troubled, frightened. Rather than fight with their friends in a zero-sum struggle, they prefer to say, in effect: I hold my absolute values; you hold yours. Thus, those who want to get along with people who are not already just like them may reveal that they have nowhere to go but into an uneasy acceptance of plural absolutes that are precisely *not* taken to be internally relative to each other. They require external rules (or determined efforts at tolerance) to allow them to coexist in their incompatible, and basically contra-dictory, separateness. Thus, both absolutism and a radical relativism defined only as its opposite make it possible, even necessary, to avoid serious engage-ment with differences. And so some differences remain unexplored, and all that we could learn with and from them—whether we come to agree or not—remains hidden. Potentially virulent unanimities that can break out into efforts to eliminate the Other remain seeded among us—as we have seen among populations that managed, when times were good, to be tolerant of each other.

In questioning knowledges still under the mantle of authoritative impar-tiality, we are precisely *not* in pursuit of a single epistemology, a single phi-losophy, a single ideology. Given that critical scholarships so often remain entangled in the very roots they oppose, I also have to say specifically what I am *not* suggesting: that because knowledges have been constructed by those in power, we should accept only, and uncritically, those constructed by the pow-erless. I am also not saying that we should embrace subjectivism rather than objectivism—or any other reversal that retains the same basic framings. Lor-raine Code, among others I have woven into this inquiry, offers a more prom-ising approach. She writes that, although women need to know for political reasons that "experts can be wrong," and that we need to recognize that "sub-jective knowers" provide alternative perspectives that are crucial, we need not choose between these polarized positions. She proposes, instead, that "knowl-edge is at once subjective and objective: subjective because it is marked, as prod-uct, by the processes of its construction by specifically located subjects; objec-tive in that the constructive process is constrained by a reality that is recalcitrant to inattentive or whimsical structurings." Thus, she also resists "radical, 'any-thing goes' relativism"—the kind that I believe is only the negative opposite of a still defining radical objectivism. She reminds us, too, that the "conflation of fiction and fact"[28] is not the goal. Distinctions remain crucial: in refusing absolutized divisions, we open space for distinctions to be made more subtly and aptly.

We are trying simultaneously to open space for free thinking and dif-fering modes of knowing; for heretofore suppressed voices to speak and be well heard in ways that may express and/or call for the creation of differing epistemologies; for critiques and reformulations of thought that has been entangled in profound errors that put us at risk of violation, and too often violence.

## Continuing Resistance to Transformation

Since these values and goals are shared (from differing perspectives) by some non-feminists, and not only those of today or of any one culture, why does the widespread discomfort unto anger persist when questions are raised about the curriculum? Does anyone really believe that centuries, even millennia, of purposeful, systemically entrenched exclusions of women—as of nonprivileged men, of whole cultures labeled "primitive" or "Oriental" or "low caste," of "inferior" ethnic or heretical "infidel" religious groups—left no significant traces? Could such exclusionary thinking have proceeded and persisted *without* creating tangles that perpetuate the original exclusions even when the will to do so has changed? That would be rather like concluding that a structural error on the ground floor of a building has disappeared because we have learned how to build the top floor differently (or, because we no longer believe in "foundationalism," we need take no account of origins, histories, archaeologies).

Yet resistance persists, and not only among those whose prejudices block their thinking, who feel their power and privilege threatened, or who fear the implications of the new scholarships for their 'private' lives. More than one man in faculty discussions of curricular change I have facilitated has sat silently through a discussion of the intellectual and ethical reasons for transforming exclusive knowledge, only to burst out suddenly with a cry that is only apparently irrelevant, such as—to quote one of them—"But my wife *likes* doing the dishes!" We can make a good guess at a source of his resistance, but such resistance is also found among those who are or have been a great deal more open.

Some early white U.S. feminist thinkers carried on a heroic struggle personally, politically, intellectually to become able to think about women by insisting on thinking for themselves *as* women, only to be accused of having carried their white, middle-class, heterosexual privilege into the defining center of a new scholarship and politics that was itself exclusive.[29] Not all took kindly to that, but many heard it, and it has had profound and continuing effects, for good and for ill. I recently overheard a young postmodern-schooled scholar say that she was shocked to find a plenary panel on racism at the National Women's Studies Association conference. "Racism!" she said. "That's such old stuff. Even Black women don't talk about *that* anymore. Things are so much more complicated." Well, I confess to thinking, yes and no. Had she heard my thoughts, she probably would have discredited me as she proceeded to write off the panelists. "Second-wave feminists," she said of them, "stuck in their old thing." That is true enough sometimes, but it is also true that crude and virulent as well as subtle racism has not disappeared because scholars have deconstructed, denied, and denounced its gross categorizations by 'kind.'

Some Black feminists courageously turned to thinking about their experiences as Black women, only to find themselves accused of betraying racial politics.[30] Some lesbian and gay scholars sought solidarity with ethnic studies scholars, only to be told that their "problem" could not be understood in the same ways in differing cultures, and even that "there are none of those in our culture." The Sisyphean rock is pushed up the hill, and then it rolls back down, by no means without damage to those who were brave enough to try to move it at all. Such criticism from allies has also spread beyond those circles. It has been taken up and used against us all. I continue to hear, from people who have not bestirred themselves to do critical or liberatory work and so are delighted to cite the dismissive judgments of others, that "feminism is racist," that "Black studies is homophobic," that "ethnic studies is sexist," that "women's studies is essentialist and passé."

We continue to be dismissed, as we have been since the new scholarships began to emerge and claim their place in the academy. This is one reason I began this book with some reminders of the situation thirty years ago, when the reasons for resisting, both given and revealed, were more direct than they are now. I do not believe the reasons have entirely or truly changed. Sometimes, at least, they are just masked by more sophisticated language and theories. Recently, an active feminist from another country told me that she was impressed by how broadly feminist theories have spread here—and how shocked she was by how often she heard them from the mouths of men sitting around a table while a woman served them coffee. Old roots continue to have their effects, even when differing growths have been grafted onto them.

Subject matter and approaches that are not very similar to the already included material or currently regnant theories still find few safe places to go—except, perhaps, as teachers tell me helpfully, into someone else's field or a specialized subfield slot that may be offered when "the basics" are covered. Feminist critiques of science? "Not 'real' science. Maybe a sociology or history course?" Feminist philosophy? "We could add on a high-level course in feminist epistemology, perhaps." "We do philosophy of mind, and there are great women in the field, but gender is obviously irrelevant to the real substance of the field." "We can't afford a full position. She could do women's studies and maybe offer a cross-listed course." Feminist economics? "Well, if there's any interest. But there's a lot of required material to cover. Our students are very professionally oriented, you know." An administrator on a campus to which I had been invited to evaluate the women's studies program told me, privately, that he really, truly did support feminism, but he hoped I would agree that, now that feminist scholarship has become established, what the women's studies people have been doing should be moved to student support offices. "They do great work," he said, "counseling students and working with the outside community." The still or again uninvited guests, like Alice at the tea party, are shuffled around the table to someone else's seat. One who steps across the boundaries of professionalized fields or currently "in" theories—or who expects the implications of liberatory knowledge to extend to home, community, academic, and political life—remains likely to be viewed as a troublemaker, as "unsound," as a "whiner" who just will not let up and get on with "serious academic work." Professionals still patrol their boundaries fiercely.

## Professionalization

The knowledge that is taught in our curricula can be changed, and it often has been, as have the disciplines themselves. At any point in its history (more in some, less in others, but always to some extent), any accepted field is ambivalent, ambiguous, or downright contradictory when all that it includes is considered. In philosophy, for example, one cannot simultaneously be an existentialist, a logical positivist, a Marxist, a Platonist, an ordinary language philosopher, and a Foucauldian. It is even difficult to draw on and use aspects of several such schools, because they arise from, draw on, and, to varying degrees tend (perhaps particularly as they move farther from their originators, who were themselves engaged with, if thinking against, other schools), to universalize such fundamentally different premises that they become mutually repellent. One can teach and use these different philosophical approaches sequentially, and one can engage them in dialogue with each other, but one cannot *espouse* all of them at once, any more than one can simultaneously be a Protestant, Muslim, and pantheist. This difficulty is, of course, a wonderful challenge to a committed teacher and inquiry-oriented scholar who practices the arts of translation, but that does not make it easy for professionals whose success can depend on establishing an identity as an authority in one specialization.

Still, one would think that teachers and scholars used to living with such conceptual diversities within their own fields would have little trouble dealing with materials deriving from different premises, developing new methods, focusing on different questions. But professional identities and ambitions, as well as personal tastes and styles, do get in the way. And here, too, practices of tolerating, rather than engaging with, differences can leave us living uneasily next door to each other but not in genuine communication. As a result, departmentalized disciplines have their own versions of outbreaks of fratricidal (and sometimes sororal) struggle. The transcript of the Harvard University faculty meeting at which women's studies was finally recognized is a fascinating and very telling document, as are the reports and position papers written at Yale when coeducation was under consideration.[31] Anyone who doubts that gender, power, knowledge, and a profession-linked sense of self are closely intertwined need only examine such documents—or, more recently, some of the antifeminist "feminist" works by women who have decided that women's studies has gone "too far" or, conversely, that it has been left behind by the other new critical fields and so should quietly fold up and disappear. The same is said about concern about racism by theorists who hold that "things are so much more complicated" and scientists who pronounce that "race" is not real.

However, cooperative transdisciplinary scholarship is possible. Most of the "classics" that continue to be taught appear in more than one department's courses (for example, Plato's *Republic* has no one obvious conceptual 'home'). We live in a time of exciting breaching and reconfiguring of academic-professional boundaries. In the face of enduring opposition that shifts its framing but preserves its purposes, feminist and other insurgent scholars have continued and are thriving. Some among them, as well as from the still dominant mainstream, fruitfully recognize and teach the unresolved tensions as sources of insight for all concerned.[32] But they do not do so everywhere, or always, or reliably. When a university appointed me visiting distinguished professor of the humanities and women's studies a few years ago, the English department generously offered to list my courses, assign classroom space, provide me with an office, and otherwise make it possible for me to do what I had been appointed to do. Women's studies—a program, not a department—could not do so. Humanities, which was taken as an umbrella term for a collection of 'real' fields, could not do so, either. And the philosophy department, tightly held within a very few schools of thought that defined others as out of disciplinary order, would have none of me.

It is hardly surprising that generations of graduate students who have wended their way through the minefields of inter- and intra-professional territoriality and competition, and the partial knowledges these protect, can, upon certification, proceed to defend views of what 'properly' constitutes their discipline with the same totalizing certitude from which they once suffered. Professionalization supported by the entrenchment of academic fields as atomistic, budget-controlling units, as well as by criteria for hiring, promotion, and tenure, contributes significantly to processes by which old roots continue to feed the "tree of knowledge," however much its vulnerable newer branches proliferate.

But, again, we are not stuck. We are retrieving the lives and works of those who have been excluded by systemic domination, colonization, exploitation, domestication, disabling. We are working with critical analyses of all of the constructions that created, mystified, legitimated such intimately oppressive relations. And so we continue to uncover where and how the knowledges of dominant traditions have been falsified. We do so not just with regard to particular points, facts, issues, ideas, but also with regard to the construction of what has been taken to be knowledge-itself.

Thinking with Zora Neal Hurston, among others, about what it means thus to "decolonize"[33] our minds, Ruel Tyson notes that "mind" is then revealed as "not simply how we think, but our tastes; not only our cognitive styles and cycles of growth, but ... the pre-reflective judgments we commonly make about the familiar and the strange; and, finally ... our desires, the baroque movements of our affections which are as much social as personal; the way we embody spirit; the dances our imaginations perform; the compulsions and elections of our will."[34]

"Decolonization" as a kind of social, moral, intellectual therapy that is both personal and political and that holds thinking, belief, and action in relation with each other is for all of us a necessary step toward the never achieved, horizonal goal of transformation. Without it, we all remain—however intricately and variously—vulnerable to the deformations of dominance-serving violation and violence-prone systems of all kinds: systems of meaning, of knowledge, of faith, of identities, and of economic, political, social, cultural systems that are legitimated by and enforce each other in circular, mystified fashion. Particular people have comprehended "mind," "reason," "knowledge" in particular ways that reflect, reinforce, question, or transcend the deeply felt reality of articulated hierarchies of power. There is something to lose in any change in what we take to be knowledge, just as there is something to gain. Power is at stake here, including the most basic power of all: the power to define what and who is real, what and who is valuable, what and who *matters*.

But "we can't read our own views back into history," a teacher insists. "People then didn't say 'he or she,' so we'll just read 'he' as generic," which suggests that it is silly to pursue the issue. However, if an important work was written by someone who used "he" as it has been used throughout most dominant traditions—to refer to males, usually a particular group of them, who were being thought about as if they were the inclusive term, the norm, and the ideal for all—that matters. Theories of the state generated from consideration only of men—and a particular group of men, at that—ought not to be studied as if they were indeed inclusive. And if it is admitted that they *were* exclusive, but their exclusivity is not then used to question all subsequent thinking and conclusions of the work or author, students learn that the exclusion and devaluation of more than half of humankind, throughout all cultural specificities, does not matter ethically, politically, or intellectually. But can Rousseau or Confucius be understood if we generously ignore, or pass off as irrelevant, or smile with benign superiority about his views concerning women, always half of humankind? Can we trust even what Foucault says in his lectures on "fearless speech," *parrhesia,* if he is actually thinking of only the few? "The one who uses *parrhesia,*" Foucault says in his published lectures, "is someone who says everything he has in mind: he does not hide anything, but opens his heart and mind completely to other people through his discourse." And then we see, in a footnote, that "responding to a student's question [about Foucault's use of "his" and "he"], Foucault indicated that the oppressed role of women in Greek society generally deprived them (along with aliens, slaves, and children, that is, the majority of the Greeks)" of the use of *parrhesia.* What, then, is Foucault's *parrhesiastes* not opening "completely to other people"?[35] Obviously, a great deal that mattered to a great many. Surely it undercuts scholarship, analysis, teaching not to take seriously such glaring and culturally, politically, historically relevant exclusions right there at the heart of a notion of "fearless speech," or any other subject, into full account.

We cannot, by fiat from the present, ignore the old hierarchical exclusions or transmute them into inclusiveness simply by making it evident that we now see them as such. The 'simple' matter of pronouns can reveal millennia of persistent errors, and there is no shortcut to fixing all they have skewed. Every time we stumble over a pronoun, we stumble over the root problem, the creation of 'kinds' of humans such that only some were allowed full participation in all the systems so long premised on their dominant centrality.

In a sense, we have come full circle. When we unwind the apparently simple observation that "he" is not and never has been genuinely inclusive, we find the same problems, the same deep and old errors, that are revealed by the most sophisticated epistemological analyses of what we take to be knowledge. Knowledge of, by, and for a part of humankind that claims to be of the whole is *partial* in both senses of the term. And the spiral of errors that began with an exclusive focus on the few continues even in the most abstract thinking, even in epistemology, even in aspects of today's critical theories. What we know now is that, in critically preparing to seek specific knowledges under the aegis of horizonal ideals of truthful justice, we are trying to comprehend differing worlds and changing times in company with many others who are truly not "us" and who also refuse to submit to dominance as the 'proper' order. If we would have transformations, and not merely palace coups or revolutions that simply bring about yet another turning upside down, we need to remember that *philo sophia*—love of wisdom—can entail desires for relations other than those of possession, mastery, dominance, certainty. And ancient Greek, rich as it is, is not the only language in which such love can be expressed.

# V

# Circling Back,
# Keeping Going

EVEN THOUGH I have indulged in raising some of the more complex epistemological questions (because I find them irresistibly interesting and because I do not think it is responsible to avoid them), there are really only a few basic realizations here. They are both easily stated and enormously complex in their many, and real, implications. Let me reiterate them so they will not be lost in the variations we have explored.

There is a *root problem* at the base of many dominant meaning systems that perpetuates systems of domination. I call it a root problem because it is deeply embedded and continues to feed all that grows from it so that, for all our pruning and grafting, it remains recognizable. The root problem we have been trying to excavate consists of dividing—not just distinguishing—beings into ontologically, ethically, politically, epistemologically significant 'kinds,' and then taking one 'kind' to be the inclusive term, the norm, and the ideal for all. That dominance-serving definitional move, which leads directly to *faulty generalizations* (from too few to many) or to *universalization,* is compounded by the consequent privileging of *singular* terms—notably, "man" and "mankind"—as well as abstractions such as "the citizen," "the philosopher," "the individual." Singularity, in turn, makes thinking of ongoing change, differences, and internal (rather than externally imposed) relations very difficult indeed. *Circular reasoning* then locks these constructions into place as standards, norms, ideals that continue to justify the original exclusions.

Together, faulty but value-freighted categorizations that lead to faulty generalizations, an emphasis on singularity, and circularity tend strongly and stubbornly to make considerations of history and place—of real, differing, always influential contexts—difficult to include in knowledge and meaning constructions. The abstract universal, singular, normative Man appears to have no limiting particularities at all. Thus, Man, with other foundational concepts, is *mystified*—made to appear what it is not—and whole systems of knowledge built with, from, and around such conceptualizations appear to have neither contexts nor consequences that should be considered to be central (rather than peripheral) to their meaning. The result is *partial knowledge* masquerading as impartial, disinterested, neutral, even as it perpetuates the hierarchical exclusiveness of the original, erroneous conceptual and political framings.

We can work on a "slow cure" of such a "disease of thought" by practicing (among other modes of critical analysis and reflection) a critical perilogical approach carried into the field of life worlds as well as books and other media. Watching for signs and symptoms of the old disorders, we can discern their presence, bring them before us in the present, think them through, and free ourselves to think and act differently. Thus, we have practiced seeing errors of *hierarchically invidious monisms* created by definitions and categorizations that move many 'kinds' of people down a scale from the normative, idealized Man toward the "rock bottom" of the natural world. We have seen such hierarchies created by and at work in 1) *faulty generalizations* (generalizing too far from the normative few); 2) *circular reasoning* (drawing on definitions, principles, standards to explain and justify the devaluations already posited by those definitions, principles, standards); 3) *mystified concepts* central to meaning systems created and sustained by the other errors; and 4) *partial knowledge* that, while held to be impartial, continues to legitimate dominance systems.

Because the dominant few were not only taken to be the inclusive term, the norm, and the ideal, but were defined and came to know themselves *in contradistinction* to all others, we cannot just add equalized 'others' onto established systems. Our cure requires reconfiguring, transforming, so that the devalued and excluded can be included not within the same systems that cast them out and down a scale of worth, but on their own, differing terms. The idea that the world is round cannot be added onto the idea that the world is flat; the idea that the sun is the center of the solar system cannot be added onto the idea that the earth is the center—and 'lower,' 'deviant' 'kinds' of humans, and other animals, and all of nature, cannot be added onto systems that took one 'kind' of man to be the center, pinnacle, and master of creation.

## From Errors to Visions

Visions of where we can go emerge from critiques of where we are and have been. When we renounce the unjustly erroneous notion that *humans are divided into 'kinds'* that hide and mystify our real differences by casting them as divisions that rank us, we free ourselves from unnecessary barriers to understanding, respect, care, cooperation. At best, these barriers have diminished us all; at worst, they have legitimated behavior and actions that nothing should or can justify. When we recognize that our predecessors *generalized too far from too few,* and too often not only generalized but universalized with only the few in mind, we open ourselves to an array of equalized diversities, with all their challenges to our minds, imaginations, hearts, and dreams with and for humankind. It becomes possible to stop confusing equality with sameness. Renouncing the false generalizations of prejudices as faulty categorical pre-judgments, we learn to think more subtly and to live and work in more appropriately complex relational ways. We begin again to create ways of thinking that support democracy instead of undermining it as the old hierarchically invidious monisms have done for so long.

When we recognize that we have been trapped in *circular reasoning,* or using assumptions, definitions, key concepts, and standards to justify the very systems of meaning—and living—from which they were erroneously derived, we can stop accepting hierarchical orderings that legitimate the dominance of the few. We are challenged to immerse ourselves in what we are studying, to suspend judgment for a while, to learn to hear new voices, and hence to emerge with new definitions and concepts and judgments that are, again, finer, more complex, more subtle, and so better suited to the interrelated worlds in which we live. We can stop pitting excellence against equity as we come to realize that without equity, we necessarily confuse excellence with exclusivity. We become able to see art in quilts and on painted mud walls as well as on canvas; to feel respect for those we may not yet understand; to admire thinking in entirely different systems of logic and meaning; to find spiritual wisdom in many forms of worship; to hear the poetry in spirituals, the literature in diaries and letters. We expand the range of human expressiveness and meaning from which all can learn.

When we release ourselves from *mystified concepts*, we become able to create new concepts that, like touchstones, help us find important knowledge where we did not even look before. We can give up, for example, the notion that we all derive from Man the Hunter and remember that we also come from Woman the Gatherer—and from societies in which the one was not more important than the other, where all together did what was necessary to sustain life. We can remember that Economic Man, the decision maker whose 'rationality' is measured by how well he plans to "maximize profits" in a capitalist economic system, is by no means universal even within capitalist systems and may be morally questionable on rational as well as other grounds. Then we can not only study but learn from others—from those who make decisions about resources out of concern for ancestors, children, respect for the land, the collective good of all rather than from narrowly construed, competitively sought self-interest. Questioning notions of moral reasoning based on mystified conceptualizations of the individual as well as of reason, we can become open to noticing that some people make moral decisions by considering the needs and values of particular individuals in the contexts of real lives that preceded and will continue after the decision has been made rather than by invoking supposedly timeless, falsely abstracted moral principles that cannot adequately connect with the interdependent particularity of the world in which we must, after all, strive to be moral.

If we uncover where and how knowledge is *partial*, we open spaces for other modes of knowing and knowledge systems. Relinquishing the notion that we 'cover' the subject matter our fields name, remembering that we teach what has been agreed on by those who were enabled to define and legitimate them— assisted by the availability of money, prestige, and access to an intellectual community denied those excluded from the academy—we become able to teach our subjects as human constructions for which we and our students are also responsible. We become better able to live up to claims we still want to value: that education means "to lead out," to liberate; that philosophy is not a list of texts or familiar problems from one tradition, but a quest for wisdom, an effort to find meanings as well as truths and to think about what that effort itself means; that history is not the story only of the powerful few, the record keepers and those the record-keepers recognized, but constructed human stories that shape the life conditions of all of us; that literature is not a particular collection of canonical works that fall into a few schools and periods and converse only with each other, but the effort of human minds and spirits to shape experience and feeling and thought into imaginative forms that speak across the boundaries that both relate and distinguish us.

With these realizations, the resources of freshly read traditions, new questions, emergent critical tools and methods, and the vast resource of all that has been excluded, we begin again the quest for knowledge, for self-knowledge. We recognize some things so obvious once they have been seen that, like the child who said, "But the emperor is naked!" we cannot but question authority. (This will get us into trouble. I suspect that child was sent to bed without supper, not instantly agreed with and granted early tenure as a reward.) But we will persist against the grain and pay very serious attention to phenomena such as racialized genderings that were long explained as 'natural' so they would be thought of as off limits for change; to the kind of privatizing that removes people(s), jobs, land, goods and services from the protections and freedoms and equality of public life, shared use, rights; to definitions of 'reason' that privilege only modes of thought that coerce agreement. And we will continue to differ as we do so.

In the familiar list of givens about Mankind, we find Man identified as the creature with speech, the creature with rationality, the political animal, and, looming large, the being who is aware of his mortality. All of these categories are limited without consideration of all of us—of how, across all groupings, gendering is shaped by and shapes them differently at different times and across cultures but shapes them all the same. All these and more can be reconsidered, transformed when we open to understanding that is not hobbled by the old errors, the old invidious divisions. What *language* has meant and means in different cultures to women, to men of nonprivileged groups, to people who are deaf becomes available to us to study and learn from. What *intelligence* can mean is expanded, enriched. What is *political* can be more accurately defined so we see the all-pervasive workings of power not only as dominance, but also as the shared empowerment that spreads among publicly gathered equals. And *mortality* can be balanced with the ongoing renewal and fresh beginnings of *natality*.

Knowledge falsely abstracted from too few, locked into circular self-validation, built around mystified concepts, and taught out of its own contexts as a human endeavor lacks the richness, and hides and mystifies the horrors, of the full human drama. Such knowledge, untransformed, remains curiously abstract and removed from the realities of our students' and our own worlds. It reduces teachers far too often to all kinds of rhetorical tricks to engage the interest of students who feel, even if they do not recognize, that they are excluded, which is painful, or, if they are of the privileged few, that too much is being claimed for them, which is frightening. Such knowledge and modes of knowing cannot adequately invite or prepare us to reach beyond ourselves toward horizonal visions of meaningful lives constantly enriched by the translational experiences and free, reflexive thinking that are central to transforming education.

Those who have been excluded are not, after all, the enemies of civilization. We are, as we have always been, essential to its very possibility. The world needs to hear all our voices. Transforming knowledges should help us envision and actually experience moments in which the possibility of the intimate but shareable communication that is the transforming heart of publicly responsible learning comes alive.

## Reclaiming Intimacy, Universality, Public Life

I have used Kant, one of my favorite philosophers, to provide an example of a great mind that was nevertheless skewed by the old errors. Let me, then, also cite him in a different spirit. Here is his call to an understanding of the humanities that could help us transcend such limitations:

> The propaedeutic does not consist in following precepts, but in cultivating our mental powers by exposing ourselves . . . to what we call *humaninora* (or: the Humanities); they are called that presumably because *humanity* (Humanitat) means both the universal *feeling of sympathy*, and the ability to engage universally in very intimate *communication*. When these two qualities are combined, they constitute the sociability that befits humanity.[1]

Here there is recognition of the responsibility of quests for knowledges to be open to all humankind in a way that makes possible an approach to (never an arrival at) communication that is both intimate and universal. To insist on both intimacy and universality, understood as regulative (or horizonal) ideals rather than possible achievements, is to insist on openness to the individual and to the particular as well as to the general and the universal. Intimacy is a mode of relation that refuses generalizations. To be intimate means to break through *what* someone is in order to become open to *who* she or he is; to experience *this* person as she or he is, not as she or he seems to be when filtered through prejudgments about the category that old hierarchies have slotted her or him into. Literatures can give us such moments of comprehension and, in so doing, suggest that the intimate and the universal are not opposites after all. Universality is a creation of thought that moves through all limitations, all particular definition, in recognition of profound connectedness. It need not come only or primarily or most convincingly through abstractions that create context-free symbols such as numbers. It can emerge from immersion in the particular, the individual, as it does in richly particularized stories, poems, paintings.

Between these ideas that call us to commune with each thing, animal, person, moment with full attentiveness and to reach for visions of connections within wholeness beyond any particular lie the richly complex social, cultural, and political realms in which we struggle to live with each other on this earth. The intimate particular and the universal both remove us temporarily from the tension of the plural, active public realm, but we need always to return to it.

Arendt wrote: "We are all the same, that is, human, in such a way that nobody is ever the same as anyone who ever lived, lives or will live."[2] She insisted on our sameness not in the usual reductive mode ("But really we're all alike"), but in the mode of uniqueness (the only way "we are all alike" is that, as unique beings, we are *not* the same) in the context of discussing action, the political. "Plurality," which is for Arendt not mere iteration, not just the presence of more than one, but a human reality that appears specifically in public, when we can see and be seen as the unique beings we each and all are, "is the condition of human action."[3] Plurality is thus a precondition, but it is also a result, a gift, of action. Without action in a public realm held open to all by rights and guarantees of equality, it is all too easy to think of uniqueness as a special quality of the privileged few—for example, to believe that there are Great Leaders, singular individuals, who appear before us, revealing themselves through what they say and do, and then there are "the masses," the "common people." This reveals the same old tangle of errors, of course. The few emerge as the only real, significant persons/personages, the history makers, the leaders, the "heads" of "bodies" politic, households, organizations. All the rest are mere "subjects," material conditions for the emergence of the Great Man whose glory is his uniqueness. To be privatized, denied equality and freedom of public action with its visibility, is to be denied the opportunity to reveal and experience one's own uniqueness and, just as important, the opportunity to recognize that we are *all* unique.

Undoing *false* universals that have given only a few the privilege of being recognized as unique is not the same as undoing the idea of universality itself. Rightly understood, "we are all the same" can be (as it is for Arendt) a highly ethical and politically sensitive claim, one that calls on us to remember human connectedness and to value it. It is dangerous when we misconstrue sameness as uniformity and interchangeability. It is particularly dangerous when we enforce sameness as unanimity. But that does not mean that we must or should give up our belief in our deepest connections. "The brotherhood of mankind" is not helpful, but that is because it is cast in partial terms, and false universals divide us; they do not connect us. In fact, they make it impossible to think universally because they falsely inflate a part into the whole.

We can learn to see the old errors of hierarchical, radically divisive dominance when we stop severing the quest for knowledge from genuine experience of public life, of action. The life of the mind and the life of action may be two different modes of human life, but that does not mean they are discontinuous rather than mutually informing.

## Thinking and Acting

What we need to comprehend is related to what we need to do; what we need to do is related to what we need to comprehend. Knowledge, untransformed, is thought for the most part to be irrelevant to citizenship, to action, because it is about 'higher' things than politics, because knowledge is 'purer' than action, because it is "impractical." But that is so because knowledge has been both misconstrued and mystified. If what we have known and the modes of knowing behind it have been derived from partial, faulty abstractions that cannot be found in, illuminate, help us deal with real, existent, particulars, or develop a feeling of universal egalitarian connectedness, or help us learn to think in the place of many others, they will, of course, seem to reference a different realm (one in which we can be precise, but too often at the cost of being inaccurate, as Kamarck put it). A transforming vision of knowledge expresses our realization that humans are natal as well as mortal—that we are born particular, changing, communicating creatures and creators of meanings; that the human condition of plurality is made visible in a free public life into which newcomers enter as they mature; that we *need* that visible plurality for self-knowledge and all knowing that honestly reaches toward comprehensiveness; and hence, that knowing is social, and intimately related to acting.

But in the realm of thinking, as in that of action, nothing is ever finally settled. Whenever thinking seems to reach a conclusion, to lead into knowledge, another thought, another question, another feeling, another voice emerges. There is always another way to turn an idea, another perspective on a phenomenon, a different conceptual approach to explore, a fresh and startlingly suggestive example to be taken into account. This, I think, is all to the good. I do not want there to be one "feminist theory," one "theory of race," one "queer theory," one "transformed knowledge." I want there to be many, so that we are recurrently called back into thinking by the multiplicity of possible ways of knowing. When we ask ourselves, What does this knowledge, this fact, this theory *mean*? we are calling on our ability to think both alone and together in a way that "unfreezes concepts," as Arendt put it, and dissolves the ideologies they anchor, preparing us to make nondeterminate judgments, to make choices, to take responsibility in and for the world we share with others who will always differ with us wherever there is even a shred of freedom.

I am aware that, to some, the open-endedness of thinking and the dissolving effects of critique seem to make action more difficult. Over the years I have been asked many times if I do not think that some kind of utopian vision, instead of or in addition to critique, is necessary for real change. I am then asked why I do not get on with envisioning alternatives. I have several responses. First, there are others whose gifts lie in imagining alternatives,[4] and there is no reason I should try to do what they do so well. But I also worry about visions emerging without ongoing critiques. I have a great respect for the power of unanalyzed assumptions and errors to continue to affect us without our realizing it, so I do not think that critique and vision should be divided. I find a great deal of positive and creative vision within critique. To uncover what is wrong is to begin to be able to see what could be right, and to do so by concentrating on what *is* so that we might really get to another 'there' from 'here.' It seems to me that we are more likely to be able to change what is if we understand it very well than if we turn from it, imagine something quite different, and then have to begin afresh to figure out what to do. Furthermore, I worry about efforts to 'get there from here' when the 'there' is too clear to us, too developed. Such visions, like accepted knowledge, can be turned far too readily into prescriptive ends in light of which present pressing realities—and too often real people—can become no more than means.

I also believe that thinking reflexively (the capacity that makes critique possible) is one of the grounds of human freedom, in part because it reveals to us that we are always both subject and object of knowing, of cultures, of our worlds. We are not just products or objects, nor are we self-contained subjects existing in a void. We are unique, related subjects whose freedom is conditioned—not determined—by worlds not of our making but in our care, open to the effects of our actions. So I believe in thinking not only as preparation for knowledge, vision, and action but as a way of being with, being open to, the realities with which knowledge, vision, and action should correspond.

When I consult with institutions and groups about changes they need to make to be truer to their missions, what we do is think together about what may be blocking their best efforts. For example, when administrators ask how they can get faculty members to do more interdisciplinary work (often because interdisciplinary programs most effectively address issues of pressing concern such as the environment, peace, a globalizing economy, human rights), I first ask questions. How is hiring done? Through discipline-based departments? How are promotion and tenure earned? Through evaluation of discipline-based scholarship? Are departments also the academic budgetary units? When institutional planning is done, are representatives of interdisciplinary programs appointed to key committees? Often enough, the institution turns out to be systemically blocking, even punishing, those who are doing what the administrators and some faculty say they want to support. The old criteria for what and who matters, while locked into the systems, continue to function unless they are deliberately changed. Add-ons do not work for systems that are actually designed to exclude any more than they do for knowledge.

To locate such institutional barriers, we need:

*Realism:* What is the actual situation?

*Critique:* What are the conditions and systems locking that situation in?

*Philosophical comprehension:* What assumptions are revealed by the system? By what logics, rules, norms, principles, values does it run?

*Strategies:* Who or what is benefiting from things as they are? Who or what is persistently harmed? What are our goals in this specific situation? Who needs to be involved? What would move them to act? Who might become allies? What could be easily changed? How would we build on that? What resources can we find to sustain our efforts?

*Flexibility:* If the first effort fails, what do we try next? If the money is cut, what other resources can we find? How do we keep building our base? When do we need to adjust our goals?

*Persistence:* Will we keep the work going?

*Honesty:* What is our own stake in learning, in change? Will we remain open and respectful?

*Imagination:* Beyond obvious alternatives, what may be possible that no one has yet suggested?

Most of all, we need to keep questioning, going deeper, figuring out what has been built into systems of all kinds—including, crucially, our own thinking within and about those systems—that keeps them going. Marguerite Kiely, one of the best organizational thinkers and consultants I know, tells a story. She was brought in to help a social-service agency solve a seriously recalcitrant problem. The key people joined her around a table for an opening discussion. After she had listened for hours to all kinds of analyses, fusses, and fumings, they asked, "What do you think?" "I have one question," she said. "What is it about this problem that you love so much that you have kept it going for all these years?"

Working for changes we think about, and for, is crucial, but if both thinking and acting are essential to freedom, as freedom is essential to them, then they should be enjoyed for their own sake as well as for what they may lead us toward. Thinking and acting together give us experiences of freedom and of community; they are not only a means to an end. That is one reason why, when people ask me how I can stand to spend so much time concerned with the injustices I feel compelled to understand, I usually find myself saying that I love the people with whom I have been privileged to think about the hardest questions—the questions before which the mind wants to stop. Those people (in books, in person, wherever they are to be found) teach me what thinking

can be; they also teach courage and responsibility. But even the saving experience of thinking and acting with such people can fail to sustain us if we are
not also open to other perspectives, if we turn in on ourselves. That is why
it is important to reach out to others, explain what we are thinking and doing,
open ourselves to responses, questions, challenges. For all engaged in it, every
such conversation is a new beginning and, indeed, an enactment, a practice
of the ends we seek.

# NOTES

## PREFACE AND ACKNOWLEDGMENTS

1. Howard Winant, *Racial Conditions: Politics, Theory, Comparisons* (Minneapolis: University of Minnesota Press, 1994), 20.
2. Anthony F. C. Wallace, *Jefferson and the Indians: The Tragic Fate of the First Americans* (Cambridge, Mass: Harvard University Press, 1999), 338. I also thank Joseph Jordan, Dawn Keller, and Valerie Jones for complicating my thinking here—although they are in no way responsible for any errors.

## INTRODUCTION

*Thinking: An Introductory Essay*

1. Alice Kessler-Harris, *In Pursuit of Equality: Women, Men, and the Quest for Economic Citizenship and Labor in Twentieth Century America* (Oxford: Oxford University Press, 2001), 35.
2. Michel Foucault, *Fearless Speech* (Los Angeles: Semiotext[e], 2001), 74.
3. For an earlier version of this sketch of the "New Academy," see "Liberal Learning and the Arts of Connection for the New Academy," a report of the American Commitments National Panel, Association of American Colleges and Universities, 1995.
4. Jean-François Lyotard, *The Postmodern Condition: A Report on Knowledge,* trans. Geoff Bennington and Brian Massumi (Minneapolis: University of Minnesota Press, 1988), 53.
5. Foucault, *Fearless Speech,* 171.
6. Linda K. Kerber, "Portraying an 'Unexceptional' American History," *Chronicle of Higher Education,* July 5, 2002, B14.

7. Elizabeth Kamarck Minnich, "Feminist Attacks on Feminisms: Patriarchy's Prodigal Daughters," *Feminist Studies* 24, no. 1 (Spring 1998).

8. Idem, "Arendt, Heidegger, Eichmann: Thinking in and for the World," *Soundings* 86, no. 1–2 (Spring–Summer 2003).

9. M. Jacqui Alexander and Chandra Talpade Mohanty, eds., *Feminist Genealogies, Colonial Legacies, Democratic Futures* (New York: Routledge, 1997), xvii.

10. Ibid.

11. See Minnich, "Arendt, Heidegger, Eichmann." See also idem, "Thinking for Herself," review of *Feminist Interpretations of Hannah Arendt*, ed. Bonnie Honig (University Park: Pennsylvania State University Press, 1995), *Women's Review of Books* 13, no. 9 (June 1996).

12. Foucault, *Fearless Speech*, 171.

13. Chris Hables Gray, "The Philosophical Implications of Postmodern War," unpublished paper presented at the Esalen Revisioning Philosophy Conference "Philosophy and the Human Future," Cambridge University, Cambridge, 1989.

14. Jane Flax, "Postmodernism and Gender Relations in Feminist Theory," in *Feminism/Postmodernism*, ed. Linda J. Nicholson (New York: Routledge, 1990), 41.

15. Wendy Brown, "The Impossibility of Women's Studies," *differences* 9, no. 3 (Fall 1997): 83–84.

16. Lyotard, *Postmodern Condition*, 67.

17. Nicholas Lemann, "Profiles: Without a Doubt," *New Yorker*, October 14 and 21, 2002, 175.

18. Malcolm G. Scully, "A Network of Global Solutions," *Chronicle of Higher Education*, September 13, 2002, B13.

19. Alexander and Mohanty, *Feminist Genealogies*.

20. Amina Mama, "Sheroes and Villains: Conceptualizing Colonial and Contemporary Violence against Women in Africa," in ibid., 51.

21. Hannah Arendt, *The Human Condition* (Chicago: University of Chicago Press, 1958), 324.

*Still Transforming Knowledge: Circling Out, Pressing Deeper*

1. William Y. Adams, *The Philosophical Roots of Anthropology* (Stanford, Calif.: CSLI Publications, 1998). I am indebted for this source, as for some of my thinking here, to Luis Galanes.

2. Carl Von Linne [Linnaeus], *Landmarks of Science*, Readex microprint (1970), courtesy History of Science Collection, University of Oklahoma, Norman.

3. Troy Duster, "The Stratification of Cultures as the Barrier to Democratic Pluralism," in *Education and Democracy: Re-imagining Liberal Learning in America*, ed. Robert Orill (New York: College Entrance Examination Board, 1997), 269–71.

4. Compare the works of Troy Duster, who has been critiquing stratification systems with particular concern for racial hierarchies for many years. He writes tellingly about how these systems are still being read into nature via genetics.

5. Pankaj Mishra, "Murder in India," *New York Review of Books*, August 15, 2002, 37–38.

6. Mokubung Nkomo, ed., *Pedagogy of Domination: Toward a Democratic Education in South Africa* (Trenton, N.J.: Africa World Press, 1990), 2.

7. Ibid.

8. Henry Friedlander, *The Origins of Nazi Genocide: From Euthanasia to the Final Solution* (Chapel Hill: University of North Carolina Press, 1995), 6.

9. James Waller, *Becoming Evil: How Ordinary People Commit Genocide and Mass Killing* (Oxford: Oxford University Press, 2002), xiv.

10. H. F. Augstein, "Introduction," in *Race: The Origins of an Idea, 1760–1850* (Bristol: Thoemmes Press, 1996), ix–x.

11. Ibid., x.

12. Karen J. Warren, "Taking Empirical Data Seriously," in *Ecofeminism: Women, Culture, Nature,* ed. Karen J. Warren (Bloomington: Indiana University Press, 1997), 12.

13. Strachan Donnelley, "Nature, Polis, Ethics . . . ," Hastings Center report, special supp., November–December 1998, S4.

14. Gloria Anzaldua, "Beyond Traditional Notions of Identity," *Chronicle of Higher Education,* October 11, 2002, B13.

15. Andy Smith, "Ecofeminism Through an Anticolonial Framework," in Warren, *Ecofeminism,* 30.

16. Benjamin M. Friedman, "Globalization: Sitglitz's Case," *New York Review of Books,* August 15, 2002, 50.

17. Patricia Williams, *The Alchemy of Race and Rights* (Cambridge, Mass.: Harvard University Press, 1991), 233–34.

18. For a discussion of "worldlessness" and "pariah" people(s), see Hannah Arendt, *The Jew as Pariah: Jewish Identity and Politics in the Modern Age,* ed. Ron H. Feldman (New York: Grove Press, 1978).

19. Alice Kessler-Harris, "The High Cost of Progress," review of Clara Bingham and Laura Leedy Gansler, *Class Action: The Story of Lois Jenson and the Landmark Case That Changed Sexual Harassment Law, Women's Review of Books,* vol. 20, no. 2, November 2002, 4.

20. As quoted in Rita Arditti, "The Grandmothers of the Plaza de Mayo and the Struggle against Impunity in Argentina," *Meridians* 3, no. 1, (2002): 19. See idem, *The Grandmothers of the Plaza de Mayo and the Disappeared Children of Argentina* (Berkeley: University of California Press, 1999), for the full story of this remarkable movement.

## I. NO ONE BEGINNING

1. Paula Gunn Allen, *Voice of The Turtle: American Indian Literature, 1900–1970,* ed. Paula Gunn Allen (New York: One World/Ballantyne Books, 1994), 5.

2. Ann J. Lane, "Mary Ritter Beard: Woman as Force," in *Feminist Theorists: Three Centuries of Key Women Thinkers,* ed. Dale Spender (New York: Random House, 1983), 347.

3. Paula Giddings, *When and Where I Enter . . . : The Impact of Black Women on Race and Sex in America* (New York: William Morrow, 1984), 5.

4. Anna Julia Cooper, *A Voice from the South,* Schomburg Library of Nineteenth-Century Black Women Writers, Henry Louis Gates, general ed. (New York: Oxford University Press, 1988), 121.

5. Jeffner Allen, *Lesbian Philosophy: Explorations* (Palo Alto, Calif.: Institute of Lesbian Studies, 1986), 13.

6. Rosemarie Garland Thomson, *Extraordinary Bodies: Figuring Physical Disability in American Culture and Literature* (New York: Columbia University Press, 1992), 51.

7. Linda Gordon, "What's New in Women's History," in *Feminist Studies: Critical Studies,* ed. Teresa de Lauretis (Bloomington: Indiana University Press, 1986), 21.

8. For other reflections on the effects of terminology in this area, see Peggy McIntosh, "A Note on Terminology," *Women's Studies Quarterly* 11 (Summer 1983): 29–30.

9. Teresa de Lauretis, "Feminist Studies/Critical Studies: Issues, Terms and Contexts," in de Lauretis, *Feminist Studies,* 3.

10. Ibid., 7. See also Elizabeth Minnich, *Toward a Feminist Transformation of the Curriculum,* proceedings of the 5th Annual Great Lakes Colleges Association Women's Studies Conference (Ann Arbor: Great Lakes Colleges Association, 1979).

## II. CONTEXTUAL APPROACHES: THINKING ABOUT

1. Frederick Rudolph, *Curriculum: A History of the American Undergraduate Course of Study since 1636* (San Francisco: Jossey-Bass, 1977), 168–69.

2. Ibid., 169.

3. Patricia Palmieri, "From Republican Motherhood to Race Suicide: Arguments on the Higher Education of Women in the United States, 1820–1920," in *Educating Men and Women Together*, ed. Carol Lasser (Chicago: University of Illinois Press, 1987).

4. Linda Kerber, *Women of the Republic: Intellect and Ideology in Revolutionary America* (Chapel Hill: University of North Carolina Press, 1980), 10.

5. Giddings, *When and Where I Enter*, 104–5.

6. For an excellent feminist analysis of the dominant tradition of thought about education, see Jane Roland Martin, *Reclaiming a Conversation: The Ideal of the Educated Woman* (New Haven, Conn.: Yale University Press, 1985). For supportive analyses of the role of education and how it might be reconceived and practiced, see, for example, Paulo Freire, *Pedagogy of the Oppressed*, trans. Myra Bergman Ramos (New York: Seabury Press, 1970); Henry A. Giroux, *Ideology, Culture, and the Process of Schooling* (Philadelphia: Temple University Press, 1981); Ira Shor and Paulo Freire, *A Pedagogy for Liberation: Dialogues on Transforming Education* (South Hadley, Mass.: Bergin and Garvey, 1987).

7. Roger Gottlieb, "Introduction," in *Racism*, ed. Leonard Harris (Amherst, N.Y.: Humanity Books/Prometheus, 1999).

8. See, for example, Barbara Christian, "The Race for Theory," *Feminist Studies* 14 (Spring 1988): 67–79.

9. Cf. Sara Evans, *Personal Politics* (New York: Random House/Vintage Books, 1979).

10. For more on the 1960s and 1970s movements, see James Miller, *Democracy Is in the Streets: From Port Huron to the Siege of Chicago* (New York: Simon and Schuster, 1987); Clayborne Carson, *In Struggle: SNCC and the Black Awakening of the Nineteen Sixties* (Cambridge, Mass.: Harvard University Press, 1981); Todd Gitlin, *The Sixties: Years of Hope, Days of Rage* (New York: Bantam Books, 1987); Wini Breines, *Community and Organization in the New Left: 1962–1968* (New York: Praeger, 1982); Sohnya Sayres et al., eds., *The 60's without Apology* (Minneapolis: University of Minnesota Press/Social Text, 1984).

11. Becky Thompson, "Multiracial Feminism: Recasting the Chronology of Second Wave Feminism," *Feminist Studies* 28, no. 2 (Summer 2002): 337–61. This is a crucial corrective to earlier versions of the history.

12. "A Kind of Memo from Casey Hayden and Mary King to a Number of Other Women in the Peace and Freedom Movements, November 18, 1965," in Evans, *Personal Politics*, 235.

13. Cynthia Washington, "We Started from Different Ends of the Spectrum," in Evans, *Personal Politics*, 238–40. See also Alice Walker's *Meridian* (Orlando, Fla.: Harcourt, 2003), a complex and fascinating novel about the Civil Rights Movement .

14. See, for example, the fine study by Harry C. Boyte, *The Backyard Revolution: Understanding the New Citizen Movement* (Philadelphia: Temple University Press, 1980).

15. Thompson, "Multiracial Feminism," 337.

16. See, for instance, Evans, *Personal Politics*; bell hooks, *Ain't I a Woman: Black Women and Feminism* (Boston: South End Press, 1984); Giddings, *When and Where I Enter*; Elly Bulkin, Minnie Bruce Pratt, and Barbara Smith, *Yours in Struggle: Three Feminist Perspectives on Anti-Semitism and Racism* (New York: Long Haul Press, 1984); Johnella Butler, "Minority Studies and Women's Studies: Do We Want to Kill a Dream?" *Women's Studies International Forum* 7, no. 3 (1984): 135–38.

17. See also Audre Lorde, "An Open Letter to Mary Daly," and other essays in *This Bridge Called My Back: Writings by Radical Women of Color*, ed. Cherríe Moraga and Gloria Anzaldúa

(Watertown, Mass.: Persephone Press, 1981); Barbara Smith, ed., *Home Girls: A Black Feminist Anthology* (New York: Kitchen Table: Women of Color Press, 1983); Florence Howe, *Myths of Coeducation: Selected Essays, 1964–1983* (Bloomington: Indiana University Press, 1984); Robin Morgan, ed., *Sisterhood Is Powerful: An Anthology of Writings from the Women's Liberation Movement* (New York: Random House, 1970).

18. For some interesting thinking on a few of the early efforts to bring change to the academy, see Charlotte Bunch and Sandra Rubaii, eds., *Learning Our Way: Essays in Feminist Education* (Trumansburg, N.Y.: Crossing Press, 1983). See also the informal publications by the Barnard College Women's Center of the proceedings of the Scholar and the Feminist Conferences. For an ongoing record of efforts to achieve institutional equity, see the publications of the Project on the Status and Education of Women, headed by Bernice Sandler of the Association of American Colleges and Universities, and the American Council on Education's Offices of Women and of Minority Affairs in these early years. For accounts of the development of women's studies in the United States, see, among other sources, back issues of *Women's Studies Quarterly*; Elizabeth Minnich, Jean O'Barr, and Rachel Rosenfeld, eds., *Reconstructing the Academy: Women's Education and Women's Studies* (Chicago: University of Chicago Press, 1988); and Carol Pearson, Donna Shavlik, and Judith Touchton, eds., *Educating the Majority: Women Challenge Tradition in Higher Education* (New York: Macmillan, 1987).

19. Cf. Jane S. Gould, *Juggling: A Memoir of Work, Family, and Feminism* (New York: Feminist Press at City University of New York, 1997). Programs of "The Scholar and the Feminist" are in Gould's appendixes.

20. See also Association of American Colleges, "Liberal Education and the New Scholarship on Women: Issues and Constraints in Institutional Change," report from the Wingspread Conference, Racine, Wis., October 22–24, 1981; and Elizabeth Kamarck Minnich, "Education for the Free Man?" *Liberal Education* 68, no. 4 (1982): 311–21.

21. Linda Nochlin, "Why Are There No Great Women Artists?" *Art News*, vol. 69, 1971, 22–39, 67–71; see also Ann Sutherland Harris and Linda Nochlin, *Women Artists: 1550–1986* (New York: Alfred A. Knopf, 1981).

22. This line spread primarily through conversations; when asked, Bunch said that the idea cited here was developed in conversations with Mary E. Hunt. See also Charlotte Bunch, *Passionate Politics: Essays 1968–1986* (New York: St. Martin's Press, 1987), 140.

23. Thomas Kuhn's work on "paradigm shifts" is relevant here: Thomas S. Kuhn, "The Structure of Scientific Revolutions," in *International Encyclopedia of Unified Science*, vol. 2, 2d ed. (Chicago: University of Chicago Press, 1962); see also idem, *The Structure of Scientific Revolutions*, 2d ed. (Chicago: University of Chicago Press, 1970).

24. Albert Memmi, *Racism* (Minneapolis: University of Minnesota Press, 2000), 175.

25. Here is an example of the root error in the familiar phrasing of "pioneer" stories: "The pioneers followed their dreams West, taking with them all their worldly goods, their wives and children." Women, then, are not included in "pioneers." Some scholarship in this area can be found in works by John Farragher, Elizabeth Hampsten, Glenda Riley, Lillian Schlissel.

26. Cf. works by Jack Forbes and, today, increasing numbers of scholars working on the co-constructions of "Negro" and "Indian" identities and mutually implicated histories—for example Sharon Holland, Melinda Micco, Naatsu Taylor Saito, Tiya Miles, Joseph Jordan. This work draws crucially on the scholarship of Native American and African American studies, while exploring more directly the relations between these fields.

## III. CONCEPTUAL APPROACHES: THINKING THROUGH

1. Simone de Beauvoir, *The Second Sex,* trans. and ed. H. M. Parshley (New York: Random House/Vintage Books, 1974), xix.
2. Thomson, *Extraordinary Bodies,* 63–64.
3. Ibid., 70–71.
4. Theodore W. Allen, *The Invention of the White Race, Volume 1: Racial Oppression and Social Control* (London: Verso, 2000), 27.
5. Ch'u Chai and Winberg Chai, eds. and trans., *The Sacred Books of Confucius and Other Confucian Classics* (New Hyde Park, N.Y.: University Books, 1965), 17.
6. For example, I made up the title *The History of Art* for the textbook cited in the next paragraph. It is intended to evoke art history textbooks required through the years, none of which adequately included women and some 'kinds' of men. Some of these texts have now been changed to some extent, but supplemental materials are often still required to transform courses.
7. I thank Patricia Rife for introducing me to the story of Lise Meitner.
8. Adam Hochschild, *King Leopold's Ghost: A Story of Greed, Terror, and Heroism in Colonial Africa* (Boston: Houghton Mifflin, 1998).
9. Amos Elon, "Israelis and Palestinians: What Went Wrong?" *New York Review of Books,* December 19, 2002, 82.
10. Ronald Takaki, *A Different Mirror: A History of Multicultural America* (Boston: Back Bay Books/Little Brown, 1993), 15.
11. Werner Jaeger, *Paideia: The Ideals of Greek Culture,* trans. Gilbert Highet, vol. 1, 2d ed. (New York: Oxford University Press, 1965), xiv.
12. Ibid., xxiv.
13. Walter J. Ong, "Latin Language Study as a Renaissance Puberty Rite," *Studies in Philology* 56, no. 2 (April 1959): 103–24. See also Elizabeth Minnich, "Institutional and Civic Responsibilities," in *Forum for Higher Education: Proceedings of the 67th Annual Conference of the North Carolina Association of Colleges and Universities, October 1987* (Raleigh: North Carolina Association of Colleges and Universities, 1987).
14. Lawrence Cremin, as quoted in Merrill D. Peterson, principal author, *The Humanities and the American Promise: Report of the Colloquium on the Humanities and the American People* (Austin, Tex.: Committee for the Humanities, 1987), 11.
15. Walt Whitman, as quoted in ibid., 9–10.
16. Ibid., 11.
17. Frederick Douglass, as quoted in ibid., 11.
18. Gunnar Myrdal, as quoted in ibid., 7.

## IV. ERRORS BASIC TO DOMINANT TRADITIONS

1. Anthony Pagden, *Lords of All the World: Ideologies of Empire in Spain, Britain and France c. 1500–c. 1800* (New Haven, Conn.: Yale University Press, 1995), 10, 22–23; emphasis added.
2. Gwyn Kirk and Margo Okazawa-Rey, *Women's Lives: Multicultural Perspectives* (Mountain View, Calif.: Mayfield Publishing, 1998), 188.
3. All but the last of these terms can be found in Michel Foucault, *The Order of Things: An Archaeology of the Human Sciences* (New York: Vintage Books, 1994), xi. The last term is in idem, *The History of Sexuality,* trans. Robert Hurley, vol. 1 (New York: Vintage Books: 1980), 11.
4. Memmi, *Racism,* 175.

*Faulty Generalization and Hierarchically Invidious Monism*

1. Cf. Rayna Rapp Reiter, ed., *Toward an Anthropology of Women* (New York: Monthly Review Press, 1975); Michelle Z. Rosaldo and Louise Lamphere, *Woman, Culture, and Society* (Stanford, Calif.: Stanford University Press, 1974).

2. I have not used labels such as "liberal feminist," "cultural feminist," "French feminist," "socialist feminist" for feminist thought, because I am exploring overlapping ways of thinking, not categorizing. For discussions that do categorize, see Alison Jaggar, Paula Rothenberg, Hester Eisenstein.

3. Hannah Arendt, "On Thinking and Moral Consideratons: A Lecture," *Social Research* 38, no. 3 (Fall 1971): 422.

4. Cf. Maria Lugones, "Playfulness, 'World'-Travelling, and Loving Perception," *Hypatia* 2, no. 2 (Summer 1987).

5. Marjorie Pryse, "Trans/Feminist Methodology: Bridges to Interdisciplinary Thinking," *National Women's Studies Association Journal* 12, no. 2 (Summer 2000): 112.

6. Adrienne Rich, "Compulsory Heterosexuality and Lesbian Existence," *Signs* 5 (1980): 657.

7. Eve Sedgwick, *Between Men: English Literature and Male Homosocial Desire* (New York: Columbia University Press, 1985), 1–2.

8. Cf. Anne Fausto-Sterling, *Myths of Gender: Biological Theories about Women and Men,* 2d rev. ed. (New York: BasicBooks, 1992), and idem, *Sexing the Body: Gender Politics and the Construction of Sexuality* (New York: BasicBooks, 2000).

9. Alice Kessler-Harris, *Out to Work: A History of Wage-Earning Women in the United States* (New York: Oxford University Press, 1982), 315–16.

10. S. H. Katz, "Is Race a Legitimate Concept for Science?" in American Association of Physical Anthropology, "Revised Statement on Race: A Brief Analysis and Commentary," University of Pennsylvania, 1995, 4–5.

11. Quoted from Troy Duster, "Buried Alive: The Concept of Race in Science," unpublished manuscript. An essay with the same title, but without the lines quoted, appeared in *Chronicle of Higher Education*, September 14, 2001, B11–12.

12. George M. Fredrickson, *Racism: A Short History* (Princeton, N.J.: Princeton University Press, 2002), 6.

13. Howard Winant, *Racial Conditions: Politics, Theory, Comparisons* (Minneapolis: University of Minnesota Press, 1994), 1.

14. Ibid., 2.

15. Paul Gilroy, *Against Race: Imagining Political Culture beyond the Color Line* (Cambridge, Mass.: Harvard University Press, 2000), 11.

16. Epigraph for Matthew Frye Jacobson, *Whiteness of a Different Color: European Immigrants and the Alchemy of Race* (Cambridge, Mass.: Harvard University Press, 1998). Brewton Berry, "A Southerner Learns about Race," *Common Ground* (1942).

17. Angela Y. Davis, *Women, Race and Class* (New York: Random House/Vintage Books, 1983), 94.

18. Hillary Rodham Clinton, as quoted by Lawrence McQuillian, Tibet Network News, September 16, 1995.

19. W.E.B. DuBois, *Souls of Black Folk* (New York: Penguin, 1989), 13; Cooper, *Voice from the South.*

20. George Walton, *Fearless and Free: The Seminole Indian War 1835–42* (Indianapolis: Bobbs-Merrill, 1977), 28–29.

21. Carol B. Stack, *All Our Kin: Strategies for Survival in a Black Community* (New York: Harper and Row, 1974), 45–46.

22. Ian Haney Lopez, *White by Law: The Legal Construction of Race* (New York: New York University Press, 1996), 225.

23. Troy Duster, "Caught Between 'Race' and a Hard Place," *Ethnicities* 2, no. 4 (September 18, 2002): 553.

24. Edwin Black, *War against the Weak: Eugenics and America's Campaign to Create a Master Race* (New York: Four Walls Eight Windows, 2003), 87–89, 277.

25. Fredrickson, *Racism*, 170.

26. For a discussion of "woman as victim," see Ellen Carol DuBois, Gail Paradise Kelly, Elizabeth Lapovsky Kennedy, Carolyn W. Korsmeyer, and Lillian S. Robinson, *Feminist Scholarship: Kindling in the Groves of Academe* (Chicago: University of Illinois Press, 1985).

27. Wendy Perron in *New York Times*, June 17, 2001.

28. Immanuel Kant, *Observations on the Feeling of the Beautiful and Sublime* (Berkeley: University of California Press, 1960), 109.

29. Ibid., 81.

30. As quoted in Vincent Harding, "Black Creativity and American Attitudes," in *There Is a River: The Black Struggle for Freedom in America* (New York: Harcourt Brace Jovanovich, 1981), 145.

31. Miriam Schneir, "Sojourner Truth: Ain't I a Woman?" and Sojourner Truth, "Ain't I a Woman," in *Feminism: The Essential Historical Writings*, ed. Miriam Schneir (New York: Vintage Books/Random House, 1972), 94–95.

32. For analyses of how we learn the deepest presuppositions of culture, some of Edward Hall's works have hardly been surpassed. See Edward T. Hall, *The Silent Language* (Garden City, N.J.: Anchor, 1973).

33. For moving stories from and analyses of teaching experiences by such teachers, see Berenice Malka Fisher, *No Angel in the Classroom: Teaching through Feminist Discourse* (New York: Rowman and Littlefield, 2001); and Esther Kingston-Mann and Tim Sieber, ed., *Achieving against the Odds: How Academics Become Teachers of Diverse Students* (Philadelphia: Temple University Press, 2001).

34. Alfred North Whitehead, as quoted in Mary Daly, *Beyond God the Father* (Boston: Beacon Press, 1973), 1.

35. Thomson, *Extraordinary Bodies*, 135.

*Circular Reasoning*

1. William James, "Monistic Idealism," in *A Pluralistic Universe* (Cambridge, Mass.: Harvard University Press, 1977), 32.

2. Jacobson, *Whiteness of a Different Color*, 15.

3. Michael Q. Patton, *Qualitative Evaluation Methods* (Newbury Park, Calif.: Sage, 1980), 21.

4. Joan Kelly, *Women, History and Theory* (Chicago: University of Chicago Press, 1984), 1.

5. The emergence of Elaine Scarry's *The Body in Pain: The Making and Unmaking of the World* (New York: Oxford University Press, 1985) from the field of literature is a telling example of thinking that refuses old boundaries and so can also think about the phenomenon of boundaries of all sorts.

6. Frank Newman, "American Education in a Competitive World," in *Forum for Higher Education*. The remark is quoted as I remember it from the 67th Annual Conference of the North Carolina Association of Colleges and Universities and from conversations with Frank Newman.

7. Peterson et al., *The Humanities and the American Promise*, 2.

8. Ibid., 16.

## Mystified Concepts

1. Sara Rimer, "Colleges Find Diversity Is Not Just Numbers," *New York Times*, November 12, 2002, A1.

2. The quotation is from a talk I heard Alan Bloom give at the Claremont Colleges in California, March 21, 1988. Cf. his *The Closing of the American Mind* (New York: Simon and Schuster, 1987). Because I am using Bloom as an example of skewed thinking, I also want to say that I admire and still use his excellent translation of Plato's *Republic*. I repeat: this work is not about wholesale rejection. It is about ferreting out errors into which most repeatedly fall because those errors are mystified and systemically efficacious.

3. Peggy McIntosh, with whom I discussed judgment in earlier years of curriculum transformation work, makes a persuasive case that the word "judgment" is so fraught with negative feelings caused by painful experiences that I should not try to retrieve it. However, I persist (supported partly by discussions with Ruel Tyson and others, as well as by Kant and Arendt) because I believe that the intellectual act of judgment is basic to action and hence to responsible freedom. It is judgment's conflation with deduction and the arbitrary imposition of inflexible rules that I, too, fear. See Elizabeth Kamarck Minnich, "To Judge in Freedom: Hannah Arendt on the Relation of Thinking and Morality," in *Hannah Arendt: Thinking, Judging, Freedom,* ed. Gisela T. Kaplan and Clive Kessler (Sydney: Allen and Unwin, 1989), 133–44.

4. Peterson et al., *The Humanities and the American Promise,* 13.

5. This was reported to me by Peggy McIntosh from conversations with Susan Van Dyne.

6. Hannah Arendt, "Introduction," in Walter Benjamin, *Illuminations,* trans. Harry Zohn (New York: Schocken Books, 1969), 50–51.

7. Cf. Sara Evans and Barbara Nelson, *Wage Justice: Comparable Worth and the Paradox of Technocratic Reform* (Chicago: University of Chicago Press, 1989); Catharine MacKinnon, *Feminism Unmodified: Discourses on Life and Law* (Cambridge, Mass.: Harvard University Press, 1987); and works by critical legal thinkers such as Lani Guinier, Patricia Williams, Derek Bell, and Cass Sunstein.

8. Jane Roland Martin, "Excluding Women from the Educational Realm," in *Women's Experience and Education,* ed. Sharon Lee Rich and Ariel Phillips, Harvard Educational Review Reprint Series no. 17 (Boston: Harvard Educational Review, 1985), 172.

9. In note 33 of the section titled "Faulty Generalization and Hierarchically Invidious Monism," I listed recent books on teaching in this spirit. See also Margo Culley, ed., *Gendered Subjects: The Dynamics of Feminist Teaching* (Boston: Routledge and Kegan Paul, 1985); the journal *Radical Teacher*, *National Women's Studies Association Journal*; the still invaluable Roberta N. Hall with Bernice Sandler, *The Classroom Climate: A Chilly One for Women?* (Washington, D.C.: Association of American Colleges and Universities, Project on the Status of Women, 1982); virtually anything by the wonderful Maxine Greene; and, along complementary lines, works by Vivian Paley, Sylvia Ashton-Warner, and John Dewey.

10. Leonard Harris, *Philosophy Born of Struggle: Anthology of Afro-American Philosophy from 1917* (Dubuque: Kendall/Hunt, 1983), ix.

11. Daniel del Castillo, "Just What the Shaman Ordered," *Chronicle of Higher Education*, November 22, 2002, A72.

12. William Ryan, *Blaming the Victim,* rev. ed. (New York: Vintage/Random House, 1976), 305.

13. Ibid., 304.

14. Ibid., 305–6.

15. A. L. Basham, *The Wonder That Was India,* 12th ed. (New York: Grove Press, 1954), 502.

16. Sara Ruddick, *Maternal Thinking: Toward a Politics of Peace* (Boston: Beacon Press, 1989).

17. For an early, and still basic, discussion of Western logic and reason, see Sandra Harding and Merrill B. Hintikka, eds., *Discovering Reality: Feminist Perspectives on Epistemology, Metaphysics, Methodology, and Philosophy of Science* (Boston: D. Reidel, 1983).

18. On this, Mariam Thalos writes: "There is a bald assumption among Kant and his supporters alike that there will be full unanimity amongst full-fledged adults who deserve calling free citizens." (That is, those who constitute rather than "merely" track "an order of status relations.") But, "Kant's list of dependents who do not qualify as citizens included children, all women, apprentices, domestic servants, domestic laborers, private tutors, and tenant farmers—persons without anything deserving to be called property.": Mariam Thalos, "Commentary," unpublished manuscript for "Feminism and Evil" panel, meeting of the Eastern Division of the American Philosophical Association, Philadelphia, 2002.

19. Harris, *Philosophy Born of Struggle,* ix.

20. Rey Chow, "Violence in the Other Country: China as Crisis, Specacle, and Woman," in *Third World Women and the Politics of Feminism,* ed. Chandra Talpade Mohanty, Ann Russo, and Lourdes Torres (Bloomington: Indiana University Press, 1991), 88.

21. Cf. Martin, "Excluding Women from the Educational Realm."

22. In addition to work by Sara Ruddick, see that by Judith Arcana, Jane Lazarre, and Adrienne Rich, among others.

23. Rudolph, *Curriculum,* 29–30. Note that "men of action" does not include "men who work with their hands."

24. Ibid., 33.

25. Cf. "Attributes of God," in sec. 48, "Benedict Spinoza": Frank Thilly, *A History of Philosophy,* 3d ed., rev. Ledger Wood (New York: Holt, Rhinehart and Winston, 1957), 323.

26. French feminist writing, including the early work of Simone de Beauvoir and other works informed by her, speaks effectively about the shaping absence of Woman. See, among others, Luce Irigary, "This Sex Which Is Not One," in *New French Feminisms,* ed. Elaine Marks and Isabelle de Courtivron (New York: Schocken Books, 1981).

27. V. Y. Mudimbe, *The Idea of Africa* (Bloomington: Indiana University Press, 1994), xi.

28. Cheris Kramerae and Paula A. Treichler, eds., *A Feminist Dictionary* (London: Pandora Press, 1985), 491, s.v. "woman" (Dennis Barron). Some sources for multiple meanings of the word "woman" beyond those in the English language and culture can be found, and traced, through publications of Zed Books (formerly Zed Press). See, for example, Ifi Amadiune, *Male Daughters, Female Husbands: Gender and Sex in an African Society* (London: Zed Books, 1987). See also Robin Morgan, ed., *Sisterhood Is Global: The First Anthology of Writings from the International Women's Movement* (New York: Doubleday, 1984).

29. Sherri Ortner, "Is Woman to Nature as Man Is to Culture?" in Rosaldo and Lamphere, *Woman, Culture, and Society ,* 67–89.

30. Cf. Suzanne J. Kessler and Wendy McKenna, *Gender: An Ethnomethodological Approach* (New York: John Wiley and Sons, 1978). For a different approach, see Gerda Lerner, *The Creation of Patriarchy* (New York: Oxford University Press, 1986). Kessler and McKenna wrote about how we "do" gender before "performativity" had become a catchword.

31. Kathy Peiss, "'Charity Girls' and City Pleasures: Historical Notes on Working-Class Sexuality, 1880–1990," in *Powers of Desire: The Politics of Sexuality,* ed. Ann Snitow, Christine Stansell, and Sharon Thompson (New York: New Feminist Library/Monthly Review Press, 1983), 74.

32. Barbara Omolade, "Hearts of Darkness," in ibid., 353.

33. Jessica Benjamin, "Master and Slave: The Fantasy of Erotic Domination," in ibid., 280.

34. Deborah Sontag, "Fierce Entanglements," *New York Times Magazine,* November 17, 2002, 62, 84.

35. For feminist 'classics' on such issues, see, for example, Nancy Chodorow, *Reproduction of Mothering: Psychoanalysis and the Sociology of Gender* (Berkeley: University of California Press, 1978); Jane Flax, "Political Philosophy and the Patriarchal Unconscious: A Psychoanalytic Perspective on Epistemology and Metaphysics," in Harding and Hintikka, *Discovering Reality*, 245–83; Juliet Mitchell, *Psychoanalysis and Feminism* (New York: Random House/Vintage Books, 1974).

36. Cf. Evelyne Accad, "Sexuality and Sexual Politics: Conflicts and Contradictions for Contemporary Women in the Middle East," in Mohanty et al., *Third World Women and the Politics of Feminism*, 237–47.

37. Sedgwick, *Between Men*, 11.

38. Judith Butler, *Gender Trouble: Feminism and the Subversion of Identity* (New York: Routledge, 1990), 146.

39. J. Glenn Gray, *The Warriors: Reflections on Men in Battle* (New York: Harper and Row, 1959), 134.

40. Arendt, *Human Condition*, 176.

41. If I were focusing on Gray's work specifically, I would also show where and how he does a remarkable job of thinking about "men in battle" in honest, fresh ways that break through and reconfigure old, limiting conceptualizations. I am in awe of his achievement. The errors I am exploring are, I repeat, so deeply rooted that they are found even in the work of the best thinkers and of those who precisely do not intend to perpetuate domination and injustices. That interests me more than their occurrence among, say, the unabashedly prejudiced. Systemic conceptualizations are not an individual matter, which is what makes them so important to locate and dissolve if and when we can.

42. Gerda Lerner, discussion comments at "Liberal Education and the New Scholarship on Women," Wingspread Conference, Racine, Wis., December 1981. For feminist analyses of war, see Cynthia Enloe, *Does Khaki Become You? The Militarization of Women's Lives* (Boston: South End Press, 1983); Judith H. Stiehm, *Arms and the Enlisted Woman* (Philadelphia: Temple University Press, 1989); the film *The Life and Times of Rosie the Riveter*, prod. and dir. Connie Field (Franklin Lakes, N.J.: Clarity Educational Productions, 1980); and "war novels" by feminists such as Marge Piercy, *Gone to Soldiers* (New York: Summit Books, 1987); Valerie Miner, *Blood Sisters* (New York: St. Martin's Press, 1981); Susan Daitch, *L.C.* (San Diego: Harcourt Brace Jovanovich, 1987). See also works by Bat Ami Bar-On, Sara Ruddick, Carol Cohn, and Claudia Koonz. The literature is significant and growing. This is the merest gesture toward a list.

43. Maria Bigoszewska, "What Then Are the Rights of Women," in *Ambers Aglow: An Anthology of Polish Women's Poetry (1981–1995)*, comp., trans., and with a critical introduction by Regina Grol (Austin, Tex.: Host Publications, 1996), 33.

44. And these 'othered' human givens have been appropriated by the makers of wars and weapons. See, for example, Carol Cohn, "Sex and Death and the Rational World of Defense Intellectuals," in *Women on War: Essential Voices for the Nuclear Age*, ed. Daniela Gioseffi (New York: Simon and Schuster, 1988): 84–99; Helena Meyer-Knapp's unpublished dissertation on nuclear seige war, Union Institute and University, Cincinnati.

45. Although, as I said earlier, categorical means to opening access are often necessary to counter categorical exclusions. Being guaranteed access, and all necessary supports in achieving truly equal opportunity in thoroughly skewed systems, does not require us to throw a group of women into shark-infested waters without thorough preparation or without appropriate exclusions of those who are unable to do this particular thing (just as males who should not be in that water should be excluded). Appropriate judgment is what we are seeking, not a mindless refusal to to take account of realities.

46. I am thinking here, as I do so often in this section, about discussions through the years with Helena Meyer-Knapp. Cf. her *Dangerous Peace-Making* (Olympia, Wash.: Peace-maker Press, 2003).

47. Chris Hedges, *War Is a Force That Gives Us Meaning* (New York: Public Affairs/Perseus Book Group, 2002), 3.

48. Karl von Clausewitz, *War, Politics, and Power: Selections from On War, and I Believe and Profess*, trans. and ed. Edward M. Collins (Washington D.C.: Regnery Gateway, 1988), 63–65. Collins, who also introduced this edition, is a colonel with the U.S. Air Force.

49. Ibid.

50. John Keegan, *The Face of Battle* (New York: Vintage Books, 1977), 18–22. In support of this book, C. P. Snow said: "None of us can afford not to be interested in war. Ignorance of all to do with it has done our kind of society much harm" (as quoted on the back cover of *The Face of Battle*).

51. Daniel Pick, *War Machine: The Rationalisation of Slaughter in the Modern Age* (New Haven, Conn.: Yale University Press, 1993), 2–3.

52. There are many anthologies that provide more names, more approaches, more differing perspectives. In front of me as I write, for example, is Lois Ann Lorentzen and Jennifer Turpin, eds., *The Woman and War Reader* (New York: New York University Press, 1998).

53. Sara Ruddick, "'Woman of Peace': A Feminist Construction," in ibid., 213–27.

54. Elizabeth Estob (1715), as quoted in Kramarae and Treichler, *Feminist Dictionary*, 175.

55. I use "second wave" here to locate the distinction between "sex" and "gender" early in the re-emergence of a women's movement in the United States. It is a distinction that will become far more complex, but it caught on and was useful in that form. I have not otherwise used the terms "first wave," "second wave," and "third wave" in this book simply because my focus is on critiques, on thinking, that is found in many of the movements and new scholarships rather than in their organizational, historical, generational locations and identities. I also have not used the "wave" categories because I think they divide us along lines that are neither adequate nor accurate. In any case, there are many other distinctions within feminisms that seem to me to have more substance intellectually and politically. I may, of course, be wrong.

56. C. T. Onions, with G. W. S. Friedrichsen and R. W. Burchfield, ed., *The Oxford Dictionary of English Etymology* (Oxford: Clarendon Press, 1966), 897.

57. *The Oxford English Dictionary: Being a Corrected Re-Issue with an Introduction, Supplement, and Bibliography of a New English Dictionary on Historical Principles Founded Mainly on the Material Collected by the Philological Society* (Oxford: Clarendon Press, 1978), 100.

58. Ibid.

59. Ibid., 114.

60. Onions, *Oxford Dictionary of English Etymology*, 214.

61. R. Bage, *Barham Downs I. 274* (1784), as quoted in *Oxford English Dictionary, Being a Corrected Re-Issue*, 100.

62. David Glenn, "Practices, Identities and Desires: Gay and Lesbian Anthropology Challenges the Received Wisdom about Culture and Kinship," *Chronicle of Higher Education*, November 22, 2002, A20.

63. Onions, *Oxford Dictionary of English Etymology*, 506.

64. *Oxford English Dictionary, Being a Corrected Re-Issue*, 100.

65. Kramarae and Treichler, *Feminist Dictionary*, 174.

66. The quotes are from Christine Hoff Sommers, *Who Stole Feminism? How Women Have Betrayed Women* (New York: Simon and Schuster, 1994), 22, 24, 51, 275.

67. Sommers's criticism of "gender feminists" is akin to works by Elizabeth Fox-Genovese, Katie Roiphe, Daphne Patai and Noretta Koertge, although her political alignment is dif-

ferent. (Sommers appears to be further to the 'right' than the others.) Patai published a new book in 2002 that extended the case she made in the 1994 book she wrote with Koertge. For further analysis of Sommers's and other such works, see Elizabeth Kamarck Minnich, "Feminist Attacks on Feminisms: Patriarchy's Prodigal Daughters: Review Essay," *Feminist Studies* 24, no. 1 (Spring 1998): 159–77.

68. Elizabeth Fox-Genovese, *Feminism Is Not the Story of My Life: How Today's Feminist Elite Has Lost Touch with the Real Concerns of Women* (New York: Doubleday, 1996), 16.

69. Sandra Harding, "Why Has the Sex/Gender System Become Visible Only Now?" in Harding and Hintikka, *Discovering Reality*, 312.

70. Rhoda Reddock, as quoted in M. Jacqui Alexander, "Redrafting Morality: The Postcolonial State and the Sexual Offences Bill of Trinidad and Tobago," in Mohanty et al., *Third World Women and the Politics of Feminism*, 135.

71. Malgorzata Hillar, "Introduction," *Readiness to Resurrection* (1995), in Grol, *Ambers Aglow*, xxvii–xxviii.

72. Ibid., xxviii.

73. Teresa de Lauretis, "Feminist Studies/Critical Studies: Issues, Terms, and Contexts," in idem, *Feminist Studies*, 9–10.

74. Diana Fuss, *inside/out: Lesbian Theories, Gay Theories* (New York: Routledge, 1991), 1.

75. William L. Leap, as quoted in "Practices, Identities, and Desires," *Chronicle of Higher Education*, November 22, 2002, A20–21. See also William L. Leap and Ellen Lewin, eds., *Out in Theory: The Emergence of Lesbian and Gay Anthropology* (Urbana: University of Illinois Press, 2002); Esther Newton, *Mother Camp: Female Impersonators in America* (Englewood Cliffs, N.J.: Prentice-Hall, 1972).

76. Fuss, *inside/out*, 7.

77. For fine reflections on the learning such teaching invites professors as well as students to explore, see Esther Kingston-Mann and Tim Sieber, eds., *Achieving against the Odds: How Academics Become Teachers of Diverse Students* (Philadelphia: Temple University Press, 2001); Fisher, *No Angel in the Classroom*.

78. Doug Marlette, presentation at the Levine Museum of the New South, Charlotte, N.C., January 22, 2003.

79. Jane Wagner, *The Search for Signs of Intelligent Life in the Universe* (New York: Harper and Row, 1986), 17–18.

80. RuPaul, *Lettin It All Hang Out: An Autobiography* (New York: Hyperion, 1995), 7.

81. Ibid., ix.

82. Ibid.

83. Kessler and McKenna, *Gender*, 164.

84. Ibid., 25.

*Partial Knowledge*

1. Katie Geneva Cannon, "Moral Wisdom in the Black Women's Literary Tradition," in *Presenting Women Philosophers*, ed. Cecile T. Tougas and Sara Ebenreck (Philadelphia: Temple University Press, 2000), 61.

2. Lorraine Code, *What Can She Know? Feminist Theory and the Construction of Knowledge* (Ithaca, N.Y.: Cornell Unniversity Press, 1991), 321.

3. Susanne Langer, *Mind: An Essay on Human Feeling*, abridged ed. (Baltimore: Johns Hopkins University Press, 1988), 63–65.

4. I heard Hilde Nelson speak on this subject at a session of the Society for Women in Philosophy meeting with the American Philosophy Association, Eastern Division, Philadelphia, December 2002. The session was held to honor Sara Ruddick, who had been selected

to receive the society's 2002 award as Distinguished Woman Philosopher. For Nelson's speech, see *American Philosophical Association Newsletter,* vol. 3, no. 1, Fall 2003, 92–94.

5.  Hannah Arendt, "Zionism and the Jewish State" (1948), in *Hannah Arendt: The Jew as Pariah—Jewish Identity and Politics in the Modern Age,* ed. Ron H. Feldman (New York: Grove Press, 1978), 182. As I write, Zionism is again under passionate attack, arousing equally passionate defense. It is thus all the more fascinating, and important, to see what the always independent Arendt wrote about it in 1948. But that is not why I am quoting Arendt on unanimity. Relating her meanings to Zionism, relating Zionism to the Holocaust, and relating the whole history of the Jewish people—enough itself to fill libraries—to the issues with which I am concerned would take many books. I am quoting Arendt here because her thinking then, as always, was indeed independent, which allowed her to see the deadly aspects of systems of all sorts that render some people(s) "superfluous," irretrievably ("naturally") different and so to be eliminated. Her thinking about Zionism, as about virtually everything else to which she turned her attention, earned her scorn, dismissal, attacks—as well as admiration and praise—even, and sometimes particularly, from those whose cause she chose to share while she could. But she never chose to support a cause if the price was to stop thinking.

6.  A. K. Dasgupta, *Methodology of Economic Research* (Bombay: Asia Publishing House, 1968), 4. All of these quotations are from Andrew M. Kamarck, *Economics and the Real World* (Oxford: Basil Blackwell, 1983), 1–3. You may have noticed that Kamarck is also one of my names. I am proud to say that Andrew Kamarck is my father.

7.  Lynn Hankinson Nelson, *Who Knows: From Quine to a Feminist Empiricism* (Philadelphia: Temple University Press, 1990), 9.

8.  Mary Midgeley, *Beast and Man: The Roots of Human Nature* (London: Routledge, 1995), 350–51.

9.  Cf. Judith Lynn Failer, *Who Qualifies for Rights? Homelessness, Mental Illness, and Civil Commitment* (Ithaca, N.Y.: Cornell University Press, 2002). See also works by Eva Feder Kittay, Hilde Nelson, Sara Ruddick, and, for legal scholarship, Martha Minow.

10.  The critical legal scholar Patricia Williams (who also critiques critical legal scholarship) is particularly eloquent and acute on the issue of property law in relation to the status of some 'kinds' of people and nature.

11.  "Translator's Preface," in Jacques Derrida, *Dissemination,* trans. Barbara Johnson (Chicago: University of Chicago Press, 1981), xiv.

12.  Ibid.

13.  Jami L. Anderson, *Race, Gender, and Sexuality: Philosophical Issues of Identity and Justice* (Upper Saddle River, N.J.: Prentice-Hall, 2002), 1, 8.

14.  Alice A. Jardine, *Gynesis: Configurations of Woman and Modernity* (Ithaca, N.Y.: Cornell University Press, 1985), 24.

15.  See Hannah Arendt, "The Jew as Pariah: A Hidden Tradition" (1944), in Feldman, ed., *Hannah Arendt: The Jew as Pariah,* 81–88, for an extraordinary reading of Kafka's *The Castle.* Although Arendt is not discussing authority in this essay, I thought of her because she captures dynamics of absolutized authority in unjust systems in such a striking way. She is, of course, thinking about the creation of "pariah" status for Jews, a world-historical instance of the injustice of creating 'kinds' of humans.

16.  Foucault, *Order of Things,* xxiv.

17.  Henry Louis Gates Jr., "Foreword: In Her Own Write," in Cooper, *Voice from the South;* emphasis added.

18.  Gayatri Spivak, *In Other Worlds: Essays in Cultural Politics* (New York: Methuen Press, 1987), 15.

19.  Flax, "Political Philosophy and the Patriarchal Unconscious," 269.

20. As quoted in Andrea Nye, "A Woman's Thought or a Man's Discipline: The Letters of Abelard and Heloise," in *Hypatia's Daughters: Fifteen Hundred Years of Western Philosophers,* ed. Linda Lopez McAlister (Bloomington: Indiana University Press, 1996), 27.

21. Robert Coles, *Children of Crisis* (New York: Dell, 1964). See also the works of anticolonialist thinkers such as the psychoanalyst Franz Fanon.

22. Mudimbe, *Idea of Africa,* 83.

23. Maurice Merleau-Ponty, "From Mauss to Claude Levi-Strauss," in *Signs,* trans. Richard C. McCleary (Evanston, Ill.: Northwestern University Press, 1964), 120; emphasis added.

24. Chandra Talpade Mohanty, "Feminist Encounters: Locating the Politics of Experience," *Copyright* 1 (Fall 1987): 42.

25. Alfred North Whitehead suggested that we use the idea of "actual occasions," or "events," to replace atomistic, unrelated, static entities/things as the basic 'parts' of reality. Cf. Alfred North Whitehead, *Process and Reality* (New York: Macmillan, 1929). Today, "relational psychology," developed in significant part by scholars associated with the Stone Center in Wellesley, Massachusetts, promotes a similar shift—although it is not extended into an ontology.

26. Cf. works by Sara Ruddick; Hilde Nelson; Nel Noddings; Carol Gilligan; Joan Tronto; Mary Field Belenky, Blythe McVicker Clinchy, Nancy Rule Goldberger, Jill Mattuck Tarule; Barbara Hilkert Andolsen et al.; Eva Feder Kittay; Margaret Urban Walker; Patrice DiQuinzio; and more. The reference sections of these authors' works suggest a coherent, expanding, multivoiced discussion of approaches that already exist and are developing.

27. Cf. works by the Pragmatists Mary Parker Follett, Jane Addams, John Dewey, William James.

28. Lorraine Code, *What Can She Know? Feminist Theory and the Construction of Knowledge* (Ithaca, N.Y.: Cornell University Press, 1991), 255. See also Satya Mohanty's work on "postpositivist realism." Both Mohanty and Code insist—rightly, in my view—that when we try to retrieve knowledge from its mystified impartial objectivity, we should not forget that knowledge emerges from encounters with realities. That is why I adduced the phenomenologists and pragmatists, among others. These are alternative epistemologies that hold knower and known in relation, submitting neither to the other.

29. Cf. Catharine R. Stimpson's critique of Betty Friedan's emphasis on the white, middle-class housewife in *Ms.,* vol. 10, December 1981, 161; see also the critiques by Arlene Avakian et al., "Women Critique Racism Conference," letter to the National Women's Studies Coordinating Council and *Off Our Backs,* March 1982, 25; Bettina Aptheker, "Strong Is What We Make Each Other: Unlearning Racism in Women's Studies," *Women's Studies Quarterly* 9 (Winter 1981): 13–16; "Black Studies and Women's Studies: Search for a Long Overdue Partnership—A Panel Presented at the Sixth Annual Conference of the National Council for Black Studies," *Women's Studies Quarterly* 10 (Summer 1982).

30. See Lorraine Hansberry, *To Be Young, Gifted, and Black* (New York: Signet/New American Library, 1970).

31. Minutes, Harvard Faculty of Arts and Sciences, Regular Faculty Meeting, Tuesday, November 18, 1986, 5ff.

32. See the work of Gerald Graf. I am thinking specifically of his presentation on a panel we shared at a Duke University–University of North Carolina conference in Fall 1988. The proceedings of that conference are published in *South Atlantic Quarterly* 89, no. 1 (Winter 1989).

33. Cf. the works of Freire, Fanon, Memmi, Cabral, and, today, the postcolonial theorists, in particular.

34. Ruel W. Tyson, "Live by Comparisons: A New Home for Reason in the University?" Sixth Annual Memorial Lecture, Society for Values in Higher Education, August 1987, published by *Soundings: An Interdisciplinary Journal* (Knoxville, Tenn., 1988), 11.

35. Foucault, *Fearless Speech,* 12.

## V. CIRCLING BACK, KEEPING GOING

1. Immanuel Kant, *The Critique of Judgment,* trans. Werner S. Pluher (Indianapolis: Hackett, 1986), no. 60, 231.
2. Arendt, *Human Condition,* 8.
3. Ibid.
4. See, for example, works by Ursula K. LeGuin and Octavia Butler, both of whom write imaginatively about utopias and dystopias. Both are critical as well as imaginative, concerned as well as hopeful, in their writings.